Semiotics and Structuralism

Semiotics and Structuralism

READINGS FROM THE SOVIET UNION

Edited with an Introduction by Henryk Baran

INTERNATIONAL ARTS AND SCIENCES PRESS, INC., WHITE PLAINS, N.Y.

Copyright © 1974, 1975, 1976 by International Arts and
Sciences Press, Inc., 901 North Broadway, White Plains,
New York 10603.

All rights reserved. No part of this book may be reproduced
in any form without written permission from the publisher.

The translations in this volume were first published in
Soviet Studies in Literature, an IASP journal edited by
Bernard L. Koten and A. J. Hollander, and Soviet Anthro-
pology and Archeology, an IASP journal edited by Stephen
P. Dunn.

Translated by William Mandel, Henryk Baran, and A. J.
Hollander.

Library of Congress Catalog Card Number: 75-46227
International Standard Book Number: 0-87332-075-1

Printed in the United States of America.

Contents

Introduction vii
Henryk Baran

Myth — Name — Culture 3
Iu. M. Lotman and B. A. Uspenskii

Theater and Theatricality in the Order
of Early Nineteenth Century Culture 33
Iu. M. Lotman

Historia sub Specie Semioticae 64
B. A. Uspenskii

Toward the Problem of Genres in Folklore 76
V. N. Toporov

Primitive Sources of Verbal Art 87
E. M. Meletinskii

A Structural-Typological Analysis
of Paleo-Asiatic Mythology 153
E. M. Meletinskii

Toward the Origin of Certain Poetic Symbols:
The Paleolithic Period   184
V. N. Toporov

Restoration of the Original Text of the Ket Myth
about the Destroyer of Eagles' Nests   226
Viach. Vs. Ivanov

Toward Formal Analysis of Plot Construction   244
O. G. Revzina and I. I. Revzin

O. M. Freidenberg as a Student of Culture   257
Iu. M. Lotman

The Origin of Parody   269
O. M. Freidenberg

The Art of the Word and the Culture of Folk Humor
(Rabelais and Gogol')   284
M. M. Bakhtin

Gogol' and the Correlation of "The Culture
of Humor" with the Comic and Serious
in the Russian National Tradition   297
Iu. M. Lotman

On the Reduction and Unfolding of Sign Systems
(The Problem of "Freudianism and
Semiotic Culturology")   301
Iu. M. Lotman

The Significance of M. M. Bakhtin's Ideas
on Sign, Utterance, and Dialogue
for Modern Semiotics   310
Viach. Vs. Ivanov

About the Editor   369

Introduction

Since the early 1960s the international scientific community has become increasingly aware of studies published by a group of Soviet researchers, members of the so-called Moscow-Tartu School. The Soviet scholars' investigations have been carried out in a number of disciplines, with special attention being paid to literary history, poetics, linguistics, art history, folkloristics, mythology, psychology, and philosophy. At the same time, notwithstanding their diversity, all of these studies have been characterized (to varying degrees) by (1) a focus on ideas and methods which pertain to structuralism in its various facets, and (2) an orientation toward the concepts of semiotics, the science whose object is the study of messages and the sign systems which underlie them. In the course of approximately fifteen years, the Soviet scholars, of whom Professor Iurii Lotman of the Tartu State University is perhaps the best known, have created a large, coherent, and interconnected body of writings. The scope of their inquiries, the boldness and originality of their formulations, and finally, the sheer magnitude of their production — all these have helped make the structural-semiotic research of the Moscow-Tartu group a major component of a broad international expansion of semiotics, which, as Sebeok shows in a recent survey, has been taking place for well over a decade (Sebeok 1974).

Semiotics and Structuralism

This volume presents a "state of the art" sample of Soviet structuralism. It brings together fifteen recent publications dealing with topics in the prehistory of the verbal and visual arts, culture theory, semantics and psychology of myth, linguistics, poetics, and history of literature. The authors of most of the studies are prominent specialists within their individual fields and have played major roles in the growth of modern semiotic-structural research in the USSR (the roles of M. Bakhtin and O. Freidenberg are discussed below). In addition to their intrinsic scientific significance, the articles are of interest in that their contents, style, and in some cases, mutual relationship are broadly characteristic of the publications of the Moscow-Tartu group as a whole. As a consequence, the selections may serve as an introduction to the movement's current major scholarly concerns and to its methods.

Before commenting on the selections included in the volume, a brief overview of the history, objectives, and methods of the scholarly milieu within which they were produced is in order. (1)

Antecedents: Modern structural-semiotic research in the USSR is indebted to a wide range of scientific and intellectual trends, both Russian and foreign. While insisting on the distinctiveness of their investigations, Soviet semioticians acknowledge that they are expanding upon and developing well-known earlier endeavors. Moreover, in keeping with their perception of themselves as participants in a scientific movement, they have sought, through publication, interpretation, and reexamination of generally unknown or unpublished works, to enlarge retroactively the tradition they see themselves as inheriting. (2)

At the core of modern semiotics in Russia and elsewhere lies structural linguistics in all its manifestations, from Saussure's Cours to Zellig Harris's descriptive methods. Three observations may be made about its relationship to semiotics. First, from its inception at the beginning of this century structural linguistics has pointed the way to a more general science of signs, in which linguistics would play a premier, but not the exclusive, part. Second, in applying semiotic methods to a variety of problems, Russian researchers have used concepts

Introduction

drawn from different linguistic schools: the Saussurean dichotomies "synchrony-diachrony," "langue-parole," and "syntagmatics-paradigmatics"; the Prague School's "goal-directedness," etc. Third, structural linguistics has influenced contemporary research not only directly but also indirectly: at each stage of its development modern linguistics has affected other disciplines and has thus provided the present generation of Soviet semioticians with precursors in fields adjacent to linguistics.

Of these predecessors the Russian Formalists, members of the OPOIaZ and the Moscow Linguistic Circle, rank among the most important. Key elements of their program, such as orientation toward the study of the distinctive characteristics of poetic language and concern with the construction of the literary (or folklore) text, have been taken up by modern researchers. In addition the latter have followed the Formalist example by involving scholars working in different disciplines in common scientific and intellectual efforts.

Even more basic for modern work is structuralism (Russian and Czech) in the 1920s and 1930s, the immediate successor to Formalist theory. The writings of Soviet scholars today reflect their appreciation and acceptance of the views of, on the one hand, Roman Jakobson and Iurii Tynianov (or more broadly, the Prague School) and, on the other hand, Mikhail Bakhtin. The elaboration of the structuralist approach in poetics and folkloristics by members of the Prague Linguistic Circle (R. Jakobson, N. Trubetzkoy, P. Bogatyrev, J. Mukařovský, etc.) laid the groundwork for the recent Soviet studies.

Other Russian scholars who earlier concerned themselves with problems which today are seen as central may be mentioned. In the nineteenth century A. Potebnia delved deeply into the interconnections between literature, folklore, and mythology. At the turn of the century A. Shakhmatov greatly advanced the theory and practice of textual reconstruction. Poetics and stylistics were developed not only by the Formalists proper but also, among others, by scholars associated with them, such as V. Vinogradov and V. Zhirmunskii. Outstanding linguists, such as L. Shcherba and S. Bernshtein, also participated in the intensive work on poetics carried out in the 1920s. G. Gukovskii and L. Ginzburg, both students of Tynianov, developed the use of typological methods in literary history. The celebrated film director Sergei Eisenstein contributed to structural analysis of film and other arts.

A special place in the line of development of modern structuralism is occupied by several internationally prominent schollars who not only have influenced Russian semioticians through their writings but also, through personal contact and participation, have given the Moscow-Tartu School an almost unique continuity with its intellectual progenitors. These are the late literary historian M. Bakhtin and the folklorists V. Propp and P. Bogatyrev, as well as, most important, the linguist and literary scholar Roman Jakobson.

Current developments: The recent spurt of semiotic research in the Soviet Union was made possible by the new intellectual climate prevailing there in the late fifties and early sixties, one in which Soviet scholars in many fields were afforded the opportunity to investigate concepts and theories which had previously been left unexplored. During this period a number of linguists made a determined effort to free their science from the aftereffects of Marrism and to bring it up to the level it had reached in the West. A hallmark of their efforts was a 1957 conference on synchronic and diachronic approaches to language. (3) Official encouragement of work in areas that are close to and, in part, dependent on modern structural linguistics (machine translation, cybernetics, information theory) facilitated their task.

Several scientific meetings devoted to problems related to the concerns of semiotics were held in 1961. Among these special attention must be paid to the conference in the city of Gorki, which had as its theme the application of mathematical methods to the study of literary language, and which was attended by both mathematicians and linguists. (4) That such a conference could be convened was a clear signal that significant work in metrics and poetics was being done in the Soviet Union.

Introduction

Quite important for the development of semiotic research was a 1962 expedition to the Ket (Yenisei Ostyak) people which was organized by linguists from Moscow University and the Institute of Slavic Studies. The expedition collected significant linguistic and ethnographic data that have since been utilized not only in Ket studies proper but also in structural-typological investigations of Slavic, Indo-European, and non-Indo-European myths and religious systems.

A symposium devoted to the structural study of sign systems (held in Moscow in December 1962) is particularly notable in the chronology of semiotic developments. The meeting was sponsored by several research groups, including, in particular, the Sector of Structural Typology of Slavic Languages, Institute of Slavic and Balkan Studies, and the Linguistic Section of the Scientific Council on Cybernetics. The large number of papers presented fell into the following broad categories: (a) the semiotic aspect of natural and artificial languages; (b) systems of writing and problems of decipherment; (c) nonlinguistic communication; (d) mythology, psychology; (e) art as sign system; (f) structural study of literary works. As we shall see below, almost all the major areas of semiotic research defined at the symposium continue to attract the attention of Soviet scholars.

The fact that the Sector of Structural Typology helped sponsor the 1962 symposium is indicative of the role played by this remarkable research center in spurring structural-semiotic investigations. The sector has maintained a leading position in Soviet structuralism thanks, on the one hand, to its imaginatively and broadly formulated long-range program of research and, on the other hand, to the extremely high caliber of its members. (5) The sector's activities, it must be emphasized, have received active support from a number of other gifted and prolific Moscow scholars. (6)

Since 1964 the Department of Russian Literature at the University of Tartu has emerged as another major center of structuralism and semiotics. Under the leadership of the literary historian Iu. Lotman, who extraordinarily effectively combines the roles of researcher, teacher, and organizer, Tartu has gained an international prominence. First indications of these developments came with the publication of Lotman's book on structural poetics, which was based on his university lectures (Lotman 1964). He has since published two other books on the structure of literary texts (Lotman 1970, 1972) as well as numerous articles. In addition to being significant contributions to poetics, all three of his volumes have helped popularize structural methods in the Soviet Union.

Although the results of Soviet semioticians' inquiries have appeared in a host of diverse (and often almost inaccessible) publications, the special series Works on Semiotics [Trudy po znakovym sistemam, abbreviated TZS], part of the Tartu University's Transactions, has served as the principal organ of the Moscow-Tartu group. (7) Many of the articles in these diverse and intellectually vital volumes were first delivered as papers at a celebrated Tartu institution, the so-called summer schools on semiotics in Kääriku. Held in 1964, 1966, 1968, and 1970, with Moscow, Leningrad, and Tartu scholars participating, these informal and open sessions served as the setting for examining methods, hypotheses, and research results and helped foster both the originality and the cohesiveness of Soviet structuralism. (8)

Finally, it must be noted that the semiotic orientation of the Tartu Department of Russian Literature has had a significant pedagogical impact. Lotman, Z. Mints, and their colleagues have trained a number of promising young researchers whose high level of work may be seen in six volumes of abstracts which to date have come from the Tartu student conferences on literature, linguistics, and folkloristics. (9)

Theory and practice: As we have noted earlier, structural-semiotic inquiries in the Soviet Union, as elsewhere, encompass a wide variety of concerns. Five major areas of study have been singled out by Soviet semioticians: (1) poetics and theory of literature; (2) myth, folklore, and religion; (3) painting, music, film, and other sign systems; (4) culture theory; (5) general semiotics. Within each of these areas, research has taken the following orientation:

Introduction

<u>Poetics and theory of literature</u>: Defining literature as a secondary modeling system, i.e., as <u>a sign system superimposed upon and dependent on natural language</u>, Soviet scholars have studied the ways in which this transformation of language is effected in a work of literature. Although important research has been done in the realm of prose (<u>10</u>), poetry has been the favored object of inquiry. <u>Organization of the different levels of the</u> poetic text (phonic, metrical, grammatical, lexical, etc.) has been investigated; in particular, attention has been focused on interlevel relationships within the <u>poetic structure</u> (e.g., on the relationship of sound to meaning). (<u>11</u>) With Tynianov's remarks on the "unity and density of the poetic series" [<u>edinstvo i tesnota poeticheskogo riada</u>] (Tynianov 1924) serving as the point of departure, study of <u>the semantics of poetic texts</u> has advanced significantly. Texts of great twentieth-century Russian poets (Mandel'shtam, Akhmatova, Blok, Pasternak) have been studied in detail principally through two approaches: (1) <u>statistical analysis of poetic lexicon</u> (either over the whole of a poet's creative biography or within given periods or collections); and (2) <u>microsemantic analysis of the individual</u> text. (<u>12</u>)

A major effort has been devoted to <u>the study of verse meter and rhythm</u>. A number of researchers (Kolmogorov, Prokhorov, Kondratov, Gasparov, Ivanov, Rudnev) have continued and vastly enriched a Russian scholarly tradition that goes back to the beginning of this century. (<u>13</u>)

<u>Myth, folklore, religion</u>: Also regarded as secondary modeling systems, myth, folklore, and religious beliefs have been investigated in detail; in addition, considerable attention has been devoted to concrete mythological and folklore <u>texts</u>. Quite interesting are the efforts of some researchers, following the example of C. Lévi-Strauss, to <u>describe the semantic structures of individual myths.</u> Of special significance is the work of Ivanov and Toporov who, using <u>an approach which combines the historical method with the typological</u>, have carried out <u>reconstructions</u>, i.e., reconstitutions by means of special operations, of texts and sign systems. In their numerous individual and

joint works, drawing on a vast array of linguistic and ethnographic data, the two scholars have re-created, among others, the ancient East Slavic mythological system (in particular, the pantheon), an archaic Indo-European mythologem, an apparently universal archaic symbol, and certain semantic universals (expressed in terms of binary oppositions such as right-left, up-down, etc.) that ultimately underlie mythological-religious systems (Ivanov and Toporov 1963, 1965, 1974; Toporov 1971, 1973).

Special note should be taken of the theory relied on by Ivanov and Toporov in their studies. Since the early 1960s they and their colleagues have regarded <u>the procedure of reconstruction as an algorithm</u> into whose terms, at least in the abstract, most of the problems faced by students of the various semiotic disciplines may be translated (this applies, for one, to the task facing the reader or the critic of a work of literature) (Ivanov and Toporov 1966; Levinton 1975; Uspenskii et al. 1973). This view has given the many Soviet semiotic investigations a certain theoretical common ground.

Within folkloristics two efforts are of special interest. First, the work done by Meletinskii and his group on <u>the structure of the fairy tale</u> is particularly noteworthy. <u>Combining the results of Propp's classic syntagmatic analysis of the fairy tale</u> (Propp 1928) <u>with Lévi-Strauss's paradigmatic approach to myth</u>, Meletinskii and his co-workers have achieved <u>a refined, semantically oriented version of the Proppian model.</u> (<u>14</u>) Second, there are G. Permiakov's provocative yet rigorous writings on <u>paremiological genres</u> (proverbs, sayings, etc.). Working with a large number of paremiological texts from differing cultures, he has succeeded in constructing an exhaustive three-level (the linguistic, the logico-semiotic, and the artistic) classificatory system and thus in laying a solid foundation for further studies (Permiakov 1968, 1970).

<u>Other artistic sign systems</u>: <u>Painting</u> has been the principal nonverbal sign system to be studied. In approaching it Soviet semioticians have concerned themselves with establishing its specific <u>language</u>, i.e., with determining <u>the set of devices used systematically to generate and transmit meaning.</u> Of major

Introduction

importance have been (1) the appearance of an unpublished article by the polymath scientist the Rev. P. Florenskii (1882-1943); (2) the publication of L. Zhegin's monograph (1970) on medieval painting; (3) Uspenskii's semiotic analyses of painting (especially medieval icons).

Study of music as a sign system has thus far been somewhat limited. Research in this field has been done principally by B. Gasparov (Tartu).

Within the last few years, in concert with a similar trend in the West (Metz, Chabrol), the language of film has attracted increasing attention. Interest in the semiotics of cinema has been dictated by the inner logic of the development of semiotic research (see Ivanov [1973b]); in addition, it has been stimulated by recognition of Eisenstein's role as a major theoretician of art and by close study of both his cinematic heritage and his many writings. Lotman (1973b), Segal, and Ivanov (1975) have all written on the cinema; the last-mentioned has also devoted a major study (as yet unpublished) to the views and practice of Eisenstein.

Culture theory: The study of the semiotics of culture is closely correlated with the previously discussed areas of research; from a broad theoretical point of view it encompasses all of them. Soviet semioticians, especially Lotman and Uspenskii, have made this field uniquely their own. Viewing culture as a plurality of mutually interacting and mutually supportive sign systems (Uspenskii et al. 1973), they have attempted to typologize different cultures. Lotman's and Uspenskii's efforts in this direction have been based principally on Russian materials. Toporov's and Segal's efforts have been far broader: the former (1973b), enlarging on the ideas of the British philosopher R. G. Collingwood and other thinkers, has differentiated between various stages in human culture on the basis of a society's attitude toward history, while the latter has based his scheme on the nature and function of ritual in a given society.

General semiotics: With the achievement of concrete results in individual disciplines, general semiotic theory has assumed greater significance for Soviet investigators. Their work, particularly in the last five years, shows a movement away from reliance on largely heuristic, intuitive definitions and toward critical examination of the logical foundations of their scientific endeavors. As Ivanov suggests (1973a), this has involved, for example, a shift in the relationship between linguistics and semiotics, with the latter ceasing to model itself solely on the former. Lotman, Revzin, Piatigorskii, and others have reevaluated basic concepts. In essence the process of semiotic analysis has itself become the object of semiotic study.

The articles selected for this collection reflect many of the points raised in the preceding discussion.
The volume opens with three articles by Lotman and Uspenskii that fall into the broad area of semiotics of culture. The selections exemplify the highly speculative, provocative approach characteristic of the two scholars' writings in this area.
In "Myth — Name — Culture" (Lotman and Uspenskii 1973) the authors suggest that one productive criterion in typology of cultures is the orientation of a particular culture toward mythological or nonmythological thought. Lotman and Uspenskii arrive at this distinction by considering myth in terms of the consciousness of either an individual or a society. They associate mythological thought with the process of nomination in natural language and claim that, from one point of view, a myth is equivalent to a proper name. Proper names may thus be seen as forming a special "mythological sphere" in language: consequently, they argue, mythological thought may be studied not only within the confines of entire societies but also through observation of the verbal behavior of children.
In the latter part of their study Lotman and Uspenskii discuss Petrine Russia and Russia at the turn of the eighteenth to the nineteenth centuries as examples of cultures oriented toward mythologization. They conclude the essay by suggesting that the common conception of the evolution of human culture, from a mythopoeic to a scientific stage, is overly simplistic — that one must speak instead of potential tendencies in any society.
Petrine Russia is also the object of attention of Uspenskii's

Introduction

(1974) "Historia sub Specie Semioticae," in which Peter the Great's behavior is treated as a text (in the broad semiotic understanding of this term). Analyzing a variety of the Emperor's public and private acts, Uspenskii suggests that such deeds had to be "read" by Russian society of the time in a very definite way (as actions of the Anti-Christ); furthermore, he raises the possibility that Peter, consciously or unconsciously, tailored his iconoclastic behavior to the expectations of his people. Uspenskii's study is but one example of an important interest of Soviet scholars: to apply concepts and methods of semiotics to problems which had hitherto been the exclusive provenance of historical research. (15)

"Theater and Theatricality in the Order of Early Nineteenth Century Culture" (Lotman 1973c) represents another excursus into individual behavior and its typology. (16) This time the criterion used is the potential relationship between life and art. In the article Lotman discusses in detail the situation in which the realm of art influences life, a condition which, he claims, prevailed in Russia and Western Europe at the end of the eighteenth century and the beginning of the nineteenth. The principal influence was that of the theater. As Lotman shows, the stage not only affected the everyday life of the individual but also transformed society's collective concerns (such as preparation for the conduct of war) into theatricalized rituals conducted on an enormous scale.

The second group of studies in the collection is devoted to varied topics in mythology and folklore. Toporov's paper (1974b) "Toward the Problem of Genres in Folklore" is a brief discussion of the problem of classification of folklore texts together with a review of relevant literature. Emphasizing the need for a typological approach to genres, the author also raises a number of significant theoretical questions. (17)

Toporov's other article (1972), "Toward the Origin of Certain Poetic Symbols: The Paleolithic Period," is, as its author indicates in the text, the first of a series devoted to the evolution of poetic symbols. Through the method of semantic reconstruction, Toporov isolates certain elements of Paleolithic cave painting that may have become components of the image of the Cosmic or World Tree at a much later time. This image is seen by

Semiotics and Structuralism

Toporov as a well-defined, universal semiotic complex (see [1973a]).

In drawing his admittedly tentative conclusions, Toporov relies heavily on the writings of two distinguished specialists in Paleolithic art, A. Leroi-Gourhan and A. Laming-Emperaire. Results of A. Marshack's subsequent research on lunar notation in Stone Age carvings (Marshack 1972) suggest alternative interpretations of some of the examples he discusses. At the same time, B. Frolov's recent analysis of representations of numbers in the Paleolithic (Frolov 1974) provides additional support for Toporov's conception.

Meletinskii's "Primitive Sources of Verbal Art" (Meletinskii 1972) surveys the essential problems that must be considered in a discussion of the origins of verbal art. In the four sections of his study Meletinskii reviews major theories on the origins of poetry (A. Veselovskii and C. M. Bowra), considers aspects of the evolution of primitive plots and character types (on the basis of Australian and Paleo-Asiatic materials), and discusses the transformation of myth into first the primitive and later the classical fairy tale.

"A Structural-Typological Analysis of Paleo-Asiatic Mythology," Meletinskii's other contribution (1974), takes up and develops some of the materials discussed in the third section of the 1972 study. The author focuses on the cycles of "Raven myths" found among the Koryak, the Chukchi, and the Itel'men peoples of Siberia and provides an analysis of the semantic structure and composition of the most important tale types. In showing how the same basic message is varied in different myths because of the use of different codes, Meletinskii brilliantly applies the methods developed by Lévi-Strauss.

The great French anthropologist's influence is also felt in Ivanov's paper (1974), "Restoration of the Original Text of the Ket Myth about the Destroyer of Eagles' Nests." Taking two variants heavily overlaid with misleading accretions and drawing on a variety of other tales, Ivanov recreates and subsequently analyzes the original Ket myth (translations of the two variants are included following Ivanov's article). As was the case with

Introduction

Toporov's article on Paleolithic symbolism, reconstruction emerges as a principal object and tool of research.
 The concern with diachrony, evident in the preceding five contributions, is absent in the brief paper by O. G. Revzina and I. I. Revzin (1973), "Toward Formal Analysis of Plot Construction." Using the formal apparatus of relation theory to describe the functioning of several works of literature, the authors obtain some interesting results. Their effort, it must be noted, is an example of the much broader work on the application of mathematical methods to the study of narrative that is currently being conducted by researchers in a number of countries.
 To show the significance for the work of present-day Soviet semioticians of the writings of earlier scholars, we have included in the volume a selection by O. M. Freidenberg, a classicist associated with the linguistic doctrines of N. Ia. Marr. Her article (1973) "The Origin of Parody," based on broad comparative materials, is preceded by Lotman's prefatory essay, "O. M. Freidenberg as a Student of Culture" (Lotman 1973a). In this introduction Lotman briefly surveys Freidenberg's published and unpublished work and attempts a difficult yet fascinating task: to lift the opprobrium surrounding Marr's discredited linguistic fantasies from his students' significant insights into literary studies, folkloristics, and the broad study of culture. (His essay is followed by a bibliography of Freidenberg's writings, which is reproduced in Russian.)
 As was noted earlier, the work of the late Mikhail Bakhtin has had a major impact on the Moscow-Tartu group. The relathionship between the following selections illustrates this. Bakhtin's essay (1973) "The Art of the Word and the Culture of Folk Humor (Rabelais and Gogol')" is actually a fragment of his 1940 dissertation. (18) Applying to Gogol' concepts developed in his study of Rabelais, Bakhtin offers a new perspective on the comic elements in the great Russian writer's works. Lotman's brief note (Lotman 1974a), "Gogol' and the Correlation of 'The Culture of Humor' with the Comic and Serious in the Russian National Tradition," contains an extension and amplification of Bakhtin's ideas.

Semiotics and Structuralism

Another of Lotman's essays (1974b), "On the Reduction and Unfolding of Sign Systems (The Problem of 'Freudianism and Semiotic Culturology')," draws a parallel between the mental processes of children and the functioning of individual societies. Taking as his point of departure Voloshinov's (Bakhtin's — see below) critical presentation of Freudian theory (Voloshinov 1927), Lotman offers a semiotic reinterpretation of the formation of childhood neuroses: he suggests they result from the child's inability to translate adult verbal and behavior texts adequately into its own code. Lotman continues by suggesting an analogy between this process of individual "translation" and the transmission of texts between cultures at different stages of development.

We have, finally, a major study by Ivanov (1973b), "The Significance of M. M. Bakhtin's Ideas on Sign, Utterance, and Dialogue for Modern Semiotics," which had initially been presented as a paper at a special 1970 symposium at Moscow University devoted to M. Bakhtin. (19)

Ivanov pursues two goals in this essay. Focusing on three key concepts in Bakhtin's thought, Ivanov reviews the many aspects of Bakhtin's heritage in general semiotics, philosophy of language, psychology, literary theory, and cultural anthropology, and he repeatedly emphasizes the fact that Bakhtin's ideas anticipated by decades a number of significant modern scientific conceptions. In addition, Ivanov uses the occasion to suggest perspectives for the future and to speculate on the directions in which semiotic inquiries shall presently proceed. (20)

One other aspect of the article must be noted. In his concluding footnote Ivanov suggests that major works written by Bakhtin himself had been published under the names of his students, V. Voloshinov and P. Medvedev. This claim, which, Ivanov notes, is backed by accounts of eyewitnesses, provides a simple explanation for the remarkable textual coincidences which have repeatedly been remarked on by scholars in discussions of the "Bakhtin School."

Henryk Baran

Introduction

Notes

1) For other, more extensive surveys, see Eimermacher (1971), Meletinskii and Segal (1971), Segal (1973), and Segal (1974).

2) The significance of such activities for contemporary Soviet structural research cannot be overemphasized. See the remarks by Lotman (1967).

3) The proceedings, characteristic of the polemics of that period, are found in Gukhman and Bokarev eds. (1960).

4) Mathematicians — Academician A. Kolmogorov and his collaborators; linguists — V. Ivanov, V. Toporov, I. Revzin, A. Zholkovskii, Iu. Shcheglov, Iu. Knorozov, etc.

5) These include or have formerly included Ivanov, Toporov, Revzin, T. Tsiv'ian, D. Segal, etc.

6) Among these have been: (1) several orientalists (A. Piatigorskii, T. Elizarenkova, A. Syrkin, B. Ogibenin, E. Semeka); (2) a group of folklorists (E. Meletinskii [Institute of World Literature], E. Novik, S. Nekliudov, and, until his emigration, D. Segal); (3) the mathematician Iu. Levin; (4) the literary historian and theoretician of verse M. Gasparov; (5) linguists such as A. Zholkovskii, Iu. Shcheglov, A. Zalizniak.

7) Lotman's 1964 monograph initiated the series; since then, several further volumes have appeared (TZS II, 1965; TZS III, 1967; TZS IV, 1969; TZS V, 1971; TZS VI, 1973; TZS VII, 1975).

8) Abstracts of papers from the summer schools have been published by Tartu University. The Kääriku tradition was extended in February 1974 with the convening of the First All-Union Symposium on Secondary Modeling Systems in Tartu (materials of the symposium are published in Lotman ed. [1973, 1974]).

9) Abstracts from the 1966, 1967, 1970, 1971, 1972, and 1973 conferences have been published by Tartu University. An additional volume from the late sixties did not appear.

10) See, for example, Uspenskii's work on composition (Uspenskii 1970) and Toporov's study of Crime and Punishment (Toporov 1973b).

Semiotics and Structuralism

11) Jakobson's exemplary analyses of poetic texts have been particularly influential in this area.

12) Study of poetic texts has been a special concern of Ivanov, Levin, Lotman, Mints, Segal, Shcheglov, Timenchik, Toporov, Tsiv'ian, Uspenskii, and Zholkovskii. A major achievement of these investigations has been the significant advance in our understanding of Mandel'shtam's and Akhmatova's works.

13) Statistical study of Russian meters was initiated by the poet A. Bely. His approach was given a solid mathematical and linguistic grounding by B. Tomashevskii, R. Jakobson, and N. Trubetzkoy. K. Taranovsky's volume (1953) represents a major culmination of their efforts.

14) A collection of translations into English of Meletinskii's and his colleagues' most important writings on the fairy tale is available (Maranda ed. 1974).

15) According to the report of the proceedings of the 1974 All-Union Symposium, at which Uspenskii's paper was delivered, his interpretation of Peter's behavior was vigorously challenged by some of the participants. See Paperno et al. (1974; 138-41).

16) The article appeared in a collection of Lotman's articles on culture theory published in Tartu; a close variant is included in Mayenowa ed. (1973).

17) A much more extensive discussion of these problems is found in Toporov (1974a).

18) The major part of the dissertation was published as (Bakhtin 1965).

19) According to O. Revzina (1971), two other papers were presented at the session. The first, by A. Dorogov, reviewed Bakhtin's biography and scholarly achievements. The second, by V. Propp, dealt with the significance of Bakhtin's conception of laughter and the carnival culture (see Ivanov [1973b]) for folkloristics as a whole.

20) Another overview of the potential future developments in semiotics is found in Ivanov (1973a).

"Dialogue & Monologue" 81-111
"On Stage Dialogue" 112-115
The Word & Verbal Art

Introduction

References

Bakhtin, M. M. 1965, Tvorchestvo Fransua Rable i narodnaia kul'tura srednevekov'ia i Renessansa, (Moscow).
*———. 1973, "Iskusstvo slova i narodnaia smekhovaia kul'tura (Rable i Gogol')," in Kontekst. 1972 (Moscow).
Eimermacher, K. 1971, "Entwicklung, Charakter und Probleme des sowjetischen Strukturalismus in der Literaturwissenschaft," in K. Eimermacher ed. Texte des sowjetischen literaturwissenschaftlichen Strukturalismus (Munich), pp. 9-40.
*Freidenberg, O. M. 1973, "Proiskhozhdenie parodii," Trudy po znakovym sistemam, VI (Tartu), pp. 490-97.
Frolov, B. A. 1974, Chisla v grafike paleolita (Novosibirsk).
Gukhman, M. M., and Bokarev, E. A. eds. 1960, O sootnoshenii sinkhronnogo analiza i istoricheskogo izucheniia iazykov (Moscow).
Ivanov, V. V. 1973a, "Edinstvo predmeta nauki o iazyke," Izvestiia Akademii nauk SSSR. Seriia literatury i iazyka. vol. XXXII, issue 3, pp. 242-54.
*———. 1973b, "Znachenie idei M. M. Bakhtina o znake, vyskazyvanii i dialoge dlia sovremennoi lingvistiki," Trudy po znakovym sistemam, VI (Tartu), pp. 5-45.
*———. 1974, "Vosstanovlenie pervonachal'nogo teksta ketskogo mifa o razoritele orlinykh gnezd," in Lotman ed. (1974), pp. 51-64.
———. 1975, "Funktsii i kategorii iazyka kino," Trudy po znakovym sistemam, VII (Tartu), pp. 170-92.
Ivanov, V. V., and Toporov, V. N. 1963, "K rekonstruktsii praslavianskogo teksta," Slavianskoe iazykoznanie (Moscow).
———. 1965, Slavianskie iazykovye modeliruiushchie semioticheskie sistemy: drevnii period (Moscow).
———. 1966, "Postanovka zadachi rekonstruktsii teksta i rekonstruktsii znakovoi sistemy," in V. V. Ivanov ed., Strukturnaia tipologiia iazykov (Moscow, 1966), pp. 3-25.

---

*Essay appears in translation in this volume.

———. 1974, Issledovaniia v oblasti slavianskikh drevnostei (Moscow).
Levinton, G. A. 1975, "K probleme izucheniia povestvovatel'nogo fol'klora," in Meletinskii and Nekliudov eds. (1975), pp. 303-19.
Lotman, Iu. M. 1964, Lektsii po struktural'noi poetike. Vvedenie. Teoriia stikha (Tartu).
———. 1967, "O zadachakh razdela obzorov i publikatsii," Trudy po znakovym sistemam, III (Tartu), pp. 363-66.
———. 1970, Struktura khudozhestvennogo teksta (Moscow).
———. 1972, Analiz poeticheskogo teksta (Leningrad).
*———. 1973a, "O. M. Freidenberg kak issledovatel' kul'tury," Trudy po znakovym sistemam, VI (Tartu), pp. 482-85.
———. 1973b, Semiotika kino i problemy kinoestetiki (Tallin).
*———. 1973c, "Teatr i teatral'nost' v stroe kul'tury nachala XIX veka," in Iu. M. Lotman, Stat'i po tipologii kul'tury (Materialy k kursu teorii literatury, vyp. 2) (Tartu), pp. 42-73.
*———. 1974a, "Gogol' i sootnesenie 'smekhovoi kul'tury' s komicheskim i ser'eznym v russkoi natsional'noi traditsii," in Lotman ed. (1974), pp. 131-33.
*———. 1974b, "O reduktsii i razvertyvanii znakovykh sistem (K probleme 'Freidizm i semioticheskaia kul'turologiia')," in Lotman ed. (1974), pp. 100-8.
Lotman, Iu. M. ed. 1973, Sbornik statei po vtorichnym modeliruiushchim sistemam (Tartu).
———. 1974, Materialy vsesoiuznogo simpoziuma po vtorichnym modeliruiushchim sistemam I (5) (Tartu).
*Lotman, Iu. M., and Uspenskii, B. A. 1973, "Mif — imia — kul'tura," Trudy po znakovym sistemam, VI (Tartu), pp. 282-303.
Lotman, Iu. M., and Uspenskii, B. A. eds. 1973, Ricerche Semiotiche (Turin).
Marshack, A. 1972, The Roots of Civilization (New York).
Maranda, P. ed. 1974, Soviet Structural Folkloristics, vol. 1 (The Hague-Paris).

*Essay appears in translation in this volume.

Introduction

Mayenowa, M. R. ed. 1973, Semiotyka i struktura tekstu (Warsaw).
*Meletinskii, E. M. 1972, "Pervobytnye istoki slovesnogo iskusstva," in Meletinskii ed. (1972), pp. 149-90.
*———. 1974, "Strukturno-tipologicheskii analiz paleoaziatskoi mifologii," Narody Azii i Afriki, no. 4, pp. 86-102.
Meletinskii, E. M. ed. 1972, Rannie formy iskusstva (Moscow).
Meletinskii, E. M., and Nekliudov, S. Iu. eds. 1975, Tipologicheskie issledovaniia po fol'kloru (Moscow).
Meletinskii, E. M., and Segal, D. M. 1971, "Structuralism and Semiotics in the USSR," Diogenes, no. 73 (January-March), pp. 88-125.
Paperno, I., Zhivov, V., Levinton, G., Lotman, M. 1975, "Pervyi Vsesoiuznyi simpozium po vtorichnym modeliruiushchim sistemam," in Lotman, Iu., Egorov, B., Reifman, P., Isakov, S., Bezzubov, V. eds. Russkaia filologiia IV. Sbornik studencheskikh nauchnykh rabot (Tartu), pp. 123-51.
Permiakov, G. L. 1968, Introduction to Izbrannye poslovitsy i pogovorki narodov Vostoka (Moscow).
———. 1970, Ot pogovorki do skazki (zametki po obshchei teorii klishe) (Moscow).
Propp, V. Ia. 1928, Morfologiia skazki (Leningrad).
Revzina, O. G. 1971, Summary in Voprosy iazykoznaniia, no. 2, pp. 160-62.
*Revzina, O. G., and Revzin, I. I. 1973, "K formal'nomu analizu siuzhetoslozheniia," in Lotman ed. (1973), pp. 110-22.
Sebeok, T. A. 1974, "Semiotics: A Survey of the State of the Art," in Sebeok ed. (1974), pp. 211-64.
Sebeok, T. A. ed. 1974, Current Trends in Linguistics, vol. 12 (The Hague-Paris).
Segal, D. M. 1973, "Le ricerche sovietiche nel campo della semiotica negli ultimi anni," in Lotman and Uspenskii eds. (1973), pp. 452-70.
———. 1974, Aspects of Structuralism in Soviet Philology (Papers on Poetics and Semiotics, 2) (Institute of Poetics and Semiotics, Tel-Aviv University).

*Essay appears in translation in this volume.

Taranovsky (Taranovski), K. F. 1953, Russki dvodelni ritmovi (Belgrade).
*Toporov, V. N. 1972, "K proiskhozhdeniiu nekotorykh poeticheskikh simvolov (Paleoliticheskaia epokha)," in Meletinskii ed. (1972), pp. 77-104.
———. 1973a, "L' 'albero universale'. Saggio d'interpretazione semiotica," in Lotman and Uspenskii eds. (1973), pp. 148-201.
———. 1973b, "O kosmologicheskikh istochnikakh ranneistoricheskikh opisanii," Trudy po znakovym sistemam, VI (Tartu), pp. 106-50.
———. 1973c, "O strukture romana Dostoevskogo v sviazi s arkhaichnymi skhemami mifologicheskogo myshleniia (Prestuplenie i nakazanie)," in van der Eng and Grygar eds. (1973), pp. 225-302.
———. 1974a, "Folk Poetry: General Problems," in Sebeok ed. (1974), pp. 683-739.
*———. 1974b, "K probleme zhanrov v fol'klore," in Lotman ed. (1974), pp. 5-16.
Tynianov, Iu. M. 1924, Problema stikhotvornogo iazyka (Leningrad).
Uspenskii, B. A. 1970, Poetika kompozitsii (Moscow).
*———. 1974, "Historia sub Specie Semioticae," in Lotman ed. pp. 119-30.
Uspenskii, B. A., Ivanov, V. V., Toporov, V. N., Piatigorskii, A. M., Lotman, Iu. M. 1973, "Theses on the Semiotic Study of Cultures (as Applied to Slavic Texts)," in van der Eng and Grygar eds. (1973), pp. 1-28.
van der Eng, J., and Grygar, M. eds. 1973, Structure of Texts and Semiotics of Culture (The Hague-Paris).
Voloshinov, V. N. 1929, Marksizm i filosofiia iazyka (Leningrad).
Zhegin, L. F. 1970, Iazyk zhivopisnogo proizvedeniia (Uslovnost' drevnego iskusstva) (Moscow).

---

*Essay appears in translation in this volume.

Semiotics
and
Structuralism

Myth — Name — Culture

Iu. M. LOTMAN and B. A. USPENSKII

I

1. <u>The world is matter.</u>
   <u>The world is a steed.</u>

One of these sentences is from a clearly mythological text (the Upanishads), while the other may serve as an example of a text of the opposite type. Despite the external formal similarity of these constructs there is a fundamental difference between them:

a) The identical copula (is) denotes here operations that are completely different in logic: in the first case the subject is a given correlation (which may be understood, for example, as the correlation of the particular with the general, inclusion in a set, etc.), while in the second the issue is one of direct identification.

b) The predicates are also different. From the point of view of a modern consciousness, the words <u>matter</u> and <u>steed</u> in these constructs belong to different levels of logical description: the first gravitates toward the level of metalanguage, and the second toward the level of object-language. And the fact is that in one case we have a reference to a category of metadescription — that is, to a certain abstract language of description (in other words, to a certain abstract construct that has no meaning outside this language of description) — while in the other case we have a reference to the same type of object, but placed at a hierarchically higher level, an ur-object, the prototype of the object. In the first case the fundamental absence of an isomorphism between the described world and the system of description is essential; in the second case, on the other hand, the recognition of such an isomorphism is essential. We shall call the second type of description "mythological" and the first, "nonmythological" (or "descriptive").

CONCLUSION: In the first case (descriptive description) we have a reference to a <u>metalanguage</u> (to a category or element of a metalanguage). In the second case (mythological description), we have a reference to a <u>metatext</u>, i.e., a text performing a metalinguistic function relative to the given one. Furthermore, the object described and the describing metatext belong to the same language.

COROLLARY: Consequently, mythological description is fundamentally monolinguistic — objects in this world are described through <u>the same type of world</u>, constructed in the <u>same</u> way. However, nonmythological description is emphatically polylinguistic — reference to a metalanguage is important precisely as reference to <u>another</u> language (it makes no difference whether it is a language of abstract constructs or a foreign language: the very process of translation-interpretation is important). Accordingly, understanding, too, in one case, one way or another involves <u>translation</u> (in the broad sense of the word), while in the other case it involves <u>recognition, identification</u>. Actually, whereas in the case of descriptive texts the information in general is defined through translation — and the translation through the information — in mythological texts the point is <u>transformation</u> of objects; and an understanding of these texts is <u>linked</u>, consequently, with an understanding of the processes of this transformation.

Thus, in the final analysis, the matter may be reduced to an opposition between a fundamentally monolinguistic consciousness and one that requires, at the very least, a pair of differently structured languages. The consciousness producing mythological descriptions we shall call "mythological."

Note: To avoid possible misunderstandings, it must be emphasized that we shall not, in the present paper, concern ourselves particularly with myth as a specific form of narrative text and, consequently, with the structure of mythological plots (nor shall we deal with the viewpoint that regards myth as a system and as a consequence centers its attention on the paradigmatics of elements). In speaking of a myth or mythologism, we always refer specifically to myth as a phenomenon of consciousness. (If sometimes we have to refer to certain plot situations characteristic of myth as text, they will interest us primarily as production of mythological consciousness.)

2. The world, seen by the mythological consciousness, should seem to be composed of objects [ob"ekt]:
1) of the same rank (the concept of logical hierarchy is, in principle, beyond this type of consciousness);
2) not divided into features (each thing is looked upon as an integral whole);
3) singular (the idea of recurrence of things presumes their incorporation into certain general aggregates, i.e., the existence of a level of metadescription).

Paradoxically, the mythological world is of a single rank in the sense of logical hierarchy, and is to the highest degree hierarchical on the semantic-value [axiological] level. Undivided into features, it is at the same time to an extraordinary degree divisible into parts (component tangible pieces). Finally, the singularity of objects does not prevent the mythological consciousness from regarding as one — in a manner strange for us — objects which are completely different from the standpoint of nonmythological thought.

Note: From our point of view, mythological thought may be seen as paradoxical but in no way as primitive, since it copes successfully with complicated problems of classification. If we compare its mechanism with our ordinary, logical apparatus, we can establish a definite parallelism of functions. Consider:

The hierarchy of metalinguistic categories corresponds to the hierarchy of objects themselves in myth and, ultimately, to the hierarchy of worlds.

Division into differential features corresponds here to division into parts (in myth a "part" corresponds functionally to a "feature" in a descriptive text but differs profoundly from it in mechanism, inasmuch as it does not characterize the whole but is identified with it).

The logical concept "class" (a set of certain objects) corresponds to the concept in myth of things which from the extramythological standpoint are many as one.

3. In the mythological world pictured in this fashion there takes place quite a specific type of semiosis, which in general amounts to a process of nomination: in the mythological consciousness a sign is analogous to a proper noun [sobstvennoe imia — literally, proper name]. Let us recall in this regard that the general meaning of proper noun is tautological in principle: any name is not characterized by differential features but merely denotes the object to which the given name is attached. A set of objects with the same name does not necessarily share any special properties other than the properties of having the given name. (1)

Accordingly, while the sentence "Ivan is a man" does not pertain to the mythological consciousness, one possible result of its mythologization might, for example, be the sentence "Ivan is Man," and specifically to the degree to which the word "man" in the latter sentence emerges as a proper noun corresponding to a personification of the object and not reducible to "humanity" (or in general to particular features of Homo sapiens). (2) Compare, on the other hand, the correspondence of the sentences "Ivan is a Hercules" and "Ivan is Hercules," in which the word "Hercules" in the former case is a common noun and in the

Myth — Name — Culture

latter is a proper name, referring to a particular individual who belongs to a different hypostasis. In the latter case what is occurring is not a characterization of Ivan in terms of some particular feature (for example, the feature physical strength) but a characterization of him through an integral whole — through naming. We readily agree that our example is somewhat artificial in character, since it would be difficult for us actually to identify a concrete person with the Heracles of mythology: for us the latter is associated with a particular cultural-historical period. However, here is a completely real example: In eighteenth-century Russia, the opponents of Peter the Great called him "Antichrist." For some of them this was a means of characterizing his personality and deeds, while others believed that Peter in actual fact was the Antichrist. Thus one and the same text can function in significantly different ways.

Hence, while in the examples considered with common nouns in the predicate construction there is a correlation with some abstract concept, in the corresponding examples with proper nouns instead there is a definite identification (correlation with an isomorphous object in another hypostasis). In languages with the article, such transformation can in some cases, apparently, be done by making the name serving as predicate determined, with the aid of the definite article. And in fact the definite article transforms a word (more exactly, a determined combination) into a name, singling out the denoted object as known and concrete. (3)

Note: It is necessary to emphasize the connection between certain typical plot situations and the nominational character of the mythological world. In this category are situations of "naming" of things that have no names, which are regarded at the same time also as acts of creation (4); renaming as reincarnation or rebirth; mastery of language (for example, of birds or animals); recognition of "true" name or its concealment. (5) No less instructive are various taboos placed on proper nouns and, on the other hand, the tabooing of common nouns (for example, the names of animals, sicknesses, etc.) which in a number of cases definitely indicates that the corresponding names are understood (and, consequently, function in the mythological model of the world) precisely as proper nouns. (6)

It may be said that <u>the general meaning of the proper noun in its ultimate abstraction resolves to myth</u>. It is precisely in the sphere of proper nouns that there occurs that identification of word and denotate which is so characteristic of mythological concepts, the features of which are, on the one hand, all kinds of taboos and, on the other, ritual changing of proper nouns (compare below, Section III-2).

This identification of the name and the named in turn determines our idea of the nonconventional character of proper nouns and of their ontological essence. (7) For this reason, the mythological consciousness can be interpreted, from the standpoint of the development of semiosis, as <u>asemiotic</u>.

Thus myth and name are directly connected in their nature. In a certain sense they are mutually defined and one is reducible to the other: myth is personal (nominational), and name is mythological. (8)

3.1. Proceeding from the foregoing, it may be considered that the system of proper nouns forms not only a categorial realm of natural language but also its specific mythological stratum. In a number of linguistic situations the behavior of proper nouns is so different from the corresponding behavior of other linguistic categories that it inevitably impels us to the idea that we are confronted by some other, differently organized language, incorporated into the body of natural language.

The mythological layer of natural language is not reducible directly to proper nouns; however, proper nouns make up its core. As a number of specialized linguistic studies have shown (currently S. M. and N. I. Tolstoi are doing work along these lines), in language one can distinguish a special lexical stratum that is characterized by extranormal phonetics as well as specific grammatical features which seem anomalous against the

Myth — Name — Culture

background of the given language. In this category one finds, among others, sound imitations, various forms of expressive vocabulary, so-called nursery words (9), forms for calling and driving away animals, and so forth. Furthermore, this stratum, from the standpoint of the bearer of the language, is primary, natural, and nonsemiotic. It is instructive, particularly, that the elements in question are used in situations of conversation with children (nursery words), with animals (calling words; also compare the naming of animals by the colors of their coats, etc.), sometimes also with foreigners, etc. It is symptomatic that such words can be conjoined with proper nouns both in form and in use. Thus in Russian, "nursery words" are formed along the lines of hypocoristic proper names (kisa, biaka; vova to denote a wolf [volk]; petia for a rooster [petiukha], etc.), while words for calling animals (tsyp-tsyp, kis-kis, mas'-mas', etc.) function, essentially, as vocative forms (of, correspondingly, tsypa, kisa, masia, etc.). No less instructive and revealing in this regard are points of contact with children's language, which is explained by the special role played by proper nouns in the world of the child (where in general all words can potentially serve as proper nouns). On this, see particularly I-5 below.

4. The mythological world has a specific mythological understanding of space. The latter is conceived not as a continuum of features but as an aggregate of individual objects bearing proper names. Consequently, in the intervals between them, space, as it were, is broken since it does not have so fundamental a quality, from our point of view, as continuity. A partial corollary of this is the "tattered" character of mythological space and the fact that a shift from one locus to another may occur outside time, being replaced by certain fixed bylina formulas, or can be arbitrarily compressed or expanded relative to the flow of time in loci designated by proper nouns. On the other hand, when it turns up in a new place, an object may lose contact with its previous state and become a different object (in some cases a change in name may also correspond to this). This is the origin of the characteristic capacity of mythological space to model other, nonspatial (semantic, value, etc.) relationships.

Semiotics and Structuralism

The fact that mythological space is filled with proper nouns gives its internal objects a finite, countable character and gives the space the attributes of delimitedness. In this sense mythological space is always small and closed, although in the myth itself one may be dealing with cosmic dimensions. (<u>10</u>)

In speaking of the delimited, countable character of the mythological world, we can refer to the circumstance that the presence of several different denotates of a proper noun in principle contradicts its nature (by creating significant difficulties for communication), while the presence of different denotates of a common noun is, generally speaking, a normal occurrence.

<u>Note</u>: The plot of myth as text is very often based on the hero's crossing the border of a "crowded," closed space and his emergence into the outer, unbounded world. However, at the root of the mechanism for the generation of such plots lies precisely the conception of the existence of a small "world of proper nouns." A mythological plot of this kind begins with movement into a world in which the names of objects are unknown to man — hence the plots dealing with the inevitability of the death of heroes who venture into the outside world without knowing the non-human system of nomination, and the survival of a hero who obtains this knowledge in some miraculous way. The very existence of an "alien," open world in myth presumes the existence of "one's own," endowed with the traits of countability and filled with objects — carriers of proper names.

5. The mythological consciousness characterized above may become the object of direct observation by turning to the world of a young child. The tendency to regard all the words in the language as proper nouns (<u>11</u>), the identification of cognition with the process of nomination, the specific experience of space and time (compare Chekhov's story "Grisha": "Until then, Grisha had known only a <u>rectangular</u> world, in one corner of which stood his bed, in another his nurse's trunk, in the third

Myth — Name — Culture

a chair, while in the fourth a lamp burned" [12]), and a number of other features that coincide with the most characteristic traits of mythological consciousness enable us to speak of the child's consciousness as typically mythological. (13) Apparently, at a certain stage of development in the child's world there is no fundamental difference between proper and common nouns, i.e., this opposition is just not relevant.

In this regard it is pertinent to recall an extremely significant observation by R. O. Jakobson, who pointed out that proper nouns are the first things infants learn and are the last to be lost in aphasic speech disorders. It is noteworthy in this respect that an infant picking up pronominal forms from adult speech — the last things to be learned, according to Jakobson's observations — uses them as proper nouns: "For example, he [the child — Iu. L. and B. U.] attempts to monopolize the first-person singular pronoun: 'Don't you dare call yourself "I." Only I am I, and you are only you.'" (14) It is interesting to compare with this the taboo use of pronouns (he, that one, etc.), evident in various ethnographic areas in naming the devil, a wood-demon [leshii], a household spirit [domovoi], or on the other hand, in naming wife or husband (when associated with the prohibition against the use by husband and wife of each other's proper names), in which the pronoun actually functions as a proper noun. (15)

No less suggestive, generally speaking, is the denotation of action in children's speech. When the child reaches a point at which an adult would use a verb, the child may switch to paralinguistic depiction of the action, accompanied by interjectional word invention. This may be regarded as a form of narration unique in children's speech. The closest model of children's narration would be an artificially assembled text in which the naming of objects would be done by means of proper nouns and the description of actions by means of inserted film shots. (16)

In this method of transmission of verbal meanings, the mythologism of thought appears with particular clarity, since the action is not abstracted from the subject, but is integrated with the agent and can emerge generally as a condition of a proper noun.

Semiotics and Structuralism

It may be assumed that an ontogenetically determined mythological layer is fixed in the consciousness (and in language), making it heterogeneous and creating, in the final analysis, a tension between the poles of mythological and nonmythological perception.

5.1. It must be emphasized that a "pure," i.e., completely consistent, model of mythological thought probably cannot be documented either by ethnographic data or by observations of a child. In both cases the researcher is actually dealing with texts of complex organization and with a consciousness that is more or less heterogeneous. This can be explained — aside from the disturbing influence of the observer's own consciousness — by the fact that a consistently mythological stage should pertain to so early a stage of development that is fundamentally incapable of being observed, both for chronological reasons and because it is basically impossible to make contact with it, so that the only instrument for study is reconstruction. Equally acceptable is another explanation, according to which heterogeneity is an inherent property of the human consciousness, for the mechanism of which the presence of at least two systems not totally translatable into each other is absolutely necessary.

When the former approach is taken, a step-by-step explanation (which in practice usually becomes evaluative) of the essence of mythologism comes to the fore, while with the second approach, its interpretation as a typologically universal phenomenon predominates. The two approaches complement each other. One might comment that from a purely formal point of view (which digresses from the essence of the question), the very principle of spatial or temporal localization of mythological consciousness (linking it with one or another stage in the development of humanity or with some ethnographically outlined area) corresponds, generally speaking, to precisely that mythological concept of space which was discussed above. And contrariwise, acceptance of mythologism as a typologically universal phenomenon corresponds completely to the conventional-logical vision of the world.

In any case, it must be borne in mind that ethnic groups at

Myth — Name — Culture

obviously early stages of cultural development and characterized by pronounced mythologism of thought may, in quite a number of situations, reveal a striking capacity to construct complicated and detailed classifications of the logical type (compare the diverse classifications of the vegetable and animal world by abstract features that one observes among the Australian aborigines). (17) One can say that in this case mythological thought coexists with logical or descriptive thinking. On the other hand, there are some situations in which elements of mythological thought may be discovered in the everyday speech behavior of modern, civilized society. (18)

6. It follows from the foregoing that mythological consciousness is fundamentally untranslatable onto the level of another description, is closed within itself, and consequently is comprehensible only from within, not from without. This follows, in particular, from the type of semiosis that is inherent in mythological consciousness and that finds a linguistic parallel in the untranslatability of proper nouns. In the light of what has been said, the very possibility of description of myth by a possessor of modern consciousness would be highly dubious if not for the heterogeneity of our thinking, which preserves some layers isomorphous with mythological language.

Thus it is precisely the heterogeneous nature of our thought that enables us to make use of our inner experience in constructing mythological consciousness. In a certain sense understanding mythology is equivalent to remembering.

II

1. The significance of mythological texts for a culture of a nonmythological type is confirmed, in part, by the persistence of efforts to translate them into cultural languages of a nonmythological type. In the realm of science this engenders logical versions of mythological texts, while in the field of art — and in a number of cases in simple translation into natural language — it results in metaphorical constructions. We must emphasize the fundamental difference between myth and meta-

phor, although the latter is a natural translation of the former into the normal forms of our thinking. In fact, in a rigorously mythological text, metaphor as such is, strictly speaking, impossible.

2. In a number of cases a mythological text, translated into the categories of nonmythological consciousness, is perceived as symbolic. A symbol of this kind (19) can be interpreted as the result of reading a myth from the standpoint of a later semiotic consciousness — i.e., interpreted as an iconic or quasi-iconic sign. It should be observed that although iconic signs are to some degree closer to mythological texts, they, like signs of the conventional type, represent facts of a fundamentally different consciousness.

In speaking of the symbol in its relationship to myth, it is necessary to distinguish between the symbol as a type of sign directly generated by mythological consciousness and the symbol as a type of sign that merely presumes a mythological situation. Correspondingly, we should discriminate between symbol as reference to myth as text and symbol as reference to myth as genre. In the latter case, moreover, the symbol may lay claim to creation of a mythological situation, for it serves as a principle of creation.

In a case in which a symbolic text corresponds to some mythological text, the latter emerges as a metatext in relation to the former; and the symbol corresponds to a concrete element of this text. (20) However, in a case in which a symbolic text corresponds to myth as a genre, i.e., to some undivided mythological situation, the mythological model of the world, undergoing functional changes, behaves as metasystem playing the role of metalanguage. Correspondingly, a symbol then corresponds not to an element of metatext, but to a category of metalanguage. From the definition given above (see I-1) it follows that the symbol, understood in the first way, does not, generally speaking, go beyond the framework of mythological consciousness, while in the second case it belongs to nonmythological consciousness (i.e., a consciousness generating "descriptive," not "mythological," characterizations).

Myth — Name — Culture

Certain texts from the early twentieth century, for example, those of Russian Symbolists, may be used as an example of a symbolism that does not relate to mythological consciousness. It may be said that here the elements of mythological texts are organized in accordance with a nonmythological principle and, in general, even pseudoscientifically.

3. While in texts of modern times mythological elements may be organized rationally, i.e., nonmythologically, the very opposite situation can be observed in baroque texts, where, on the contrary, abstract constructs are organized according to the mythological principle: the elements and properties can act as characters from the mythological world. This is explained by the fact that the baroque arose against a background of religious culture, while the symbolism of modern times has been engendered against a background of rational consciousness, with its normal connections.

Note: This, incidentally, is why the argument about what the baroque represents historically — a phenomenon of the Counter Reformation, an exaltation of intense Catholic thought, or the "realistic," "optimistic" art of the Renaissance — is essentially pointless: baroque culture, as a transitional type, simultaneously is correlated with both cultures, the Renaissance culture being expressed in the system of objects, and the medieval in the system of connections (figuratively speaking, Renaissance culture determines the system of nouns, while the medieval determines the system of verbs).

4. Since, as has been said, a mythological text under the conditions of nonmythological consciousness generates metaphoric constructs, the tendency toward mythologism may be implemented in a process of opposite direction: realization of metaphor, its literal interpretation (which destroys the very metaphoricity of the text). A device of this kind characterizes surrealist art. The result is an imitation of myth outside mythological consciousness.

Semiotics and Structuralism

III

1. For all the diversity of its concrete manifestations, to some degree mythologism may be observed in the most diverse cultures and, in general, shows marked stability in the history of culture. Its forms can be relicts or results of regeneration; they may be unconscious or deliberate.

Note: It is necessary to differentiate spontaneously arising mythological layers and segments in the individual and social consciousness from conscious attempts, undertaken for whatever historical reasons, to imitate the mythogenic mind by means of nonmythological thought. From the standpoint of nonmythological consciousness, texts of the latter kind may be regarded as myths (or even not differ from them). However, their organic incorporation into the nonmythological circle of texts and their total translatability into nonmythological languages of culture indicate the illusoriness of this coincidence.

1.1. In a semiotic aspect, the stability of mythological texts can be explained by the fact that, being the product of specific nominational semiosis — in which signs are not ascribed but recognized, and the very act of nomination is identical with the act of cognition — myth, in its further historical development, began to be perceived as an alternative to semiotic thinking (compare above, I-3). Inasmuch as the semiotic consciousness accumulates social relationships within itself, in the history of culture the struggle against various forms of social evil often becomes the negation of particular sign systems (including one so all-inclusive as natural language) or of the principle of semioticity as such. Recourse, in such cases, to mythological thought (and along with it, in a number of cases, to the consciousness of childhood) is a rather common fact in the history of culture.

2. From a typological standpoint, even if one considers the inevitable heterogeneity of all the cultures actually recorded

Myth — Name — Culture

in texts, it is useful to discriminate cultures oriented toward mythological thinking from cultures oriented toward extramythological thought. The former may be defined as cultures oriented toward proper nouns.

One observes a certain parallelism, not without interest, between the character of changes in the "language of proper nouns" and a culture oriented toward mythological consciousness. The very fact that it is precisely the subsystem of proper nouns that forms in natural language the special layer that can be subjected to change and conscious (artificial) regulation by the bearer of a language (21) is, in itself, sufficiently suggestive. In fact, while semantic motion in natural language bears the character of gradual development — internal semantic shifts — the "language of proper nouns" moves like a chain of conscious and sharply delimited from each other acts of naming and renaming. A new name corresponds to a new state. From the mythological point of view, the transition from one state to another is conceived in the formula "and he saw a new sky and a new earth" (Apoc., XXI, 1) and simultaneously as an act of complete replacement of all proper nouns.

3. An example of orientation toward a mythological consciousness in relatively recent times (which is usually associated with the rejection of old concepts) could be the Petrine period's vision of itself and the understanding of this epoch in Russia during the eighteenth and early nineteenth centuries that was imposed by the era's inertia.

If we consider the interpretation of the Petrine period by its contemporaries, we are struck by the extremely rapid establishment of a mythological canon that, not only for subsequent generations but to a considerable degree for historians, was transformed into a device for coding the real events of the time. One must note above all the profound belief in the complete and absolute rebirth of the country, a belief that naturally stresses the magical role of Peter — the demiurge of the new world.

> One does not drop from his hands the wise Petrine rulings,
>   By which we became <u>suddenly</u> a <u>new</u> people.
>
>   (Kantemir)

Peter I appears in the role of the sole creator of this new world:

> He was God; he was your God, Russia!
>
> (Lomonosov)

"Augustus, the Roman emperor, as he was dying, uttered an extraordinary paean to himself: 'I inherited a Rome of brick, but am leaving one of marble.' For our Glorious Monarch it would be vanity, not praise, to utter this; it is fitting, in truth, to say that he inherited a Russia of wood but created one of gold" (Feofan Prokopovich).

This creation of a "new" and "golden" Russia was viewed as a general renaming — a complete replacement of names: a replacement of the names of the state; transfer of the capital and giving it a "foreign" name; a change in the title of the head of the state and in the designations of ranks and institutions; a reversal of the places occupied by "native" and "foreign" languages in everyday life (22); and the associated complete renaming of the world as such. (23) At the same time, there occurred a monstrous expansion of the realm of proper nouns, since the majority of socially active common nouns in fact functionally shifted to the class of proper nouns. (24)

4. We could present other, but in their own way no less vivid, manifestations of mythological consciousness at the opposite social pole of the eighteenth century. Its features may be seen, in part, in the pretender movement. Simply asking the question of which of the names in the pair "Peter III — Pugachev" is "legitimate" reveals a typically mythological attitude toward the problem of name (compare Pushkin's note: "'Tell me,' I said to D. P'ianov, 'how Pugachev came to be sponsor at your wedding?' The old man answered me angrily: 'To you he is Pugachev, but to me he was the great lord Peter Fedorovich.'"). No less characteristic is the story of the alleged "royal signs" on the body of Pugachev. (25)

But perhaps the most striking example is the famous portrait of Pugachev in the collection of the State Historical Museum in Moscow. As was determined, this portrait was painted by an unknown artist <u>over</u> a portrait of Catherine II. (<u>26</u>) If a portrait is seen as the parallel in painting of a proper name, the re-painting of a portrait is equivalent to an act of renaming. Many analogous examples could be given.

5. It would be quite an intriguing task to describe for various cultures the realms of actual functioning of proper nouns, the degree of cultural activity of this layer and its relationship, on the one hand, to language in general and, on the other, to its polar antipode — the metalinguistic sphere within the confines of the given culture.

IV

1. The opposition between the "mythological" language of proper nouns and the descriptive language of science can, apparently, be associated with its antithesis: poetry and science. In the usual conception, myth is associated with metaphorical speech and, through it, with verbal art. However, in the light of what has been said above, this connection appears dubious. If we hypothetically assume the possibility of the existence both of a "language of proper nouns" and of the type of thought associated with it as a mythogenic substratum (such a construct may in any case be regarded as a model of one of the linguistic tendencies that actually exist), then a demonstrable corollary will be the assertion of the <u>impossibility of poetry at a mythological stage</u>. Poetry and myth emerge as antipodes, each of which is possible only if the other is negated.

1.1. Let us recall the well-known thesis of A. N. Kolmogorov, who defined the amount of information in any language, H, in the following formula:

$$H = h_1 + h_2,$$

where h_1 is the diversity that makes it possible to transmit the entire volume of differing semantic information, and h_2 is the diversity that expresses the flexibility of the language, the possibility of transmitting a certain equivalent content in a number of different ways, i.e., linguistic entropy itself. Kolmogorov commented that precisely h_2 — i.e., linguistic synonymy in the broad sense — is the source of poetic information. When $h_2 = 0$, poetry is impossible. (27) But if we imagine a language consisting of proper nouns (a language in which common names perform the function of proper nouns), and behind it a world of unique objects, then the absence of any room for synonyms in such a universe becomes obvious. Under no circumstances is mythological identification synonymy. Synonymy presumes the existence of several interchangeable designations for one and the same object and, consequently, relative freedom in using them. Mythological identification has a fundamentally extra-textual character, and it arises on the basis of the indivisibility of the name from the thing. Here one should not speak of a substitution of equivalent names, but of a transformation of the object itself. Each name pertains to a specific moment in the transformation, and thus in one and the same context it cannot substitute for another name. Therefore, names denoting different hypostases of a changing thing cannot substitute for each other, are not synonyms; and without synonyms poetry is impossible. (28)

1.2. The breakdown of mythological consciousness is accompanied by processes that proceed tempestuously: the reinterpretation of mythological texts as metaphorical and the development of synonymy at the expense of periphrastic expressions. This immediately leads to a sharp growth in the "flexibility of language" and thereby creates the conditions for the development of poetry.

2. The picture thus drawn, although confirmed by numerous examples from archaic texts, is in substantial measure hypothetical, inasmuch as it rests on reconstructions that re-create a period of remote chronological distance not directly recorded in any texts. However, the same picture may be viewed not from a diachronic, but from a synchronic, standpoint. Then natural language will seem to us a kind of synchronically orga-

nized structure at whose semantically opposite poles are found proper nouns and groups of words functionally equivalent to them, which we discussed above (I-3.1), and pronouns, which are the natural basis for the development of mythogenic models, on the one hand, and metalinguistic models, on the other. (29)

2.1. To our consciousness, cultivated in that scientific tradition which formed in Europe from Aristotle to Descartes, it appears natural to assume that no motion of cognitive thought is possible outside a two-stage description (in accordance with the pattern "concrete — abstract"). However, it can be shown that the language of proper nouns that served archaic groups proves quite capable of expressing concepts corresponding to our abstract categories. Let us limit ourselves to a single example from A. Ia. Gurevich's The Categories of Medieval Culture. The author discusses specific phraseologisms encountered in ancient Scandinavian texts and constructed on the principle of combining pronoun and proper noun. Agreeing with S. D. Katsnel'son, Gurevich feels that they concerned stable kin groups denoted by a proper noun. (30) The proper noun — the sign of a separate individual — here plays the role of kin name, which for us would require the introduction of some metaterm of a different level. An analogous example might be cited from the use of coats of arms in chivalric Poland. By its nature, a coat of arms is a personal sign, because it can be borne only by one living representative of a clan and is handed down by inheritance only after his death. However, the coat of arms of a magnate, while remaining his personal heraldic sign, simultaneously performs the metafunction of group designation for the gentry fighting under his banner.

2.2. The indivisibility of the levels of direct observation and logical construction under which proper nouns (individual things), while remaining themselves, were elevated in rank, replacing our abstract concepts, proved to be quite favorable for thought constructed on directly perceived modeling. The stupendous achievements of ancient cultures in constructing cosmological models and in accumulating astronomical, climatological, and other knowledge are apparently connected to this.

Semiotics and Structuralism

2.3. While not giving logical-syllogistic thought a chance to develop, the "language of proper nouns" and the mythological thinking associated with it stimulated the capacity to establish identifications, analogies, and equivalencies. For example, when a bearer of ancient consciousness built a typically mythological model, in accordance with which the cosmos, society, and the human body were regarded as isomorphic worlds (isomorphism could extend as far as establishing relationships of similarity between individual planets, minerals, plants, social functions, and parts of the human body), he thereby <u>developed the idea of isomorphism</u> — one of the leading concepts not only of modern mathematics but of science in general.

The specificity of mythological thought lies in the fact that identification of isomorphic units occurs at the level of the objects themselves, not at the level of their names. Accordingly, mythological identification assumes transformation of an object, which occurs in concrete space and time. Logical thought, however, operates with <u>words</u>, possessing relative independence — outside time and space. The idea of isomorphism is present in both cases, but under the conditions of logical thought a relative freedom of manipulation of the initial units is attained.

3. In the light of the foregoing, one can dispute the traditional conception that human culture has moved from a mythopoeic initial period to a logical-scientific one that follows. With regard to both synchrony and diachrony, poetic thought occupies some middle position. Further, it is necessary to emphasize the profoundly conventional character of the stages identified. From the moment culture made its appearance, the system of combinations within it of oppositionally organized semiotic structures (the multichanneled nature of social communications) appears to have been an immutable law. One can only speak of the dominance of certain cultural models or of a subjective orientation toward them by a culture as a whole. From this standpoint, poetry, like science, has accompanied humanity along its entire cultural path. This does not contradict the fact that particular periods of cultural development can proceed "under the sign" of semiosis of one or another type.

Myth — Name — Culture

Notes

1) Compare R. O. Jakobson: "Proper names... take a particular place in our linguistic code: the general meaning of a proper name cannot be defined without a reference to the code. In the code of English, 'Jerry' means a person named Jerry. The circularity is obvious: the name means anyone to whom this name is assigned. The appellative 'pup' means a young dog, 'mongrel' means a dog of mixed breed, 'hound' is a dog used in hunting, while 'Fido' means nothing more than a dog whose name is 'Fido.' The general meaning of such words as 'pup,' 'mongrel,' or 'hound,' could be indicated by abstractions like 'puppihood,' 'mongrelness,' or 'houndness,' but the general meaning of 'Fido' cannot be qualified in this way. To paraphrase Betrand Russell, there are many dogs called 'Fido,' but they do not share any property of 'Fidoness.'" (See R. O. Jakobson, "Shiftery, glagol'nye kategorii i russkii glagol," Printsipy tipologicheskogo analiza iazykov razlichnogo stroia, Moscow, 1972, p. 96; compare R. Jakobson, "Shifters, Verbal Categories, and the Russian Verb," in R. Jakobson, Selected Writings, II, The Hague and Paris, 1971, p. 131.)

2) The history of the scriptural expression Ecce homo (John, XIX, 5) is rather interesting in this connection. There is reason to believe that this sentence was actually uttered in Aramaic; but at that time it apparently would originally have meant simply "Here he is," because the word expressing the idea "man" was used in Aramaic in its pronominal sense, in approximately the same way as the word man is employed in modern German (oral communication from A. A. Zalizniak). Subsequent reinterpretation of this sentence has to do with the fact that the word "man" (presented in the corresponding translation of the scriptural text) came to be understood, generally, as analogous to a proper noun, i.e., underwent mythologization.

3) The connection between the proper noun and the category of definiteness, expressed by the definite article, is revealed in the native Arabic grammatical tradition. Proper nouns are

regarded there as words whose definiteness has always been inherent in them by virtue of their semantic nature. See G. M. Gabuchan, Teoriia artiklia i problemy arabskogo sintaksisa, Moscow, 1972, pp. 37 ff.

It is characteristic that in the Grammatika slavenskaia of Fedor Maksimov (St. Petersburg, 1723, pp. 179-80), the mark titlo, which in Church Slavonic texts indicated the sacralization of a word, compares semantically with the Greek article: both carry the meaning of uniqueness.

4) Compare V. V. Ivanov, "Drevneindiiskii mif ob ustanovlenii imen i ego parallel' v grecheskoi traditsii," Indiia v drevnosti, Moscow, 1964; I. M. Trotskii (Tronskii), "Iz istorii antichnogo iazykoznaniia," Sovetskoe iazykoznanie, II, Leningrad, 1936, pp. 24-26.

5) Also compare the conception, characteristic of mythological consciousness, of the world as a book, in which cognition is equated with reading, based precisely on the mechanism of decodings and identifications. See Iu. Lotman and B. Uspenskii, "O semioticheskom mekhanizme kul'tury," Uch. zap. Tartuskogo un-ta, Issue 284, Tartu, 1971, p. 152.

6) Thus, for example, to name a disease (aloud) could be interpreted specifically as invoking it: the disease might come if it heard its name (compare in this connection such colloquial expressions as "to summon disaster, disease," etc.). See the extensive material of this type gathered in the following monograph: D. K. Zelenin, Tabu slov u narodov Vostochnoi Evropy i Severnoi Azii (Part I in Sbornik Muzeia antropologii i etnografii, Vol. VIII, Leningrad, 1929, pp. 1-144; Part II, ibid., Vol. IV, Leningrad, 1930, pp. 1-166).

7) Compare, in this connection, the ancient Greek concept of the correctness of names by nature (see I. M. Trotskii, op. cit., p. 25).

8) Further confirmation of the fact that in the mythological world the common name of an object is also its individual proper name can be found in a number of texts. Thus, for example, in the Younger Edda, in the story about how Odin (calling himself Bulwerk) set off to obtain the mead of poetry, we read:

Myth — Name — Culture

"Bulwerk took an auger named Rati." In a footnote the editors state: "This name also means 'auger'" (<u>Mladshaia Edda</u>, edition prepared by O. A. Smirnitskaia and M. I. Steblin-Kamenskii, Leningrad, 1970, p. 59; compare analogous notes on pp. 72 and 79). See the special analysis of this aspect of Homeric language in M. S. Al'tman, <u>Perezhitki rodovogo stroia v sobstvennykh imenakh u Gomera</u>, Leningrad, 1936. Furthermore, a different variant of the same tendency appears in assigning names to swords, which is typical of chivalric epics: Roland's sword was called Durandal, and Siegfried's was Balmung.

9) We have in mind the special lexical forms used by adults in conversing with children.

10) The concept of the dependence of man's behavior on his <u>locus</u> is expressed particularly vividly in one of the early medieval Armenian legends, which has come down to us in the <u>Istoriia Armenii</u> by Pavstos Biuzand. It relates an episode that occurred in the fourth century, when Armenia was divided between Byzantium and Sassanid Persia. Since the Arshakid dynasty of Armenian kings continued to exist for a while in eastern (Persian) Armenia as vassals of the Persian kings, while at the same time it continued to struggle for restoration of the country's independence, the legend is quite original, for while remaining within the framework of mythological ideas, it revealed the possibility of a person's dual behavior as a consequence of moving from one locus to another. The Persian King Shapukh, wishing to know the secret intentions of his vassal, the Armenian King Arshak, ordered that half of his tent floor be covered with Armenian soil and the other half with Persian. Inviting Arshak into the tent, he took him by the arm and began to pace back and forth with him: "And when, walking around the tent, they stepped on Persian soil, he said: 'Armenian King Arshak, why did you become my enemy? I loved you like a son, wanted to give you my daughter in marriage and make you my son; but you grew fierce against me and on your own, against my will, made me your enemy....' King Arshak said: 'I sinned and am guilty before you; for, although I overtook and won victory over your enemies, killed them and expected from you the

reward of life, yet my enemies led me into error, frightened me with regard to you and compelled me to flee. But the oath that I swore to you led me to you, and so here I am before you. And I am your servant, am in your hands; do as you will with me; if you wish, kill me, for I, thy servant, am very guilty before you and deserve death.' And King Shapukh, again taking him by the arm and pretending to be naive, walked along with him and led him toward the side where the floor was covered with Armenian soil. And when Arshak came to the place and stepped on Armenian soil, he, becoming very indignant and proud, changed his tone and began to speak: 'Get away from me, you evildoer — you servant who became lord over your lords. I do not forgive you, and I will take vengeance upon your sons for my ancestors.'" This change in Arshak's conduct is repeated many times in the text, depending on whether he is walking on Armenian or Persian soil. "And so from morning to evening he [Shapukh — Iu. L. and B. U.] tested him, and each time Arshak stepped on Armenian soil he became arrogant and he threatened; but when he trod on the local [Persian — Iu. L. and B. U.] soil, he expressed contriteness" (see <u>Istoriia Armenii Favstosa Buzanda</u>, translation from the Old Armenian and commentary by M. A. Gevorgian, Erevan, 1953, pp. 129-30).

It must be emphasized that the concepts "Armenian soil" and "Persian soil" are here isomorphic with the concepts "Armenia" and "Persia" and are perceived as metonyms only by the modern mind (compare analogous use of the expression "Russian soil" in Russian medieval texts: when Chaliapin carried a suitcase full of Russian soil with him on trips abroad, it naturally fulfilled for him the function not of poetic metaphor but of mythological identification). Consequently, Arshak's behavior changes depending on what proper noun he is acting as a part of. Note that the medieval ceremony of becoming a vassal, accompanied by a symbolic act of surrender of some domain and of receiving it back, was semiotically deciphered as a change in the name of the domain (compare the custom, prevalent in Russia before 1861, of changing the name of an estate when it was purchased by a new owner).

Myth — Name — Culture

11) Hence the vocative case can appear in nursery words as morphologically original. Compare, for example, bozha or bozia (i.e., bog [God]), which are clearly formed from the vocative bozhe (example provided by S. M. Tolstaia). Entirely analogously, kisa may be taken as derivative from kis-kis, and so forth.

12) Emphasis in the quoted texts is ours, here and below — Iu. L. and B. U.

13) Compare in this regard the characterization of "complex thinking" of a child by L. S. Vygotskii in his book Myshlenie i rech' (L. S. Vygotskii, Izbrannye psikhologicheskie issledovaniia, Moscow, 1956, pp. 168 ff).

14) R. O. Jakobson, op. cit., p. 98. Compare, in this connection, God's words in the Bible: "I am the same Who said: here am I!" (Isaiah, LII, 6, compare: Exodus, III, 14). Compare in the Upanishads (Brihad-āranyaka, I, $4._1$): "In the beginning [all] this was only Atman.... He looked about him and saw no one but himself. And before all else he uttered: 'I am.' That is how the name 'I' arose. Therefore, even today, he who is asked, begins by answering: 'I am' and then goes on to give the other name he bears" (see Brikhadaran'iaka upanishada, translation, preface, and commentary by A. Ia. Syrkin, Moscow, 1964, p. 73). It should be observed that the word "Atman" may be used in the Upanishads as the pronoun "I," "myself" (see commentary by Syrkin, op. cit., p. 168, and also S. Radhakrishnan, Indiiskaia filosofiia, Vol. I, Moscow, 1956, pp. 124 ff.).

15) See D. K. Zelenin, op. cit., Part II, pp. 88-89, 91-93, 108-9, 140.

16) An analogous type of narration may also be observed in ritual dances.

17) See P. Worsley, "Groote Eyland Totemism and Le Totémisme aujourd'hui," in E. Leach., ed., The Structural Study of Myth and Totemism, Edinburgh, 1967, pp. 153-54. Characterizing the features of thought of Australian aborigines in L. S. Vygotskii's terms, the author states: "The totemic classification we have examined is based on 'complex thinking' or 'congeries thinking' [terms proposed by L. S. Vygotskii (op. cit.,

pp. 168-80); according to Vygotskii, unification on the basis of congerie is one of the varieties of complex thinking — Iu. L. and B. U.], but not on 'thinking in concepts.' I do not want to say, however, that aborigines are incapable of thinking in concepts. On the contrary, the systematization of flora and fauna, i.e., ethnobotanical and ethnozoological models, they developed independent of totemic classification specifically reveals an obvious capacity on the part of aborigines for conceptual thought. In one of my works I have listed hundreds of species of plants and animals that were not only known to aborigines but had been classified by them into such taxonomic groups as, for example, <u>jinungwangba</u> (large animals living on dry land), <u>wuradjidja</u> (those which fly, including birds), <u>augwalja</u> (fish and other sea animals), etc. At the same time, various species are combined in ecologically related groups. It is precisely for this reason, of course, that Donald Thompson — a natural scientist by training — was able to state that the analogous ethnobotanical-zoological systems of the aborigines of Northern Queensland 'bear a certain resemblance to a simple Linnaean classification.'" Worsley, who evaluates such classification systems as "proto-scientific" (while emphasizing their fundamentally logical character), concludes: "Thus we have not one but two classifications, and it would be wrong to think that totemic classification is the only way to organize objects in the external world in the minds of the aborigines."

18) Compare Vygotskii's observations on the elements of "complex thinking" (observed primarily in children) in the everyday language of adults (L. S. Vygotskii, op. cit., pp. 169, 172 ff.). The scholar observes, in part, that when speaking, for example, of tableware or clothing, an adult often has in mind not so much the corresponding abstract concept as a set of concrete things (as is typical, generally speaking, of a child).

19) We are not referring here to the special meaning given this term in Ch. Pierce's classification.

20) Of course, in the sense of "sign-design," not "sign-event" (compare R. Carnap, <u>Introduction to Semantics</u>, Cambridge, Mass., 1946, Section 3).

Myth — Name — Culture

21) However, cases in which attempts at renaming are extended to particular common nouns (for example, in the Russia of Paul I) may indicate specifically the incorporation of such nouns into the mythological sphere of proper nouns, i.e., of a definite expansion of the mythological consciousness.

22) The linguistic phenomenon observed by Pushkin:

> And on their lips did not our native language
> Become foreign?

was a direct consequence of conscious orientation of organized efforts. Compare the instruction: "One's desire should be decently presented in accepted and courteous words, as if one had had occasion to speak with some foreign person" (Iunosti chestnoe zertsalo, ili pokazanie k zhiteiskomu obkhozhdeniiu, sobrannoe ot raznykh avtorov poveleniem E. I. V. Gosudaria Petra Velikogo, St. Petersburg, 1767, p. 29). Also compare Trediakovskii's observations in "Razgovor ob ortografii" on the special social function of a foreign accent in Russian society in the middle of the eighteenth century: "'A person from a foreign land' here says to a 'Russian': 'If well-known rules concerning your stresses are found, then we all will learn well how to utter your words; but in this perfection we shall lose the right to be a foreigner, which in truth is more important for me than a proper pronunciation of your language'" (see Sochineniia Tred'iakovskogo, Vol. III, St. Petersburg, 1849, p. 164).

The depth of this general attitude in the culture of the "St. Petersburg period" of Russian history appears most vividly, perhaps, in its influence on the social circles imbued with the Slavophile attitude in the mid-nineteenth century. Thus V. S. Aksakova reacted in 1855 to the appearance of a number of progressive publications (in the Morskoi sbornik) with the following diary entry: "One breathes more comfortably, as if one were reading about a foreign country" (Dnevnik V. S. Aksakovoi, 1854-1855, St. Petersburg, 1913, p. 67. Compare V. A. Kitaev, Ot frondy k okhranitel'stvu. Iz istorii russkoi liberal'noi mysli 50-60kh godov XIX veka, Moscow, 1972, p. 45).

Semiotics and Structuralism

23) Part of this was the practice of renaming traditional toponyms by order (and not custom) that was established after Peter. It must be emphasized that we are not talking about a conventional connection between a geographic point and its name, permitting the sign to be changed without changing the thing itself, but about their mythological identification, since the change of the name is conceived of as destruction of the old thing and the birth in its place of a new one, more nearly satisfying the requirements of the initiator of this action. That such operations were commonplace is confirmed by a story in the memoirs of S. Iu. Witte. In Odessa, the street on which he had "lived when a student," then called Dvorianskaia, "was renamed Witte St. by order of the municipal Duma" (S. Iu. Witte, Vospominaniia, Vol. 3, Moscow, 1960, p. 484). In 1908 a Black Hundred municipal Duma, writes Witte, "decided to rename the street bearing my name to Peter the Great St." (ibid., p. 485). Aside from the desire to please Nicholas II (every order to give a street the name of a member of the royal house undoubtedly became known to the tsar, because it could go into effect only with his personal approval), here one clearly felt the notion that the act of renaming the street was associated with efforts to destroy Witte himself (at that time the Black Hundreds made several attempts on his life; it is suggestive that the author of the memoirs himself classifies these actions as synonymous). But the author of the memoirs does not note that the naming of the street for Witte was also done in a renaming process. (After the Revolution the street was renamed Komintern St., but after the war the name Peter the Great St. was reinstituted.) Witte also communicates another, no less vivid fact: After Prince V. A. Dolgorukov, governor-general of Moscow under Alexander III, fell into disfavor and was replaced in his post by Grand Duke Sergii Aleksandrovich, the Moscow municipal Duma, demonstrating that the time of Dolgorukov had been succeeded by that of Sergii, "issued a resolution on renaming Dolgorukov Alley [today it is Belinskii St. — Iu. L. and B. U.], which passes by the house of the governor-general of Moscow, as Grand Duke Sergei Aleksandrovich Alley" (ibid., p. 486).

Myth — Name — Culture

True, the renaming did not take place, for Alexander III countermanded it with a resolution: "How base!" (ibid., p. 487).

24) The trend toward "mythologization" permeates Petrine society all the more because it regarded itself as moving in the opposite direction: its ideal of "regularity" presumed the building of a state machinery "correct" and legitimate throughout, in which the world of proper nouns was replaced by numerical orderliness. Indicative in this regard were the efforts to replace the names of streets (proposed canals) with numbers (the "lines" on Vasilevskii Island in Petersburg) and the introduction of numerical order into the system of official hierarchy (the table of ranks). Orientation toward the number was typical of Petersburg culture and distinguished it from that of Moscow. P. A. Viazemskii wrote: "Lord Yarmouth was in Petersburg in the early 1820s. Speaking of the pleasures of his stay in Petersburg, he commented that he often visited an amiable lady of the sixth class who lived on the Sixteenth Line" (P. Viazemskii, Staraia zapisnaia knizhka, Leningrad, 1929, p. 200; compare, in the same source, p. 326).

This mixing of opposite tendencies generated so contradictory a phenomenon as the post-Petrine government bureaucracy.

25) See K. V. Chistov, Russkie narodnye sotsial'no-utopicheskie legendy, Moscow, 1967, pp. 149 ff.

26) See M. Babenchikov, "Portret Pugacheva v Istoricheskom muzee," Literaturnoe nasledstvo, No. 9-10, Moscow, 1933.

27) See the presentation of A. N. Kolmogorov's concept in I. I. Revzin, "Soveshchanie v g. Gor'kom, posviashchennoe primeneniiu matematicheskikh metodov k izucheniiu iazyka khudozhestvennoi literatury," Strukturno-tipologicheskie issledovaniia, Moscow, 1962, pp. 288-89; A. K. Zholkovskii, "Soveshchanie po izucheniiu poeticheskogo iazyka (Obzor dokladov)," Mashinnyi perevod i prikladnaia lingvistika, Issue 7, Moscow, 1962, pp. 93-94.

28) If poetry is connected with synonymy, then mythology is realized in the opposite linguistic phenomenon — homonymy (compare comments on the fundamental connection between myth and homonymy in M. S. Al'tman, Perezhitki rodovogo

stroia v sobstvennykh imenakh u Gomera, Leningrad, 1936, pp. 10-11, passim).

29) It is remarkable that an essentially analogous understanding of poetry can also be found in texts directly reflecting the mythological consciousness. See the definition of poetry in the Younger Edda ("Iazyk poezii" — see the edition cited above, p. 60):

"What kind of language is suitable for poetry?"
"The language of poetry is created in a threefold way."
"How?"
"Each thing can be called by its name. The second kind of poetic expression is that which is called substitution of names [reference is to synonymy — Iu. L. and B. U.]. And the third kind is called kenning. It consists of our saying 'Odin' or 'Thor' or some other Aesir or alv, to which we then add the denotation of a feature of another As or one of his deeds. Then the entire naming pertains to this other, not to the one who was named [reference is to a special kind of metaphor — Iu. L. and B. U.]."

30) A. Ia. Gurevich, Kategorii srednevekovoi kul'tury, Moscow, 1972, pp. 73-74; S. D. Katsnel'son, Istoriko-grammaticheskie issledovaniia, Moscow and Leningrad, 1949, pp. 80-81 and 91-94.

Theater and Theatricality in the Order of Early Nineteenth Century Culture

Iu. M. LOTMAN

In Memory of P. G. Bogatyrev

In his article "The Folk Theater of the Czechs and Slovaks" [Narodnyi teatr chekhov i slovakov], Bogatyrev wrote: "One of the principal and basic theatrical characteristics of any theatrical performance is reincarnation: the actor exchanges his personal appearance, costume, voice, and even psychological character traits for the appearance, costume, voice, and character of the person he portrays in the play." (1) It is not only the actor who undergoes reincarnation: the whole world, when it becomes a theatrical world, reorganizes itself according to the laws of theatrical space, entering which, things become the signs of things.

In his works Bogatyrev repeatedly examined the processes by which the extratheatrical world influences that of the theater, and vice versa. The "theatricalization" and ritualization of certain aspects of the extratheatrical world, the situation in which the theater becomes a model for actual behavior, constantly drew his attention. This is what the author of the present work had in mind in dedicating it to the memory of Petr Grigor'evich Bogatyrev.

Semiotics and Structuralism

* * *

Although objectively art always reflects phenomena of life in one way or another, translating them into its language, the conscious attitude of the author and the audience in this regard may be of three kinds.

First, art and extra-artistic reality are regarded as realms between which the difference is so great and fundamentally insuperable that even comparing them is impossible. Thus, for example, until the last war there was a portrait of Empress Elisabeth (by Caravaque) (2) in the Ekaterina Palace at Tsarskoe Selo in which the face, painted to closely resemble the subject, was joined to the nude body of Venus. To the artistic consciousness of later periods such a canvas would have had to appear indecent and, considering the status of the person depicted, simply audacious. However, eighteenth-century viewers saw the picture differently. It could never have even occurred to them to see in the nude female body a depiction of the real body of Elisabeth Petrovna. They saw in the picture a combination of texts with two different standards of convention: the face was a portrait and, consequently, related to a specific external reality as an iconic depiction of it, while the body fell within the norms of allegorical painting, which operated with emblems that were symbols and not depictions of objects. Just as the face of Catherine II and the eagle at her feet in the well-known painting by Levitskii provide a different degree of convention (the face depicts a face while the eagle depicts power), so the face and body in the portrait of Elisabeth were differently correlated with the world of extra-artistic reality.

Thus where the imitative fine arts or theater (as, for example, in ballet) operate with obviously conventional signs and the relationship between depiction and content is determined not by similarity but by a historical convention, the possibility of "confusing" these two levels is excluded, and an insuperable barrier arises between canvas and viewer, stage and audience. Artistic and extra-artistic space are separated by so sharp a border that they can only refer to each other, but not interpenetrate.

Theater and Theatricality

Second, the realm of art is regarded as a region of models and programs. Active influence is directed from the realm of art to the region of extra-artistic reality. Life chooses art as an example and hastens to "imitate" it. *Oscar Wilde*

Third, life serves as the region of modeling activity — it creates the examples that art imitates. While in the second case art provides the forms for people's actual behavior, in the third the forms of actual behavior determine behavior on the stage.

While recognizing the total conventionality of such a characterization, one can compare the first case with classicism, the second with romanticism, and the third with realism.

Historians of literature and art often speak of the "classicism" or "neoclassicism" of the culture of the early nineteenth century. B. V. Tomashevskii spoke of the "Empire" style as a rebirth of classicism in the literature and architecture of the early nineteenth century. (3) L. Ia. Ginzburg writes: "The followers of Karamzin are, of course, not classicists in the content and form of their art, but they are classicists in their historical function, in the role they had to play in the literature of the 1810s, into which they introduced the spirit of system and organization, the norms of 'good taste,' and logical discipline. To solve these problems they found themselves in need of the harmonious, stylistic hierarchy of classicism (naturally, in modified form)." (4)

Students of culture note a new wave of passion for antiquity. (5) In this connection they usually cite a well-known passage from the memoirs of Vigel': "The new Brutuses and Thymoleons desired, finally, to re-create in their own land an antiquity they regarded as exemplary....Everywhere there appeared alabaster vases with carved mythological scenes, censers and little tables in tripod form, curule chairs, long couches where one's hands rested on eagles, griffons, or sphinxes." (6) "The passion for classicism was so strong in Russia that every artist working in this style enjoyed enormous success among his contemporaries. Martos and Count F. Tolstoi mark the boundaries that encompass the history of the Empire style in Russia." (7)

Semiotics and Structuralism

In his memoirs S. Glinka made an interesting comparison between the cult of antiquity of the 1800s and, on the one hand, the sense of civic duty and love of freedom and, on the other hand, the cult of military glory that in the first years of the new century assumed the form of Bonapartism (the national interests of Russia and France had not yet come into conflict: note the Bonapartism of Pierre and Andrei Bolkonskii at the beginning of War and Peace): "The voice of the virtues of ancient Rome, the voice of the Cincinnatuses and the Catos, resounded loudly in the fiery young souls of the cadets....Ancient Rome became my idol too. I did not know under what kind of government I lived, but I knew that liberty was the spirit of the Romans." And further: "He who from youth had studied the heroes of Greece and Rome was then a Bonapartist." (8) This "martial classicism" determined, for example, the interpretation of Russian Empire architecture at the beginning of the nineteenth century: "Monuments, facades, and the cornices of houses are decorated à la grec, with lions' heads, helmets, shields, spears, and swords. The attributes of war appear even on the walls of churches." (9) The turn toward classicism was even more pronounced in Western European culture. In France, where classicism, going beyond the limits of the culture of a particular period, acquired the significance of a national tradition, this tendency was essentially not interrupted but merely changed its coloration with the transition from Revolution to Empire. Even Germany, having survived Stürmer's negation of the classic forms of culture, turned to them again in the work of the later Schiller and Goethe.

Thus it might appear that the tradition of classicism either continued without interruption (France) or was restored in comparatively unchanged form (Russia, Germany). Such a conclusion would be quite wrong.

A number of studies have already noted the fact that "neoclassicism" was, despite its declarations, essentially camouflaged romanticism (see, for example, the works of G. A. Gukovskii). For the special purposes of the present article we need not examine this question in full; we shall consider but a single aspect of it.

Theater and Theatricality

Despite the similarity, in a number of cases, of the structure of the text of works of classicism and neoclassicism, immanent examination of them decisively changes the pragmatics of the text, the attitude of the audience toward it, and the formula of correlation to extratextual reality.

As I have already noted, classicism erected an impenetrable barrier between art and life. This meant that, even when enraptured by theatrical characters, the viewer understood that their place was on the stage and that he could not imitate them in life without risking seeming ridiculous. The stage was ruled by heroism, life by propriety. The laws of both were strict and absolute for artistic and real space. Let us recall Heine's joke when he said that a modern Cato, before stabbing himself, would sniff to make sure the knife did not smell of herring. The meaning of this witticism lay in the mixing of the irreconcilable realms of heroism and good taste.

When Sumarokov, in the heat of his clash with the commandant of Moscow, Saltykov (1770), wrote a letter filled with pathos to Catherine the Great, the empress sharply upbraided him for the "indecency" of transferring into life the norms of a theatrical monologue: "It will always be more pleasant for me," she wrote to the playwright, "to see the presentation of passions in your plays than to read them in letters." And the Grand Duke Konstantin Pavlovich, raised in the same tradition, wrote many years later to his tutor La Harpe: "No one in the world fears and loathes more than I do actions for effect, whose effect is calculated beforehand, or dramatic and enthusiastic actions." (10)

Meanwhile, the barrier between art and the everyday behavior of the viewers was broken in the early years of the nineteenth century. The theater invaded life and actively reshaped people's everyday behavior. The monologue penetrates the letter, the diary, and everyday speech. What yesterday would have seemed pompous and ludicrous, because it was ascribed solely to the realm of theatrical space, becomes the norm in everyday speech and behavior. People of the Revolution conduct themselves in life as on the stage. When Gilbert Romm, sentenced to the guillotine, stabs himself and, tearing the dagger from the wound,

Semiotics and Structuralism

hands it to a friend, he repeats a feat of antique heroism known to the people of his era from numerous depictions in the theater, poetry, and the fine arts. (11) Art becomes the model life imitates.

Examples of how people at the end of the eighteenth and the beginning of the nineteenth centuries built their personal behavior, everyday speech, and in the final analysis, their destiny around literary and theatrical examples are quite numerous. Anyone who has studied the history of everyday texts of that period knows how sharply their style changes as they approximate the norms developed in the purely literary realm.

Let us present only one example, taken from the previously cited memoirs of Sergei Glinka and interesting because of its dual encoding: The norms of antique heroism, drawn from literary texts, become the model toward which is oriented the real behavior of people drawn into practical, mundane situations of Russian life in the 1790s. But this behavior is presented to us in a verbal version. The narrator could have interpreted the content of the story from different points of view: He could have spoken about his hero as a bearer of old-fashioned virtue (in antithesis to the "fops" and fashionable cynics), as an eccentric or even madman, or in some other way. But he chooses the "antique" key, harmonizing the viewpoint of the narrator with the position of the person being discussed. "We had our Catos, our imitators of the valors of the ancient Greeks; we had our Philopoemens. We had our Cato in Gine, who went from cadet to the officer corps and on to become a teacher of mathematics. Had he been in the position of Regulus, he too would probably have had to petition the Roman Senate from a military camp to plow and cultivate his field. Other than his salary he had nothing; but he had a brother whom he valued above all treasures. The love they bore each other was like that of Castor and Pollux. But these are heroes of fable. In terms of historical brotherly love, Gine was on a par with Cato the Elder, who, to the question thrice put to him 'Who is your best friend?' answered: my brother, my brother, and my brother. The brother of our Cato-the-officer served at Kronstadt and fell dangerously ill. The

news of his brother's illness shattered our Cato-Gine.
"The crackling frosts of Christmas were raging. The gulf was firmly bound under its icy cover. A sled could not be hired at any price, but there was a spirit that moved both legs and heart, and Gine set off on foot to see his brother, wearing only boots and even without stockings. Could one have obtained warm boots and money from someone? But what does it mean to ask? Go into debt. The ancient Roman suffered but did not beg. Gine crossed the gulf in something over a day and a half, visited and embraced his brother, and returned to his corps in time to go on duty. And although the signs of fever appeared, although he was urged to rest and others offered to relieve him, he replied: 'I shall not betray my post.' He did his turn and lay down in bed. In the delirium of a terrible fever he constantly saw his brother, spoke with him, and uttered his name with his last breath." And further: "And a hero of 1812, Kul'nev, entered the corps in the footsteps of Fabricius and Epaminondas. Like the Theban Epaminondas he loved his mother and shared his salary with her; like Philopoemen he was simple in his clothes and in public life....Reviving Epaminondas and Philopoemen in himself, and becoming spiritually akin to Fabricius, Kul'nev treasured his poverty and called it 'the grandeur of ancient Rome.' When his comrades would invite themselves to dinner, he would reply: 'Cabbage soup and kasha there is, but bring your own spoons.' He was inseparable from Plutarch: He slept with the <u>Lives</u> on his modest cloak, traveled with them on the post wagon, and gained from them that feeling which found grandeur in life's needs and poverty." (<u>12</u>) This <u>"Roman" poetry of poverty</u>, which lent a theatrical grandeur to material need, was subsequently <u>characteristic of many Decembrists</u> (for example, F. Glinka), but it was <u>rejected outright by</u> the intellectual-commoners [<u>raznochintsy</u>] of the next generation. S. Glinka's interpretation of Kul'nev's conduct is of further interest because other contemporaries "decoded" his acts in an entirely different key, seeing in them, for example, "eccentricities" like those of Suvorov. Compare the well-known lines by Denis Davydov:

Semiotics and Structuralism

> Tell of the deeds of the moustached hero,
> Oh muse, tell how Kul'nev did battle,
> How he wandered in the snows in his shirt
> And appeared in battle in a Finnish cap.
>   Let the world hear
> Of Kul'nev's eccentricities
>   and the thunder of his victories. (13)

In <u>The Eighteenth Brumaire of Louis Bonaparte</u> K. Marx wrote about the social causes of the "antique masquerade." However, "Roman pomp" (Belinskii) was part of a wider movement, the center of which was <u>literary romanticism and which transformed artistic texts into programs for real behavior:</u> Pushkin's Silvio imitated not ancient heroes but characters in Byron and Marlinskii; but the principle of imitating literature remained. It is interesting that the heroes of Gogol, Leo Tolstoy, or Dostoevsky, i.e., of texts that themselves imitate life, did not evoke imitation by readers.

Theater played a particular role in the culture of the early nineteenth century throughout Europe. This is all the more revealing because in this period <u>the role of the theater</u> is not in any way proportional to the place of dramaturgy in the total system of literary texts. <u>The epoch as a whole is theatricalized. Specific forms of stage behavior leave the stage and subject life to themselves.</u> This is true above all of the culture of Napoleonic France. When Russian travelers found themselves in Paris after Tilsit, they were astounded by the ritualization and splendor of the Tuilleries court, which was very remote from the deliberate simplicity of Petersburg court life under Alexander I (people of the older generation, accustomed to the splendor of Catherine's court, saw this as a sign of stinginess on the part of the emperor). In his memoirs Count E. F. Komarovskii provides a detailed description of the impressions left by the court ritual of Paris on Russian travelers: "The gathering in the palace was extraordinarily crowded; the entire diplomatic corps, all the elite, military, civil, and courtiers, made up a court splendid in the extreme. Several marshals in mantles, full uniform, and each with staff in hand gave it an even greater grandeur. The court uniform was red, with silver trim on breast and cuff. In the middle of this court, resplendent in gold and silver, Napoleon, in the simple uniform of a chasseur regiment, created the greatest nuance....Nothing was grander and, at the same time, more martial than the sight of grenadiers of the emperor's guard, courageous and martial in appearance, decorated with medals and chevrons, in their bearskin hats, standing on both sides of each step of the tall staircase of the Tuilleries Palace." He goes on to describe the ritual of presentation to Empress Josephine and the princesses: "When the partners for cards had been chosen, both halves of the door were opened, and all the gentlemen and ladies had to proceed, one at a time, to make — as it is called — obeisance to the empress and to both queens: of Spain, of Holland, and to Princess Borghese, all of whom would respond with a slight bow. Meanwhile, Napoleon stood in the same room and seemed to everyone to be making an inspection....For the ladies this ceremony was quite a nuisance, since they had to maneuver without turning but merely pushing aside with their legs the extraordinarily long trains of their dresses. The empress's table was alone, set against the lateral wall of the room, and the other three along the longitudinal wall. As a consequence, three curtsies had to be made while walking directly toward the empress's table; then, turning slightly to the right, one curtsy each had to be made to each of the queens and the princess while moving sideways from one to the next, and then backward to the doors." (14)

Genlis has provided an interesting explanation for the theatrical quality of court life under Napoleon: "After the fall of the throne, an etiquette and court rules were established in accordance with what had been observed on the march and as foreign kingdoms were devastated. The titles 'highness,' 'excellency,' and 'gentleman of the bedchamber' became just as common among us as in Germany and Italy....In the Tuilleries one could see a strange mixture of foreign etiquettes. Court ceremony was further supplemented by many things taken from theater customs. A wit commented at the time that the ceremony of presentation

Semiotics and Structuralism

at court was an exact imitation of the presentation of Aeneas to the Queen of Carthage in the opera Dido. It is known that people often turned to a certain well-known actor for advice about the costumes to be devised for solemn occasions." (15)

However, court etiquette was not the principal realm in which an aesthetic and theatrical factor penetrated into nonartistic life — that realm was war.

The Napoleonic era brought into military actions, in addition to the factors inherent in them, an indisputable element of the aesthetic. Only if we consider this will we understand why writers of the following generation — Merimée, Stendhal, Tolstoy — needed such creative energy to de-aestheticize war, stripping from it the cloak of theatrical beauty. In the total system of culture of the Napoleonic era, war was an enormous spectacle (of course, not only and not primarily that). The contrast between the court at the Tuilleries and the generals in their theatrically splendid uniforms on the field of battle, on the one hand, and the emperor in his everyday "working" uniform, on the other hand, immediately excluded Napoleon from theatricalized space and underlined who were the actors and who the director of this enormous spectacle. Let us recall that the conditions and norms of war in those years meant that not every open space was suitable to be a "space for war." A gigantic natural amphitheater, like the fields of Austerlitz or Borodino, was regarded as most appropriate. The commanders-in-chief, ranged on the heights, were in the position of both directors and audience. Feofan Prokopovich, speaking about the personal participation of Peter [the Great] in the Battle of Poltava and the emperor's bullet-riddled hat, had long ago noted the possibility of the positions "viewer" and "actor" in a battle, and he directly compared them to theater: "Not from the side, as one stands at a spectacle, but himself in the action of such a tragedy." (16)

"Such a tragedy" played out on the fields of Europe actively shaped the psychology of men of the early nineteenth century; it particularly accustomed them to see themselves as the dramatis personae of history, "enlarged" them in their own eyes,

Theater and Theatricality

taught them an awareness of their own grandeur; and subsequently, this could not but make itself felt in their political self-consciousness. It is suggestive that even Denis Davydov, seeking to define the essence of partisan warfare, resorted to a simile emphasizing the aesthetic perception of "minor warfare": "This enacted field of poetry demands romantic imagination and a passion for adventure, and does not content itself with dry, prosaic bravery. It is a stanza from Byron!" (17)

True, Denis Davydov, demonstratively rejecting the "antique" interpretation of the War of 1812 (typical of Russian Empire style, for example, in the well-known bas-reliefs by F. Tolstoi) (18), did not fashion his personal conduct after Roman models. The example for him was not the Russian gentleman who conducted himself like Cato or Aristides but the Russian gentleman who imitated in his behavior a man of the people: "I learned from experience that in a people's war one must not only speak the language of the rabble but adapt oneself to its habits and clothing. I put on a peasant's caftan, let my beard grow, replaced my Order of St. Anne with an image of St. Nikolai, and spoke with them in the language of the folk." (19)

One could compare this with Ryleev's proposal that, in taking to the square on December 14, 1825, the "Russian caftan" be worn. As was also the case later among the Slavophiles, what was significant here was the very fact of reincarnation; for Ryleev, of course, did not think that anyone would take him in such a costume for a man of the people. It was no accident that Nikolai Bestuzhev called this plan a "masquerade." (20)

The aesthetic, play essence of such behavior lay in the fact that the Russian gentleman, taking on the character of Cato, Brutus, Pozharskii, the Demon, or Melmoth and conducting himself in accordance with this self-adopted role, did not cease to continue simultaneously to be precisely a Russian gentleman of his time. This duality of behavior, so characteristic of an entire generation and vividly manifested, for example, in Iakubovich, evoked much censure, by no means always just, on the part of men of the era of Dobroliubov and Bazarov.

One of the vivid manifestations of the "theatricality" of everyday behavior was <u>a sharpened sense of the entr'acte</u>. It should be noted that <u>the perception of theatricality as a change in the scale of conventionality in behavior</u> was particularly characteristic of the culture of the eighteenth and early nineteenth centuries, with its <u>habit of combining in one theatrical performance tragedy, comedy, and ballet</u>, while "one and the same performer declaimed in tragedy, made jokes in vaudeville, sang in opera, and posed in pantomime." (<u>21</u>) In order to understand the full poignancy of the <u>sense of reincarnation</u>, it should be added that the theater buff of this period knew the actor or actress as a person and was fond of going backstage during intermission. It should also be remembered that it was precisely this act of reincarnation, which made makeup an obligatory component of theater, which was <u>held in high esteem in the actor's play</u>. What was valued in an actor was <u>the ability to abandon his own system of behavior and switch to the conventional-traditional behavior prescribed for the particular type of character</u>. The evaluations of actors' performances made by so experienced a theatergoer as S. T. Aksakov are very significant: "After <u>The Two Figaros</u>, the most interesting spectacle was a short comedy, <u>The Two Crispins</u>, that would be performed along with some play. The two Crispins were played by the famous and noble rival actors F. F. Kokoshkin and A. M. Pushkin, who, like Kokoshkin, had translated one of Molière's comedies, <u>Tartuffe</u>, and also adapted it to fit Russian manners. Lovers of theatrical art long remembered this 'battle of artists.' One had to win and one to be defeated; but the public divided into two equal halves, and each regarded its hero as the winner and proclaimed him as such. Pushkin's admirers said that Pushkin was much better than Kokoshkin because he was adroit, lively, courteous, simple, and natural to the highest degree. All this was true, and in this regard Kokoshkin could not bear comparison with Pushkin. But Kokoshkin's admirers said that he, poorly or well, played Crispin, while Pushkin played Pushkin; and that was also entirely true, from which one must conclude that both actors were unsatisfactory as Crispin. Crispin is a familiar character on the French stage; he was and is (if he still is) played traditionally.

Theater and Theatricality

That is how Kokoshkin played him, but, in my opinion, unsuccessfully, precisely because he lacked naturalness and life; for even in the performance of traditions there has to be a naturalness and inspiration of a certain kind. Pushkin forthrightly played himself or, at least, a contemporary, clever rogue. He did not even put on the familiar costume in which Crispin had always appeared on the stage: in a word, there was not even a shadow of Crispin here." (22)

The change in type of play behavior, sharpening the sense of convention, and the problems of the entr'acte and the footlights — the limits of the play space on the boards of the theater and in time — are organically linked.

For the everyday behavior of the Russian gentleman at the end of the eighteenth and the beginning of the nineteenth centuries also characteristic are a fixing of a type of behavior to a specific "stage area" and a gravitation toward the "entr'acte" — a break during which the semioticity of behavior is reduced to a minimum. In order to evaluate these properties fully, it is necessary to recall the behavior of the "nihilist" of the 1860s, whose ideal was "truth to self," constancy in one's life image and everyday conduct, adherence to identical norms within the family and in public, in "historical" and personal life. The requirement of "sincerity" presumed abandonment of emphatically semiotic systems of behavior and, at the same time, eliminated the need for breaks in which "to be oneself."

Gentry life at the end of the eighteenth and the beginning of the nineteenth centuries was built not only on the basis of a hierarchy of conduct, created in turn by the hierarchical nature of the political order of post-Petrine governmental structure, organized by the table of ranks, but also as a set of possible alternatives ("service/retirement," "life in the capital/life on one's estate," "Petersburg/Moscow," "military service/civil service," "the Guards/the army," etc.), each of which presumed a particular type of behavior. One and the same person would conduct himself differently in Petersburg than in Moscow, in his regiment than on his estate, in female than in male company, on the march than in barracks, and at a ball than "at the hour of a bachelor's carouse." Moreover, unlike the peasant's life, in which individual behavior changed in accordance with the calendar and the cycle of farm work, as a result of which the type of behavior did not depend on individual choice (23) and character consequently became nakedly social and lost individuality, the life-style of the gentry presumed the constant opportunity to choose a type of behavior. At the same time, while the peasant physically lacked the opportunity to practice "nonpeasant" behavior, for a gentleman "nongentry" behavior was ruled out by the norms of honor, custom, government discipline, and class habits. The inviolability of these norms was not automatic but in each individual instance constituted an act of conscious choice and a free manifestation of one's will. However, "gentry behavior" as a system not only admitted but presumed some departures from the norm that were structurally isomorphous with entr'actes in performances. The striving of a gentleman to gain access to a different existence for brief periods — life in the theater wings, of the camp, of folk festivals (compare in bourgeois life the analogous function of the picnic, of going out "into the lap of nature," accompanied by a pronounced simplification of social ritual; in the twentieth century an analogous role is sometimes played by sports and, in particular, by tourism) — generated breaks in normed behavior and its replacement by behavior performing a function not normed by society. However, this absence of norms was purely functional within the bounds of the given system. Outside it the same behavior appeared highly normed. This is evident simply from the fact that the types of such violation were rigorously classified in accordance with the age and status of a person in the social hierarchy. Society distinguished clearly between "correct" (permissible) and "incorrect" (impermissible) deviations from the norm.

An interesting indicator of the theatricality of everyday life is the fact that the amateur performances and household theaters that were widely prevalent in gentry life at the beginning of the nineteenth century and entry into the professional theater were perceived as a departure from the world of the conventional and insincere life of "society" to the world of genuine feelings

Theater and Theatricality

and directness, i.e., as a reduction in the level of semioticity of behavior. (24)

The persistent effort to interpret the laws of the life of gentry society through the prism of the most conventional forms of theatrical spectacle — masquerade, puppet comedy, and buffoon shows [balagan] — which we constantly encounter in the literature from the end of the eighteenth to the start of the nineteenth centuries, is quite revealing. (25)

* * *

We have already observed that, in examining the culture from the beginning of the century, it is impossible to ignore the military actions of massed troops, just as one cannot eliminate the circus from the spectacle culture of Rome or bullfights from the analogous system in Spain. As we know, in all these cases the fact that real blood flows in the course of the spectacle does not eliminate the factor of aesthetization but is a condition for it. In the long chain of transitions that separate the theater boards from the chivalric tournament or professional boxing, the horrible and beautiful are in a special relation for each gradation. At the extreme links of the chain they change places: in tragedy the beautiful is perceived as terrible, and in a real battle, aesthetically perceived, the terrible is seen as beautiful.

However, in the army of Paul's and Alexander's times there was yet another form, oriented to an incomparably greater degree toward spectacle but perceived as the antipode and total opposite of battle. It was the parade. The parade was, of course, oriented toward the spectacular to a much greater degree than combat. In a certain sense precisely here lay the barrier that divided the military men of that period into two camps: some saw the army as an organism destined for battle, while others saw its highest calling to be the parade. It is natural that in the former case the practical function was advanced into the foreground, while in the latter it was totally displaced into the background. However, while the aesthetic function in the former case was present only as a barely detected nuance changing the coloration of the picture but not its outline, in the latter it burst forth, pushing aside all practical considerations.

Behind the orientation of the army toward combat and toward parade lay two different military-pedagogical and military-theoretical doctrines, and in the final analysis, two philosophical concepts as well. (26) Their sociopolitical opposition is just as obvious as the opposition in orientation toward classicist and romantic culture. In another aspect one of them was perceived as "Prussian" and the other as national-Russian. At the intersection of all these oppositions there also arose the great difference in the aesthetic experience of these two principal factors in the life of the army of those years.

Participation in wars, having become an important part of the biography of an entire generation of young people in Europe, a feature without which the life image of the Decembrist is impossible, significantly influenced type of personality. Although battle was realized as a kind of organization (it was determined by the general disposition, and the place and role of the individual participant were determined by the assignment of his unit and the nature of the duties placed upon him by rank and post), it afforded considerable freedom for personal initiative. The organization of battle, drawing together people quite different in their place in the social hierarchy and simplifying the forms of contact among them, in a certain sense repealed the social hierarchy and was perceived as its simplification. Where, except on the field of Austerlitz, could a junior officer see an emperor weeping? Moreover, the atoms of the social structure proved in battle to be considerably freer in their orbits than in social life, oppressed by bureaucratic law and order. The "accident" that made it possible to bypass the middle steps of the social hierarchy, leaping from the bottom directly to the top, and that in the eighteenth century was associated with the empress's bed, at the beginning of the nineteenth century called to mind the image of Bonaparte at Toulon or on the bridge of Arcoli (compare Prince Andrei's "my Toulon" in War and Peace). There were changes not only in means but goals: the ambitious man in the eighteenth century was an adventurer dreaming of

Theater and Theatricality

personal advancement, but his counterpart at the beginning of the nineteenth century also dreamed of a place in the pages of history. The meteoric ascents and falls that, having become so characteristic in Catherine's reign, were brought by Paul to the level of caricature were virtually unknown at Alexander's court. Only war, which unchained the initiative of hundreds of junior officers, taught them to regard themselves not just as blind implementers of another's will but also as men in whose hands the fate of their homeland and the lives of thousands of people had been placed. Participation in the Patriotic War and activation of civic self-awareness merged enterprise in battle with political desire for liberty. Pushkin distinctly emphasized the connection between liberalism and the military past of this generation:

> They who, set free at age fifteen,
> In three wars became used only to powder and the field
> (UP, pp. 246 and 365).

A parade was exactly the opposite: it rigorously regimented the behavior of each person, transforming him into a silent cog in an enormous machine. It left no room whatever for variation in the conduct of the individual. Moreover, the initiative was transferred to the center, to the person of the commander of the parade. Starting with Paul, this was the emperor. Timothy von Bock wrote: "Why does the emperor so passionately love parades? Why is the very man whom we knew during military service as an ill-starred diplomat transformed in peacetime into an ardent soldier who casts everything aside the moment he hears the roll of the drums? It is because a parade is the triumph of the nonentity, and every warrior before whom he had to drop his gaze on a day of battle becomes a mannequin in a parade, while the emperor seems the divinity who alone thinks and commands." (27)

While battle was associated in the minds of contemporaries with romantic tragedy, a parade was clearly oriented toward the corps de ballet. Nicholas I's balletomania is suggestive. Alexander I was indifferent to the dramatic and operatic theater

— of all forms of performance he preferred the parade, in which he awarded himself the role of director, while the army of many thousands was a huge ballet troupe. "Drill" [frunt] was simultaneously a science and an art; and considerations of beauty, of "order," were always that supreme criterion to which all of Paul's sons sacrificed the soldier's health, their own popularity in the army, and the army's capacity to fight. Of course, it would be foolish to see in this stubborn inclination only a manifestation of the strange personal qualities of Paul and his sons: the parade became an aestheticized model of the ideal not only of military but of general governmental organization. It was a grandiose spectacle daily affirming the idea of autocracy.

However, one must not lose sight of the fact that although the mania for drill met virtually unanimous condemnation among the battle officers (documentary proof of this is voluminous and eloquent), the science of drill was part of the subtle knowledge of the secrets of the service, and no military man could ignore it. Pestel' was a connoisseur of the formation, and the Decembrist Lunin won the favor of the fanatical proponent of the drill Grand Duke Constantine not only by his chivalry and insane valor but also by his subtle knowledge of the mysteries of parade-ground service. The aesthetics of parade could not be entirely foreign to any professional soldier, and even in Pushkin's Bronze Horseman it evoked lines devoted to its "monotonous beauty" (which did not prevent Pushkin from recognizing the connection between monotony and slavery; compare: "Like the monotonous song of slaves"). Both the aesthetics of parade and the aesthetics of ballet had a deep, common root — the serf order of Russian life.

For all their obvious differences there is also a significant similarity between the situations of "Napoleon on the field of battle" and "Paul I on parade." It consists of the fact that what occurred was divided into two spectacles. On the one hand, the spectacle consists of a mass (in battle or in a parade), while the audience is represented by one man. On the other hand, this same man is a spectacle for the mass that here appears as an audience. With this, however, the similarity ends. Let

Theater and Theatricality

us examine the two sides of this dual spectacle.

If we abstract from the facts that Napoleon and Paul I were not only observers but actors, and that their actions were fundamentally different in character, and if we regard them only as an audience, we cannot fail to discover a fundamental difference in their attitude toward the spectacle. Paul I views a spectacle with an "iron scenario" (Eisenstein's term): all details are foreseen in advance. The beautiful is equivalent to adherence to rules; and deviation from norms, even the slightest, is regarded as aesthetically deformed and punishable under disciplinary procedure. The highest criterion of beauty is "orderliness," i.e., the ability of different people to move in identical fashion, in accordance with rules prescribed beforehand. Here orderliness and beauty of motion interest the connoisseur more than plot. The question "How does it end?" assumes secondary significance both in ballet and on parade. The viewer of a battle resembles the viewer of a tragedy whose plot he does not know: no matter how gripping the grandeur of the spectacle, interest in its denouement is overriding.

Even greater are the differences in the spectacle from the position of the masses. Before the eyes of his soldiers, an astounded Europe, and generations to come, Napoleon performed the play "A Man in the Struggle against Destiny," or "The Triumph of Genius over Fate." Linked to this were the markedly human appearance of the main character (the simplicity of his costume and the role of "simple soldier") and the inhuman vastness of the obstacles in his path. In his behavior and destiny (determined in considerable measure by the historical role he had chosen for himself) Napoleon anticipated the problematics and range of plots of a whole branch of romantic literature. Genius could thereafter be interpreted differently in plots — as anything from a demon to one or another historical personage — and the barriers standing in its path could also be given different names (God, feudal Europe, the inert crowd, and so forth). But the pattern had been set. Of course, Napoleon did not invent it: he had picked up his role from the same literature. But, embodying it in the play of his life, he returned this role to literature with that increased power with which a transformer returns to the circuit the electrical impulses it has received.

Paul I played a different role. Commanding parades in crown and emperor's mantle (under Catherine the command of the trooping of the colors was regarded as a corporal's, not a tsar's, business; the regalia of royalty were used only in exceptional parade situations, and even in such cases Catherine sought to replace the crown by a symbol for the crown — a light, jeweled ornament in the form of a crown), he tried to show Russia the spectacle of God. Paul tried to embody in a splendid and awesome spectacle Lomonosov's metaphorical expression about Peter: "He was God, he was your God, Russia!" In this sense it is absolutely no accident that in Marin's parody Paul was replaced by Lomonosov's God from the "Ode Selected from Job."

Alexander I did not like the theater and avoided splendid ceremonies. The modesty of his personal life often gave reason to accuse the emperor of stinginess. The young emperor's manner was winning in its simplicity and directness. He seemed the embodiment of his father's opposite, and the beginning of his rule should have been the end of the era of theatricality.

However, the deeper we penetrate into the meaning both of the politics and the personality of Alexander Pavlovich, the more often we pause, even with a certain disbelief, before the profound continuity between father and son. Not only was Alexander not averse to games and reincarnations but, on the contrary, he loved to change masks, sometimes extracted practical advantages from his ability to play different roles, and sometimes yielded to the pure artistry of changing appearances, evidently enjoying the fact that he confused his interlocutors, who mistook play for reality. Let us cite but a single example.

In the middle of March 1812 Alexander decided, for a number of reasons, to remove Speranskii from affairs of state. What interests us here are not the political and governmental aspects of this event (which, by the way, have been well explained in the scholarly literature) but the character of the ruler's personal behavior in these circumstances. Having on the morning of March 17 summoned the director of the chancellery of the

Theater and Theatricality

Ministry of Police, Ia. de Sanglen, who was one of the mainsprings of the intrigue against Speranskii, the emperor said, with apparent regret: "However much it pains me, it is necessary to part company with Speranskii. He must be sent away from Petersburg." That very evening Speranskii was called to the palace, had an audience with the emperor, and was then sent into exile. On the morning of March 18, Alexander, receiving de Sanglen, said to him: "I raised Speranskii to high office, brought him close to me, had unbounded faith in him, and was compelled to banish him. I wept....Men are scoundrels. Those who yesterday morning sought his smile today congratulate me and rejoice in his banishment." The monarch took a book from the table and angrily threw it back down on the table, saying with indignation: "Oh, villains! Those are the ones who surround us unhappy rulers!" (28)

That very day the emperor received A. N. Golitsyn, whom he regarded as his personal friend and in whom he had unbounded confidence, and expressed himself in the same spirit. Upon seeing the extreme gloom on the face of the tsar, Prince Golitsyn inquired about his health and received this reply: "If your hand had been cut off, you would certainly scream and complain that it hurts: last night they took Speranskii away from me, and he was my right hand!" (29) Upon which the emperor wept. And he also wept when he bid Speranskii farewell. But today we know for a certainty that no one had cut off Alexander's right hand: Alexander, making use of several stupid and senseless denunciations, gradually made up the entire intrigue personally and in all respects. When Speranskii all but succeeded in breaking up the stagy removal from office planned by the tsar by submitting his resignation, Alexander not only considered it necessary to reject the resignation but raised his already doomed victim even higher. (30) But another scene is even more astounding. At the time when this whole affair was played out, Professor G. F. Parrot, rector of the University of Dorpat, happened to show up in Petersburg. Distinguished by a rare nobility of soul, Parrot was one of the very small group of people whom the suspicious Alexander trusted. It was precisely because he was not a courtier or favorite, rarely saw Alexander, and never turned to him with any requests that he had grounds to consider himself a personal friend and confidant of the emperor. On the evening of March 16 he was summoned to the palace. "The emperor," wrote Parrot, "described to me Speranskii's ingratitude with an anger I had never seen in him, and with emotion that brought his tears. Setting out the proofs he had received of this betrayal, he said to me: 'I have decided to shoot him tomorrow and, wishing to know your opinion on this score, have invited you here.'" (31)

Parrot begged the emperor to give him time to think. On the morning of March 18, in a special letter, he tried to soften Speranskii's fate. The emperor responded to him graciously; and Parrot left for Dorpat, confident that he had saved Speranskii. But it is obvious that Alexander Pavlovich had no intention of shooting Speranskii; and when he thanked Parrot for the letter and seemed to take his arguments favorably, Speranskii's fate had already been settled and he was on his way to exile.

Shil'der, relating this story, not without a certain disbelief — a feeling that almost never leaves students of Alexander's personality — sums up: "In the correspondence between de Sanglen and M. P. Pogodin the following curious comment of Emperor Alexander about Parrot is to be found: 'These scientists all see things obliquely, do not hit the target, and have little knowledge of life, although he is a man of the world.' Pogodin, in turn, adds: 'Parrot was misled, like everyone.' Our historian, when he wrote these lines, did not even suspect what a great truth he had uttered, for he was completely unfamiliar with the deliberate comedy played out on March 16 by the central figure of this truly Shakespearean drama in modern Russian history." (32)

It is no accident that terms from the theater here come to the mind of the historian. There is only one point on which we cannot agree with him: Alexander did not play out a "Shakespearean drama" — it was an unbroken "theater for one actor." In each of the emperor's reincarnations subtle calculation showed through; but it is impossible to rid oneself of the feeling that the very ability to change masks gave him, all other things aside,

Theater and Theatricality

deep, "disinterested" satisfaction. Napoleon demonstrated deep penetration in calling him the "northern Talma."

Alexander's "theater" was closely linked to his style of solving political problems: on principle he did not distinguish interests of state from his personal interests, and he systematically transformed political into personal relations (in this regard, despite the weakness of Alexander's character, he adhered consistently to the despotic system and was a true son of his father). In the field of foreign policy this engendered that style of personal diplomacy which Alexander was able to impose on the courts of Europe and which enabled the Russian emperor to score a number of diplomatic triumphs. In domestic policy he staked his bets on personal devotion to the monarch, which appeared hopelessly archaic at the beginning of the nineteenth century and caused the final downfall of Alexander's entire domestic policy.

Alexander's "game" [play] missed the style of the age: romanticism required a constant mask that became grafted to the personality, so to speak, and became the model for its behavior. Such a style of shaping a personality was perceived as majestic. Alexander's "Proteanism" was perceived by his contemporaries as "cunning" and a lack of sincerity. The verb "to swindle" often appears in evaluations of the tsar, even by those in his immediate circle. By changing his masks in order to "captivate" everyone, Alexander only repelled everyone. One of the most talented actors of his era, he was the least successful actor.

* * *

There are periods in which art imperiously invades daily life, aestheticizing the everyday course of life. Such were the eras of the Renaissance, the Baroque, Romanticism, and the art of the early twentieth century. This invasion has many consequences. The explosions of artistic talent that occurred during these periods seem to be associated with it. Of course, it was not only theater that exercised a powerful influence on the penetration of art into the life of the epoch that interests us. Here sculpture and, particularly, poetry played no less a role. Only against the background of the mighty invasion of poetry into the lives of the Russian gentry at the beginning of the nineteenth century can the colossal phenomenon of Pushkin be understood and explained. However, this problem goes beyond the framework of the present article.

It is necessary to pay attention to yet another aspect of the question: the course of daily life and its literary reflection provide the individual with different degrees of freedom of self-expression. A man freezes into everyday existence like one of Dante's sinners in the ice of Caina. He loses freedom of movement and ceases to be the creator of his own behavior. The men of the eighteenth century already lived in considerable measure under the sign of custom. The supraindividual course of everyday life automatically predetermined the behavior of the individual. And although adventurism, which in the eighteenth century gained unprecedented sway, provided the most active men of the age an outlet beyond the limits of the routine of everyday life, it was, on the one hand, a fundamentally unique path and, on the other hand, openly and demonstratively amoral: it was the course of personal affirmation of life through preservation of its bases. The hero of a picaresque novel did not destroy the life around him. All his energy and his skill in breaking out of the social yoke were directed merely at fitting into that very yoke, but in the most advantageous and pleasant way for him. His activity objectively did not destroy, but affirmed, the general order of life.

It is precisely because the life of theater differs from everyday existence that the view of life as spectacle gave a man new possibilities for behavior. When compared with theatrical life, everyday life seemed stagnant: events and occurrences either did not take place in it at all or were rare departures from the norm. Hundreds of people could live their entire lives without experiencing a single "event." Moved by the laws of custom, the everyday life of the ordinary Russian eighteenth-century gentleman was "plotless." Theatrical life represented a chain of events. A man was not a passive participant in an inchoate passage of time: liberated from everyday life, he led the existence of a historical personage — he himself chose his type of behavior, actively influenced the world around him, perished or achieved success.

The view of real life as a spectacle not only gave a man the opportunity to choose his role in individual behavior but also filled him with an expectation of events. Plot [suzhetnost'], i.e., the possibility of unanticipated occurrences, of unexpected turns of events, became the norm. It was precisely awareness of the fact that all types of political upheavals were possible that shaped the perception of life by youth at the beginning of the nineteenth century. The revolutionary consciousness of the romantic gentry youth had many sources. Psychologically it had been prepared, partially, by the habit of viewing life "theatrically." It was precisely the model of theatrical behavior, transforming a person into a character, that liberated him from the automatic power of group behavior, of custom. A short period of time shall elapse, and the literariness and theatricality of the behavior of the imitators in life of the heroes of Marlinskii or Schiller themselves will appear to be a group norm blocking individual manifestation of personality. The man of the 1840s to 1860s will seek his own identity by spurning literariness. This does not change the fact that the period of the beginning of the nineteenth century, a period that lived under the sign of the invasion of art — primarily the theater — into Russian life, will always remain a notable epoch in the history of Russian culture.

Notes

1) P. G. Bogatyrev, Voprosy teorii narodnogo iskusstva, Moscow, "Iskusstvo" Publishing House, 1971, p. 14.

2) I take this opportunity to express my gratitude to V. M. Glinka for his valuable advice.

3) See K. Batiushkov, Stikhotvoreniia, Leningrad, 1936, pp. 28-29; B. V. Tomashevskii, Pushkin i Frantsiia, Leningrad, 1960, p. 107.

4) L. Ginzburg, O lirike, Moscow and Leningrad, "Sovetskii pisatel'" Publishing House, 1964, pp. 18-19.

5) Mara Kazoknieks, Studien zur Rezeption der Antike bei russischen Dichtern zu Beginn des XIX Jahrhunderts, Munich, 1968, p. 73.

6) F. F. Vigel', Zapiski, Vol. 1, Moscow, 1928, pp. 177-79.

7) Igor' Grabar', Istoriia russkogo iskusstva, Vol. 5; Baron N. N. Vrangel', Istoriia skul'ptury, Moscow, undated, I. Knebel' Publishing House, p. 171.

8) Zapiski Sergeia Nikolaevicha Glinki, St. Petersburg, 1895, pp. 61-63 and 194.

9) Igor' Grabar', p. 171.

10) Sb. RIO, Vol. V, St. Petersburg, 1870, p. 66.

11) Compare Radishchev's words:

>And her Arria the sharp steel
>Boldly plunges into her bosom:
>Accept, my dear Pactus,
>No, it is not painful...
>(Vol. 1, pp. 111-112)

12) Zapiski Sergeia Nikolaevicha Glinki, pp. 61-63.

The famous duel between Chernov and Novosil'tsev may be taken as an example of the active influence of the "antique" model on the real behavior of men of that era. The very conditions for the duel were unusual and colored in severe, almost Roman tones of citizenship and duty: Novosil'tsev was required to duel to the death, by shooting, with the brothers of his bride by order of age, and if he succeeded in killing them, then with their aged father. This bore no resemblance to the duels of high society, in which the victim was

>a young friend
>Who by immodest glance or rejoinder,
>Or some other trifle,
>Had insulted you over the bottle.

Theater and Theatricality

More likely, contemporaries were reminded of the fight between the Horatii and the Curiatii. The parallel was all the more evident because Titus Livius also had patriot brothers fighting against the enemies of Rome who were required to kill their sister's groom. Chernova herself took her own life, as had Lucretia.

13) Denis Davydov, Soch., Moscow, 1962, p. 64.

14) Count E. F. Komarovskii, Zapiski, St. Petersburg, "Ogni" Publishing House, 1914, pp. 159-64.

15) Mme la Comtesse de Genlis, Dictionnaire critique et raisonné des étiquettes de la cour...ou l'ésprit des étiquettes et des usages anciens, comparés aux modernes, Vol. 1, Paris, 1818, pp. 18-19. This dictionary does not justify its resounding title. In it factual information is often replaced by banal moralizing. The "famous actor" was Talma.

16) Feofana Prokopovicha, arkhiepiskopa Velikogo Novgoroda i Velikikh Luk, sviateshego pravitel'stvuiushchego sinoda vitse-prezidenta, a potom perventstvuiushchego chlena Slova i Rechi, Part I, 1760, p. 158.

17) Denis Davydov, Opyt teorii partizanskogo deistviia, 2nd ed., Moscow, 1822, p. 88.

18) Compare his statement: "Disputed issues between states are today not settled by battles between Horatii and Curiatii," ibid., p. 46.

19) Denis Davydov, Soch., p. 320.

20) Vospominaniia Bestuzhevykh, Moscow and Leningrad, 1951, p. 36.

21) Leonid Grossman, Pushkin v teatral'nykh kreslakh. Kartiny russkoi stseny 1817-1820 godov, Leningrad, 1926, p. 6.

22) S. T. Aksakov, Sobr. Soch. v 4-kh tt., Moscow, 1956, pp. 47-48. Sosnitskii was famous as a character actor. In 1814, while still a young actor, he astounded the audience by playing eight different roles in a comedy. While the appearance of Kokoshkin and the Kleinmikhel family, all dressed as Georgian peasants, falling at the feet of Arakcheev and thanking him for their happy lives, at an unmasked ball in Petersburg at the beginning of the 1820s, was an example of gross invasion of

theatricality into the sphere of nontheatrical, everyday life, it is also possible to cite examples of a fine sense of stage convention and theatrical semiotics: Only under conditions of a very high theatrical culture as a special sign system could a spectacle have arisen whose piquancy lay in an individual's transformation into a sign of himself. Aksakov recalls an intermezzo put on by actors and theatergoers of Moscow on the birthday of D. V. Golitsyn: "This intermezzo was marked by the fact that some people played themselves: A. A. Bashilov played Bashilov, B. K. Danzas — Danzas, Pisarev — Pisarev, Shchepkin — Shchepkin, and Verstovskii — Verstovskii, after initially feigning being the retired chorister Reutov" (S. T. Aksakov, Sobr. soch., Vol. 4, pp. 125-26).

There is a fundamental difference between this and A. M. Pushkin's "playing himself." Pushkin depicted his own self unwillingly, because he was unable to abandon his characteristic behavior. As a consequence, the semiotic behavior (role) was reduced to ordinary behavior. At the evening in Golitsyn's honor the actors played themselves, i.e., they elevated their customary behavior to the level of signs of their own personalities.

23) Compare: "Rain in the courtyard: one must sit at home; fine weather: one must make hay, reap, etc. Not responsible for anything, not inventing anything himself, man lives only by obeying, and this obedience every minute and every second, which is transformed into labor every moment, is what life consists of" (G. I. Uspenskii, Vlast' zemli, in Sobr. soch. v 10-i tomakh, Vol. 5, Moscow, 1956, p. 120. Emphasis in the original.).

Uspenskii's assertion, based on many years of careful observation of Russian life, cannot, however, be accepted without significant amendments. On the one hand, here one clearly perceives that the world-view adhered to by Uspenskii himself in the early 1880s has exercised an influence. On the other hand, Uspenskii's observations pertain to a folk life that had undergone profound historical transformation. The structure of Russian peasant life had taken shape, for the most part, in pre-Petrine times. On the one hand, there was the abundance of

Theater and Theatricality

ritualized holidays and, on the other, a stable ritualization of daily life and work itself, produced by the need to transmit from generation to generation the habits of the most desirable activities at work, leading to a substantial transformation of behavior in life in accordance with the laws of performance. This rigorous monotony of behavior, whose causes Uspenskii saw in the "power of the land" and which he was inclined to poeticize (although he had the insight to associate it with poverty and the bitter struggle for a piece of bread), was not at all an inherent feature of the people's life. It was the result, in the first place, of a century and a half of servitude as serfs and, secondly, of impoverishment after the emancipation. As a consequence, the people's life became primitivized (one of the results of this destructive process was the disappearance of folklore, the beginning of which dates specifically to the post-reform period).

Whereas in folklorized peasant life the alternative to labor was a holiday, with its own, strictly ritualized, norms of behavior, there no longer was an alternative to the daily round observed by Uspenskii. Therefore, a holiday was associated not with changeover to a different kind of behavior, but with a realization of nonbehavior. This is the origin of the replacement in holiday behavior of subjective orientation toward "decency" by orientation toward "disorder," as was noted by all observers of folk life in those years, accompanied, on the one hand, by an increase in the consumption of alcohol and, on the other, by a change in the function of "drunken" behavior: having become the sole alternative to an individual's being bound by the conditions of life, it simultaneously acquired the characteristics of complete freedom and total ugliness.

24) Compare the famous words of the theater-lover Pisarev about actors, preserved in Aksakov's memoirs: "Now it is with such people I want to live and die — with actors imbued with love for art, who love me as a man with talent! Am I going to weary myself with the boredom in the drawing rooms of your proper society people? Am I going to die of melancholy, listening to banalities and encountering the ignorant understanding of

the artist by your, if you please, most honorable people? Your most humble servant says no! I shall not set my foot anywhere but in the theater, in the homes of my friends, and in the poor quarters of actors and actresses, who are better, kinder, more honest, and simply more frank than the bon ton lady arbiters" (S. T. Aksakov, Vol. III, p. 89). Compare the assertion, in A. N. Ostrovskii's Les, that comedians are not actors, but their audiences are gentlemen.

25) One of the earliest comparisons of society to a masquerade ball may be found in Krylov's "Pochta dukhov": "I do not know whether they dress up in such a manner in order to show themselves in their true aspect, according to the disposition of their souls, which resemble, perhaps, the ugliness that is so acceptable to them, or whether they like to be unrecognizable and always appear to be different than they actually are. If this observation is valid, it might be said...that this world is nothing but a great building in which a tremendous number of masked people are assembled, of whom perhaps the larger part, beneath outward masks, bear deception, malice, and perfidy in their hearts" (I. A. Krylov, Soch., Vol. I, Moscow, 1945, pp. 60-61).

26) See E. A. Prokof'ev, Bor'ba dekabristov za peredovoe russkoe voennoe iskusstvo, Moscow, 1953; M. V. Nechkina, A. S. Griboedov i dekabristy, Moscow, 1947, pp. 248-82; Iu. M. Lotman, "Voennye vzgliady A. N. Radishcheva," Trudy po filosofii, 4, Uchenye zapiski Tartuskogo gosudarstvennogo universiteta, Issue 127, Tartu, 1958.

27) A. V. Predtechenskii, "Zapiska T. E. Boka," in Dekabristy i ikh vremia, Moscow and Leningrad, 1951, p. 189.

28) N. K. Shil'der, Imperator Aleksandr Pervyi, ego zhizn' i tsarstvovanie, Vol. 3, St. Petersburg, 1897, pp. 38 and 48. Compare Russkii arkhiv, 1871, p. 1131.

29) Ibid., p. 49.

30) All the threads were gathered in the emperor's hands to such an extent that even the most active participants in the conspiracy against Speranskii — the above-named Ia. de Sanglen and Adjutant-General A. D. Balashov (who was among the individuals closest to the emperor), when sent to Speranskii's

Theater and Theatricality

home to take him away after he returned from the palace following the audience with the tsar — admitted to each other with sad amazement that they were not sure whether they would be arresting Speranskii or whether the emperor would issue orders to him to arrest them. Under these circumstances it is obvious that Alexander was not yielding to anyone's pressure but merely pretending to do so, while in fact he was firmly pursuing the course he had himself chosen and, as always, was being cunning, changing masks, and "setting up" the next scapegoats.

31) Shil'der, pp. 38-39.
32) Ibid., p. 368.

Historia sub Specie Semioticae

B. A. Uspenskii

In a semiotic perspective the historical process may be conceived of as a process of communication in which a constant influx of new information determines one or another response reaction on the part of the social addressee (the socium). Serving as code in this case is some "language" (taken, of course, not in the narrow linguistic but in the broad semiotic sense) that determines the perception of various facts — either real or potentially possible — in the corresponding historical-cultural context. Thus events are ascribed meaning: the text of events is read by the socium. One might then say that in its elementary phase the historical process appears as a process of the generation of new "phrases" in some "language" and their reading by the social addressee (socium).

The corresponding "language," on the one hand, unifies a given socium, determining the possibility of communication between its representatives and of an identical reaction to the events occurring. On the other hand, it organizes the information itself, determining the selection of significant facts and the establishment of a specific connection between them: what is not described in this "language" is, as it were, not perceived by the social addressee at all, simply dropping from his field of vision.

Historia sub Specie Semioticae

The "language" of a given society changes over time, of course; but this does not rule out the possibility of isolating synchronic cross sections that permit its description precisely as an operative mechanism (compare the theoretically analogous situation with natural language).

The identical objective facts, constituting a real event text, can be interpreted differently in different "languages": in the language of the corresponding socium and in some other "language" pertaining to a different space or time (this can be determined, for example, by a different articulation of events, i.e., by unequal segmentations of a text as well as by a difference in establishment of the cause-and-effect relationships between the corresponding segments). In particular, what is significant from the standpoint of a given period and a given cultural area may have no significance at all in the system of ideas of another cultural-historical area, and vice versa. Furthermore, it is necessary to bear in mind that it is precisely the system of ideas of the socium that acts as the social addressee which determines the direct mechanism of unfolding of events, i.e., of the historical process as such.

For description of the "language" of some cultural-historical area, particular significance attaches to conflict and controversy situations that are determined by the clash of different "languages" with respect to one and the same reality and that reveal the generally inadequate perception of the same events. In the extreme case a situation is possible in which the sender and receiver of a message are in essence using different "languages," despite the same external means of expression. In particular, rich material for description of the system of associative links in pre-Petrine Rus' is provided by the Petrine period, specifically thanks to its internal contradictoriness, cultural heterogeneity. At the same time, examination of this system from the given standpoint appears immediately interesting for a characterization of the personality of Peter himself. One of the possible interpretations of this era will in fact be an admission that the sender and receiver of a message (Peter and the socium) were using fundamentally different

Semiotics and Structuralism

"languages." Below we shall see, however, that such an interpretation is not the only one possible. We face, in any case, a clearly expressed conflict situation, inasmuch as the activity of Peter and his associates was evaluated by the broad masses of the populace quite negatively, in extremely negative terms. As we know, Peter was perceived by his contemporaries (and in part by subsequent generations, if one considers the Old Believers [1]) as the Anti-Christ, and this in turn determined a whole series of acts against Peter. A considerable number of documents (of various types) exist that testify to such a perception. At the same time, analysis of these documents allows us to uncover the directly formal, semiotic ("language," sometimes even in the narrowly linguistic sense) reality of such a reaction. We may firmly assert that Peter's deeds could not have been perceived otherwise. A considerable number of his actions more or less unambiguously predetermined the corresponding perception in the system of background ideas of pre-Petrine Rus', with approximately the same accuracy as if Peter himself had proclaimed it about himself.

In certain cases this semiotic determination of this kind of perception is particularly evident. Let us examine but a few of the facts pertinent to this, while consciously centering our attention specifically on the formal "linguistic" factors.

Thus Peter's marriage to Catherine evoked a sharply negative reaction not only because Peter married a second time while his first wife, forcibly tonsured, was still alive: there had at least been similar precedents before (albeit in exceptional cases). Unprecedented was the mixture of spiritual and carnal relationship. The point is that when Catherine converted to Orthodoxy, Tsarevitch Aleksei Petrovich acted as her godfather. Consequently, Catherine was Aleksei's goddaughter (since Catherine was named "Alekseevna" for her godfather, i.e., this could be regarded as a patronymic in the strict meaning of the term!); and in relationship to Peter himself she became, in spiritual terms, a granddaughter. Furthermore, spiritual kinship in this case was not distinguished from the carnal but only held even higher. Thus by marrying Catherine, it was

Historia sub Specie Semioticae

as though Peter had married his own granddaughter. This could not be regarded as anything but a kind of spiritual incest, a blasphemous violation of fundamental Christian laws.

It is not hard to see that the corresponding reaction was determined in the final analysis by the semantics of the word "father." The semantics of this word also played a vital role with respect to the church reforms of Peter and Feofan Prokopovich.

In 1721 Peter assumed a new title: he began to officially call himself "Emperor," "the Great," and at the same time, "Father of the Fatherland." The last title had actually been applied to Peter earlier as well: for example as early as 1709 Feofan Prokopovich had called him "father of the fatherland" in his "Panegyric" [Pesnia pobednaia], dedicated to the triumph at Poltava. (2) This expression is nothing but a translation of the Latin pater patriae, the honorary title of the Roman emperors. However, in the Russian cultural context it sounded different. Inasmuch as fatherhood could be either blood or spiritual, and Peter obviously could not be the father of the people in the sense of blood kinship, this title was understood precisely as a claim to spiritual kinship. But only an ordained priest could be a spiritual father. In turn, the title "father of the fatherland" could be applied only to an "archpastor" — a bishop (archbishop) and primarily to a patriarch. (3) And that is actually what the ecumenical patriarchs (of Constantinople and Alexandria) were called. Inasmuch, further, as the official adoption of this title coincided with the abolition of the patriarchy and the subsequent proclamation of the monarch as "Supreme Judge" by the Spiritual College (4), to that extent the title could be perceived in the sense that Peter had become head of the church and had declared himself patriarch. And that is just how it was perceived. But according to canonical rules, governing the church required the powers of episcopal rank (that is, of extending and withholding grace); it was Patriarch Nikon who had previously proclaimed the intrusion of secular power into church government to be a manifestation of the spirit of the Anti-Christ. Accordingly, Peter was accused of willfully

Semiotics and Structuralism

"usurping unto himself episcopal power, he named himself father of the fatherland." It must be emphasized that, in its formal aspect, this conclusion agrees to some extent with the opinion of Peter's apologists. For instance, Feofan Prokopovich, in his "Essay on the Pontifex" [Rozysk o pontifekse] (1721), set himself the task of specifically justifying that in a certain sense Christian monarchs could be called "bishops" and "archbishops." Feofan, of course, did not have in mind the rigorously canonical meaning of these terms, but this casuistic distinction was fundamentally unacceptable to one who held traditional views. (5) All this fell exactly into the well-known image of the Anti-Christ occupying the episcopal throne.

In polemical anti-Petrine writings, Peter is accused of having "usurped unto himself" not only spiritual (episcopal) but also divine authority, and consequently was called "pseudo-Christ." It must be recognized that from the standpoint of the pre-Petrine worldview, there were ample grounds for this conclusion as well. Peter actually did permit himself to be called "God" and "Christ." Thus in a considerable number of the writings of Feofan Prokopovich and of Feofilakt Lopatinskii (some of these works having been edited by Peter himself!) the thesis is justified that monarchs are "gods and christs"; and Peter is titled accordingly. Here the word "christ" is employed in the sense of "the anointed"; but it is quite obvious that it was meant to be perceived by contemporaries primarily as a proper, not a common, noun. Peter's own conduct, particularly the ceremony surrounding him, also served this purpose to a considerable degree. Thus in Moscow after the triumph over the enemy (December 21, 1709), Peter was welcomed with the words of church singing addressed to Christ on Palm Sunday: "Blessed is he who cometh in the name of the Lord, Hosannah in the highest, Lord God appear to us...," i.e., Peter, as it were, personified Christ entering Jerusalem. (6) Similarly, during Peter's exits from the Spasskoe Monastery, he was greeted with the singing of "Hosannah in the highest...," i.e., once again he was addressed as God would be. Moreover, he appeared in a crown that could have been associated with the

Historia sub Specie Semioticae

crown of thorns. It is characteristic that the same manner, an equally facile attitude toward sacral texts, emerged in daily life. Thus Feofan Prokopovich was able to welcome Peter, who showed up at Feofan's during a night carouse with his friends, with the words of a troparion: "It is the bridegroom who cometh at midnight." Similarly, B. P. Sheremet'ev, drawing in a letter to Peter a picture of the drunken revelry on the occasion of the news that a son had been born to the tsar (1715), could take an image from the Gospel story of the descent of the Holy Ghost to the apostles ("And when they heard the universal joy, and there was noise and turbulent exhalation among us, and, giving praise to God and his divine Mother, they began to make merry"); and Men'shikov, in a letter to Peter of December 10, 1709, calls St. Petersburg "the holy land." Whereas in the context of the baroque theatricalized culture similar phenomena could pertain exclusively to the expression plane, in the eyes of Peter's contemporaries all this looked like explicit blasphemy: Peter had publicly proclaimed himself God, had declared that he was God if not directly linguistically, then semiotically. And, in fact, cases are known of almost religious worship of Peter. For example, one of Peter's associates, the invalid Kirillov, kept a portrait of Peter among the images in his votive corner and bowed to it as to an ikon: kissed it each day, placed a candle before it, and so forth. Compare Krekshin's later address to Peter in the form of a prayerful glorification: "Our Father, Peter the Great! Thou led us from nonexistence into existence; until thou camest we were in ignorance.... Before thee all called us the last, and now we are called the first," and so forth. Thus his contemporaries could not fail to see in Peter's behavior claims to divine prerogatives — and this behavior, in turn, corresponded exactly to their idea of the conduct of the Anti-Christ (as found in the New Testament itself: Matthew, XXIV, 5).

The activity of the "Most Drunken Synod," which also had a direct relationship to the examples just cited, could not be perceived as other than scoffing ridicule of the church and church services. It is important to note that this carnival play included genuine elements of sacral ritual, which in the corresponding context assumed, as it were, the opposite meaning. Thus during the mock marriage of the patriarch on December 13, 1715, the marriage rite was performed in a church by a genuine clergyman (of the Cathedral of the Archangel), an old man of ninety. It is noteworthy that not only the observers but even the participants in similar plays could perceive them as something analogous to a Black Mass, i.e., as a ritual having a negative — satanic — force (see the eyewitness report of Prince I. I. Khovanskii: "They took me to Preobrazhenskoe and, before the entire court, Mikita Zotov raised me to metropolitan and gave me a scroll for renunciation, and in accordance with that writing, I renounced, and in the renunciation they asked, 'Do you drink?' instead of 'Do you believe?' and by this renunciation I lost more than my beard by not challenging it, and it would have been better for me to accept the crown of martyrdom than to perform such a renunciation").

The idea that the tsar had proclaimed himself a spiritual or even holy person was undoubtedly greatly enhanced by the fact that Peter had ordered that he be named without patronymic; after all, spiritual figures — or even saints — were thus named. An even stronger impression must have been made by calling himself the First, which indubitably had to seem a claim to sanctity. Pre-Petrine culture was characterized in general by a mythological identification of various persons and objects with corresponding persons and objects in a hierarchically primary hypostasis, which were in this sense "the first": ontologically initial. Thus, for example, Constantinople and Moscow were identified with Rome and called, accordingly, the second and the third Rome. Ivan III was called the second Constantine, etc., etc. The point is precisely identification, which, as it were, reveals the true ontological essence of whoever is named in such a way. (It is indicative that in certain cases a person could be named directly for his namesake saint. Thus Metropolitan Paisius Ligarid, when addressing Tsar Aleksei Mikhailovich, could call him "Aleksei, Man of God," i.e., he seems to see in Aleksei Mikhailovich the manifestation of the

Historia sub Specie Semioticae

essence of his patron — Saint Aleksei, the man of God in whose honor the tsar had been christened. In the same sense, for example, the Paulicians in their day called themselves by the name of the apostle Paul and his pupils and associates, regarding themselves as incarnations of those figures.) It is natural that, given such a system of views, the title "Peter the First" would have to be perceived as an unjustified claim to being the point of reckoning, the beginning, which was permissible, generally speaking, only in the realm of the sacral (or at least that which had been sanctified by tradition). That Peter began to call himself "the Great" was in the eyes of his contemporaries a good deal less immodest than that he began to call himself "the First."

There is no need to pause in detail on such well-known facts as the forced shaving of beards and replacement of Russian dress by German. We note only that beard shaving and German dress acquired a special meaning in the eyes of his contemporaries because demons were depicted in ikons in corresponding form. (7) Thus the corresponding image was not at all something new for the Russian: for him it was specifically a sign that fell into a fully defined iconographic conception: in the words of contemporaries, Peter "dressed people like demons." The shaving of beards could be directly linked with heresy. It is characteristic that Patriarch Filaret cursed in synod "the doglike ugliness" and that both patriarchs of Peter's time, Ioakim and Adrian, opposed it, the latter directly threatening beard shavers with excommunication. As far as the counterposing of Russian and Western dress is concerned, it is indicative that as early as 1652, foreigners living in Russia were forbidden upon pain of punishment to put on Russian dress; the patriarch (Nikon) specifically insisted upon this. On the other hand, it must be borne in mind that in pre-Petrine Rus' German dress was for amusement (for masquerade). Thus in this period tsarevitches and their entourage could wear German dress. On the other hand, in Peter's day the weddings of the jesters Shanskii and Kokoshkin were celebrated in Russian garb, which now assumed the character of masquerade costume (precisely as in a later time gimnazium and university students were punished by being garbed in peasant, i.e., Russian national, dress). One might thus say that the opposition of Russian and Western dress is preserved, but the signs are changed into their opposites.

The facts presented could be greatly multiplied, but they already provide a basis for certain conclusions. From a certain point of view, Peter's behavior appears not as a cultural revolution but as antitexts, minus-behavior within the bounds of the same culture. In any case, that was how his contemporaries could regard it, and this fact is fundamentally important. In other words, Peter's behavior, paradoxical as it might seem, for the most part did not go outside the bounds of traditional ideas and norms. It fit entirely within these limits, but with a minus sign. Accordingly, in the "language" of the period Peter's actions could not be perceived in any other way. In the eyes of contemporaries Peter seemed to proclaim publicly that he was Anti-Christ.

But, of course, Peter knew this "language" and consequently could anticipate the effects of his actions. One possible explanation of his behavior would be to recognize that Peter consciously ignored his native "language" as incorrect, regarding the imported "language" of Western European cultural ideas as the only correct one. In his very attitude toward "language" — which was nearly irrational — Peter still remained a loyal son of his culture: the adoption of a "correct" language and abandonment of an "incorrect" one prove subjectively to be a more important factor than the possible consequences of the corresponding deeds. From this explanation it follows that Peter consciously created texts in another language from that in which they were read (by the socium). This can be traced, generally speaking, even in the narrowly linguistic sense (see above, for example, about the expression "father of the fatherland," which is used as translation of the Latin pater patriae, despite the fact that in Russian texts this expression has a different meaning. Certain other facts presented above can be treated in the same way). (8)

However, it is also necessary to bear in mind that there

Historia sub Specie Semioticae

existed in Russia a clear tradition of "reverse behavior" (antibehavior), the influence of which to some degree — albeit unconsciously — Peter might have felt (as, perhaps, Ivan the Terrible had in his day). The magic, black culture (reflected in particular in incantations, etc.) was in considerable measure built on antithetical opposition to church culture. The motif of disguise, of splitting the personality, so characteristic of Peter's everyday behavior, is curious in this regard. It is no less significant that Peter's actions in a number of cases seem to justify the attitude of the socium toward him, i.e., Peter seemingly submits to what they think about him. In the first place, his actions entirely correspond to the eschatological expectations of the times. The coming of the Anti-Christ was expected in 1666. When that did not happen, people began to expect him in 1699 (1666 + 33 = 1699). And just a few days before the beginning of that year (August 25, 1698; it must be borne in mind that the new year began on September 1), Peter appeared from his first journey abroad, and his arrival was immediately marked by a whole series of cultural innovations (forced shaving of beards began the very next day; New Year's Day of 1699 was also marked by the elimination of beards; and it was then, too, that the struggle against Russian national dress and a number of other reforms of the same order began). It was natural to link to this the rumor that the real Peter had been murdered abroad, and it is noteworthy that these rumors began before Peter's return. One must conclude that the legend of the "surrogate tsar" was promoted by the carnival masquerade of Peter, who during the voyage adopted the role of Sergeant Peter Mikhailov. It is even more striking that the rumors of Peter's attempt on the life of Tsarevitch Aleksei came in advance of, as it were, anticipated, the actual event by more than ten years (as K. V. Chistov has shown). (It is noteworthy that on the basis of these rumors, the first self-proclaimed Pseudo-Aleksei appears six years before the execution of the tsarevitch.) Thus Peter's deeds entirely fit into the images that had previously existed.

But, regardless of the inner motivations of Peter's behavior,

Semiotics and Structuralism

the result of the reading of corresponding texts in the "language" of the socium seems entirely legitimate. The consequences of this are known — they are the inorganic nature of the Petrine reforms, which is evident even much later.

Notes

1) It must be borne in mind that in the Petrine period this idea clearly had quite a mass character and was by no means exclusively associated with the Old Believer socium. Furthermore, it is important to bear in mind that in Peter's day the Old Believer community considerably changed its makeup, with opponents of Peter's innovations being added to its ranks. It is for this reason that subsequent Old Believer ideas could reflect the general mood of the Petrine period.

2) This was the first meeting between Peter and Feofan Prokopovich, which played a major role in Feofan's subsequent advancement. Prokopovich's speech of welcome given on the occasion of the victory at Poltava so pleased Peter that he immediately ordered its publication in Russian and Latin.

3) The word otechestvo could carry the meanings both of "homeland" and "paternity," including "spiritual paternity."

4) This appelation first appears in the oath of the members of the Spiritual College (1721), which was edited by Peter himself. The words about the "Supreme Judge" were added in Feofan Prokopovich's own hand. A corresponding expression then passed into the oath of the members of the Synod, which was withdrawn only in 1901.

5) Thus one might say that Peter's apologists and his opponents are not so far from each other in their formal characterization of Peter but diverge substantively in their attitudes toward that characterization.

Significant in this regard is the influence this idea had on Russian monarchs' subsequent perception of their powers. Thus Paul I in the legislative act on inheritance of the throne, April 5, 1797, wrote: "The Russian monarchs are the Head of the church"; and this became part of the Legal Code of Laws.

Historia sub Specie Semioticae

Catherine II also called herself "head of the church."

Paul I and, subsequently, Alexander I were in a position to conduct rituals that, strictly speaking, only a clergyman could perform: thus, according to legend, they could celebrate the mass. In precisely the same way Paul was able to be the head of the monastic Maltese Order. However paradoxical it may seem, this would appear to be a reflection of precisely the perception of Peter's innovations that was under discussion above.

6) It is necessary to bear in mind that only a very short time earlier (and specifically in Moscow!) there had been a special church ritual of the patriarch's ride on a young ass on Palm Sunday, in which the patriarch mystically personified Christ during the entry into Jerusalem. It must be assumed that elements of this ritual were used in the ceremony of Peter's triumphant welcome (the tsar was greeted by children, dressed in white hyposticharions, "with fronds and branches"), which aggravated the blasphemous nature of this ceremony. If one further takes into account that this ritual had been abolished specifically under Peter, the accusation against Peter that he had arbitrarily appropriated to himself the functions of patriarch (see above) has an even more persuasive ring.

7) Compare Gogol's image of the devil in German dress, in which one can see a certain iconographic tradition.

8) In general it must be borne in mind that as a result of contacts with foreign languages, numerous translated constructions (all sorts of calques, translations of phraseologisms, etc.) appear in texts originating with Peter and his entourage. This, in turn, made possible figurative, metaphorical use of Russian words (for tropes, strictly speaking, may also be regarded as translations from some other language). However, the polyglot socium legitimately understood the corresponding metaphors literally. Such a situation provided in principle the opportunity to actualize metaphors.

Toward the Problem of Genres in Folklore

V. N. TOPOROV

Among the problems in folkloristics that have recently been attracting increasing attention on the part of researchers one must undoubtedly class those that relate to clarifying the nature of genres, to the internal segmentation of the entire corpus of texts (typology of genre), and to cross-genre relationships.

The usefulness and applicability of modern classifications in the field of folklore are determined by the fact that they help clarify relationships between at least <u>two series of facts</u>, one of which is directly connected with the folklore text and the other with various kinds of space-time and of cultural-historical criteria. Scientific classification as such sets narrower limits for itself: it establishes the relationships between <u>two</u> (or, naturally, more) <u>series of folklore structures</u> and consequently presumes the ability, in the first place, to differentiate between these two (or more) series and, in the second, to distinguish in each of them groups of facts forming (or understood as) a structure. As a consequence, a classification of this kind ideally yields both the segmentation of a given folklore tradition into genres and the segmentation of a text of a given genre into particular structures, which in turn presumes knowledge of units, levels, and categories. Thus the possibility arises of describing a genre through a group of more specific features or

Genres in Folklore

more general criteria. With respect to folkloric material, we can be certain that such a segmentation is determined not only and not so much by convenience of description as by the natural organization of the entire corpus of texts and of each individual text. The significance of this segmentation is the greater in that it is fully perceived (particularly with regard to genres) by the bearers of the living folklore tradition. Still more important is what remains unperceived or, at least, does not get clearly formulated — the criteria by which one genre is opposed to others. These criteria, which to a certain extent are comparable with distinctive features in phonology (and even more so at higher levels of language structure), make it possible to reveal in folklore the concrete forms of what has been called cultural patterning and, consequently, the determinative categories of each given culture. The parallel with linguistics can be extended. Each language possesses a set of units particular to it alone, which linguists seek to describe, assuming some universal set. The universal set itself is corrected by the data of all the individual languages known to us. A similar situation is observed in folklore with respect to genres, where there is also an interdependence between a universal scheme and schemes of particular traditions. As a consequence of this state of affairs, it is necessary to examine cases in which it proves incorrect to juxtapose what seems like the same genre in two different folklore traditions, for the same reasons that in linguistics substantively identical elements can be put in different classificatory schemes. By virtue of the fact that the genre "space" of each tradition is structured in its own way, the problem of differentiation and structural description of genres becomes more or less acute. However, in any case the problem of genre must not and cannot be eliminated or dissolved in general analysis of style and structure. It is hardly accurate to assert that genres can be distinguished only after analysis of form and structure, on which the identification of genres is actually based. Naturally, there are no grounds for doubting that analysis of structure offers highly serious and reliable criteria for differentiation among genres, but it is possible even without such analysis (to be more precise, prior to it) to differentiate genres within the given tradition. In any case, the starting point for genre analysis is the idea that texts in any oral tradition do not constitute "a uniform mass as far as its nature and information value are concerned" (L. Honko), despite attempts by a number of scholars (particularly if the traditions of "primitive" peoples are at issue) to define all forms of oral creation through one or more supragenre languages. The particular structure of each genre and its particular extrafolkloric (general cultural) motivation contribute to the fact that precisely genre analysis leads to the most complete and natural classification of all the material within a given oral tradition. In preliminary classification of genres it is necessary to rely on the local indigenous traditions, with their own nomenclature (compare "Listen to the natives!" as B. Malinowski puts it), and also on analysis of situations in which the given genre is actualized and acquires its highest value. Exhaustive analysis of genres presumes the use of different criteria linked with study of content, form, style, function, origin, chronology, distribution, relationship to music, and so forth. These indicators, like some others, cannot be ignored in developing a universal scheme of criteria for different genres. However, one gets the impression that quests for a maximum number of genre-differentiating criteria within a given tradition often lead to redundancy that obscures the structural characteristics of the genre and the hierarchy of criteria. Thus for the moment one prefers classifications that are usually more particular but incomparably more rigorous, which are built on the basis of singling out truly relevant features. Such is the two-dimensional scheme for "narratives" in which the different meanings (yes, no) of two pairs of features, "fabulous-factual" and "secular-sacred," make it possible to differentiate between folktale, myth, and historical or sacred-historical tradition, and to oppose them all to legend (or saga) (C. Scott Littleton). It is curious that many characteristics prove in this case to be derivative from the results of the two-feature classification. W. Bascom uses partially similar principles when he constructs a quasi matrix to differentiate three types of narrative prose —

myth, legend, and folktale. A classificatory scheme for oral traditions transmitting historical content has been constructed by J. Vansina, who uses less operationalist categories. Particular significance attaches to works in which attempts are made to consider the entire genre range of a given tradition and to provide criteria for differentiating it. The latter task is more complex, and its solution often remains unclear even when the genres are known. However, a number of new techniques for solving the problem have recently been proposed (R. Austerlitz and others). It is interesting that in a case where there exists a description of all the genres of the given folklore tradition, and further, the local nomenclature of genres is known and/or the conditions of their existence, it proves possible to establish a system of distinctive features for genres that turns out to be entirely satisfactory, at least on the operational level. It is characteristic that establishing this system of features is simpler the more ritualized the genres, i.e., the more deeply they are incorporated in general contexts defined by the action of cultural patterns. It is precisely under these conditions, when each genre may be conceived of as a bundle of distinctive features, that it is pertinent to speak not about a set of genres in a given tradition but about their system, inasmuch as the distinctive features themselves impose the structure of the genre space and the possible principles of hierarchical organization. It is not excluded that in some cases it would appear desirable also to introduce quantitative characteristics for determining the place of the given genre in the particular tradition (or the distance between two genres in the genre space). In any case, it is quite obvious that the genre space of the folklore tradition (this in fact may pertain to literary traditions as well) must be characterized by such criteria as the degree of its differentiation, the degree of depth (distance between the most and least specialized genres in terms of distinctive features), the degree of flexibility (the number of genres capable of transmitting a given content; the problem of synonymy), and so forth. To conceive of genres in a given tradition as a system not only makes it possible to define the explanatory force of the tradition and the cor-

Semiotics and Structuralism

responding load of each genre and, consequently, the details of the functioning of this system, but it creates conditions for solving problems of diachronic folkloristics; in particular, it allows us to turn to internal reconstruction of the genre space (which to a certain degree recalls analogous tasks in linguistics).

Regrettably, folklore studies in the realm of genre quite clearly make inadequate use of the extremely rich experience accumulated in this regard by literary scholarship. The theoretical importance of the problem area of genre is explained by the fact that genres are based on the structure of common human existence (which is inevitably reflected in the structure of each individual text), and, as a consequence, they "may be regarded as institutional imperatives which both coerce and are in turn coerced by the writer" (N. H. Pearson). Therefore, in folklore studies, as in literary scholarship, one must regard as mistaken efforts to view the problem of genres as immaterial or bearing purely on classification. It is possible that the folkloristic theory of genres would gain additional support with the introduction of some more general concepts of a stylistic character (relatively speaking) — compare the lyrical, epic, and dramatic in E. Staiger's conception, which in this case goes back to the ideas of Novalis. Introduction of these concepts makes it possible to establish a more direct connection with the system of differential features (than when we are dealing with genres as already given forms) and to indicate more concretely ways of generating the genre. When this approach is taken, it turns out that it is easier to provide a linguistic (or formal) characterization precisely for these general concepts than for given genres, each of which may be derived, as a special type, from these concepts or may be regarded as the result of their interaction. Hence the most characteristic case, in which a type appears in a text not in pure form. Naturally, in folklore the problem of genres assumes a simpler form than in literature; however, in folklore too one is constantly running into texts that can be regarded as creolized in terms of styles (compare the combination of the epic and lyric principles in the ballad, the dramatic and epic in the fairy tale or complex forms of riddles, the lyric and

Genres in Folklore

dramatic in a number of varieties of songs, and so forth). This creolization appears most completely and concretely on the level of structural organization of the text, which presumes stressing the <u>morphology</u> of the given text taken as a whole. In this sense it is characteristic that both in folklore studies and in literary research, the ideas of "type," "metamorphoses," "mobile structure," and the like, which originate in Goethe, begin to acquire special significance (compare Propp's morphology of the fairy tale, on the one hand, and morphological literary studies since the early 1940s). It is understandable that both in folklore and literary scholarship (as a consequence of the methodological principles described above), the point of view begins to take root that empirical research in the field of classification of genres cannot lead to the development of the concept of type as understood today, in the first place, and that the problem of genre classification is a typological question, in the second place. In other words, folkloristics, faces the same problem that had long ago emerged in linguistics — the relationship between particular and general descriptions (compare B. Nathorst's argument against the presumptively universal definition of the riddle by A. Dundes and R. A. Georges). Considering that formally similar texts in different traditions are incorporated in different cultural contexts (for example, a song can be included in ritual and be an object of faith in one culture while in another it is looked upon as something improbable and entertaining), one has to agree with the principal conclusion of this polemic, according to which it is better for the time being to leave aside the requirement of "universal validity of generally valid definitions and categories."

If we turn to the typology of oral poetic genres and their finer segmentations, it turns out that one must regard as most promising those studies of recent years in which cases that are "mobile" (in various respects) are analyzed. By the latter we mean those examples that presume a different term of comparison and a more or less close relationship between the two terms of comparison. Such "mobility" is created when a genre is transitional (under conditions in which it has recently been isolated

Semiotics and Structuralism

from some other genre or shows a tendency to identification with it in the near future) or when there are two (or more) interacting culture areas, two (or more) chronological cross sections fixing various stages in the evolution of the genre, changes in the environment in which the given genre has currency, etc. In this connection the overriding interest (if one is speaking of oral poetic folklore) in the <u>ballad</u> and similar forms, against a background of study of the poetic epic and song, is quite characteristic. While with respect to the epic specialists are mainly attracted by essentially historical problems, and from the standpoint of structure by the theme of formulaic construction, with respect to song (except for works on poetics) the central concern is the practical classification of types, most often for the purposes of cataloging. Since (generally speaking) the ballad occupies an intermediate position between the epic and the song, indexing and cataloging it is more complicated and, in part, presumes the kind of preliminary analysis in which significant features of one genre are revealed. Indicative in this regard is a study by G. List, in which he proposes to index ballads by means of so-called "dramatic-narrative elements" (elements of a similar kind have already figured in part in the classifications by T. P. Coffin, G. M. Laws, Jr., and also by F. J. Child, in which, however, they were neither unique nor self-sufficient). The isolation of a five-member schema (1. exposition; 2. episode; 3. development, crisis, and solution; 4. episode; and 5. secondary crisis and solution) and the selection as a basis for the classification of so-called "plot gists" is associated, in particular, with the special role of point 3 in the transition from one variant to another. In general, analysis of all cases and types of transition from variant to variant is significant in that it leads to the problem of change in the elements of structure of a genre and the boundaries of a genre upon transition from one cultural tradition to another (the same problems arise upon analysis of new genres associated in one way or another with the ballad and with the influence of literary, professional, regional, and other factors — compare L. Shepard, A. B. Friedman, O. Brand, B. R. Jonsson, and others), and also upon analysis of the balladic treatment of historic or contemporary material that yields to more or less precise dating. Naturally, many of these problems have a direct relationship to the topic of the diachronic existence of genre schemes, to which the best studies in the field of the ballad are devoted (A. Taylor, J. Kemppinen, H. O. Nygard, L. Vargyas, and others). One must regard as the most valuable results of these studies the establishment of the fact that the ballad, in the course of historic development, forced out the heroic epic (or the old mythological ballad, which in turn arose within the depths of archaic mythopoeic cultures) and the disclosure of methods of contentual and formal transformation upon transition from epic to ballad. These achievements must be reflected as well in tasks of cataloging and specifying genres of the ballad. It is no accident, therefore, that the question of creation of an index of types of ballads for a more or less broad and heterogeneous area is being raised more and more frequently (R. W. Brednich). The creation of an index of this kind would be an event of epochal importance. Moreover, its results would bear not only on folklore (epic and song, in particular) but also on literature.

Establishment of the system of genres within a given tradition (and, consequently, of the rules of transition from one genre to another) and the successes in typological study of genres undoubtedly will set scholars the task of cross-genre analysis, understood as the identification of genre structures (transforms) communicating a given content. One may hope that such analyses can, ideally, be constructed as calculations, from which follows the possibility of prediction in folkloristic and cultural anthropology studies. Cross-genre analysis is called upon to play, with regard to the content of folklore forms, approximately the same role as transformational analysis in linguistics, which permits a rigorous description of meaning by indicating a set of syntactic transforms. In any case, in folklore studies (as in linguistics) transformational theory will once again lead the researcher to semantic problems, but in this case on a more formal and, consequently, more readily verifiable basis. Just as cross-genre analysis defines the boundaries of a given genre

Semiotics and Structuralism

from without, i.e., from the standpoint of the entire system of genres in the given tradition, analysis of different variants of texts in a given genre defines the <u>internal</u> boundaries of the genre as well as the internal boundaries of a given type of text (which leads scholars to the problem of the invariant and variants in folkloric material, which is not examined here).

Naturally, very broad opportunities are opened here for internal reconstruction of the <u>given</u> genre and of the entire genre space of the corresponding tradition. Yet it must be taken into consideration that a maximum of information about the semantics and pragmatics of a genre is extracted in those traditions in which links with ritual are retained or where one finds a consistent introduction of folklore genre in teaching and raising children (vocabulary development, elementary predication, mastery of the concepts of sound and sense identity and opposition, question-response patterns, the problem of differing descriptions of a single object and a single description of different objects — synonymy and homonymy, a minimal plot, the connection of motifs in a chain, basic actions and characters, and so forth). Under these conditions, particular importance attaches to an understanding of all texts of different genres within a given tradition as <u>a single text</u>, the different parts of which realize some common content, transmitting it in accordance with a set of concrete rules of transformation. Thereby it is presumed that it is possible, within the bounds of the entire text, to identify mutually correlatable elements and the transitions between them. The carrying out of these two operations will lead not only to uncovering the transformational aspect of the structure of genre space but to revealing connections of a historic nature. It is significant that in contemporary folklore studies, isolationist tendencies continue to be so strong that, despite their obviousness, one often ignores connections between elements that have the same designation. The new approach makes it possible to eliminate all doubts that a common series of regular transformations unites God the Thunderer and Il'ia the Prophet in the snake-fighter myth; God and Il'ia in ritual spring songs, in which they appear in an economic function ("And St. Il'ia/Walked

Genres in Folklore

along the field bounds, / Walked along the field bounds, / And caused the grain to sprout: / 'Engender, God, / Dense grain...' "; compare in the same source: "Where the goat's horn was, / There is hay by the rick" along with: "Il'ia walks... / Waves here... / The grain grows" and so forth); Il'ia in spells against snakes; Il'ia Muromets in byliny (his fight with Solov'ei the Robber) and in fairy tales (such as "raz Illiushku," in which, having triumphed over Prazhor, the hero says: "... I will command the thunderclouds! "); the old man Il'ia with the goat (and shooting at it with arrows) in texts associated with popular acts (such as the Slovak Turon') which are a degenerated ritual, and so forth; and perhaps as far as humorous epitaphs and children's folklore ("I said to you: / 'Don't eat mushrooms, Il'ia.' / You didn't listen / And ate everything, / And died like a pig" in the context of a myth about children being changed into mushrooms, about eating children — in connection with the Thunderer or his father [Kronos], and so forth). Such series take on greater significance in that they can couple or intersect with other series. Compare with these examples the link between the Virgin Mother and Praskov'ia ("The Virgin Mother herself / Went out into the street... / Carried out the keys, / ... And opened up the summer... / Oh, God, give us summer, / Cause the grain to sprout, God! / ... Little Praskov'iushka, / She reaped the grain standing up."). It is indicative that Praskov'ia appears particularly frequently in the text of ritual songs, performed in the spring for newlyweds (compare the cliches: "With his young wife / And with young Paraskov'ia. / The fine young groom, / The new bride, oh, so young! "). If one takes into consideration that this song, as it continues, contains the lines: "I picked the last weft into the cloth / ... I wove, I spun, / I sewed with silk..." — the suggestion becomes quite credible that behind the image of Praskov'ia, correlated to the Virgin Mother, there may be seen Paraskeva Piatnitsa (the latter competed with the Mother of God in North Russia, as may be seen from two-sided ikons depicting them both). Yet Paraskeva is the successor to the pagan Mokosha (with, in particular, the same functions), who, according to a likely hypothesis, might at one time have been the wife of the Thunderer, punished by him for bad behavior (compare mokos'ia — a woman of loose morals, and so on). Naturally, such examples derive directly from orientation toward cross-genre analysis. They require that the question of sources of diachronic research in folkloristics be posed in a new way.

Primitive Sources of Verbal Art

E. M. MELETINSKII

1. On the Origin of Verbal Art

Archeological material that provides so much for the history of visual arts helps very little in the study of the roots of verbal art. For the latter we must turn to the data of ethnography, which is a considerable inconvenience, inasmuch as the prehistory of the verbal art of some peoples has to be judged on the basis of the archaic folklore of others, assuming here the concept of uniform, general regularities of social development.

Verbal art apparently arose later than some other forms of art, inasmuch as its material, its primary element, is the word, speech. Naturally, all arts could appear only after man mastered articulate speech, but the appearance of verbal art required a high level of development of language in its communicative function and the existence of quite complex grammatical-syntactic forms. Apparently, visual art appeared earliest. The first decorated wood and bone objects (female statuettes — the Paleolithic "Venuses") date approximately to 25,000 B.C. The classical monuments of European cave painting (the depictions of animals in the Aurignacian, Solutrean, and Magdalenian) date to between 25,000 and 10,000 B.C.

Visual art arose in the Upper Paleolithic (the final stage of the Old Stone Age), when man did not in any way differ constitutionally from modern man, when he possessed speech, had a clan organization based on dual exogamy (division of the social group into two halves, within each of which marital ties were forbidden), made refined implements of stone, bone, and horn, and possessed primitive religious concepts. But less-advanced tools had already been made by man in the Middle and Lower Paleolithic, at least 400,000 years earlier.

In the process of work the hand was becoming perfected; it could now give utilitarian-purposeful shape to natural materials, and subsequently could use the object it had made in an equally purposeful manner. "Intellectual" use of the hand (and eye) sharpened the abilities that made articulate speech and human thinking possible. The shape of the tools made was becoming a plastic realization of human thought, idea, and design, and corresponded to the emerging aesthetic taste. A sense of proportions and symmetry was being generated both through man's observation of animals, plants, and himself and through the technique and rhythm of work activities. Even prior to the creation of the first bone sculptures and cave "canvases," the manufacture of implements of labor more elegant and refined than was necessary to satisfy daily needs indicated the appearance of an aesthetic sense.

Paleolithic cave painting bore a sharply pronounced "realistic" character. Only at the stage corresponding to the Azilio-Tardenoisian archeological culture did the depictions of animals become more conventional and schematized. But the Paleolithic and — even more — the Neolithic know not only representational, figurative art but also the art of ornament, which decorates implements of labor, objects used in daily life, and in all probability, the human body (tatooing, temporary coloring), and, subsequently, objects of worship, and which emerges as a rhythm of forms and colors. Some models of ornament originate directly in the techniques of plaiting, pottery, and weaving; others are reflections of geometric forms in nature, expressions of man's sensory experience. The convergence of representational and ornamental art in the Neolithic was one of the causes of the wide dissemination of conventional, stylized depictions. Certain

Primitive Sources of Verbal Art

ornaments did in fact arise as the result of stylization of realistic depictions of natural objects, but more often their symbolic interpretation arose on the basis of much later associations. It may be that convention and schematization in depictions were connected with the development of pictography — writing in the form of drawings. The development of mythology undoubtedly also promoted the appearance of symbolic and fantastic images. There is virtually no doubt that Paleolithic cave painting not only synthesized observations of animals — objects of the hunt — and in this regard represented a means of "mastering" them, but also had magical significance as a means of attracting and subjugating the hunter's quarry. This is indicated by depictions of spears stuck into the figures of animals. The "animation" of rock drawings or drawings on the ground by the Australian aborigines during rituals meant to cause multiplication of the given species of animal certainly is magical in character. Visual art was also widely used in more complex rituals, intimately associated with early religious beliefs. However, visual art could exist that was not closely connected to religious-magical purposes (as is confirmed by practices of the same Australians).

In the famous Trois Frères Cave there is a picture of a masked man with reindeer horns, dating to the Magdalenian, i.e., the period when Paleolithic painting flourished in Europe. This and similar figures undoubtedly indicate the existence at that time of hunting dances that apparently already had a magical purpose. Dance — the living plastic art — is not only one of the most ancient forms of art but one that attained a high level of perfection precisely in the primitive period.

While in the most ancient visual art there was an interweaving of expressive, figurative depiction with ornamental motifs, in the dance the dynamic reproduction of scenes of the hunt, labor processes, and some aspects of daily life were inevitably subordinated to strict rhythm; and the rhythm of the movements was from time immemorial supported by sound rhythm. Primitive music is virtually inseparable from dance, and was for a long time subordinate to it. For the most part, musical instruments beat time, and even in singing the rhythmic element was

Semiotics and Structuralism

markedly dominant over the melodic. The rhythmic principle, the development of which was promoted by work practices, was itself an important factor in organizing work and ordering psychophysical energy and in synchronizing various structures of the nervous system. Moreover, rhythm, by breaking up into its elements the flow of visual, sound, and motor perception, and by identifying the individual "frames" in it, promotes the creation of artistic images.

Reproduction of the hunt, the gathering of roots, and later of other work processes, detached from the actual performance of these labor processes, opened the road to free reproduction and generalization of reality — the most important principles of art. If work practices prepared the way for art, then separation from the actual processes of labor was a necessary prerequisite for the development of art as a unique form of creative activity, reflecting and at the same time transforming reality. At the primitive stage the transforming role of art was often naïvely identified with a utilitarian goal attainable not by work but by magic.

Depiction of the hunt in dance (and such hunting dances are widespread among a number of culturally backward peoples) was no mere game, not merely a physical exercise and dress rehearsal before a hunt. It was a ritual act, which was supposed to directly attract game and to influence the course of the hunt in the future. More complex magic rituals were supposed to promote the multiplication of animals and the growth of plants, to maintain the regular succession of the seasons, in which the period of cold and scarcity was followed by a time of warmth and abundance. As animist and totemic conceptions, the worship of ancestors, tutelary spirits, and the like developed and grew more complex, the primitive magic ritual changed into a religious cult.

The link between the dance and magic ritual and, subsequently, the religious cult proved to be closer than in visual art, inasmuch as the dance became the principal element in the ritual act.

Ritual folk games, including elements of the dance, pantomime,

Primitive Sources of Verbal Art

music, and sometimes visual art (and subsequently poetry), became, in their syncretic unity, the embryo of theater. A distinguishing feature of primitive theater was the use of masks, which genetically originated in disguise as a device of the hunt (clothing oneself in the hide of an animal in order to approach the quarry without arousing suspicion). Dressing up in an animal skin is widely practiced in hunting dances among the North American Indians, certain African peoples, and others. Imitation of the habits of animals, accompanied by the use of animal masks and body painting, attained particular development in the totemic rituals associated with the corresponding conception of a special kinship between a group of people (particular clans) and some species of animals or plants and of their descent from common ancestors (usually pictured as beings of semihuman-semianimal nature). In Australia, the classic land of totemism, such rituals were performed either with the magical object of multiplying the animals of one's totem (rituals of the Intichiuma type) or with a cognitive-educational purpose during the rites of initiation of youth as full members of the tribe. During these rituals (initiations) youths, after passing rigorous trials (symbolizing temporary death and rebirth), became the viewers of various pantomimed scenes and dances performed before them by adult men.

It is interesting to note that these performances included scenes of a grossly grotesque character. The image of the animal (first an object of the hunt, and then the revered totem) precedes in "theater" (as in the rock painting) the image of man. Human masks first appear in burial and memorial rituals in connection with the cult of ancestors (or of deceased kin). Secret male societies, well preserved in Africa, Melanesia, Polynesia, and the northwest of America, played a special role in the preservation and development of the primitive "theater" traditions. Members of such societies always performed masked; the masks represented human ancestors, sacred animals, and various spirits, often in highly fantastic form (to frighten the uninitiated, and also under the influence of a developed animist world-view). In the period when clan society was in decay,

Semiotics and Structuralism

shamanizing and analogous acts of sorcery among certain peoples provided an example of syncretic theatrical ritual activity, with the use of masks, imitation of animals, etc. The Tsam mystery performed in prerevolutionary times in Lamaist monasteries of Mongolia is descended in considerable measure from shamanic activities.

The bear festival, widespread among the peoples of the North, combines hunting magic and the complex bear cult with a vivid, motley, theater spectacle, including not only cult scenes but others having to do with everyday life, even satirical, serving exclusively for entertainment.

Among many peoples the marriage ritual has features of a unique kind of ritual syncretic act and marked elements of theatricality. The same must be said of various calendrical agrarian ritual folk plays depicting the replacement of winter by spring or summer in the form of a fight or dispute between two forces, in the form of a "funeral" of a doll or actor incarnating conquered, dying winter. More complex forms of calendrical agrarian mysteries are associated with the cult of the dying and reborn deity. Such are the ancient Egyptian cult mysteries of Osiris and Isis, the ancient Babylonian New Year's celebrations in honor of Marduk, and the ancient Greek mysteries in honor of the fertility gods Demeter and Dionysus. (Such, in essence, are the medieval Christian mysteries in their genesis.)

The origin of theater in classical antiquity is associated with the Dionysian mysteries. In uncovering the primitive heritage in the ancient Greek tragedy and comedy, A. D. Avdeev, in his book The Origin of the Theater (Avdeev, 1959), offers the hypothesis that initially the basis of tragedy was a zoopantomime, while the dithyramb of the Dionysian legend became the source of its further development as a dramaturgical genre.

The "primitive" heritage is even more obvious in the traditional theater of Indonesia (the Javan topeng), Japan (the medieval Nō theater), China, India, Burma, and other countries of the Far and Middle East, in which the connection with the cult of ancestors is distinctly traced, masks are used, and zoomorphic images, demons, and the like hold a large place.

Primitive Sources of Verbal Art

In archaic forms of theater the pantomime element dominates over the verbal text, and in a number of cases a minor verbal part is given to a special "actor" (this characteristic has been preserved to this day in the traditional theater of Japan and Indonesia); the transformation of a ritual-theatrical performance into drama occurs even in historically developed society by means of a break from ritual and through a very much more intensive penetration of elements of verbal art, often already with the aid of written language.

* * *

Let us proceed directly to verbal art.

K. Bücher, in his well-known book Work and Rhythm (Russian translation: Bücher, 1923), basing himself on an extensive collection of work songs of various peoples, offered the hypothesis that "at the lower stages of development, work, music, and poetry represented something united, but the principal element of this trinity was work" (p. 264); that poetic meter originates directly from work rhythms and that the principal types of poetry — the epic, lyric, and drama — gradually developed from the work song. This hypothesis presents the link between work and poetry one-sidedly and in a vulgarized fashion. It has already been observed above that it was precisely the transition from genuine productive activity to its generalized reproduction in folk ritual games that was the important premise of the development of art, or in any case of dance, music, and theater.

The distinguished Russian scholar A. N. Veselovskii, in his Historical Poetics, saw specifically in folk ritual the roots not only of dance and music but of poetry. Primitive poetry, according to his conception, initially consisted of the singing of a chorus accompanied by dance and pantomime. In song the verbal element, naturally, was united with the musical. Thus poetry developed, as it were, in the depths of a primitive syncretism of types of art united by the framework of folk ritual. At the outset the role of the word was negligible and entirely subordinated to rhythmic and mimetic principles. The text was improvised for the occasion, until it finally assumed a traditional character.

Veselovskii assumed the primitive syncretism not only of types of art but of genres of poetry. "We viewed the epic and lyric as consequences of the breakup of the ancient ritual chorus" (Veselovskii, 1940, p. 291). In his opinion, along with the separation of song from ritual, a differentiation of its genres occurs; first the epic emerges, then the lyric and drama. He regards the lyric-epic character of the early forms of epic to be the fruits of its primitive syncretism. As for lyrical poetry, it, in Veselovskii's opinion, arose from the emotional cries of the ancient chorus and shortened formulas of varied content. as an expression of "collective emotion," of "group subjectivism"; and it emerged from ritual syncretism, primarily from the spring ritual games. He links the final emergence of the lyric to an individualization of poetic consciousness greater than in the epic. Veselovskii traces drama to folk ritual that had succeeded in adopting the form of a developed cult. He sees poetic creation as collective in the literal sense, i.e., as choral, in its genesis. The poet is descended from the singer and ultimately from the leader of the ritual chorus.

Within the framework of this evolution Veselovskii places various types of singers (the Finnish laulaia, the ancient Scandinavian tul and skald, the Anglo-Saxon scops, the Celtic fili and bards, the ancient Greek Aedes and rhapsodes, the medieval wandering singers: spielmann, jongleur, skomorokh, etc. [non-Russian terms transliterated from the Russian where necessary]).

Analyzing the corresponding lexicon, Veselovskii demonstrates the semantic kinship in the genesis of concepts of song–tale–theatrical performance [deistvo]–dance, and also of song–incantation–divining–ritual act.

Veselovskii traces some ancient features of the folk-poetic style, such as verse parallelism, to the choral-ritual roots of poetry, particularly the amoebaean (i.e., with the participation of two half-choruses or two singers). But "psychological parallelism" (comparison of phenomena of man's spiritual life with the state of natural objects) in his opinion has its roots in the primitive animist world-view, which regards all of nature as

Primitive Sources of Verbal Art

animate. Veselovskii traces a number of typical narrative motifs and plots to certain features of the primitive world-view and way of life (animism, totemism, exogamy, matriarchy, patriarchy, blood brotherhood, and so forth). Veselovskii's "historical poetics," which arose on the basis of generalization of an enormous amount of material accumulated by classical ethnography and nineteenth-century folkloristics, is the only such, in its own way, consistent theory of the origin of verbal art.

However, Veselovskii's concept, too, requires revision in the light of the present state of science. Veselovskii traced quite fully the role and evolution of elements of verbal art in folk rituals and correctly domonstrated the gradual increase in the role of the verbal text in ritual syncretism. Folk ritual, which played an exceptional role in the development of the dance-music-theater complex, cannot be regarded as the sole source of the origin of poetry. Also an exaggeration is the thesis that the epic, lyric, and drama intitially formed a total, syncretic unity. The descent of drama from cult mysteries is beyond doubt. As already stated, it is chiefly the prehistory of drama that relates to the preliterate period and ritual syncretism. In order for it to take final shape, not only was its separation from the cult needed but a rather advanced level of development of narrative folklore as a source of plots. Veselovskii's theory is most productive for understanding the origin of lyric poetry. The folk lyric is entirely sung, and song by its very nature reflects a syncretism of music and poetry. Veselovskii, and simultaneously with him the prominent French philologist Gaston Parisse, persuasively demonstrated the connection between the medieval chivalric lyric and the traditions of folk songs from the spring ritual cycle.

In its genesis the epic is much less intimately linked with ritual syncretism. True, the song form, which is characteristic of epic poetry, probably originates, in the final analysis, in the ritual chorus; but narrative folklore has, since the most ancient times, also been transmitted in the form of the oral prose tradition and in mixed song- or verse-prose form, the share of prose in archaic times being greater (not less, as would follow

Semiotics and Structuralism

from the theory of the primitive syncretism of types of art and genres of peotry). This is explained by the fact that although the role of the word in primitive rituals is considerably less than the role of the mimetic and rhythmic principles, even among the most "primitive" tribes, including the Australian aborigines, there exists along with ritual a developed tradition of prose narration that in the final analysis originates not in the expressive but in the purely communicative function of speech. Mythology, which can in no way be entirely elminated from poetry, occupies an enormous place in this narrative tradition.

Studies on the origin and early stage of poetic creation are very few in number.

In the three-volume monography by the British scholars C. and M. Chadwick, The Growth of Literature (Chadwick, 1923-1940), which is rich in material, the problem of initial genesis remains in the shadow. The book is useful thanks to the effort to classify a large number of archaic genre forms and their distinctiveness among different peoples. A serious attempt to reconstruct the very origin of poetry and its first steps is found in the study by the English academic C. M. Bowra, Primitive Song, which uses material from the folklore of Australian aborigines, Negritoes, Andaman Islanders, Bushmen, and other primitive hunters and gatherers of wild grains. Like Veselovskii, Bowra consciously adopts "evolutionary study by comparative methods" (Bowra, 1962, p. 265); but unlike Veselovskii, Bowra examines the course of formation of song both within and outside ritual. Bowra's general picture of the establishment of poetry is quite similar to that drawn by Veselovskii. Bowra believes that poetry originates genetically from rhythmicized actions and begins with the addition of words to the rhythm of music and pantomime (song is preceded by melody with fixed sounds of the voice that lack, however, direct meaning). According to Bowra, the initial unit of song was, when accompanied by dance, the entire line and, in the absence of dance, the poetic line suggested by the melody and internal rhythm of the structure itself. In the latter case further growth of the "text" proceeds "line by line," some lines being merely

Primitive Sources of Verbal Art

repeated to increase the magical power of the word. Repetitions have, from the very outset, a tendency to vary and lead to parallelism. Alliteration and rhyme appear sporadically as nonobligatory ornamentation, while the fixing of the number of syllables (whether stressed or unstressed) is a means of working out the meter.

Bowra, the results of whose studies confirm many of Veselovskii's guesses, has a clearer picture of the full complexity of the interrelationship between primitive song and narrative poetry. He does not regard primitive song as the immediate embryo of the epic. "Narrative poetry, in the full meaning of the word, is absent among the primitives, and its place is taken by drama" (p. 54); "Song is not the normal means for narrating myths. They are usually narrated in prose tales" (p. 236).

And in fact, familiarization with samples of the poetry of culturally backward tribes (1) shows that this poetry is primarily ritual-lyrical. Here one finds such genres as sorcerers' healing incantations and hunters' songs; war songs; songs associated with agrarian magic that accompany both the work operations of the farmer and the corresponding spring ritual; funeral laments, songs of death; wedding and love songs; "shaming" songs and humorous, sung disputes; various songs accompanying dances and constituting one of the elements of complex ritual ceremonials; and prayer-incantations addressed to various spirits and gods. In the poetry of culturally backward peoples one can find specimens of striking lyricism; but on the whole, their poetry is not rigorously lyrical, and it contains many descriptive elements, rhetoric, and ritual symbolism (this, however, is not syncretism with the epic in the literal meaning of the word, as Veselovskii imagined).

Both the content and the form of the primitive lyric are rigorously canonized. In the old ethnographic literature, particularly in all kinds of "travel narratives," the primitive lyric is often erroneously described as free improvization for the occasion, a direct, "naïve" expression of impressions and emotions. However, in the majority of cases these songs are not spontaneous self-expression, even of "collective subjectivism," but

Semiotics and Structuralism

purposeful activity based on faith in the power of the word. From this point of view one can understand the words of a certain Indian (Navajo) that he was so poor a man that he did not have a single song.

Many songs have a magical purpose, for example, sorcerers' incantations, songs about the growth and multiplication of plants, hunting songs in which a hunter usually calls on animals as their "friend," and love "calls." Most love songs have precisely such a character. A whole series of songs that do not pursue "magical" goals are meant to encourage and inspire those who sing them or to demoralize an enemy. This is true, for example, of war songs, with their self-glorification, or "shaming" songs that denigrate enemies. Deliberately merry songs, glorifying life, are sung for analogous reasons under conditions of hunger, forced isolation, and so forth. A special case is songs sung by warriors at moments of mortal danger or after receiving a fatal wound. These songs express great courage, the inevitability of one's death, and revenge on the enemy.

In agrarian songs and prayers to spirits there are often inspired hymns to nature, poetic expressions of spring flowering and of the might of the "masters" of various types of natural forces. In ritual and lyric songs a descriptive narrative element sporadically penetrates, in the form of an explanation of the causes of illness (in sorcerers' incantations), a deed by a god of war (in war songs); information on the deeds of "spirits" and even presentation of the mythical picture of the creation (in ritual songs); and feats of valor of a dead leader (in funeral and memorial songs). In Polynesia a special genre of panegyric developed from funeral and wedding songs. Among some peoples (for example, Eskimos or certain African tribes) competition in songs is practiced, sometimes in the form of humorous disputes.

Songs are usually seen as the collective property of male societies, ritual societies, and more rarely, of individuals. The Pueblo Indians associated the origin of song with the kingdom of death and the chthonic snake (when the snake was cremated, the shreds of his body became songs). The source of a song is

Primitive Sources of Verbal Art

often regarded to be the suggestion of spirits, usually in the form of a dream "vision." In the past the Nivhkhi believed in a special spirit who sits on the tip of the singer's tongue when he performs a song. Poetry without music is unknown in the preliterate period.

Ritual and lyric poetry are known only in song form, very often in combination with a theatrical-dramatic element. From the standpoint of elegance of stylistic structure, ritual poetry ranks first, followed by strictly lyric songs. Songs can be quite brief and consist of a single word (for example, characterizing a particular animal) or of two words (for example, the word "warrior" and the name of a warrior), but they can also be quite long.

In songs the musical element predominates; rhythm, approximating meter, is dominant in them. In a number of cases rhythmicization is achieved by lengthening or adding new syllables and also all kinds of emphatic particles, exclamations, etc. Rhyme is not characteristic of primitive poetry. Its principal feature is the repetition not of sounds but of meaning complexes. The element of repetitiveness is supported by belief in the power of the word, as an accumulation of this power. But repetition of thoughts has to vary, because literal repetition is often regarded as dangerous. Sometimes, in the ritual poetry of American Indians, ritual models require repetition of a phrase for each quarter of the compass, but with replacement of the existing symbolic meaning of the name of a flower, animal, plant, etc. We also find repetition of lines in any enumeration.

The combination of repetition and variation leads to semantic-syntactic parallelism.

In parallel lines the device of contrast is often found (of the following type: the white light of morning and the red light of evening; falling rain and standing rainbow). Similar contrasts (day and night, man and woman, red and white falcon) are extremely typical of "primitive" songs. Along with contrasts, the accumulation of synonyms is a typical stylistic feature of primitive poetry.

In the lyric one finds not only parallelism but, very often, refrains, repetitions that are literal or with variations. Repetition of a word at the end of one line at the beginning of the next line (polylogy — picking up) is one means of singling out an important word. In oratory, speeches are repeated many times in addressing different persons, new situations, and so forth.

Metaphors are found in primitive poetry. They are also common in oratorical prose when describing the greatness of leaders or warriors. Some metaphors owe their origin to the taboo on reference to death and disease. Fixed metaphorical formulas emerged in ritual poetry.

In its genesis the epic is considerably less tied to ritual syncretism than is the lyric. The classical epic monuments of the European and Asian peoples are for the most part poetic, but in the more archaic monuments of the epic (for example, the tales of the peoples of the Caucasus, the heroic poems of the Turko-Mongolian peoples of Siberia, Irish epic poetry, etc.) the share of prose is greater, and the so-called mixed form, i.e., a combination of prose and verse, is often encountered. The speeches of characters and solemn epic descriptions are most often presented in verse. Certain plots have come down to us in both prose and verse forms. On the other hand, one often finds in the tales of quite different peoples verse intrusions that can be interpreted as a relict of the same mixed form.

If we address ourselves directly to primitive folklore, we will be convinced that the narration here, as a rule, is present not in the form of songs, but precisely in the form of oral prose with verse inserts. Moreover, the verse inserts often coincide with speeches by the characters and retain a rather clear-cut connection with ritual examples. They are prayer, incantation, call to battle, lament for the fallen, ritually fixed exchange of remarks, etc. However, the basic prose portions contain no traces of a link with music or rhythm. They are transmitted in ordinary speech and stylistically are much less firmly fixed and polished than the verse inserts. Although the song form of the heroic epic probably originates in the final analysis in primitive lyric-ritual song, narrative folklore has from the most ancient times been transmitted primarily as a prosaic or primarily prosaic (mixed) tradition. The combination of prose and verse

Primitive Sources of Verbal Art

(song) in the mixed tradition is, of course, something quite different from lyric-epic song as understood by Veselovskii.

The origin of verbal art cannot be investigated merely "from without," in its relationship to ritual and other forms of existence. The internal aspect of this problem leads us to myth. In twentieth-century Western scholarship (Frazer, Robertson-Smith, Harrison, Raglan, Hook, James, and others), the "ritualistic" tendency (2) to identify myth with ritual to the maximum degree and even entirely, and to see myth purely as an echo of ritual, is very strong. The "ritualists" have tried to trace literature itself directly to ritual: St. Ives in the case of the fairy tale; Miro, Levin, Carpenter, and others with respect to the epic. There is no question as to the intimate connection between myth and ritual in both primitive and early Eastern cultures, and certain myths actually did originate directly in rituals (for example, the myths about dying and reborn gods). However, there are also myths that are clearly independent of ritual in their genesis and even lack ritual equivalents. Fragments of myths that had arisen quite independently were often staged within rituals. In Australia there is evidence of both interrelated myths and rituals, nonritual myths, and rituals lacking mythic correlates (on which, see below). We know that, for example, mythology is considerably richer than ritual among the Bushmen and certain groups of American Indians. The same applies to Ancient Greece, as distinct from Egypt or Mesopotamia. The question as to the relationship of myth and rituals on the genetic level is equivalent to the problem of the chicken and the egg (which came first?!). And the deep connection between them, their "intellectual" unity and structural homogeneity are typical of primitive culture. Mythology pertains not to the realm of behavior, but to the area of thought; and that, naturally, does not exclude mutual conditionality of these two realms.

Syncretism is manifested in primitive culture not only in forms of activity but in forms of thought, of ideology. Ancient myths contain in an as yet undeveloped unity the embryos of art, religion, and prescientific conceptions of nature and society. Mythology was undoubtedly the "cradle" and "school" of poetic

Semiotics and Structuralism

fantasy and in many respects anticipated its properties, although the complete identification of mythology and literature suggested by "ritual-mythological" literary studies (Bodkin, Frye, Chase, and others) is unquestionably unacceptable.

Contrary to the dominant nineteenth-century concept of myths as merely naïve rational explanations of the surrounding world, Lévy-Bruhl emphasized the significance of affective elements of "collective ideas" and postulated their prelogical character in view of the tendency to mystical "participations." Ernst Cassirer interpreted mythology, along with language and art, as an autonomous, symbolic form of culture, marked by a particular modality and a particular means of symbolic objectivation of sensual emotions. But only Lévi-Strauss was able actually to describe mythological thought in its aspect of generation of semiotic modeling systems and, unlike Lévy-Bruhl, showed the intellectual capacity of myth to classify and analyze, while simultaneously explaining those of its specific features that bring it close to art: thought at the sensual level; thought attaining its objectives by indirect paths ("bricolage") and using a kaleidoscopic rearrangement of an available set of elements; and purely metaphorical thought — some myths prove to be metaphorical (more rarely — metonymic) transformations of others, transmitting the same "message" through different "codes"; transformations of mythological texts become a means of revealing symbolic (but not allegorical) meaning.

The significance of mythology is very great in the development of various aspects of the arts and in the very genesis of artistic-imaged thinking; but it goes without saying that mythological narration had particular importance for the formation of verbal and, above all, narrative art. Susanne Langer was not quite right in saying that myth has no language and meter and can be "drawn," "danced," and so on — that it has an equal relationship to all the arts (Langer, 1953). Thanks to the properties of visual art, drawing, even on a distinctly mythological theme, is somewhat freer in the concrete-pictorial resolution of this theme and even in the selection of impressions of actual reality in the quality of material, the model. The same ap-

Primitive Sources of Verbal Art

plies to dance-pantomime, and so forth.

But narrative poetry, having language and plot as its primary elements, also possesses a relative independence to a minimal degree.

The essence of primitive myth lies in the fact that conceptions about the organization of the world are transmitted in the form of narration about the origin of various of its elements. Moreover, events in mythical time from the lives of the "ancestors" are presented as the ultimate causes of the present state of the world. From the standpoint of science, events and persons are determined by the state of the world; but from the viewpoint of myth, the state of the world is the result of particular events and the deeds of particular mythical personalities. Thus a narrational quality enters the essence of the primitive myth. Myth is not only a world-view but a narration — hence the special significance of myth for the shaping of verbal art, primarily narrative.

2. The Folklore of the Australian Aborigines

To obtain a more concrete view of the oldest state of verbal art — narrative art above all — let us turn to the folklore of the indigenous population of Australia, whose culture some scholars have tentatively compared with the Azilio-Tardenoisian culture of the Mesolithic in Europe.

The central place in the verbal art of the indigenous population of Australia is held by myths, in which the action is set in some ancient, prehistoric period (<u>alchera</u> among the Aranda tribe, <u>mura</u> among the Dieri, <u>djugur</u> among the Aluridja, <u>bugari</u> among the Karadjeri, <u>ungud</u> among the Ungarinjin, <u>wingara</u> among the Warramunga, <u>mungai</u> among the Binbinga, etc.). In this prehistoric era mythical heroes were in action; and their deeds determined the appearance of the earth's surface, called people, plants, and animals into life, and determined various customs.

Such location of action in a particular prehistoric period is a characteristic sign of myth not only among the Australians but also among American Indians (according to the observations of Boas) and among other peoples.

A number of Australian tribes denote this mythical time by the same word they use for "dream" (in Anglo-Australian ethnography this generally accepted denotation is dream time). The association with "dreams" shows that the issue is a time that is not only prehistoric but extrahistoric, a time "out of time." It can be re-created in dreams and also in rituals in which the performers identify themselves with their mythical ancestors. The latter are conceived of as eternal and not created by anyone. They lived their life cycles in the alchera (altjira) time and were ultimately transformed into cliffs, trees, or stone and wooden sacred tjurungas. These sacred objects (natural or created by human hands) continue to this day, in the minds of Australian tribes, to retain the magical creative power of their mythical ancestor and may be the means for multiplication of animals, the source of the souls of newborn babies who, in certain tribes (the Aranda), are thought of as reincarnations of ancestors. The life of the ancestors is described in quite commonplace forms: they sleep, eat, hunt, argue with each other, have love affairs, and perform rituals; the quest for food predominates. It should be noted that in most cases the ancestors are successful in the hunt. "Dream time" is pictured as an epoch of abundance and, in this sense, a kind of golden age.

The basic meaning of "dream time" is, however, not in idealization of the past, but in the creation of the world by the ancestors.

Both the very structure of the world and the events determining it are very simple in Australian mythology. Its fantasy lacks the whimsicality and hyperbolism that mark the myths of the Indians, Polynesians, and others. The local group (the fundamental social unit of Australian society, with kinship reckoned through the father, usually coinciding with the totemic clan that Western observers sometimes call, quite inaccurately, a "horde") is closely connected with a given food territory beyond which it does not go, for all practical purposes. The folklore vividly reflects the Australian's love for this territory as his native land. And in the myths the major attention is directed not toward the universe, but precisely toward this "microcosm."

Consequently, the most prevalent Australian myths bear the character of local legends explaining the origin of all somehow notable places and natural objects in the food territory — hills, lakes, springs, cliffs, pits, large trees, and so forth. Very often the myths relate the wanderings of their forebears in "dream time" along specific trails. Various features of topography, vegetation, and the like prove to be the result and "monument" of the activity of the mythical hero, the trace of his camp, the fruit of his creative activity, or the place where he was transformed into a tjurunga. The placement of certain objects in a locality supposedly reproduces certain scenes from the history of the ancestor. The myth lists and describes with great exactness places through which the hero passed, his route. Some of the mythic trails cross the territories of several local groups or even entire tribes. In this situation one local group proves to be the guardian only of part of the myth. The mythic trails usually run from north to south, which probably corresponds to the direction in which the continent was populated.

The mythological heroes are, for the most part, totemic ancestors, that is, the original forebears or founders simultaneously both of a given species of animals (less often, plants) and of the human group that regards the given species of animals as its totem, i.e., its kin, its "flesh."

Totemism is a unique ideological superstructure in early clan society. It applies to surrounding nature (from which man has not yet learned to "isolate" himself entirely) conceptions about clan social organization (see Tokarev, 1964). People's relations with each other appear as the relationship of man to nature. On the other hand, conceptions about animals and plants well known to man, and their names, are widely used as material for the elaboration of a unique and, of course, rather cumbersome "code," making it possible to classify both natural and social phenomena (Lévi-Strauss, 1962). This, in considerable

Semiotics and Structuralism

measure, explains the fact that along with the basic (clan) totem there are all kinds of individual subtotems, sex totems, etc., etc. The principal totem usually corresponds to the requirements of exogamy (prohibition of marriage within a given totem) and the alimentary taboo (prohibition against eating the meat of the totem animal except for special moments in ritual). Both exogamy and the alimentary taboo are often violated in the ancestor myths.

Apparently, totemic centers, whose creation is also described in the myths, are localized in places where a particular species of animal or plant is most prevalent. In totemic centers members of the given totem periodically perform magical rituals meant to multiply the totemic species of animal or plant. In the scholarly literature these rituals are called, not very accurately, Intichiuma. During such rituals (and also during the initiation ritual) plots of corresponding myths about totemic heroes are usually acted out.

In the myths totemic ancestors appear as beings of a not completely differentiated dual zoo-anthropomorphic nature, in which, however, the human principle is clearly predominant. For the most part these are people who, in case of need, can readily transform themselves into the corresponding species of animal. In the beginnings of myths of certain tribes one sometimes finds this form: "It was in the time when the animals were still people." Sometimes wanderings end with this transformation. Thus among the Murinbata (according to Stanner) myths often end with the word demɲinoi, which means "to change body" and also "to transform oneself from a man into an animal," and "to flee into the water." Certain events in the lives of totemic ancestors motivate and explain particular features of the corresponding animals and plants (their coloration, shape, habits). In such cases the etiologism (explanatory function) of the myth includes not only the features of the locality but also properties of the fauna and flora. Such etiologism is widespread in the mythology of the most diverse peoples of the world.

Myths about the wanderings of totemic ancestors appear in their classic form in the folklore of the tribes of central Aus-

Primitive Sources of Verbal Art

tralia. The scientist-missionary Carl Strehlow (Strehlow, 1907-1908), an outstanding authority on the language, folklore, and culture of these tribes, wrote down the myths and translated them accurately from the languages of the Aranda and Loritja. (3) Strehlow's collection includes myths on the ancestors of the red kangaroo, gray kangaroo, emu, eagle, wildcat, spiny anteater, bat, duck, crow, frog, snail, various snakes, birds, grubs, fish, etc.

The totemic myths of the Aranda and Loritja are virtually all built on a single pattern: that of the totemic ancestors returning individually or in a group to their native land — to the north (less often, the west). The places they pass, their searches for food, their feasts, the organization of campsites, and encounters en route are listed in detail. Not far from their homeland, in the north, they often encounter the local "eternal people" of the same totem. Upon reaching their goals, the wandering heroes disappear into burrows, caves, springs, under the ground, having transformed themselves into cliffs, trees, tjurungas. The reason offered for this is often fatigue.

Totemic centers are established at the sites of their camps and, particularly, at the place of their deaths (or, more exactly, departure into the earth). In some myths (for example, about wildcat people) the totemic heroes carry with them tjurungas, cult staffs (which are used as weapons or to hew a path through cliffs, i.e., as an instrument to create topography), and other cult objects.

Sometimes the narrative deals with leaders' taking with them groups of youths who have just gone through the initiation ritual — the consecration as full members of the tribe. En route the group performs cult ceremonies to increase its totem. It also happens that wandering bears the character of flight and pursuit. For example, a large gray kangaroo flees from a person of the same totem; the man, with the help of youths, kills the animal, but it is reborn, and then both become tjurungas; or a red and a gray kangaroo flee, pursued by dog-people and then by a falcon-man; a fleeing emu is torn apart by dog-people; swimming fish are pursued by a crab and then a cormorant; two snakes are

Semiotics and Structuralism

pursued by people of the same totem. In these cases it is difficult to tell who is the subject: animals, people, or beings of dual nature. For the most part it is the last.

The totemic myths of the Aranda and Loritja also include a small number of tales about heavenly luminaries. The moon is seen as a man who initially belonged to the opossum totem. The motion of the moon across the sky is explained as follows: It ascended to the sky with a stone knife, made its way to the west, descended to the earth to hunt opossums, and then climbed to the sky once again on a tree. Having eaten opossums, the moon becomes large (the half-moon); fatigued, it assumes the form of a gray kangaroo and in that guise is killed by youths (the new moon), but one of them keeps a bone of the kangaroo, from which the moon grows once again. The sun is a girl who has climbed a tree to the sky; the Pleiades are also girls, from the bandicoot totem, who had witnessed the initiation ceremonies of youth and thus had been transformed into stones, and then into stars, and so forth. As has already been noted, heavenly phenomena did not attract among the Australians, particularly among the Aranda and Loritja, as much attention as in more advanced mythologies. The mythology of the Aranda knows the image of the "master" of the sky (Altjira, according to C. Strehlow), but this personage is quite passive and plays no special role in the Aranda myths.

During their wanderings some of the totemic ancestors of the Aranda introduce various customs and rituals and play the roles of so-called culture heroes. Fire was obtained by a representative of the gray kangaroo totem from the body of a gigantic gray kangaroo he had hunted. In this connection one cannot but recall the Karelo-Finnish rune about how Väinämöinen obtained fire from the stomach of a fiery fish. A similar myth is typical of a primitive economy in which the gathering of ready natural products predominates. Two falcon-men coming from the north to the Aranda country taught others to use the stone axe; rules of marriage, which people had forgotten, were reestablished by one of the ancestors of the tree-climbing kangaroo, named Katukankara. The introduction of marriage rules is also ascribed to an emu-man.

Primitive Sources of Verbal Art

The introduction of initiation rituals, which play a very important role in the lives of the Australians, and of the ritual operations on the body associated with them, is ascribed to wildcat ancestors and to fly-catching lizard ancestors (the use of the stone knife for these operations replaced, according to the myth, the use of burning sticks).

The "eternal people" of <u>alchera</u> times, who subsequently became fly-catching lizards, play a particularly important role. The tales of their wanderings take on the character of an anthropogenetic and in part cosmogonic myth. Tradition places their wanderings among the very earliest. However, in reality they probably mark a less primitive stage in the history of mythology, inasmuch as what is treated here is the origin not of a single totemic group, but at the very least of several; and the point is not only the scattering of tjurungas but the initial emergence of "humankind."

According to this myth, the earth was initially covered by the sea (a mythological concept very widespread throughout the world); and on the sides of the cliffs projecting from the water there were not only the "eternal" mythical heroes but also so-called <u>rella manerinya</u> (i.e., "pasted people"), according to Strehlow, or <u>inapatua</u>, according to Spencer and Gillen — bunches of helpless beings with fingers and teeth pasted together, closed ears and eyes. Other similar human "grubs" lived in the water and resembled raw meat. After the earth dried out, a mythical hero — the totemic ancestor of the "lizards" — came from the north and with a stone knife separated the human embryos from each other, cutting out for them eyes, ears, a mouth, a nose, fingers, and the like. With the same knife he circumcised them (this reflects in part the idea that only the initiation ritual "completes" a man), taught them to make fire by friction, to prepare food, gave them the spear, the spear-thrower, the boomerang, provided each with his personal tjurunga (as guardian of his soul), divided people into phratries ("earth" and "water") and marital classes. Before us appears a typical cultural hero-demiurge: the central figure in primitive mythology.

The conception of human development from imperfect, helpless

Semiotics and Structuralism

beings is also known to other Australian tribes and to many other peoples. An echo of this idea is the familiar old Scandinavian myth, retold in the Elder Edda, of how the gods found on the seashore the unbreathing bodies of the first human beings in the form of pieces of wood and how they breathed life into them. Along with this "evolutionary" mythological concept of human origin, the selfsame Aranda, in certain myths, have the "eternal" heroes of the "dream time," also functioning as genuine forebears — creators of people and animals. Thus in a myth of the bandicoot totem there is the tale of an ancestor named Karora, from whose armpits there first emerged bandicoots and, in the days that followed, his sons, human beings who began to hunt the bandicoots. (Identically, giants were born from Ymir's armpits in Scandinavian mythology.) This anthropogenetic and, at the same time, totemic myth is interwoven with a cosmogonic myth: in the beginning of time was darkness, and the unending night pressed down on the earth like an impenetrable curtain; then the sun appeared and dissipated the darkness over Ilbalintja (the totemic center of the bandicoots, see Strehlow, 1947, chapter I).

Analogous tales about the wanderings of totemic ancestors and culture heroes exist among other Australian tribes as well, but they have been recorded less fully. Moreover, the influence of totemism does not appear anywhere with such force as among the Aranda and Loritja. Among the Dieri and other tribes living to the southeast of the Aranda, around Lake Eyre, there are numerous tales known from Howitt's classic works (4) about the wanderings of certain Mura-mura — mythical heroes analogous to the "eternal" people of the Aranda but having weaker zoomorphic features. Various landscape features, the introduction of exogamy and totemic names, the use of the stone ax for circumcision and for producing fire by friction, as well as the "finishing" of imperfect human beings, are also associated with the wanderings of the Mura-mura. One of the Mura-mura, who ascended to heaven, became the moon. As for the sun, it is a woman who had dug a pit and set off into the sky to find her lost child; ever since then she periodically travels the same

Primitive Sources of Verbal Art

route. According to another tradition, the sun was born of an affair between a Mura-mura and a Dieri girl, and so forth.

The ancestor myths do not always tell of their wanderings. Some ancestors (among the Aranda, for instance) do not make prolonged journeys. A good collection of the myths of a northeastern tribe (the Munkan), associated only in part with wanderings, was collected by Ursula Macconel (Macconel, 1957). This collection contains many myths about the establishment of totemic centers after the totemic ancestors' (pulwaiya) "departure under the ground." Departing under the ground is often preceded by arguments and fights among the pulwaiya, in which they injure or kill each other. Although the ancestors are depicted as purely anthropomorphic beings, the descriptions of their behavior reflect observations on the way of life and the habits of the corresponding animals; and certain features in the lives of the ancestors explain qualities of these animals. Many of the features of the physical aspect of animals are motivated by crippling injuries dealt them by pulwaiya in ancient times when the animals had human appearance: sharks have small eyes because of sand thrown at them by pulwaiya of the oyster; the screech-owl has a flat head because of a blow from a digging stick, and so on and so forth. The local breed of storks have red legs because a pulwaiya of the stork applied red clay to spears he was holding on his knees. Although the story is devoted not to storks but to their purely anthropomorphic ancestors (of the time when storks were still people), in the description of how an ancestor clambers onto a "sleeping platform" or in the pose of the ancestor sitting in a tree, observations of the habits of these birds are vividly manifested. In identical fashion the myth of the opossum's anthropomorphic ancestors accurately relfects the sleepiness and love of honey characteristic of this animal. There are many similar examples. Relationships of friendship and hostility of pulwaiya correspond exactly to the mutual relations among various animals and plants. Some pulwaiya engage in cultural acts: for example, the ancestor of one of the predacious birds that feed on fish invented the fishing net and spear.

* * *

Semiotics and Structuralism

The myths of the northern and southeastern tribes have not only totemic ancestors but more complex, more generalized, and apparently, later developed images of "supratotemic" mythical heroes. In the north there is the "old woman-mother" (Kunapipi, Kliarin-kliari, Kadjari, etc.), a matriarchal forebear symbolizing the fertile, fecund earth, and associated with her (and with fertility and multiplication), the image of the rainbow snake. (5) In the southeast there is, on the other hand, the patriarchal image of the universal "father." He is Nurrundere, Koin, Birral, Nurelli, Bunjil, Baiame, Daramulun. The uninitiated call him simply "father" (for example, papang). He lives in the sky and acts as culture hero and patron of initiation rituals (see Howitt, 1904; Mathews, 1905). The mother also has a relationship to initiation and performs in culture acts. Mother and father do not necessarily belong to some single totem, but often to many at once (for example, each part of their bodies may have its own totem), and are consequently a common ancestor, i.e., in the aborigines' understanding, the carrier and primal source of the souls of various groups of people, animals, and plants.

In myths (as distinct from ritual, which will be discussed below) there is usually not one mother but several, sometimes two sisters or a mother and daughter. These tales (and ritual) are associated with one of the moieties (phratries) of the tribe (specifically of the Dua), which permits the hypothesis about partial genesis of these mothers from concepts of phratrial ancestral mothers.

Among the Yulengor, who live in Arnhem Land (According to Chaseling), the mythical ancestors who came from the north were the Junkgowa, sister-women. They floated on a sea they themselves had created. In their boat they brought various totems which had to be hung on trees to dry out. Then the totems were hidden in work bags and gradually distributed in various places during their wanderings. The Junkgowa gave birth to ten children who originally were sexless. Later, however, those hidden in the grass became men and those hidden in the sand — women. For their descendents they made yamsticks, feather

Primitive Sources of Verbal Art

belts, and other ornaments, introduced the use of fire, created the sun, taught the children to use particular types of food, gave them weapons and magical devices, taught them totemic dances, and introduced the initiation rite for youths.

According to this myth, initially the keepers of ritual secrets were women, but men took away their totems and secrets, and the ancestresses were driven away by singing. They continued on their way, forming topographical features, new food territories, and kin groups of human beings. When they again reached the sea in the west, they set off toward islands that had previously arisen from the lice they threw from their bodies.

Long after the disappearance of the Junkgowa in the west, another two sisters, the Wauwilak, appeared, were born in the shadow behind the setting sun. They completed the work of their two predecessors, founded marital classes, and introduced the famous rite of the great mother — Gunapipi (Kunapipi) — in which their deeds are partly dramatized. The sisters settled in a certain place, built a hut, and began to gather food. One of them was pregnant and gave birth to a child. The sisters tried to cook yams, snails, and other food, but the plants and animals came alive again and jumped out of the fire, and it began to rain. The sisters tried by dances to drive away the rain and the terrible rainbow serpent that approached them and gulped down first the totemic animals and plants (the sisters' food) and then both women and the child. Finding themselves in the belly of the serpent they tormented him, and he spit them out, while the child was brought back to life by ant bites. This myth is widespread among the tribes of the northeast.

The Wauwilak sisters (as they are called by the Yulengors and certain other tribes) are also associated with the Dua phratry. They are a special variant of the ancestral mothers who embody fertility. The myth also contains the terrible rainbow serpent — an image widely known over the greater part of Australia, as Radcliffe-Brown has shown. This special mythological image combines the concept of the spirit of water, the snake-monster (embryo of the dragon concept), and the magic crystal (in which the spectrum of the rainbow is reflected) used by sor-

Semiotics and Structuralism

cerers. The swallowing and spitting out of people by the snake is unquestionably associated (as among other peoples) with the initiation ritual (the symbolism of temporary death and renewal). The snake changing its skin naturally becomes the symbol of renewal. R. M. Berndt also sees in the snake's swallowing of the Wauwilak sisters erotic symbolism connected with fertility magic. It is curious that in one of the myths of the Murinbata tribe (and the corresponding rite), the old woman Mutjiŋga herself swallows children entrusted to her by parents who have gone off to look for food. She calms the children, looks for lice in their hair, but then swallows them, one after the other. After the old woman's death the children are freed alive from her womb. Among the Mara tribal group there is a story of a mythical mother who murdered and ate the men attracted by her daughters' beauty. In this demonic form we do not recognize the mighty ancestral mother. Rather, it resembles the legendary witch, something like Baba Yaga. However, not only among the Australians but among other peoples (for example, the Kwakiutl Indians, according to Franz Boas's materials), the myth of an evil, cannibalistic old woman is associated with the idea of initiation of youths as full members of the tribe (as among the Australians) or a men's society (among the Indians). In some myths the rainbow serpent accompanies the "great mother" in her wanderings.

The Yirrkalla tribal group has a myth about Djanggawul who wanders with his sisters, with whom he is in an incestuous relationship. Among the Murinbata a rainbow serpent named Kunmaŋgur himself appears as the ancestor, the father of the father of one half of the tribe and the father of the mother of the other. He is believed "to have made us all" and still "looks after the people" (Stanner, 1966). Kunmaŋgur's son violates his sisters and then inflicts a mortal would on his father. Kunmaŋgur wanders in search of a place where he can be cured. In desperation he collects all the fire belonging to people and extinguishes it by casting it into the sea. Another mythical personage again obtains the fire (the idea of rebirth).

The myths of the rainbow serpent and, particularly, of the

Primitive Sources of Verbal Art

ancestor mothers are closely connected to the complex ritual mystery held before the beginning of the rainy season in honor of the earth-mother Kunapipi, embodying fertility.

Let us now turn to the image of the tribal "great father" among the southeastern tribes, which was well investigated as early as by Howitt. Tokarev quite correctly traces its origin from a number of more primitive images: the personification of the sky of the Altjira type among the Aranda, the phratry totem, the culture hero, the patron of initiations and frightful spirit, who transforms boys into adult men (only the initiated believe in him). (6) These personages contain only the embryo of the properly religious concept of god the creator. Virtually all of them figure as great ancestors and teachers of people, who lived on earth and were later transported to heaven.

This transportation to heaven of earthly mythological heroes also corresponds, in the mythology of other peoples as well, to the process of deifying folkloric personages.

Bunjil, in the Kulin tribe, was pictured as an old tribal leader married to two representatives of the black swan totem. His very name means "eagle" or "hawk" and simultaneously serves as the name of one of the two phratries (the other, Waang, i.e., crow). Bunjil is pictured as the creator of the earth, trees, and people. He warmed the sun with his hands, the sun warmed the earth, people emerged from the earth and began to dance the corrobboree.

Thus in Bunjil the features of the phratry ancestor, a demiurge and culture hero, predominate.

Daramulun, among the tribes of the southeastern coast (the Yuin and others), was regarded as the supreme being, while among the Kamilaroi, Wiradjuri, and Euahlayi he occupied a position subordinate to Baiame. According to certain myths, Daramulun and his mother (the emu) planted trees, gave laws to people, and taught them the rites of initiation. During these rites Daramulun is drawn on the ground or on bark, the sound of a whistle represents his voice, and he is perceived as the spirit transforming boys into men.

In the Kamilaroi language the name of Baiame is associated with the verb "to make" (Howitt, 1904, p. 494), which would seem to correspond to the idea of a demiurge and cultural hero. Mathews associates the etymology of this name with the idea of human and animal semen (Mathews, 1905, p. 138), while Langloh-Parker asserts that in the language of the Euahlayi this word is understood only in the sense of "great" (Langloh-Parker, 1905, pp. 6-7). Euahlayi speak of the time of Baiame as the Aranda do of the "dream time." In ancient times, when only animals and birds were on earth, Baiame came from the northeast with his two wives and created human beings in part of wood and clay, while part of them was transformed from animals; and he gave them laws and customs (the ultimate motivation for everything: "Thus spake Baiame"). Mathews presents a myth of the Wiradjuri and the Wongabon to the effect that Baiame went out wandering in search of wild honey after a bee to whose leg he had tied a bird feather. (Let us recall the most important cultural achievement of Odin of ancient Scandinavia — the obtaining of the sacred honey!) Baiame's place of residence in ancient times was held to be in a region of exposed granite 460 kilometers from Sydney. Among a long list of tribes Baiame is the focal point of all rites of initiation (the so-called bora), the chief teacher of novices passing through the rigorous initiation trials.

Thus far we have been speaking of myths. It is clear from our presentation up to this point that the myths of the Australian aborigines are intimately associated with rituals. This connection is quite clear; various myths are reproduced in theatrical form, are dramatized during the initiations of youths as a means of familiarizing them with the "sacred history" of the tribe and as a transmittal of tribal wisdom. On the other hand, some myths and rites have the same heroes: myths serve in considerable measure as explanations of the ritual mysteries, while rites commonly use the language of myth. This direct connection exists between totemic myths and the rituals of the Intichiuma; between myths of the heavenly phratrial ancestor-culture hero (Baiame) and the ritual ordeals of the bora; between myths of ancestral mothers and the cult of Kunapipi, etc. However, this does not justify the conclusion that the role of myth among

Primitive Sources of Verbal Art

the aborigines amounts to commentary on ritual and that a myth is merely ritual translated into narrative form. There is no more intimate interweaving of myth and ritual than in the theme of Kunapipi and the rainbow serpent. However, there are stories of the rainbow serpent that have no ritual equivalent: the myth of the Wauwilak sisters is closely linked to ritual, not to just one, but to three different ritual ceremonies (Berndt, 1951, p. 35). This myth does not coincide with any one of them. According to Stanner, among the Murinbata there is not only the myth of Mutjiŋga, which has a ritual equivalent in the form of the punj ritual, but there have also been recorded myths having no ritual equivalent about Kunmaŋgur and Kukpi (the father of one and the mother of the other half of the tribe), as well as circumcision and funerary rites having no mythological equivalent (Stanner, 1966, chapters IV and V).

It is another matter that, as Stanner has quite persuasively demonstrated, the rituals and myths of the Murinbata are isomorphic and have identical structures of the mystery type. In both cases the equilibrium of life is violated, voluntarily or not (by death, by the onset of sexual maturity in boys, by the departure of parents, little children, or daughters of Kunmaŋgur in quest of food, by the dissatisfaction of Kukpi seeking a place for herself, and so forth). The lack of food in the myth of Mutjiŋga corresponds to the lack of wisdom (food of the spirit) among youths in the corresponding ritual (punj). The violated equilibrium is gradually restored, moreover at a higher level, as the result of a spiral motion. This spiral motion includes the same stages: the individual in question is taken out of the normal and everyday (boys are taken into the woods or are abandoned to the tutelage of Mutjiŋga, a dead body is carried out of the village, the children of Kunmaŋgur leave their home, Kukpi abandons familiar places, and so forth). Thus the personage of the myth-ritual is isolated, as it were, and then partially destroyed (the sacrifice of boys' foreskin, the destruction of the decaying body of a corpse, the dealing of ritual blows to initiates, their being swallowed by an old woman, the murder of men due to Kukpi's perfidy, the violation of his sisters by Kunmaŋgur's son and his attempt to kill his father, and the destruction of the emblems of the old social status).

Next follows transformation — the salvation of the person and his return to the normal round of existence at a higher level (children are saved or return to their homes as individuals who have been initiated and attained a new social status; the wise old man guesses the identity of and neutralizes Kukpi, obtaining the whistle; the dead man's spirit is liberated from the body and becomes an object of reverence, and so forth). The ultimate emergence from the conflict situation is also dual; ascent to a higher level is attained at the price of losses, and life is renewed by means of death, sacrifice, or suffering: fire is saved thanks to the death of Kunmaŋgur (the father), while the lives of children and their initiation are purchased not only at the price of tormenting trials but also by the death of Mutjiŋga (the mother).

Stanner's interesting analysis does not, of course, justify the conclusion that myth is genetically dependent on ritual. Much here is explained by the ideological syncretism characteristic of primitive culture, which we have previously pointed out. Moreover, the material presented by Stanner can also be used to identify particular differences between myth and ritual which he did not discuss and which exist even if myth and ritual are directly interconnected (as in the punj). It goes without saying that in the present cyclically repeated ritual acts correspond to a single mythical event that occurred in the remote (prehistoric) past. Both the time of the ritual and the time of the myth exist outside the normal, commonplace system of reckoning and conceiving time; but the ritual is oriented toward a special break in the flow of time, and myth to a period prior to the beginning of this flow of time and its reckoning. The randomness and, sometimes, the unintendedness of the mythical event stand opposed to the rigorous obligatoriness and intentionality and organization of ritual on the part of the tribal authorities. The parents who left their children to Mutjiŋga did so out of hunger and, as it were, were unaware of the danger. In the corresponding ritual children were consciously and forcibly taken into the forest in the power

Primitive Sources of Verbal Art

of the old woman. In Australian myths the initial situation is often associated with the search for food, while the need to make youths party to the tribal wisdom, i.e., to sate them with food for the spirit, is the premise for initiation rites. The difference between myth and the punj ritual may be additionally determined, in its genesis, by a break between the esoteric and exoteric versions: the patron of the initiation appears to the uninitiated as a demonic being who steals children. Curiously, the obvious evil coming from Mutjiŋga and similar figures (Kukpi and others) corresponds to secret good in the ritual. (7) The false friend in the myth proves to be the false enemy in the ritual. The false friend — Mutjiŋga — calms children in order to make them easy prey, but the leaders of the ritual frighten youths with the sound of the whistle. The myth of Mutjiŋga ends with vengeance on the old woman, while the ritual ends with the acquisition of wisdom by youths.

Further analysis of the differences between Australian myths and rituals might lead to a more rigorous identification of the differential features by which myths and rituals contrast to each other. To the foregoing it must be added that even when particular myths and rituals resemble each other and are associated to the maximum, performance of the myth is not necessarily a part of the ritual; it may not accompany the ritual at all or do so only in part, because what is sanctified in the myth is not the ritual act as such, with which it is linked, but the verbally expressed content, particular information, names, and the like. The myth, as it were, sanctions and reinforces the ritual and clarifies its meaning; but in performance a myth is relatively freer than the dance, music, or even songs, which often directly constitute the sacred action. This largely determines the distinctiveness of myth. But the specific characteristic of myth as the embryo of narrative art is determined, of course, not just by the degree of freedom from ritual at the moment of performance. Among the Australians, even beyond the bounds of ritual an intimate thematic link ties various forms of art and genres of poetry. The same hero of "the dream time" is told about, sung about, danced about, and painted in ochre on sand

Semiotics and Structuralism

and rocks; but it is not at all required that these be done at the same time, nor within the framework of a single ritual act. The essence of the various arts and genres of poetry is clearly revealed, for example, upon comparative analysis of the myths, songs, and dances of the Aranda recorded by C. Strehlow and by Spencer and Gillen, or in the case of the myths, songs, and dances of the Kunapipi cycle recorded by Berndt.

In principle, dance, song, and myths all depict the wanderings of heroes of "the dream time." However, the essence of the myth of totemic ancestors among the Aranda lies, above all, in the information about places they visited in the course of their wanderings and in explanations of landscape features. The essence of songs (which are fundamentally devoted to the same wanderings) is their unique "lauding" of mythical heroes. In the songs the entire "geography" of the wanderings is greatly compressed or even dropped. In the songs about the wanderings of the great mother, only a single old woman figures, not several (as in the myths); and her arrival, accompanied by the rainbow snake, the manner in which she makes food grow by touching with a magic yamstick, and how she scatters the souls of people and animals, etc., are narrated in highly generalized form. Primarily emphasized is her might (Harney and Elkin, 1949, pp. 29-32). It goes without saying that all details of plot, which we encounter in individual variants of the myths, are lacking in the songs. The songs are quite different from prose myths in form as well. Strehlow describes in detail the performance of songs among the Aranda and cites many examples (Strehlow, 1910).

Songs are performed in chorus by old men, in the form of melodious nasal chanting. One of two unstressed syllables is followed by a stressed one, regardless of the stresses used in ordinary speech. All the words in a stanza are pronounced as a single word. The songs contain many words that are of an archaic nature or that have been borrowed from the language of neighboring tribes and are therefore little understood.

In the songs the semantic-syntactic parallelism of two lines, in which the second repeats and explains the first, appears with extraordinary clarity. As is known, such parallelism is widely

Primitive Sources of Verbal Art

encountered in songs of various peoples throughout the world, particularly in epic songs, for example, in Karelo-Finnish runes. The songs of the Australian aborigines about the feats of their mythical ancestors have a sharply expressed lyrical-epic character. They have a powerful emotional effect on both audience and performers. Sometimes the old men themselves cry in ecstasy (as the great singer Väinämöinen cried in the Kalevala). It is understood that the song has magical singificance and should help achieve the object of the ritual. Such rigorous poetic organization of a song depends in considerable measure on its simultaneity and coordination with dance. The dance also has its specific characteristics. Although the running or stamping of the dancers across sacred ground near the totemic center depicts the wandering of totemic ancestors over extensive territory in ancient times, a specific element — imitation of totemic animals, their external appearance and habits — predominates in the dance. With the same object in mind the actors paint their bodies with ochre, blood, and charcoal and build complex hairdos of their own hair, down, and twigs. The naturalism of direct imitation is combined with the carrying of ritual objects (_knatanya_, _kalgaranga_, _waninga_), symbolizing some part of the ancestor's body (heart, stomach, spine, and sometimes the ear of a kangaroo, the wing of a bat, a spiderweb, and falling drops of rain). The same purpose is served by the wearing of tjurungas decorated with spiral circles and parallel lines or chains of little circles joining these circles. This ornamentation is also interpreted as a depiction of parts of the body of the totemic animal or as the camp of the totemic ancestor and the path of his wanderings (the parts of the animal's body are also depicted in stylized form on the ground and on rocks).

Thus songs and dances actually do, for the most part, appear in syncretic unity, but this does not extend to prose exposition of myths. The myths are related in prose sometimes in part and sometimes in their entirety. The elders actually do narrate something during the ritual, not for magical purposes, however, but to explain what is being depicted, in the form of a special commentary. Parts of myths are also presented upon visits to secret caves, forbidden to the uninitiated, where the tjurungas are kept (see Strehlow, 1947), or during the initiation trials through which youths are put to transmit the tribal wisdom to them, but with no direct connection with the initiation ritual as such. The myths are related in ordinary language lacking rigorously prescribed stylistic structure. Thus in manner of performance myths are considerably freer than songs and less ritualized. But their principal content, particularly the description of the mythical trails of the heroes of "the dream time," is sacred and has to be kept secret from the uninitiated, i.e., women and children. It is precisely the sacred, hidden knowledge, not the rituality, that is the important feature of the aborigine myths. Comparison of different variants of the same myths in the publications of C. Strehlow, and also of Spencer and Gillen, reveals a certain freedom of invention in the realm of plot details compared with the songs, since most of the songs are constrained by ritualized performance. But the sacred content prevents further development of plot invention. From this standpoint the recording of myths from the mouths of the uninitiated — old women, for example — is of great interest. The content of the myths reaches the uninitated one way or another. The particularly sacred portion of the myths — information about the mythical trails and the routes followed by the heroes in their wanderings — is an exception. At the same time, the myths told by the uninitiated, not to transmit wisdom but rather for amusement, are enriched by freer plot invention. This is one of the ways legendary epics take shape.

However, a myth, even when it has partially lost its sacred significance, continues for a long time to preserve other distinguishing features of the myth — such as depiction of the world in the form of a story about the origin of its elements. We find good examples of this in the collection, referred to above, of Munkan myths recorded by Ursula Macconel, in considerable measure from women. We have already observed that the collection contains few statements on the wandering of totemic heroes; and even in places where the fact of wandering exists, the route does not appear, inasmuch as it is the object of secret knowledge of the initiated.

Primitive Sources of Verbal Art

Macconel's collection contains many stories about how the totemic centers came into being and about the origin of various characteristic features of animals (examples have been presented above), i.e., of genuine etiological myths. A typical feature of these stories is that the fantasy of the storytellers is concentrated on depiction of the family life of totemic ancestors, and in this field the narrators or, to be more precise, narratrices, display no less power of observation than in their sketching of the habits of animals. Totemic animals appear in family groups (which is absolutely not the case in the sacred myths of the Aranda recorded by C. Strehlow). Even parts of one and the same plant — the water lily (stalk, rootstock, rootlets) — turn out to be husband, wife, and children. The wife of the totemic ancestor of the yam refused to bring him water, which led to an argument. In the same manner, the ancestor of the oyster totem quarreled with his wife — the ancestor of the turtle totem — because the wife refused to dig a source of pure water in the sand. Or again, two sisters, the pulwaiya of the sea and land turtles, quarreled over refusal to fulfill a request.

Complex relationships and fateful quarrels arise among the families of totems of various fish, ants, and owls as a consequence of wives' infidelity. Wives' unfaithfulness and the pursuit of the seducer occur among the ancestors of bird totems, and so on and so forth. All this familial thematics gradually undermines the myth, for the principal interest of a myth lies not in the fates of individuals (which is more typical of fairy tales), but in the origin of the world, man, animals, customs, and so forth.

Here a certain contradiction arises that may be resolved, in the long run, by the fact that plots that have recently come into being about family relationships and conflicts in social mores shall become detached from the images of the mythical ancestors and the "dream time" and shall become the genuine fairy tale (animal, if the totemic appellations are retained, or magical).

However, because it is so archaic, the aborigine folklore shows almost no instances in which this process is completed.

Semiotics and Structuralism

Only the corresponding tendencies are known to it. Here the qualification must immediately be made that the secularization of myth is not the sole source of the formation of the fairy tale. The other ancestor of the fairy tale is the primitive true story [bylichka], i.e., stories of encounters in the recent past between human beings and various spirits, "masters," who brought them evil or good. Such stories may rest, in the final analysis, on actual events (fact), interpreted in the light of the dominant mythological conceptions. In this class of tales it is also necessary to put the stories with which mothers "frighten" children — about evil cannibal spirits, including the spirits who (in the minds of the uninitiated) kidnap boys who have reached puberty to transform them into grown men — full members of the tribe.

In Australian folklore the aborigines themselves distinguish between myths and tales. Tales lack sacred significance, are available to the uninitiated, and may be told for amusement and also to frighten, so as to keep the uninitiated obedient. In this last case tales play the role of myths for the uninitiated. This is a peculiarly Australian trait. However, very few such stories have been recorded (apparently they are considerably fewer in number than myths), and this, naturally, makes their analysis difficult. C. Strehlow cites a few tales in his great work. Tales are carefully distinguished in the recordings of Arnhem Land folklore by Capell (1960, pp. 31-62).

In C. Strehlow's compilations a number of fairy tales are devoted to wondrous beings (tneers and indatoa), which are referred to in myths but are not subjects of particular reverence. The fairy tales tell of the battle between these beings and evil spirits. One of the fairy tales deals with little beings, twanyirrika, that torture little boys during initiation (initiates do not believe in these beings). Capell cites a number of interesting fairy tales that do, in fact, fall into the category of mythologized true stories. The principal characters are not mythical beings but ordinary people who, in the course of hunting turtles (if it is about men) or gathering snails (if about women), have various adventures: they meet evil spirits, fall victim to old women

Primitive Sources of Verbal Art

cannibals, die because of breaking a taboo, and so forth.

3. Cultural Heroes and Mythological Tricksters — the Central Figures of Primitive Narrative Folklore

Within the framework of the present study we are not able to pause to survey the folklore of various culturally backward peoples. (8) We shall deal only with a few of the most general questions, and above all the principal figures.

The most important phenomenon of narrative folklore in primitive communal society is stories about first ancestors, demiurges, culture heroes, which are genetically associated with etiological myths (and more broadly with myths of creation) about the origin of various elements of nature and culture, but which later, in the process of cyclization, include also plots of a fairy-tale nature (animal, magical, protoheroic). Despite the inclusion in these stories of elements that are nonhomogeneous with respect to genre, they can justly be called mythological epics, since a mythical personage stands at the center of their cyclization. It must be emphasized that in primitive society only a mythical personage could be a hero, since he alone possessed, in the eyes of members of the primitive community, the required freedom of independent action. At the same time, a hero could be only a personage who modeled not the forces of nature (as, say, various master spirits), but the clan-tribal group itself.

This is the case with the founder of a tribe (conceived also as the ancestor of all mankind, inasmuch as in primitive communal society tribal boundaries subjectively correspond to those of humanity as a whole) and a culture hero.

The conceptions of first ancestors, culture heroes, and demiurges are intimately interwoven, and sometimes identical, in primitive folklore. It would seem that the images of first ancestors are the first to acquire sharp outlines, as the Australian material seems to show.

In more archaic cultures culture heroes are almost always first ancestors, phratrial and clans ancestors (this is true of

Semiotics and Structuralism

the Australian aborigines, Papuans, the Melanesian Gunantuna, the northeastern Paleo-Asiatics, and Paleo-African primitive tribes of Central and South Africa). Among the less archaic (some of the Indians of North America, Polynesia) the features of the first ancestor in the image of the culture hero are merely relics.

Everywhere in the islands of Oceania there are cycles of stories of culture heroes who are often thought of as ancestors (but not as gods). In various parts of Melanesia they are called Qat, Tangaro, Warohunuga, or To Kabinana.

In Polynesia the brothers Tangaroa and Rongo are endowed with features of culture heroes; but, unlike the Melanesian Tangaro, Tangaroa has been converted into one of the great gods of the Polynesian pantheon.

However, in Polynesia, in addition to Tangaroa there is the well-known, nondeified Maui, who is a favorite personage of Polynesian narrative folklore. Maui is a prematurely born foundling discarded in bushes or the sea.

Of Maui's numerous feats the most famous are dredging up fish-islands from the bottom of the sea, the snaring of the sun and the theft of fire, which was vigilantly guarded in the underground world by the old woman-ancestress. Maui even tried to overcome death but was defeated himself. Among the Indians of North America, the features of culture heroes are distinctly present in such popular characters as Raven, Mink, Hare or Rabbit (Manabozho), Coyote, Old Man, and others (names apparently of totemic origin). Raven, for example, procures light, fresh water, the tides, creates certain species of fish, and also participates in the creation of men. To perform his culture feats Raven often resorts to magical transformations and shrewd tricks. Thus he transforms himself into a pine needle swallowed by the daughter of the master of the heavenly bodies. From this needle she bears Raven. The newborn screams heartrendingly until he is given as toys the sun, the moon, and the stars. Lulling the guardian of fresh water to sleep, Raven then falsely accuses him of having soiled his bed and, in the form of compensation, drinks water from the stone vessel and then

Primitive Sources of Verbal Art

spits it out as rivers and lakes. The Raven cycle contains innumerable etiological motifs. It also contains anecdotal stories about how gluttonous Raven deprives other animals of their catch or even turns them into a catch. Similar anecdotes can be found in the stories of Mink, Coyote, and others (on this, see below).

Raven is also the central figure in the folklore of the northeastern Paleo-Asiatics (Chukchi, Koryaks, and Itel'mens). Ekva-Pyrishch, the hero of the folklore of the Ob River Ugrians, has much in common with Raven.

Features of culture heroes, albeit not as vividly expressed, are sometimes present in relict form in the beloved heroes of African folklore. Some of them are zoomorphic (Hare, Spider, Jackal, Mantis, Chameleon, Turtle) or semizoomorphic (Pu, Uhlakanyana). In African folklore the features of culture heroes and miraculous blacksmiths are sometimes combined.

Sometimes a culture hero is one of many brothers (as in the cases, for example, of Qat, Tangaro, and Maui in Oceania); very often culture heroes are twin brothers, competing with or hostile to each other (Ioskeha and Tawiscara among the Iroquois, To Kabinana and To Karvuvu among the Gunantuna of Melanesia, and many others); less often they help each other ("the little boy from the wigwam" and the "little boy from the bushes" who defeat monsters, among the Indians in the southern parts of North America). Such twins are often simultaneously the phratrial ancestors. "Twinship" itself is a further proof of the initial identity of first ancestors with culture heroes. According to the well-argued interpretation of A. M. Zolotarev and S. P. Tolstov, culture hero-twins, like other pairs of twins in mythology (the Ashvins and Dioskuri, Romulus and Remus, etc.), originate in the final analysis in the dual-clan organization that existed everywhere at a given stage of primitive society (see Zolotarev, 1939, 1964; Tolstov, 1948).

The unique realm of activity of the culture hero is the obtaining of fire and domesticated grains, and invention of various objects of culture needed by man in his struggle with nature. By virtue of the undifferentiated character of nature and culture

Semiotics and Structuralism

in the primitive world-view (for example, concepts of the acquisition of fire by friction, the origin of thunder-lightning, of sunlight, and the like tend to be equated), there is no sharp boundary between the culture hero and the demiurge.

In more ancient versions, reflecting the properties of a gathering economy, the hero acquires the benefits of culture and sometimes the natural elements by simply finding them or <u>stealing</u> them from the original guardian (see above, examples of myths on the procuring of fire by various totemic beings among the Australian aborigines, and also its having been stolen by Maui, Raven, Prometheus, and the like). Later, the idea arises of the <u>manufacture</u> of all these things by the demiurge with the help of potter's or smith's tools. At the dawn of the age of metal, for example, among the Paleo-African peoples, the culture hero often appeared in the form of a miracle-working smith.

These myths are to a certain degree a chronicle of the triumphs of human labor and technical inventiveness over nature; but this chronicle (partly by virtue of the slow pace of technological progress) is projected back into mythical times of creation, such as the "dream time" of the aborigines.

The example of the culture hero — the central figure of primitive mythology and folklore — is specifically associated with primitive ideological syncretism. This image can also evolve into a god-creator (in which case the primitive myth is transformed into an exclusively religious myth-legend). But in the majority of cases it does not become a genuine object of religious worship but is transformed into a beloved legendary-epic hero. Culture heroes are for the most part classified by the aborigines themselves not as gods; they usually fall into the same category as spirits and outstanding people of the past, to a certain degree in order to differentiate them from gods and at the same time to emphasize their magical power (<u>mana</u>) and significance. A vivid example of the difference between undeified and deified culture heroes is the Polynesian god Tangaroa and the Melanesian hero Tangaro. From this standpoint it merits attention that, unlike Tangaro, Tangaroa does not occupy a significant place in folklore, while throughout Polynesia the favorite folk-

Primitive Sources of Verbal Art

lore hero is Maui, who all the same did not enter the supreme pantheon of Polynesian gods. Let us remember that the renowned Prometheus was not admitted to Olympus and remained outside the Olympian pantheon.

The special realm of activity of first ancestors, culture heroes, and demiurges coincides with the boundaries of the myths of creation, i.e., myths that are etiological in the broad sense of the term.

Also on the borderline of strictly etiological myths are such deeds, often associated with culture heroes, as battles with monsters which disturb the peaceful life of human beings and gods. The battle against monsters may be one of the aspects of overcoming the powers of chaos and the organization or ordering of the structure of the world, i.e., part of the process of creating the contemporary world. Sometimes the world is created from the body of the defeated chthonic monster itself. In such a case the ritual of sacrifice becomes a model of creation. Moreover, the struggle against monsters is sometimes associated with the mythical concept of the historical succession of generations of gods or spirits. Such myths of creation are not characteristic of primitive mythology as such but are typical of developed mythologies of the Babylonian type (the myth of the combat between Enlil or Marduk with Tiamat), the Indian (the creation of the world from the body of Purusha), the Chinese (P'an-Ku), the Scandinavian (the world from the body of Ymir, Thor's battle with the world snake), the Mayan (the world from the body of the earth goddess), and so forth. However, a more primitive struggle with monsters, unrelated to the concept of generations and not always having clear-cut etiological results, is encountered quite frequently in primitive folklore, particularly in tales about culture heroes (the Indian twin brothers from the "wigwam" and the "bush," Maui in some areas of Polynesia, Raven among the Koryaks, and many others).

In the plastically precise ancient Greek mythology, this new aspect of the cultural hero is well represented in Hercules (unlike Prometheus).

In myths about struggle against monsters, the idea of over-

Semiotics and Structuralism

coming chaos gains a new direction — not merely the ordering of sunlight, the tides, the seasons of the year, the relationships among the various animals, the prohibition of incest and other taboos, the introduction of marital classes and rituals needed to sustain the normal natural and life cycle, but also the constant struggle with natural forces threatening to overthrow "order." This dual note in the overcoming of chaos is typical of mythology as a whole, and also explains much as well in the genesis of verbal art. In essence, nearly every work of art is aimed at overcoming life's chaos by artistic reorganization of reality.

Concepts of spontaneous forces of nature (by virtue of the identification of nature and culture, and also of one's own tribe as "real people" with mankind as a whole) often sharply converge and even coalesce with images of aliens. Thus the culture hero acquires, as it were, an epic mission and the features of a hero, while the tales themselves, going beyond the bounds of etiological myths, become a kind of heroic story.

Stories of culture heroes are marked by archaic forms of idealization, in which the heroic features are not so much physical force and boldness as intelligence and shrewdness, and powers of magic and sorcery.

In the folklore of many peoples, as has already been observed, one often finds a paired image in the form of twin brothers. Such twin brothers sometimes represent the heroic pair of fighters against monsters. But more often, only one of the brothers retains his lofty essence, while the other is endowed with demonic and simultaneously (paradoxical as this may seem) comic features. If both brothers take part in the creation myths, one of them commits serious and useful deeds, and the other either consciously creates harmful and useless objects and phenomena or does so unwittingly, as the result of unsuccessful imitation (for example, To Kabinana and To Karvuvu in Melanesia: compare Prometheus and Epimetheus in ancient Greek mythology). In episodes not associated with creation, the brother or brothers of the culture hero often appear as pitiful, malicious rivals (for example, Maui's brothers).

When the hero has no brother, mischievous tricks are often

Primitive Sources of Verbal Art

ascribed to him in addition to serious culture deeds. These tricks are sometimes parodic reinterpretations of his serious acts (among the Indians of the western portion of North America and others).

Sometimes the mythological rogue does not coincide with the serious culture hero. The mischievous stunts of the mythological rogue (trickster in the terminology of American ethnographers studying Indian folklore) (9) serve to satisfy his greed or lust. Greed dominates among some tricksters, lust among others. Thus, for example, in the folklore of the Indians of the northwest Pacific coast, Raven is specifically a gluttonous trickster, while Mink is carnal. Identically, in the folklore of Dahomey, Legba is marked by hypereroticism, and Io by gluttony. Seeking to satisfy his insatiable desires (or simple hunger), the trickster turns to deception, violates the most rigorous norms of customary law and the community morality. Tricksters engage in incest with daughters or sisters, shrewdly use cordial hospitality, deprive their nearest kinfolk and members of their own families of food, gobble up communal reserves for winter, and so forth. In other cases their violations of taboos and all kinds of profaning of things sacred bear the character of something like complacent gluttony. Wakdjunkaga, trickster among the Winnebago Indians, has an affair with a woman during the sacred ceremony of preparation for a military campaign (a violation of a taboo of the highest importance), destroys the boat that he had earlier invited the participants in the campaign to board, and destroys ritual objects — all this while being the chief of the tribe. Here the explicit profanation of things sacred assumes the character of a parody of ritual preparation for the campaign. In another case he parodies the extremely important ritual of acquiring a protector spirit. Among the eastern Paleo-Asiatics Raven often performs tricks that are obvious parodies of the acts of shamans, not to speak of the fact that many of Raven's tricks are jesterlike imitations of his own serious creative acts.

Acting in a manner that is fundamentally antisocial and frankly profaning things sacred, the trickster nonetheless often triumphs and settles accounts mercilessly with those who submitted to his deception. Sometimes, however, the trickster himself suffers a fiasco. Raven, for example, experiences failure when he violates the communal standards of morality or perverts human nature itself; but from this it is not yet possible to derive rules binding on all tricksters.

It merits attention that the trickster combines in himself the characteristics of a triumphant knave (acting out of selfishness), an unbridled troublemaker, and a madman, and that he often continues, moreover, to be thought of as a culture hero, a benefactor of mankind. True, indigenous storytellers can differentiate between serious myths of creation relating the deeds of culture heroes and anecdotes for amusement (which merge with animal stories when the trickster is partially zoomorphic). But the fact that the culture hero and trickster are identified therein is beyond doubt. The question arises: How did this combination of culture hero and trickster, of myths of creation and anecdotes with knavish tricks, of shamanic legends and rituals with their humorous profanation, sometimes reaching satiric jest, become possible?

A purely formal factor is of a certain significance: With the cyclization of primitive narrative folklore around a culture hero, various plots and genre formations were combined, and everything was ascribed to the first and only folkloric hero. Different properties were, so to speak, compelled to cohabit within a single image, creating its contradictoriness and whimsy. But this formal consideration is not enough. Here there must be deeper reasons. (10)

The figure of the trickster — that remote ancestor of medieval jesters, the heroes of picaresque novels, the colorful comic characters in the literature of the Renaissance, and so forth — is extremely archaic. However, in the most archaic mythologies (the Australian aborigines, the Papuans) there is no such figure. The primitive syncretism of the culture hero and the trickster can be recognized only in a certain sense, can be accepted only with substantial qualifications.

The most ancient mythical heroes (totemic ancestors, culture

Primitive Sources of Verbal Art

heroes, demiurges) often act by shrewdness and guile only because the mind is, in the primitive consciousness, not separated from shrewdness and sorcery, and moral criteria themselves are highly archaic and unique. Even in the Homeric epic or the Edda, the gods are a great deal less fastidious in their means than the epic heroes. Of course, we are speaking of lack of fastidiousness from the standpoint of later moral valuations. The most ancient mythical heroes participate in the creation of the world, and virtually every step they take has etiological consequences. Not only their purposeful activity but even their random deeds make a contribution to the ordering, the organization of the structure of the world. Their very behavior often lacks conscious purpose, in the Promethean enthusiasm for serving mankind. At times striving to satisfy their own needs they acquire fire, light, and so forth.

However, such primitive heroes of myths are not yet tricksters. Only to the degree to which, in the very consciousness of the bearers of folklore, there arises the conception of the opposition between shrewdness and reason, deception and noble directness, lofty spirituality and base instincts, enthusiasm for conscious service to clan-tribe interests and egotistic asocialness, organization and chaos — only to the degree to which these distinctions are realized — does the figure of the mythological rogue as the double of the culture hero (his brother or "second face") develop. Many of the tricks performed by this figure (but by no means all) are genetically descended from the serious mythical deeds of culture heroes and demiurges, in certain rituals, shamanic miracles and tricks. But all of these deeds and actions are reinterpreted parodically or are even directly ridiculed.

Along with the parodic reinterpretation of the old mythic plots, a great number of new and often anecdotal plots arise or are attached to the image of the trickster. If the trickster preserves his semizoomorphic character, as for the most part happens, anecdotes about him approximate animal stories in type.

Awareness of the differences between serious mythical deeds and tricks, between myths and fairy tales, between culture heroes and tricksters, gives special sharpness to and emphasizes the duality of the mythical figure who is, at the same time, both the serious creator of the organized world order (natural and social) and a jester-rogue, constantly bringing chaos into the very organization he created, violating the taboo, deceiving or killing other beings to satisfy his own base instincts. This combination in a single individual of culture hero and trickster, of organizing and chaos-inducing elements, is possible only because the action, in the fabular-mythological cycles, is placed in the time before a rigorous world order had been established. This placing in mythical time legitimizes the trickster's mischief-making to a considerable degree. Apparently, trickster plots are a unique safety valve (legitimized because they are related to mythical times) in a strictly regulated society, such as clan-tribal society unquestionably is.

The overemphasis on base instincts, on all kinds of "dirty" details associated with greed, eroticism, and defecation, is opposed in particular to primitive spirituality, which acquired a considerably, albeit primitive, embodiment in shamanism. Ridicule of shamanic practice and of obligatory rituals sometimes goes very far and lacks any trace of good-natured kidding; it even contains elements of social criticism.

However, this does not mean that here are expressed a lack of belief in shamanism, an abandonment of the ritual life of the tribe, and the like. It is beyond question that the trickster anecdotes exist in the same milieu as serious myths, shamanic legends, and so forth.

Ridicule is quite universal in trickster stories: it is merciless to the victims deceived by the trickster and to the trickster himself when he is trapped. It is aimed at both shamanic spiritualism and the base lack of self-control of the trickster himself, as well as at his attempts to change the natural, to violate the primitive communal morality, i.e., at the manifestations of his antisocialness. This universal comedy is related to the carnival quality that also appeared in the elements of self-parody found in the rites of the aborigines, in Roman saturnalia, and in medieval "festivals of fools," with the overthrow of hierarchical order, the jester's re-creation of the church service,

Primitive Sources of Verbal Art

and so forth. M. M. Bakhtin regards this kind of "carnival quality" as a most important feature of folk culture, widely reflected in the literature of the Middle Ages and the Renaissance (Bakhtin, 1964).

The most ancient first ancestors, the culture heroes whom we are forced rightfully to consider the first literary characters, thus appear in archaic folklore as syncretic images, often (but of course not always) combining three aspects: the mythical creator, the comic trickster, and the archaic hero who cleanses the earth of monsters. These three aspects correspond to a well-known genre syncretism: myths of creation — animal tales and anecdotes about tricksters — protoheroic stories. This genre syncretism is externally expressed in the prevalence of unitary cycles of a kind of mythological epic.

Along with the gradual differentiation of narrative genres within the framework of this mythological epic about culture heroes and the like, the development of genre variations, even in the earliest stages, follows the same paths also outside these cycles (in the true stories cited above, local legends, etc.). A significant difference arises only when the impersonal figure of the primitive true story is displaced by the active and powerful character in the heroic fairy tale.

Thus far we have examined archaic narrative folklore and have chiefly taken the images of central heroes as point of departure. Now let us turn to our material from the point of view of the historical morphology of the genre. In view of the fact that the process of differentiation of genres is interwoven with a certain sequence of stages in the area of development of genre and style, it is impossible to separate study of the history of the oral literature of primitive society from the genesis of narrative genres that, in primitive folklore, are in a state of emergence, of development, and have not yet finally broken away from the primitive syncretism under the aegis of myth. Analysis of this dual process presents great difficulties.

4. From Myth to Tale

Myth was dominant in the only partially articulated generic

Semiotics and Structuralism

syncretism that was characteristic of the state of the narrative art in archaic societies. The point is not just that myths and tales were combined in single cycles centered on popular mythical heroes. Myths and tales only then began to be differentiated, and some sort of intermediate form was in fact dominant. Such experts as Franz Boas or Stith Thompson have repeatedly spoken of the difficulties of differentiating between myth and tale in primitive folklore (see, for example, Thompson, 1955, No. 270).

Primitives themselves, however, often distinguish between two forms, for example, the adaox and malesk among the Tsimshian, pynyl and lymnyl among the Chukchi, hvenoho and heho among the Fon (Dahomeyans), liliu and kukvanebu among the Kirivina in Melanesia, and so on and so forth. We can correlate these two forms with myths and tales only very tentatively. They differ fundamentally along the line of sacrality and nonsacrality, and strict reliability and loose reliability (i.e., the admissibility of some relative freedom of invention). Boas demonstrates that the first form, i.e., myth, is rigorously bound to placement of action in mythical times. Moreover, leaving aside local classifications, there can be no doubt that myths are typified by a basic etiologism of plot, while in fairy tales, even if etiological endings remain, they acquire a purely ornamental character. The opening formulas indicating mythical times: "It was when people were still animals," or the opposite, "When animals were still people," and closing formulas of etiological character in primitive folklore are widely disseminated in both myths and tales.

These stylistic clichés originate genetically in myth and therefore in primitive folklore are most often found in real myths, but also penetrate into the fairy tale. Note that in European folklore the situation is precisely the opposite — etiological legends are artless, while the fairy tale gleams with stylistic rituality.

In primitive folklore myth and folktale unquestionably have the same morphological structure in the form of a chain of losses and acquisitions of certain cosmic or social values. This

Primitive Sources of Verbal Art

is also recognized by the structuralists (Dundes, for example, or the Marandas). The difference, however, lies first in the fact that in myth acquisition is usually initial appearance, origin, i.e., etiology in the very broadest sense, while in the fairy tale it is redistribution of whatever benefit the hero has acquired either for himself or for his limited community. In the second place, in myth these acquisitions themselves are cosmic in character: light, fresh water, fire, and so forth; acquisition can also appear in negative form as reduction of the number of heavenly bodies, the cessation of a flood, and so forth, but the point does not change as a result. In the fairy tale the objects sought and the goals achieved are not elements of nature and culture, but rather food, wondrous objects, women, and the like, constituting the hero's good fortune. These differences — etiologism at the plot core or, better, in the form of a decorative pendant, cosmic or family-clan, collective or individual — are still more significant for discrimination between myth and tale than the distinction between sacrality and nonsacrality.

The mythic culture hero obtains fire or fresh water by stealing it from its primeval guardian (an old woman, a frog, a snake). The point here is the origin of fresh water on land inhabited by human being. The folktale hero steals the living water needed to cure his sick father (in Hawaii, for example) or obtains fire with the help of animals for his hearth (for example, in Dahomey). The folktale zoomorphic rogue (Hare) by guile steals for himself alone water from a well dug by other animals (in the folklore of many African peoples). Between the <u>loss of</u> and the <u>acquisition of</u> values stands the creative action of the demiurge-culture hero, or the <u>feat-ordeal</u> of a tale hero, or the cunning <u>trick</u> of a trickster. The true difference, however (within the confines of primitive folklore), does not lie in the character of the deed itself. The demiurge, for example, often resorts to adroit tricks. Reference has been made above to how Raven transforms himself into a child and screams to demand the luminaries as balls to play with; or how Maui deliberately puts out the fire and then again wheedles it out of his great-grandmother. But in these cases the issue is <u>the origin</u>

of fire and a benefit for all, as distinct from the seekers of living water, fresh water, and fire in the tales referred to above. The altruism of the Hawaiian good son obtaining the water of Kane for his father and the egotism of the Hare are equally contrary to the collectivism and etiologism of myth. However, here, too, in practice we find many intermediate cases. They include a majority of the stories about the stunts of mythological rogues, inasmuch as these rogues are still mythical personages who, moreover, have also performed serious, creative deeds. The Indians, it is true, can distinguish the serious deeds of the Raven-demiurge and the humorous stunts of Raven-trickster.

But among the Dahomeyans the cycle of the trickster Legba, associated with the pantheon of the higher gods, is classed with hvenoho (sacral myths), while the cycle of the trickster Io is classed with heho (tales).

It is very significant that the primitive folktales, although they are somewhat freer than myths in the sense of individual invention and ritualism of performance, are also associated with actual beliefs, with concrete mythology; their fantasy has a strictly ethnographic and in no way conventional character. The point is not only the difficulty in discriminating between myth and tale but the very syncretism frequently mentioned above. One and the same text can be interpreted by one tribe or group within a tribe as myth and by another group as tale, can be included in some sacral-ritual system or excluded from it. Moreover, one and the same text can, before one and the same audience, function as both myth and folktale, for example, if it simultaneously describes some link in cosmogenesis, sanctions a given ritual, demonstrates the bad consequences of violation of taboo, and at the same time inspires and amuses listeners with the bold or cunning escapades of the mythical hero. Therefore, it is necessary to work out a method for multilevel analysis of primitive texts — narrative-syntagmatic and symbolic-paradigmatic.

If one proceeds from synchrony to diachrony, i.e., to historical perspective in the shaping of a fairy tale, it is quite obvious

Primitive Sources of Verbal Art

that the transformation of a myth into a fairy tale facilitates its deritualization (if the myth was attached to ritual), its desacralization (for example, the sacred information on ancestral routes in Australian folklore is omitted or "declassified"), demythologization of the hero himself (abandonment of a totemic or semidivine hero, sometimes even with the loss of his name), demythologization of the time of the action (appearance of fairy-tale indefiniteness of time); switching from cosmic scale to the depiction of the lives of individuals, weakening or abolishing of etiologism; detachment of conventional fairy-tale fantasy from actual beliefs, weakening of reliability, and conscious admission of poetic invention. This transformation is not finally concluded within primitive culture, but a considerable degree of genre differentiation is nonetheless achieved.

As already observed, tales about mythological rogues are closely connected with the formation of <u>animal tales</u>. In practice, the trickster is the main character of such tales in the folklore of the indigenous population of Africa and America, and the escapades of zoomorphic rogues are the principal elements of most animal stories. A premise for the development of this genre is desacralization of totemic personages while their zoomorphic nature is preserved. As totemic beliefs are forgotten, animal stories are enriched with motifs from daily life, including some that are anecdotal. Observations of the habits of animals are combined with depiction of family and social relationships. Reference was made above to the major significance of the egotism of the trickster, his hyperbolic greed and readiness to violate any social norms for his personal advantage.

We find the classical form of animal tale in Africa. There (as distinct from the Indians, Melanesians, and others) these tales are quite clearly distinguished from myths. Etiological motifs and, to an even greater extent, cultural deeds are retained there only in rudimentary form. Tricksters' escapades serve as a manifestation of their cunning but no longer of sorcery. Episodes in which tricksters appear as madmen are very rare. A majority of the tricks (playing dead, intimidation by nonexistent powers, persuading other animals to agree to be tied up or

Semiotics and Structuralism

cooked for the sake of illusory benefits, proposals to care for the children of others, etc., etc.) are encroachments on the common catch or that of others and, as in the folklore of the American Indians, usually serve to satisfy hunger. But in African tales the moralizing emphasis is strengthened: the actions of the trickster destroy the initial friendship of the animals and are evaluated as ingratitude. Etiological endings are usually supplanted by moralizing. Elements of moral admonition open the road to the fable, which was so popular in Eastern literatures and, in part, in Europe as well. However, in African animal tales there are as yet no set masks representing specific human characters, no pure allegorism and didacticism.

The classical animal tale is the precursor not only of the fable but of the tale of everyday life. It is very likely that the tradition of folklore "tricksteriads" and of the animal story (and naturally the ancient fable) had a decisive influence on the literary animal epic, such as the medieval novel of Reynard.

A necessary premise for the development of the <u>magical</u> and the <u>magical-heroic fairy tale</u> is, in the first place, complete anthropomorphization and a certain degree of idealization of the hero and, in the second place, his demythologization. Here it would appear necessary to consider the interaction of myths, true stories, and local legends. The hero of the fairy tale is no longer seen as demigod or totemic ancestor, although he often retains divine parents (his distinctive and, of course, archaic form of idealization). The heroic twin brothers mentioned above — destroyers of chthonic monsters in the folklore of the American Indians — are a transitional stage. Among the Indians of the Northwest, alongside the unique mythological epics about Raven, Mink, and the wandering twins, there are folktales, highly colored with mythological fantasy, about extraordinary ordeals that the son-in-law of the sun or a youth pursued by envious uncles triumphantly undergoes. These are a kind of heroic fairy tale, but the heroic quality here still has a character of sorcery and shamanism. The future son-in-law of the sun is found in the stomach of a pike, can himself be transformed into a pike and obtain help from a pike (the totemic

Primitive Sources of Verbal Art

motif). By means of a sack with the winds given him by an old woman, the hero puts out the fire started by the sun, hunts for the daughters of the sun who have taken on the appearance of goats or birds, and flies off with them to the earth. Similarly, a pursued nephew saves himself from persecution by his uncle by means of magic objects, in the end marries the daughter of the chief, and avenges himself on the evil uncle.

The Polynesian tales of Tahaki and his clan, which originate from a heavenly female cannibal who has descended to earth, are similar in nature. Her son Hema, his children Tahaki and Karihi, grandson Rata, and the other characters in this cycle are fundamentally different from the culture hero — the trickster Maui. Tahaki is perceived as an ideal example of a Polynesian sacralized chief acting through his sorcerer's power or the magical help of ancestors, spirits, and so forth. The principal motifs associated with Tahaki, Rata, and the others are heroic childhood, miraculous betrothal, and particularly, a vendetta for the sake of which the hero has to ascend to heaven and descend into the underground world, defeating crafty spirits and monsters. These are typical for heroic fairy tales.

Along with such heroes, who retained the aura of myth, there appear, as early as in archaic folklore, heroes "who are not promising" and are victims of social injustice. This is true, for example, of the poor orphan treated badly by his closest clan and tribal kin, who thus violate the commandment of mutual help among kin. Such tales of poor orphans are popular among the Melanesians, the mountain tribes of Tibet and Burma, the Eskimos, the Paleo-Asiatics, North American Indians, and others.

In Melanesia the little orphan is the victim of his uncle's (his mother's brother's) wives, while in fact, according to clan morality, the uncle should have been his principal protector. Among the Indians the dirty orphan "burnt belly," living with his grandmother at the edge of the settlement, who eats leavings along with the dogs, is an object of contempt and ridicule on the part of the entire village.

However, with the aid of spirits, his sorceress-grandmother, or his dead parents, the orphan becomes a great hunter, warrior, and shaman (among the Indians) or attains high degrees in the secret men's society (in Melanesia).

The intervention of mythical beings in the life of a poor orphan is not so much the result of his rigid adherence to ritual regulations as the consequence of sympathy for the socially deprived who has become victim of the decline of clan-tribal norms of customary law and morality. If the tales of the son or son-in-law of the sun and similar "lofty" heroes seem like archaic analogues to Russian tales about Ivan Tsarevich, then the poor little orphan, the "dirty kid," reminds one of Ivanushka the Fool and Cinderella.

The plots of archaic magical-heroic fairy tales on the one hand reveal a clear-cut connection with primitive myths, rituals, and tribal customs and, on the other, anticipate the principal plot types of European and Asiatic magical fairy tales.

This is the case, for example, with the cited plots about the acquisition of marvels, elixirs, and wondrous objects, which originate in the myths about the stealing of cultural benefits by a mythical hero (No. 550, as well as Nos. 560 and 563, in the Aarne-Thompson plot index) or the story of marriage to a miraculous totemic being that has temporarily discarded its animal form, which is known to the very broadest range of peoples. The magical wife (in later variants, husband) grants success in the hunt to the one she chooses but abandons him as a result of violation of marital prohibitions, after which the hero seeks and finds his wife in her country and, in order to get the runaway back, has to go through a series of traditional marital trials (compare Nos. 400, 425, and some others in the Aarne-Thompson index).

Other examples: the story of a group of children who have fallen into the power of a cannibal and who are saved thanks to the resourcefulness of one of them, apparently reflecting the customs of initiation (see No. 327); the plot of the killing of a mighty snake, initially to acquire its magical power or to gain deliverance from chthonic demons (compare No. 300 and others); the plot of visits to "other" worlds or the kingdom of the dead

Primitive Sources of Verbal Art

to liberate female captives there, by analogy to the wandering of a sorcerer or shaman in search of the spirit of a sick or dead person (compare No. 301), and others. Later, motifs of familial and clan relationships are appended to these very ancient plots. The fairy-tale family is undoubtedly a generalized depiction of the clan or "extended family," and plots describing family quarrels to a certain degree reflect the social-historical process of decay of the clan system and the transition from communal distribution to family isolation. But in the archaic folklore, as we have seen, the family theme is barely suggested. The classical form of the magical fairy tale took shape very much later than the classical form of animal tale, well beyond the boundaries of primitive culture. We know this classical form only from the folklore of civilized peoples of Europe and Asia.

The shaping of this classical form of magical fairy tale was prepared by the decline (albeit incomplete) of the mythological world-view and the detachment of fairy-tale fantasy from concrete tribal ethnography.

One should note the characteristic schism in European folklore between the special conventional fairy-tale mythology and prevalent superstitions reflected in true stories. Associated with this is frank acceptance of <u>invention</u> in the magical fairy tale, unlike both the European true story (synchronically) and the primitive fairy tale (diachronically). This orientation toward invention is formalized in the beginnings of fairy tales (references to an indeterminate place and time) and their endings (reference to fable [<u>nebylitsa</u>] through the category of the impossible). The beginnings and endings of the classical fairy tale are the polar opposites of the initial and final formulas of the primitive (syncretic) tale that originates from myth. The fairy tale poetization of mythology encompasses not only images of mythical beings (typical of the fairy tale are Baba Yaga, Zmei, Kashchei, and others) but also magical transformations and acts of sorcery. The success or failure of the hero is no longer a direct consequence of adherence to magical formulas and the ordeals of shamanism, of family or marital ties with spirits, but only the result of the goodwill of miraculous forces, thanks to adherence to specific and rather abstract rules of behavior or direct displays of kindness to miraculous persons and objects. Miraculous helpers and objects, when they have taken the hero under their protection, already act to a certain degree in his stead.

Consequently, there appear <u>structural differences</u> between the primitive-syncretic tale and the classical fairy tale. (<u>11</u>) The structure of the archaic, mythological folktale acts as a type of metastructure with respect to the magical folktake as such. In the archaic folktale the chain of acquisitions and losses may consist of an indeterminate number of links, while a positive, happy ending (acquisition), although found more often than an unhappy ending (loss), is not obligatory. All links are more or less equivalent. In the classical magical fairy tale there emerges a rigorous hierarchical structure of two, or more often three, tests of the hero. The first trial (<u>preliminary</u> — verification of behavior, knowledge of rules), leading to acquiring the miraculous instrument, is a step toward the <u>basic</u> and concluding principal feat — the elimination of a calamity-lack. A third stage often consists of a <u>supplemental test for identification</u> (it explains who performed the feat, and it is followed by the disgracing of competitors and impostors). The obligatory happy ending includes, as a rule, marriage to the princess and receipt of half the kingdom.

Thus far we have been discussing the morphology of the fairy tale on the level of plot. Questions of historical poetics and stylistics of the fairy tale, and of the stylistic features of narrative folklore in archaic societies, have been very little studied.

The style of the narrative folklore of the Indians of the Northwest has been illuminated in the works of Franz Boas, and his observations on the folklore of the Kwakiutl and Tsimshian tribes were used by him to characterize the primitive art of the word in his classic work <u>Primitive Art</u> (1927). Interesting findings resulting from study of Chinook style is provided in a monograph by M. Jacobs, <u>The Content and Style of an Oral Literature</u> (1959). Jacobs emphasizes in every way the theatrical

Primitive Sources of Verbal Art

elements in the Chinooks' performance of fairy tales. The stylistic features of myths and fairy tales are the same, but myths have been polished to a greater degree and must contain formal beginnings and endings. The beginning includes reference to the name and place of habitation of the hero, and sometimes mention of his kinfolk. A characteristic of myth is the addition: "I do not know how long ago...," which hints at orientation toward mythical times. The ending includes the formula "now let us separate" (it is assumed that the parting is with the characters of mythical times), and one is told which of the characters have been transformed into whom or what (stars, animals, and so forth). The ending terminates with the words "myth, myth" or "story, story." Jacobs lists in detail numerous loci communis in the narrative folklore of the Chinooks. Such are, for example, the means of localizing or expressing distance, indicating time, symbolizing of various themes, the simplest emotions, and description of typical personages. For example, the narrative may speak of entering the last house in the village, where a poor youth or old woman lives; or on the other hand, a traveler asks children where the house of the chief is, which is always in the center of the village. The village is described from above, and it is either very populous or entirely empty. The number five is adopted to express a large number: "five villages" or "five mountains" indicates a great space or the fact that the traveler has been journeying for a long time. The breaking of a bow or a root-digger indicates misfortune; anger or depression are expressed in stylized manner by the news that the hero cannot eat or cannot speak; and so forth. In addition to identically expressed, verbal loci communis, Jacobs records a considerable number of recurrent motifs, situations, and so forth.

Subtle observations of the poetics of the Chukchi fairy tale, moreover in evolutionary cross section, may be found in the classical works of Bogoraz and, particularly, in the articles of Nikiforov (see Nikiforov, 1935, 1937, pp. 207-13).

The "real fairy tales" of the Chukchi are extraordinarily colorful. Their exceptionally rich fantasy has its roots, on the one hand, in the Chukchi-Eskimo sea demonology, with numerous images of spirit-masters of the sea, and so forth, and on the other hand, in shamanic mythology, with its complex cosmology, animal spirit helpers, and magical transformations. Bogoraz emphasized the striking difference between the ocean monsters of Chukchi fairy tales (dolphin-lycanthropes, the bear Kochatko whose trunk is of mammoth bone, the shaman Whale, giant cannibals from across the sea, and so forth) and the "Uralo-Altaic" one-eyed, one-armed, iron demons (Bogoraz, 1900, p. 1).

Nikoforov correctly observes that transformations, i.e., the changing of characters into various objects and beings, as well as their movement through a multilevel universe (making multilinearity of the action possible), are the principal springs and devices for constructing a plot in the Chukchi folktale. From the standpoint of historical poetics, the same Nikiforov identifies in the Chukchi folktale examples of three stages of evolution: (1) narrative-magical incantatory stories lacking the structure of the primitive tale (according to Bogoraz's data, the plot of "magical flight" — with the throwing of stones and grass that are transformed into mountains, seas, and forests — acquires a magical use in the funeral ritual); (2) "complete telling" [doskazka], in which the magical function is lacking, but an artistic poetics is barely marked, as a true story [byval'-shchina]; and (3) the fairy tale with more or less developed artistic means (among more "cultured" narrators known to Bogoraz, such as Chene, Aivan, and Keutebyn). The formula with the verb "was," obligatory for the beginning of cosmogonic myths ("Once upon a time it was dark," etc.), indicating mythical times, is found in fairy tales only in the third stage. The formulas for ending stories are: "I killed the wind" (a relict of the magical function of the fairy tale) and "they began to live." The tales contain a number of loci communis, such as, for example, the dialogue between the hero and the person he meets. The developed Chukchi folktale is characterized by repeated sequences and the law of fives.

Interesting observations on the poetics of the narrative folk-

Primitive Sources of Verbal Art

lore of Oceania may be found in the works of Lessa and Fisher referred to above.

Notes

1) See, in particular, the brief but brilliant characterization of "primitive" poetry in Boas's classical work (Boas, 1927), and compare the introductory articles to anthologies of the poetry of the Australian aborigines and American Indians: Harney and Elkin, 1949; Astrov, 1950; Day, 1951; and others.

2) For details on this see Kluckhohn, 1942, pp. 145-79; Hyman, 1955, pp. 462-72; Raglan, 1955, pp. 454-61; and James, 1958.

3) Compare the exposition of totemic myths in the final monograph by the classic scholars in Australian studies, Spencer and Gillen (1927, pp. 301-90).

4) See Howitt, 1904, pp. 475-88, 779-806, for exposition of these stories.

5) See Radcliffe-Brown, 1926; Berndt, 1951; Chaseling, 1957; Stanner, 1966.

6) See Tokarev and Tolstov, 1956, pp. 240-44.

7) In other myths and rituals as well, the express evil (for example, incest between the children of Kunmaŋgur) of the myth is often an allowable, even obligatory action in the ritual.

8) From the enormous and, for the most part, purely descriptive literature, one must single out the very valuable classic works of Franz Boas on the Indians of the Northwest (particularly Boas, 1916), of the Russian scientists V. Bogoraz, V. Iokhel'son, and Shternberg on the Paleo-Asiatics, as well as the articles of A. I. Nikiforov, and the lengthy works on the Indians by Thompson (1929, 1946). Among postwar writings the following on the Indians are particularly noteworthy: Radin, 1956; Radin, 1954-1956; Jacobs, 1959; Dundes, 1964; Lévi-Strauss, 1964-1971; Hultkrantz, 1957; Luomala, 1949, 1955; Lessa, 1961; and also articles by Fisher. On various peoples see the collections of articles (Jacobs, 1966). For North Asia, see the works of the Soviet scientists A. F. Anisimov, G. M. Vasilevich, M. G. Voskoboinikov, Z. N. Kuprianova, and others. Interesting thoughts

based on materials in Ket folklore can be found in writings by
V. V. Ivanov and V. N. Toporov. Some information can be found
in my works (Meletinskii, 1957, 1958, 1959, 1963).

9) See the seminal work by Paul Radin on materials from the
folklore of the Winnebago and other prairie Indians (Radin, 1956).

10) P. Radin believed that the trickster was, from the outset,
a combination of a divine culture hero and a divine jester from
the very time when man as a social being became differentiated
from the animal. In the story of the Winnebago trickster named
Wakdjunkaga, Radin sees a conscious depiction of the evolution
of man from primitive spontaneity to heroic consciousness.
One is inclined, however, to the belief that Radin is exaggerat-
ing, on the one hand, the primordial nature of this dual figure
and, on the other hand, the evident intellectual conception in
Winnebago tales as a depiction of the development of the individual. K. Kerenyi also regards this figure as very ancient, but
at the same time associates it with the late archaic period, when
by virtue of features not of content but of style itself, powerful,
brutal factors of entertainment obtrude. The connection between
the archjester and the archmadman seems to Kerenyi to be
primeval. Cunning, moreover, emphasizes stupidity, including
the stupidity of the cunning individual. Jung, in accordance with
his general theory of archetypes, sees in the trickster a "psy-
chologeme" of exceptional antiquity — a copy of undifferentiated
human consciousness that has barely left the animal world, the
embodiment of all the lowest character traits in the individual.
However, only an overcoming of absolute psychological ignorance,
he believes, could have induced such a glance backward by the
ego into the remote past of the collective consciousness. The
trickster is a figure who allegedly stands simultaneously both
higher than man (supernatural forces) and lower than him
(thanks to unconsciousness and spontaneity).

11) The presence of similar structural divergences strikes
one, particularly, upon comparing the structural description of
the Russian fairy tale in Propp's Morfologiia skazki (1928) and
Dudes's description of folktales of North American Indians
(1964), which is identical in method.

Primitive Sources of Verbal Art

Bibliography

ASTROV 1950: Margot Astrov, ed., The Winged Serpent, An Anthology of Indian Prose and Poetry, 1950.
AVDEEV 1959: A. D. Avdeev, Proiskhozhdenie teatra, Moscow, 1959.
BAKHTIN 1964: M. M. Bakhtin, Tvorchestvo Fransua Rable i narodnaia kul'tura srednevekov'ia i Renessansa, Moscow, 1964.
BERNDT 1951: R. M. Berndt, Kunapipi. A Study of an Aboriginal Religious Cult, Melbourne, 1951.
BÜCHER 1923: K. Bücher, Rabota i ritm, Moscow, 1923.
BOAS 1916: F. Boas, "Tsimshian Mythology," Report of the Bureau of American Ethnology, No. 31, Washington, 1916.
BOAS 1927: F. Boas, Primitive Art, Oslo, 1927.
BOGORAZ 1900: V. G. Bogoraz, Materialy po izucheniiu chukotskogo iazyka i fol'klora, sobrannye v Kolymskom okruge, Part I, St. Petersburg, 1900.
BOWRA 1962: C. M. Bowra, Primitive Song, London, 1962.
CAPELL 1960: A. Capell, "Myth and Tales of the Nunguburuyn," Oceania (Sidney), Vol. XXXI, 1960, No. 1.
CHADWICK 1932-1940: H. M. Chadwick and N. K. Chadwick, The Growth of Literature, Vols. I-III, London, 1932-1940. Reprinted, London, 1971.
CHASELING 1957: S. Chaseling, Yulengor, Nomads of Arnhem Land, London, 1957.
DAY 1951: A. Grove Day, ed., The Sky Clears. Poetry of the American Indians. New York, 1951.
DUNDES 1964: A. Dundes, The Morphology of the North American Indian Folktales, Helsinki, 1964 (F. F. Communications, No. 195).
HARNEY AND ELKIN 1949: Songs of the Songmen, retold by W. E. Harney and A. P. Elkin, Melbourne, 1949.
HOWITT 1904: A. W. Howitt, The Native Tribes of Southeast Australia, London, 1904.
HULTKRANTZ 1957: A. Hultkrantz, The North American Orpheus Traditions, Stockholm, 1957.
HYMAN 1955: S. E. Hyman, "The Ritual View of Myth and the

Mythic," Journal of American Folklore, 1955, No. 270.
JACOBS 1959: M. Jacobs, The Content and Style of an Oral Literature. Clackamas Chinook Myths and Tales, Chicago, 1959.
JACOBS 1966: Melville Jacobs, comp., The Anthropologist Looks at Myth, London, Austin, 1966.
JAMES 1958: E. O. James, Myth and Ritual in the Ancient Near East, London, 1958.
KERENYI 1946: K. Kerenyi, Prometheus, Zurich, 1946.
KLUCKHOHN 1942: C. Kluckhohn, "Myths and Rituals: A General Theory," Harvard Theological Review, XXXV, 1942.
LANGER 1953: S. Langer, Feeling and Form, New York, 1953.
LANGLOH-PARKER 1905: K. Langloh-Parker [sic], The Euahlayi Tribe: a Study of Aboriginal Life in Australia, London, 1905.
LESSA 1961: W. A. Lessa, Tales From Ulithi Atoll, Berkeley and Los Angeles, 1961.
LÉVI-STRAUSS 1962: C. Lévi-Strauss, La pensée sauvage, Paris, 1962.
LEVI-STRAUSS 1964-1971: C. Lévi-Strauss, Les mythologiques I-IV, Paris, 1964-1971.
LUOMALA 1949: K. Luomala, Maui-of-a-Thousand-Tricks, Honolulu, 1949.
LUOMALA 1955: K. Luomala, Voices of the Wind, Honolulu, 1955.
MACCONEL 1957: U. Macconel, Myths of the Munkan, Melbourne, 1957.
MARANDA 1971: E. Maranda and P. Maranda, Structural Models in Folklore and Transformational Essays, The Hague and Paris, 1971.
MATHEWS 1905: R. H. Mathews, Ethnological Notes on the Aboriginal Tribes of New South Wales and Victoria, Sydney, 1905.
MELETINSKII 1957: E. M. Meletinskii, "Mifologicheskii i skazochnyi epos melaneziitsev," in Okeaniiskii sbornik, Moscow and Leningrad, 1957.
MELETINSKII 1958: E. M. Meletinskii, Geroi volshebnoi skazki, Moscow, 1958.
MELETINSKII 1959: E. M. Meletinskii, "Skazanie o Vorone u

narodov Krainego Severa (o drevnikh fol'klornykh sviaziakh Azii i Ameriki)," VIMK, 1959, No. 1.
MELETINSKII 1963: E. M. Meletinskii, Proiskhozhdenie geroicheskogo eposa. Rannie formy i arkhaicheskie pamiatniki, Moscow, 1963.
NIKIFOROV 1935: A. I. Nikiforov, "Struktura chukotskoi skazki kak iavlenie primitivnogo myshleniia," Sovetskii fol'klor, 1935, No. 2-3.
NIKIFOROV 1937: A. I. Nikiforov, "Chukotskie skazochniki i russkaia skazka," in Pamiati V. G. Bogoraza, Moscow and Leningrad, 1937.
PROPP 1928: V. Ia. Propp, Morfologiia skazki, Leningrad, 1928.
RADCLIFFE-BROWN 1926: A. V. Radcliffe-Brown, "The Rainbow Serpent Myth in Australia," Journal of the Royal Anthropological Institute of Great Britain and Ireland (London), Vol. 56, 1926.
RADIN 1954-1956: P. Radin, "The Evolution of an American Indian Prose Epic," A Study in Comparative Literatures, Parts I and II, Basel, 1954-1956.
RADIN 1956: P. Radin, The Trickster. A Study in American Indian Mythology, London, 1956.
RAGLAN 1955: F. R. S. Raglan, "Myth and Ritual," Journal of American Folklore, 1955, No. 270.
SPENCER AND GILLEN 1927: W. B. Spencer and F. Gillen, The Arunta. A Study of a Stone Age People, Vol. 2, London, 1927.
STANNER 1966: W. E. H. Stanner, On Aboriginal Religion, Sydney, 1966.
STREHLOW 1907-1908: C. Strehlow, Die Aranda- und Loritja-Stämme in Zentral-Australien, Vols. I and II, Frankfurt on Main, 1907-1908.
STREHLOW 1910: C. Strehlow, Die Aranda- und Loritja-Stämme in Zentral-Australien, Part Three (Die totemistischen Kulte), 1910.
STREHLOW 1947: T. G. H. Strehlow, Aranda Traditions, Melbourne, 1947.
THOMPSON 1929: S. Thompson, Tales of the North American

Indians, Cambridge, Mass., 1929.
THOMPSON 1946: S. Thompson, The Folktale, New York, 1946.
THOMPSON 1955: S. Thompson, "Myth and Folktale," Journal of American Folklore, 1955, No. 270.
TOKAREV 1964: S. A. Tokarev, Religiia v istorii narodov mira, Moscow, 1964.
TOKAREV AND TOLSTOV 1956: S. A. Tokarev and S. P. Tolstov, eds., Narody Avstralii i Okeanii, Moscow and Leningrad, 1956.
TOLSTOV 1948: S. P. Tolstov, Drevnii Khorezm, Moscow, 1948.
VESELOVSKII 1940: A. N. Veselovskii, Istoricheskaia poetika, Moscow, 1940.
ZOLOTAREV 1939: A. M. Zolotarev, Rodovoi stroi i religiia ul'chei, Khabarovsk, 1939.
ZOLOTAREV 1964: A. M. Zolotarev, Rodovoi stroi i pervobytnaia mifologiia, Moscow, 1964.

A Structural-Typological Analysis
of Paleo-Asiatic Mythology

E. M. MELETINSKII

I

Study of the folklore of the Paleo-Asiatic peoples, the most ancient inhabitants of the north of Asia, and particularly study of the underlying semantics of their myths, is, in our opinion, one of the key approaches to study of the culture of the Asian continent. It must not be forgotten that the Paleo-Asiatics of the Chukchi-Kamchatka group came from the south and that analysis of their nonmaterial culture may also perform a service in the study of the more southerly, particularly the maritime cultures of Asia.

The mythology of the Paleo-Asiatics of the Chukchi-Kamchatka group, and in some respects that of the Indians of the American Northwest, is focused in the image of Raven and his people (family). Explicitly or implicitly Raven — the culture hero and trickster (mythological rogue) — serves as universal "mediator" between heaven and earth, the dry land and the sea, and more broadly, between the dry and the wet, the fresh and the salt, meat and vegetable foods, the male and female principles, man and animal, winter and summer — in the final analysis, between life and death, nature and culture. For it is a chthonic bird, nonmigratory, feeding on carrion, which obtains a lump of earth from the primeval ocean and, suffering from thirst, begs fresh water from the masters of the salt sea; it easily changes from from man into bird and vice versa; it is capable of changing sex ("the shaman of 'transformed sex' ") and represents natural chaos and cultural orderliness. The marital ties of Raven's children with various natural forces and beings also have a mediative function.

Among the Paleo-Asiatics and Indians there is a partial coincidence of the plots of the most ancient etiological "raven" myths (stealing of the heavenly bodies-balls, the acquisition of fresh water, the origin of Raven's black color and the coloring of birds by each other, the creation of the first people and animals), certain anecdotal motifs representing the "carnival" interpretation of certain "tricks" of the shamans (false death, change of sex), and also the persistent combination in the image of Raven of the features of the demiurge — the culture hero, shaman, and trickster. There are also pronounced differences between the folklore of the Paleo-Asiatics and Indians. For example, the Paleo-Asiatics had no myths about controlling the tides or about Raven obtaining fire. Typical for the Paleo-Asiatics is a myth about the acquisition not of fire but of light by drilling through the celestial firmament. This may possibly conceal allomorphs in a state of transformation and complementarity: heavenly light in place of earthly fire; clawing through the celestial firmament with a beak so that the light could break out, instead of retention of fire in the beak so that it could not break out; in the place of the etiology of the black beak, the etiology of a short one.

The Indians of the Northwest are characterized by the arrangemeant of "raven" tales into a biographical cycle, while a "family" cycle is typical of the Koryaks and Itel'mens. The similarity between the Asian and American "raven" cycles reflects not only typological but genetic similarities, as well as contact con-

Paleo-Asiatic Mythology

nections in the past. (1) In Eskimo folklore "raven" motifs are borrowed, for among the Asian Eskimos they are reminiscent of Chukchi and Koryak folklore, while among the Alaskan they resemble the folklore of the Tlingits. "Raven" motifs among the Aleuts and Yukaghirs are clearly peripheral, and perhaps borrowed.

The unitary "raven" mythology that probably existed among the northeastern Paleo-Asiatics in the past is now sharply differentiated between the Chukchi, on the one hand, and the Koryaks and Itel'mens on the other. Among the Chukchi, "raven" mythology has been partially displaced by the influence of Eskimo folklore, but the Chukchi have retained genuine myths of creation, in which Raven is the major figure, although the word "creator" is formally applied in Chukchi folklore to a different mythological figure. Among the Koryaks, on the other hand, Raven retains the name of "creator," but in fact only relicts of actual myths of creation remain. One such is the tale of how Raven obtained fresh water from the people of the sea and about the creation of the rivers (IK, 117, 134; Stebnitskii, pp. 15-18, 92-93; compare II, 12). (2) There is a remote echo between the etiological myths of Indians about the "liberation" or acquisition of fish of the salmon family thanks to marriage with the mistress of the salmon — the cloud-woman — and the Koryak story (IK, 104) about an unsuccessful attempt on the part of Raven to betray his wife with the salmon-woman who fed him spawn.

Certain etiological myths are directly inverted — for example, the one about the stealing of the heavenly bodies, known to the Chukchi and Indians. Big-Raven does not obtain light, but some ordinary Raven-man (Val'vamtilan) swallows the sun, which leads to darkness and a cessation of economy activities. The daughter of Big-Raven makes him laugh by tickling him and thus makes him spit out the Sun (IK, 82, BK, 1). The demonic-comic image of Valvamtilan is also preserved in other episodes (BK, 1; IK, 10). This kind of parodistic inversion is doubtless the consequence of the Koryak Big-Raven's loss of the features of demiurge and culture hero. Fundamentally, among the Koryaks Raven appears not as a demiurge but as progenitor, patriarch, and shaman of the Raven people. Raven's skills as a shaman are manifested in the healing of children threatened by evil spirits (kalau, kamaks, ninvits), in the struggle against these evil spirits (IK, 1, 2, 3, 8, 13, 14, 15, 22, 24, 29, 30, 32, 37, 39, 51, 54, 56, 57, 62, 73, 74, 75, 78, 101, 103, 105, 118; compare IK, 4), and in Big-Raven's calming of bad weather, rain, and storm (IK, 9; Stebnitskii, pp. 9-12, 91-92). Certain "tricks" by means of which Raven obtains food are shamanistic in character thanks to the devices used (for example, he travels to the wind-man or to reindeer breeders on a sled pulled by teams of mice or foxes — IK, 9; IK, 65; he creates a river in the house and catches fish, etc.). Here pride of place must be given to themes associated with hunting and fishing festivals and the corresponding group of concepts: Raven hunts for sea animals but lets them all go, one after the other, until a whale or the son of the master of the sea appears (IK, 119, 139). This "sending back" of a guest from the sea in the hope that he will send others in his place is the basic symbolic concept of the whale, seal, and similar festivals. Some of Raven's tricks also show his talents as a shaman; but nevertheless, these plots appear to be a kind of parody of genuinely shamanistic actions (he changes sex, plays dead in order to eat ritual food, restores its hide to a rabbit as an act of sorcery, and so forth), or even of acts of creation (Quikynniaqu makes kinfolk out of rotten fish, a beautiful girl out of feces, dogs or workers out of his sexual organs, catches fish in his own innards, etc.). The parodistic nature of such activities is emphasized by ultimate failure and the use of what might be called "antimaterials."

Along with such shamanistic tricks, many tricks are ascribed to Raven that are based on deceit, guile, and perfidy. He sometimes also uses such tricks in the struggle against evil cannibal spirits, but much more often in a clash with other "beasts," or more precisely, fox-men, wolf-men, bear-men, mice-girls, and so forth. Raven's tricks commonly succeed when they are directed against "outsiders" (evil spirits, reindeer breeders, other "beasts") and end in fiasco when aimed against "his own" community.

Paleo-Asiatic Mythology

The "raven" folklore of the Koryaks has much in common with the "raven" folklore of the Itel'mens, in which, however, there are fewer anecdotes and more elements of the fairy tale. The organization of Koryak and Itel'men folklore into family cycles differentiates it sharply from that of the Chukchi. In most of the myth-folktales of the Koryaks and Ite'mens, the sons and daughters of Raven take an active part.

Virtually all such myth-folktales may be divided into three broad groups, making up a kind of unitary system. In the narration about the struggle with evil spirits (kamaks, ninvits, kalau), Raven's children fall victim to these spirits, and Raven rescues them. In the story about the unsuccessful tricks of the hungry Raven in seeking food, his illusory, "paradoxical," and unsuccessful "economic" activity is contrasted with the normal activity of that kind by his sons, who provide the "raven" people with food by successfully hunting wild reindeer. In the story about the marital adventures of Raven's children, he plays the role of magical helper to his sons and daughters and facilitates marriages with beings representing useful natural forces.

The present article makes an attempt to provide an analysis of the semantic structure and its compositional expression in the second and third groups of myth-folktales of the Koryaks and Itel'mens.

Let us demonstrate the unfolding of the narrative structure of mythological anecdotes about Raven among the Koryaks (and in part among the Itel'mens). We will be concerned with Raven's tricks against the background of family. The general model can be seen in Diagram 1. Diagram 2 shows its concrete form.

In Diagram 1 the "separation" and "uniting" of personages are quite significant, for these phenomena create a certain division in the flow of the narrative. In the case in question the "separation" is profoundly meaningful, inasmuch as it is two "separations" — one positive and one negative — that are compared. Quikynniaqu's abandoning Miti is not only a preparation for action but an attempt at self-isolation from the family (the community), with the idea that he will obtain food for himself alone. Therefore, the "separation" also occurs when Quikyn-

Diagram 1

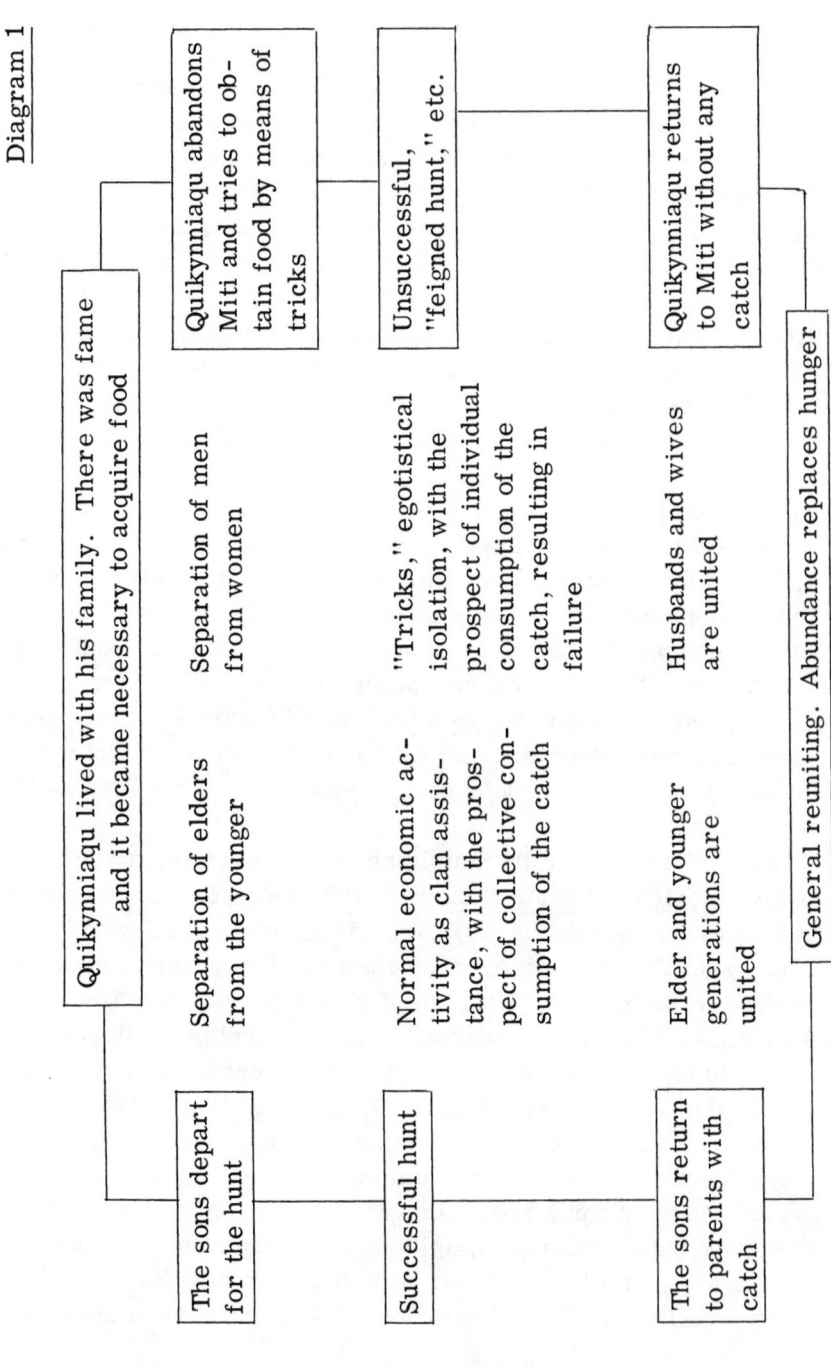

Diagram 2

	"Separation" (family splits up)	Food, its "givers" or the "antimaterial" objects from which it is obtained	Tricks of deception, sometimes with transformations	Exposure and fiasco	Unification
IK, 25	Quikynniaqu leaves for the coast	Miti makes "brothers" from the "shameful" parts of her body	Quikynniaqu seeks a wife among the reindeer breeders	Miti, in the form of a "house," awaits him, admits him into her anus-door, and carries him back	Reconciliation of spouses and general reunification of family
IK, 45	The sons leave to hunt wild reindeer	Quikynniaqu makes "parents" of rotten salmon	Quikynniaqu changes sex and pretends to be a girl from the reindeer breeders	Miti also changes sex and pretends a young man is courting her, making her husband jealous	Reconciliation and reestablishment of family in normal form; reunification with sons
IK, 27			Quikynniaqu changes sex and departs to the reindeer breeders	Miti also changes sex and follows to "court" him, but an attempt to have sex after changing sex does not succeed	Reconciliation and restoration of family in normal form
IK, 31	Quikynniaqu and his son settle separate from his wife and daughter	Quikynniaqu makes "little people" from his sexual organs to gather berries. He	The men gather berries and fish, while the women hunt sea mammals	The men's fishing fails, the "little man" cannot gather berries (which	Reunification of male and female parts of family

IK, 7 (compare IK, 23)	The children disperse over the tundra, and Quikynniaqu goes to the seashore	Quikynniaqu and Miti make "little dogs" from sexual organs to run errands (maintain contact) during the hunt	and Miti treat each other to a dish of mashed sexual organs	(a purely male job)	the daughter does anyhow). Miti seduces walruses erotically. Quikynniaqu eats the mashed sexual organs; Miti does not	Return of sons and reunification of family. Competition between shore people and reindeer breeders; victory of former
				The "little dogs" or "little people" transmit orders incomprehensibly (speak poorly); no contact is established	
IK, 42	Sons leave to hunt wild reindeer		Quikynniaqu, his wife, and daughter "fish" in their own insides by putting their heads there	Quikynniaqu eats feces	Return of sons and reunification of family
IK, 121		Quikynniaqu (Kutq) makes a girl of feces to be his wife		The girl of feces melts, giving off a stink	
IK, 120			A pine cone girl invites Quikynniaqu into her home-tree, filled with food	He eats and chokes from greed	
BK, 23			Quikynniaqu brings a salmon-woman home as a new wife	Miti cooks her rival, salmon-woman, three times	Reconciliation with wife

Diagram 2 (cont'd.)

	"Separation" (family splits up)	Food, its "givers" or the "antimaterial" objects from which it is obtained	Tricks of deception. sometimes with transformations	Exposure and fiasco	Unification
II, 1; II, 37			Kutq gives fish and heads to his mistress, fox	Miti kills fox by driving a stake into her	Reconciliation with wife
IK, 131	Kutq goes to hunt in a separate house		Quikynniaqu hides his hunting catch from Miti	Miti teaches the partridges to tease him and exposes him	Reconciliation with wife and reunification
IK, 35	Quikynniaqu pretends to go to town for tobacco but stays in the storehouse		Quikynniaqu eats the family's winter food supply	Miti exposes him with the help of her shaman-brother	Reconciliation with wife and reunification
IK, 35 (compare II, 21)	The sons go fishing		Quikynniaqu plays dead and eats their ritual food	Miti exposes him or he himself pretends he has been resurrected	Reconciliation and reunification

niaqu does not in fact depart but only makes believe he is doing so. He says he is going to town for tobacco, but in fact goes to the storehouse that holds the family's reserves for the winter (feigned departure).

"Separation" may also take the form of feigned arrival: Quikynniaqu changes his sex, creates "parents" for himself from rotten fish and "reindeer" out of sand, and pretends to be a girl from the reindeer breeders come as a guest. But most often Quikynniaqu actually does go away, to rich reindeer breeders, for example, or settles down with them separately from Miti and their daughter. Quikynniaqu's return to Miti is a result either of his failure or of activity on her part. She makes him jealous by transforming herself into a youth who allegedly pays court to her or into a house that is entered by Raven, who has no idea of what is going on, and so forth.

"Separation" may take on distinctive expression in loss of verbal contact ("information") between Raven and his wife: "little dogs" or "little people" made out of sexual organs (a comical transformation of the sexual "code" into the linguistic) speak incomprehensibly and are unable to maintain contact between themselves at a distance during the pretended hunt at sea. In the Itel'men myths Kutq's unexpected "flight" into the other world is preceded by the following scene: Kutq and Miti collect pine cones and call to each other. Suddenly Miti falls silent, and it is then that the raven flies away.

Departure from Miti is often accompanied by quests for another, more "advantageous" wife, or in the cited Itel'men myths, a wife for his son; but Miti cuts short these efforts and kills the new wife. Thus quests for food run, as it were, parallel with quests for amatory adventures.

Two tricksters coexist among the Indians of the Northwest — Raven and Mink; the former is gluttonous, the latter is lustful. Among the Paleo-Asiatics there is Raven alone, and therefore his greed can be transmitted simultaneously at both these levels and be expressed in both the food and erotic codes. For example, the story of the violation of the division of labor by sex in the quest for food can be compared to a story of change

Paleo-Asiatic Mythology

of sex or exchange of sexes with Miti. A metaphorical confusion of the two codes can be seen in the motif of mutual offering of feasts of sex organs or their use to make "little people" for the purpose of collecting berries, stealing fish, etc. In reality, however, these "levels" are far from being equivalent. Raven's chief goal is the satisfying of hunger, from which the entire family, the community, suffers (among Indians it is usually not general famine which is spoken of, but the peculiar personal gluttony of Raven, which begins after he has eaten the scab from a bone). Everything else is merely a means of sating his gluttony. Inasmuch as marriage brings with it mutuality with the other "clan" and exchange relationships, marriage proves to be a means toward the acquisition of food. This, for example, is the meaning of the marriage to the salmon-woman, who feeds her husband roe and who is cooked several times by the vengeful Miti. The encounter with the pine cone-woman, who opens for Quikynniaqu a tree with an inexhaustible supply of food, in which Raven chokes from greed, has analogous meaning. The "totemic" wife is the mistress of corresponding forms of food acquisition by hunting and gathering. However, she is not the personal owner of this food but a representative of the corresponding "clan." It is no accident that the pine cone-woman leads Quikynniaqu into the trunk of the tree which was her grandmother. Even on the level of daily life as such, every kind of prosperity, wealth, and mutual assistance, particularly under Arctic conditions, is associated with the presence of relatives by blood and marriage, who may be the direct "givers of food," and are in any case "givers of a wife." For this reason, Quikynniaqu curses Miti as being "kinless" and she, to calm him, makes brothers for herself out of parts of her body (the wife of Raven's son, a shell-woman, when she hears a similar criticism, brings in her real kin — animals of the sea — as "guests," to provide food for Raven's family). And it is in part for this reason that Quikynniaqu creates imaginary parents for himself out of rotten fish. These motifs emerge in two variants of a single plot and are in symmetry with each other, differing by opposition: the initiative of Quikynniaqu the husband or of Miti the wife, kinship in the "horizontal" dimension (via brothers) or in the "vertical" (through parents).

Thus quests for food are replaced by searches for a wife as "the giver of food"; and quests for a wife, by quests for "the giver of a wife." Here the food code changes not into the erotic but into the familial-clan (social), and the very transformations constitute a process of metonymization, inasmuch as the wife or relatives provide the food and in-laws provide the wife. True, the normal situation is inverted in all this from the very beginning, in the sense that Raven is changed from a giver of food to his wife and her kin and strives to become a receiver.

Another, even more direct course is metonymic substitution: instead of simple quests for food there is the creation of agents for acquiring it ("the little dogs" or "little people" who gather berries, transmit orders from Raven to Miti, and so forth) or forms of organization of economic activity (for example, change in the division of work by sex). Here the food code is replaced by an "economic" one. But inversion and violation of norms occur at all levels, with the consequence that, in the final analysis, hunger is not satisfied. The food itself or agents for acquiring it are made from inedible, inappropriate materials, or else its givers or "the givers of its givers" are. Other alternatives are that social norms are violated in the process of obtaining food (division of labor by sex), or biological norms are violated in the search for food givers (change of sex), or again (and this is the most important, always presumed here at least implicitly) social norms are violated not in production but in distribution, as Raven hides the take of the hunt, eats everyone's winter reserves, the ritual food for the dead, and so forth. Inversion also appears in the substitution of the top and the "lofty," the spiritual, by the bottom and the "low," the materially vile.

The plots analyzed demonstrate clearly how by means of various codes one and the same message about the unsuccessful attempts of the hungry Raven to obtain food for himself, by means of various codes, is transmitted in various ways and is realized in somewhat different plot forms.

Paleo-Asiatic Mythology

The examples shown reveal the similarity of plot structure not only paradigmatically but syntagmatically.

2

The motifs of the mythological folktales about the marital ties of Raven's children are in a certain sense the opposites of mythological anecdotes about the tricks of Raven, particularly in the stories of his attempts to be unfaithful to Miti. These attempts on Raven's part are socially destructive, while the marital ties of Raven's children are socially constructive.

Let us indicate the principal plot subtypes, with references to the sources:

1) The tale of the two consecutive marriages of Raven's elder son and elder daughter (IK, 17, 20, 107, 83, 53, 81, 106 in Koryak folklore.

2) The tale of the marriage of one and then another of Raven's children (IK, 19, 75, 80) in Koryak folklore.

3) The tale of the threat (usually feigned, "theatrical") of marriage to a monster and the subsequent normal marriage of Raven's elder daughter or elder son (IK, 4, 5, 60, 66, 87, 91) in Koryak folklore.

4) The tale of the preliminary betrothal of the sister or father of the hero and of the subsequent marriage of Ememqut (II, 2, 5, 17, 41; IK, 136) in Itel'men folklore.

5) The tale of the marriage to a beast (a monster who becomes handsome, etc.) and its unskillful imitation by envious kin (compare the Itel'men: II, 10; IK, 138; and Koryak: IK, 18, 21, 33, 48, 101).

6) The tale of how Raven's elder daughters or niece reject a groom "who does not offer hope," or who frightens them, while the youngest daughter accepts him and benefits by this (II, 16; IK, 55, 58).

7) The tale of the unskilled marital tests of one of the grooms and the skilled tests of another (IK, 82, 46; BK, 1; Baboshina, 72, 73).

8) The tale of the temporary loss of a wife as the result of

disputes, insults, and the like, and of how she is regained after trials (II, 13, 15; IK, 52, 116).

9) The tale of the unsuccessful attempt to destroy the hero and to take away his wife (II, 26; compare IK, 8).

10) The tale of the loss of Raven's daughter's husband, who is forced to marry a girl from the "lower village," and of his return (IK, 93, 94).

11) The tale of the "substitution" of a wife and her new acquisition (II, 1, 14, 32, 38; IK, 64; Baboshina, 32; Stebnitskii, pp. 36-42).

Plot type 12 stands by itself. It is the story of how Raven's eldest daughter, to whom no one wishes to be betrothed, takes as husband, one after the other, various unworthy beings and objects (II, 28; compare II, 40).

Plots 5-11 are more stereotyped than 1-4 and 12 and have close parallels in the international plot index. There is a deep internal connection between these plots, definite relations of symmetry, direct or inverse. Among the compositional mechanisms of the type of plot being analyzed, a major role is played by violation of taboos of the various kinds.

In Koryak myths, death and resurrection, for which any of the characters can be responsible, are a special kind of operator of change of state. Often the heroine is killed and immediately resurrected by a figure who wants to marry her, for example, the cloud-man (IK, 83) or the grebe-man (IK, 80). It also happens that one kills her, another resurrects her, a third marries her — for example, Ememqut kills her, a wolf resurrects her, and the cloud-man marries her (IK, 81). Naturally, in a number of cases the "enemy" kills and the "friend" saves, but this is not obligatory, for it is the act that is important and not its performer; what is important is realization of the function of change of state through temporary death. The aspects of space and time are tied together in the act of temporary death, inasmuch as change of state is almost always a change of fate and "locus."

As compared to the European folktale, the syntagmatics of which has been described by V. Ia. Propp and his modern followers, the Koryak and Itel'men mythological folktale with a marital theme

Paleo-Asiatic Mythology

(which is so typical and obligatory for the European fairy tale) lacks the preliminary trial before obtaining a magical helper (even though such a helper is sometimes found, for example, in the form of a little old spider-woman; this personage is also known to American Indians), as well as a further test for identification. Moreover, marriage is not an end in itself and not a means of overcoming conflicts at the family level thanks to improvement of one's family status, but a means of establishing social contact with natural forces. This final difference is not syntagmatic (not rigorously narrative), although it is reflected in the composition of the mythological tale. Finally, the very referral of the action to mythical time and attachment to mythical personages — the children of Raven — differentiates the Itel'men-Koryak myth-folktales from the European fairy tales and characterizes them as "myths."

On the level of composition these mythological folktales are distinguished by "duality" — for example in the form of two "movements" describing the first and second marriages of the hero (heroine) or the two marriages of Raven's various children. If the former marriage is to be preferred, the second (or attempt at a second) is followed by return to the first marriage partner.

If in fact the story is about a single marriage, two compositional movements are nonetheless retained. This is determined either by the threat of a suit from a highly undesirable marriage partner (sometimes this is merely the jesterlike "mask" of a monster), or the first appearance of the groom in deformed ("bestial") form, or the preliminary suit of the sister or father in the name of the hero, or the temporary departure of the insulted wife and her later reconquest, or a comparison of the suits of two suitors.

Compositional "duality" is a feature of the syntagmatics of these plots and of the very organization of the narration. But this duality leads to a certain counterposing of persons, deeds, and elements of the cosmos, behind which the semantic paradigms of the Koryak-Itel'men myth-tale are revealed; moreover, plots more remote from European stereotypes (and particularly plots that are in general less stereotyped) are semantically richer.

As far as the characters are concerned, these myth-tales, as can be seen, either set in opposition the first and second marital partners (and one of them may only "threaten" or temporarily "replace" her), or present two competing suitors passing through trials of marriage, or two brides making choices of suitors, or two suitors (or brides), one an ugly or unsuccessful rival and unskillful imitator.

The syntagmatic "duality" of mythological tales about the marital advantures of Raven's children corresponds to semantic paradigms in the form of oppositions: endogamy (incest, cousin marriage) and exogamy (the family-clan — i.e., the social code); the basic components of the cosmos, i.e., sky and earth or the underground world (the cosmological code); or useless (or harmful) and useful natural objects that control the sources of food and the conditions for successful economic activity (the economic code).

In the Koryak stories of the two consecutive marriages of the children of Quikynniaqu (plot 1), the changing of marriage partners is often reducible to transition from endogamous to exogamous marriage. The issue is chiefly incest (the ultimate form of endogamy, i.e., marriage within one's own family-clan group). There is a story that Ememqut and Yiñea-ñeut, when still little children, were abandoned by their parents (after a misfortune: a whale that had been killed did not wish "to go away" back to the sea, and as a consequence they were threatened with starvation) in different places and grew up not knowing that they were brother and sister. Ememqut, to whom their parents left a bow and arrows, learned to hunt wild reindeer, while Yiñea-ñeut laid snares for marmots. Encountering each other accidentally they married, but animals started to tease them, and later Ememqut exchanged wives with the Strong-One or the Big-Kamak (clearly not an evil spirit but an amulet — the protector of the clan), whose wife was also called Yiñea-ñeut (IK, 17, 20).

Stories of incestuous marriage between brother and sister, the first people to master the hunt, are found in the folklore of

Paleo-Asiatic Mythology

various peoples, including the Chukchi, among whom such stories are not at all associated with the children of Raven, and the heroes are consequently nameless. A story about incestuous marriage between Raven's children also exists among the Kereks, who until recently were regarded as identical to the Koryaks. One can cite examples of uncompleted incestuous marriage (IK, 66), which is equated with the possibility of marrying a monster (within the framework of plot 3). In relict and comically softened form, the incest motif is associated with Illa: by mistake he always finds himself in bed with his sister or mother (IK, 48). In Itel'men folklore there are a number of "texts" in which one can see a more or less veiled hint at the incestuous marriage of Ememqut and his sister Sinanewt (II, 13, 18, 2, 40, etc.).

These plots are comparable with the plot about how a brother or father tried unsuccessfully to destroy Ememqut and take his wife away (II, 26).

The majority of variants involving incest tell of how it is avoided or overcome and about the change from endogamous to exogamous marriage. It is emphasized in every possible way that endogamous marriage with newcomers from afar, and so forth, occurs by means of exchange: Ememqut gives the Strong-One or Big-Kamak his Yiñea-ñeut, and receives their Yiñea-ñeut. The entire plot acquires the character, as it were, of an "etiological" myth about the rejection of incest and the introduction of exogamy, and thereby the principles of social organization. This kind of marriage by exchange in the form of a "folded" motif is also present in other stories about the marital ties of Raven's children, where there was no talk of incest. Moreover, there is frequent reference to the fact that from that time on the groups that had thus become kin wandered together, or all settled down together with Raven's family, and so forth.

For all the unusual clarity of this plot, marriages that were at all remote, by kidnapping or exchanges, were very rare among the Koryaks and Itel'mens in historical time; and marriages to a brother's sister-in-law and vice versa, which are frequent in myths, were virtually forbidden.

It is curious that incestuous marriage in the Koryak version

(IK, 20) is preceded by the failure of a whale to go away after the whale festival and by the threat of famine. In other versions, in which Raven's children enter normal exogamous marriage, this is followed by successful whale hunting: the social code is interwoven with the economic.

Along with incestuous marriage, Koryak folklore quite often refers to marriage of cousins as more common and normal. "The Creator married Ememqut and Illa to cousins and ordered them to disperse over the tundra" (IK, 7). There are frequent references to the fact that Ememqut is married to the female shaman Kilu, daughter of Quikynniaqu's sister (IK, 7, 14, 53, 83, 106, 107, 109), while Yiñea-ñeut is married to Illa, Kilu's brother (IK, 7, 106). Marriage to the daughter of one's mother's daughter, or to the daughter of one's father's sister (cross-cousin marriage), is the foundation of the classical forms of marriage in archaic societies. However, as early as the eighteenth century, marriages between cousins were also apparently forbidden. It is precisely for this reason, one has to conclude, that tales exist to the effect that after his first marriage to Kilu, Ememqut (either because she was childless or without any stated motive) was married again to the grass-woman (IK, 53) or the cloud-woman (IK, 83).

The plots of two consecutive marriages are not reducible to the avoidance of incest or cousin marriage. Comparison of the two consecutive marriages isolates negatively marked ones (monsters, disease spirits, close kin, the silver fox, the lizard, the fly-agaric, and others) and those marked positively, which were particularly preferred. Ememqut prefers the white-whale-woman over other wives (IK, 116). He becomes convinced of the virtues of marriage to the shell-woman, who (although termed "kinless") brings her kin, the animals of the sea, to be objects of the hunt for Raven's sons; he returns to her after a brief affair with the wolf-woman (IK, 52). Ememqut is glad to rid himself of the lizard and to regain his ramson-wife (wild garlic) (II, 14, 38) or to triumph over the machinations of his kinfolk and return to the raspberry-woman (II, 26). Ememqut proceeds from marriage to his sister or cousin to marriage with the

Paleo-Asiatic Mythology

the grass-woman, the daughter of the man-root. The grass-woman is most frequently called Ememqut's wife (IK, 3, 5, 11, 67, 75; Stebnitskii, 36-42, 108-11, etc.). There is a single variant in which Ememqut goes from Kilu to a bumble bee-woman, to a fisherwoman (IK, 107). Yiñea-ñeut in the final analysis often turns out, on her second round, to be the wife of fog, of sun-man, or principally, of cloud-man (IK, 19, 114, 80, 81, 94).

Negatively evaluated marital partners have no relationshp whatever to economic activity, sources of food, and favorable climatic conditions. On the contrary, it is emphasized that it is necessary to feed fish to the fox, that the lizard seeks ways to acquire food in Ememqut's name, that Czelkutq's departure to take up with the amanita-girls leads to the beginning of a hungry existence (for the female spider leads all the animals away into the sky). Kamaks bring sickness, sexual intimacy with one's sister leads to the breaking of arrows and failures in the hunt, and so forth. Preferred marriages are associated with the hunt for sea animals and in part with fishing, the gathering of grasses and berries, and with factors in the weather, which are so important, particularly for sea hunting. The white-whale-woman is directly associated with the hunting of whales. According to one version, Ememqut's mother, Miti, also was a white whale, so that both Raven and his son took wives from the white-whale clan (in another version Miti is the daughter of Magpie). Of the shell-woman it is said that she had called her kin, the animals of the sea, and that the ocean had thrown up cauldrons and dishes, and a whale festival followed (a celebration that can be held only after a successful hunt of the whale-visitor). The bumble bee-woman is also associated with fishing, and the ptarmigan (white partridge), which Raven's younger daughter took as husband, is associated with reindeer breeding. Raven's daughters find marriage partners in the woods — hunters (dressed in wolfskins and bearskins).

Ememqut's marriage to the raspberry-woman, the ramson-woman, and particularly to the grass-woman, indicates a connection with life-giving vegetative forces and the renewal of nature in spring of which grasses and berries are a sign (a metaphorical expression). The son of

Ememqut and the grass-woman bears a name that is deciphered as "Reborn," which corresponds to Koryak beliefs in the rebirth of ancestors in later generations and simultaneously ties together the rebirth of vegetation and the cycle of the generations. Fog and clouds undoubtedly bear a relationship to weather, as do sun, frost, twilight, wind, and the very mistress of weather herself, all of whom are cited less often. The significance of the cloud-man in Paleo-Asiatic mythology goes beyond purely "metaphorical" bounds: cloud-people are the children of the master of the sky (sometimes identified with the sun). They govern family life (lovers appeal to the cloud-man!), weather, the hunting of sea animals, and fishing. Among the North American Indians, cloud-people are "specialized" masters of fishing. Therefore, it is not surprising that Yiñea-ñeut, too, goes from the fog-man to the cloud-man (IK, 81).

There is also a story of how Kilu's first marriage, to Ememqut (endogamous cousin marriage), was succeeded by Kilu's marriage to the cloud-man and Ememqut's marriage to the cloud-woman, followed by a successful hunt for whales and the whale festival. The successful hunt for whales was a consequence of the cloud-people's power over them (compare the whales' refusal to go away in the face of incest between brother and sister). Thus the story of the two consecutive marriages of Raven's sons or daughters is revealed both from the compositional-syntagmatic and the semantic-paradigmatic aspects. Two plot movements correspond to definite opposition of the marriage partners and their semantic characterization on the family-clan, i.e., social (exogamy-endogamy), or economic-natural levels. The connection between these levels is very intimate and deep, as the marriages of Raven's children "socialize" natural forces and the exogamous nature of marriages and their "exchange" character (marriage of a sister to a cloud-man involves marriage of a brother to a cloud-woman, and so forth); they demonstrate the possibility of exchange of "wives" for certain economic benefits, and thereby the social "armature" of the corresponding myths becomes clear.

Paleo-Asiatic Mythology

The transition from the first marriage to the second, or from a "temporary" one to a lasting one, marks a certain progress in the sphere of social organization and the establishment of contacts with the most important natural forces and objects: the masters of success in hunting and fishing, climatic factors, and the powers of calendrical vegetative renewal. Nevertheless, cases are possible in which transition from a first marriage to a second is not evidence of progress of any kind. Here, too, syntagmatic duality corresponds to a very rigorous meaning. In one variant (IK, 4) Yiñea-ñeut's marriage to the cloud-man is followed by her fall from the sky to the kamaks in the underground world (Ememqut creates a tempest) and by her marriage to a kamak, i.e., the sequence appears to be directly the reverse of the normal one and fundamentally "regressive." However, this is not the case. The point is that after the marriage of Raven's daughter to a kamak, Raven exchanges the kamaks' "cannibal" stomachs for those of seals, and the kamaks cease to be cannibals. This means, in practice, victory over the diseases and death that evil spirits bring to human beings — to the "raven" people. This result is equivalent to the success of the family-marital ties of Raven's children to the cloud-people: the animals of the sea become food for people (positive), and people cease to be food for cannibals (negative). Thus there is no retrogression. Nor is there progress, and the meaning of "duality" is revealed here as an opposition of "the high" and "the low," the sky and the underground world, and as mediation between high and low, as the global scope of the natural forces by the "mediative" marital ties of the raven people (clan, family).

It was pointed out above that aside from myths-folktales about how one of Raven's sons (or daughters) exchanged marital partners (Plot 1), we find "two-movement" narratives about two marriages of two different representatives of the Quikynniaqu family (Plot 2). Here it is as though the rigor of composition has been weakened but the semantics of the plot is revealed even more deeply. In this case the "duality" is quite significant, and the connections that, at first glance, seem to be random, the result of violation of a more rigorous traditional plot, in fact

Semiotics and Structuralism

reveal a deep ethnocultural and logical motivation.

There is a story (IK, 75) very similar to the one examined, with its opposition of "high" and "low," but differing from it in two particulars. It is not the sky and the underground world that are counterposed, but the earth and the world below. In the first "movement," the narrative has to do with Ememqut's marriage to the grass-woman, and in the second with the marriage of Quikynniaqu ("White Light"), Ememqut's younger brother, to a kamak woman (he found himself there together with Ememqut's son, having violated his elders' instructions to stay as far away from the river as possible). From the grass-woman to the kamaks is the same kind of "regression" as from the cloud-man to kamaks; but here, too, marital contact with the kamaks leads to their being rendered harmless: the kamaks are killed by throwing down their throats whale-meat, food which is normal for human beings but apparently deadly to them. They are then resurrected, but no longer as cannibals. The fact that different people get married in the first and second movements is not so important as that both are children of Raven, and the point here is the group social ties of the raven family, the mediating between opposite parts of the cosmos, and so forth.

Let us turn to a myth-folktale (IK, 80) whose structure can be revealed only by means of ethnocultural commentary. The first episode tells of how Quikynniaqu asked a grebe-shaman (pochard duck) for means to calm the disturbance of the sea and on his advice married Ememqut to a woman from the middle of the sea. The episode ends by telling us of a whale hunt and the whale festival. The second episode begins with Čanai-ñaut and Kilu gathering sedge for the whale festival and Čanai-ñaut beginning to imitate the shaman song of the grebe. The grebe-shaman had heard her and carried off her heart, but later himself resurrected and married her. Her older sister Yiñea-ñeut married the fog-man.

At first glance this plot seems chaotic. In reality the narration is rigorously organized in its semantics. The hunt for sea animals, which was the Koryaks' basic source of livelihood until the appearance of reindeer breeding (under the influence of

Paleo-Asiatic Mythology

their neighbors of the Tungus linguistic group), is in direct and strong relationship to weather. Ememqut's marriage to the mistress of the weather gives the raven people power over the weather and provides the opportunity for successful hunting of the whale, with the whale festival that follows (just as does marriage of Raven's daughter or niece to the cloud-man). Therefore, the whale festival is entirely in place here. Marriage to the mistress of one or another natural force is the principal means of influencing nature for economic purposes in Koryak-Itel'men mythology.

There is an Itel'men myth about the marriage of Raven's daughters to a northwind-man and to a southwind-man, a myth about the establishment of good weather (IK, 133), and also stories about how Quikynniaqu pacified the weather by giving a drink to the mistress of weather, who lived on an island in the middle of the sea, and by cutting off her hair (Stebnitskii, 9-12), or about how mice ate through the harness of the wind-man's sledge (IK, 40). The mistress of weather and the wind are male and female hypostases of the same natural force. This is confirmed, inter alia, by the identical mode of Raven's arrival where they are (on a boat or sledge to which mice are harnessed). Gnawing through the harness or cutting hair are variations of the same motif, alternative (or supplementary) to pacifying the weather through marital ties. These plots constitute a definite system in which "redundancy" is overcome by varying the sex of the master of weather (strictly speaking, the mistress of ocean weather or the wind-man) in the singular or the plural (there is a single mistress of the weather, but two winds), and by varying the means of pacifying him (cutting off the source of turbulence of the sea or the wind).

In this system the identical "message" (pacification of the weather) is transmitted, to employ Lévi-Strauss's terminology, by the use of different kinds of "armatures." The degree to which mythical thought was occupied with management of the weather among the Paleo-Asiatics is also demonstrated by other variations on this theme: cessation of rain due to Raven's roasting the drum struck by the master of the sky and the

Semiotics and Structuralism

mistress of rain (a metaphor for the sexual act: see IK, 9), use of the plugging of a hole in the land of the sunrise to calm a tempest as a marital test of the little bird-man who is offering himself as a suitor to Quikynniaqu's daughter (IK, 11 [10?]), the pushing asunder of the clouds in an Itel'men tale not associated with Raven's family, and the like. Thus the initial episode of the story (IK, 80) which we have examined fits rigorously into the given semantic system and pertains to the "meteorological" code which holds a privileged position in Paleo-Asiatic mythology. In fact, all the motifs and episodes of the mythological tale we have analyzed (IK, 80) are brought together and organized by a "meteorological" code. This immediately makes comprehensible the reference to the marriage between Yiñea-ñeut and the fog-man at the end of the story, neither Yiñea-ñeut nor the fog having previously been mentioned at all.

The grebe, which flies in springtime and nests in sedge, has a direct relationship to weather, and particularly to the spring break in the weather. Its flight marks spring and the beginning of the whaling season, while its cry signals the change in weather. That is why it is presented in myths as prophet and shaman.

Lévi-Strauss shows that the semantic interpretation of pochards and loons shows very wide variation in the mythology of the North American Indians, but that these birds are, in mythology, invariably associated with changes in weather or in the seasons, with the onset or cessation of rain, wind, and the like, and that much attention is given to their cries. The death of Čanai-ñaut is punishment for violation of the stillness and for mimicking of the cry of the grebe-shaman. When one considers the synchronicity of the cries of the grebe in the sedge and the opening of the whale hunt (the celebration of the whale festival as this is described in myths), the disturbance of the silence has a dual significance here. The first half of the whale festival occurs in silence, which is then replaced by noisy celebration. But the gathering of grass by girls is an act of preparation for the festival and pertains to its beginning and thus to the period of sacral quiet.

After killing a girl, the grebe-shaman immediately resurrects

Paleo-Asiatic Mythology

and marries her. Grebes nest in May on the Kamchatka and Chukotka peninsulas, so that renewals in nature, the economy, and family life naturally coincide in the plot. It is probable that the symbolism of "temporary death" of the whale in the whale festival will prove to be in harmony (metaphorically) with the "temporary death" of the heroine, marking a change in her state. Thus the story of the marriage of Ememqut to the mistress of the weather, and the story of the marriage of Čanai-ñaut to the grebe (marking the change in weather and the spring renewal), is actually a doubling of the same theme and, moreover, in the same "meteorological" code.

For the Paleo-Asiatics the emergence into the foreground of the meteorological aspect as such was typical, so that the calendrical aspect remains in the shade, as it were, in the latent state (as distinct from the situation among the Indians, where in similar cases we find myths not only of triumph over weather, storms at sea, and the like, but also about regulation of the tides, the seasons, and the winds, even within the framework of the Raven cycle). This latent calendrical aspect comes through more vividly in another plot (IK, 114), in which the "astronomical" code is dominant. This plot is also quite unique, and in terms purely of story line it differs greatly from the Koryak-Itel'men stereotypes; but a certain semantic integrity is to be found in it as well.

The heroine of this story, as of many others, is Yiñea-ñeut, the name which the Koryaks give to one of the stars in the Pleiades. Yiñea-ñeut rushes across the tundra on skis, and by disturbing the quiet of the night, by her "stellar" nocturnal activity attracts the attention of the people of the sky — the Moon and the Star. Quikynniaqu punishes his daughter by leaving her alone in the tundra for the summer after cutting off her leg. Lévi-Strauss used a number of examples to show that removed limbs often indicate the use of an "astronomical" code. In fact, Yiñea-ñeut's removed leg, and she herself, later turn up in the sky. Yiñea-ñeut flies there with the help of a goose wing which she substitutes for her missing limb, and one must conclude that she changes there into a star. In the sky the cloud-man marries her (as in other stories about Yiñea-ñeut's marriages). But real power over the take of the hunt as the result of marrying the cloud-man is here expressed in a negative way: having been mistreated by her father, Yiñea-ñeut collects the animals and plants in a hide and does not permit them to descend to earth, which produces famine there. After a certain lapse of time she is reconciled with her father, and Ememqut is also married to a cloud-woman. The "astronomical" code is quite clear, but here a calendrical aspect is also clearly present in the references to the time of year (summer) and the temporary removal of the take of the hunt (for the winter?).

Our hypothesis is confirmed when one compares this myth to certain Itel'men texts on the theme of the marital ties of the "raven" clan.

In one variant (II, 8, 33) Kutq treats his daughters badly, and they flee to the Kutq of the sea, spend the winter there, and return in spring with meat and hides. Subsequently, they marry hunters who have shot through the hides of the reindeer and bear in which they had been clothed. Here the motif of flight from the insults of Raven, their father, coincides with references to the seasons of the year and the appearance of meat and hides in the spring, after the temporary absence of the daughters. Furthermore, the marvelous trip to the sky, to the people of the clouds, and to the stars with the help of a bird's wing is transformed, as it were, into a sea voyage to the master of the sea, by means of a sea animal (whale). The temporary absence of the animals corresponds, as it were, to temporary absence of the daughters themselves, clothed in animal skins, and one may draw the conclusion that the daughters' bringing of meat and the like followed the temporary absence of sea game during the course of the winter.

Even more important, however, are other comparisons, primarily with Itel'men tales of "substituted" wives. Sinanewt, after her husband Czelkutq has gone away to the amanita-girls, ascends a mountain to the sky, with the help of a female spider, and takes all the animals with her, with the consequence that famine sets in on earth and Czelkutq starves. After recon-

Paleo-Asiatic Mythology

ciliation, Sinanewt also helps her husband climb the mountain. She had earlier poured water on it to make it slippery and cut the straps that Czelkutq tried to hold on to (II, 1, 32). Here the coincidence is virtually complete, except that the individual who dealt out bad treatment was not the father but the husband, and it is not the animals that return from heaven to earth but the husband who rises from earth to heaven (as Ememqut does to reach the cloud-woman).

In another story (II, 38) Sinanewt's place is taken not by amanita-girls but by an evil female lizard who takes away her clothing and tries to kill her. There is also a variant (II, 34 [14?]) of the same plot in which the heroine (in the text we know she is called Maroklnawt and is the wife of Ememqut), having been left alone by her husband (who is temporarily in the power of the evil lizard-woman), gets married again to Goose, who has flown in for the summer to his usual place. She has a son by Ememqut and another by Goose. In winter Goose flies off again, but the next summer he returns to her. However, he is killed by a hunter, the son of the heroine and Ememqut. In the end Goose is brought back to life, the lizard is exposed and driven away, and Maroklnawt divides into two women, the wife of Ememqut and the wife of Goose.

In this variant the motif of marriage to Goose is very important, and the calendrical character of the tale of Goose is emphasized. He flies away for the winter and returns in spring for the summer, and later is even killed during the period of seasonal hunting for water fowl. His death and resurrection are comparable to the deaths and resurrections of the target animals hunted at sea in the ritual of the corresponding "festivals." The ultimate meaning of the comparisons and the transformations we have noted becomes clear when one introduces one more link — the popular story (II, 6) about how Sinanewt became the wife of Goose's eldest son after she took care of his younger son. The gosling's wings did not grow, and he was not able to fly away with his parents to warm places for the winter. Sinanewt built a pond in the house for the gosling, kept him and fed him there, and in the spring she herself made him wings (out of a grass whisk and the like), so that he could fly

Semiotics and Structuralism

away with his parents. In order to return from this plot to the original Koryak text (IK, 114), one needs only its complete "inversion." Here the gosling has been left alone for the winter by his parents, without food or wings, and Sinanewt makes him a wing and thus helps him fly away into the sky; while in the other story Yiñea-ñeut (Sinanewt) is left by her father to fend for herself, without food and lacking a leg, but she makes use of a goose wing to fly to the sky. One motif strictly inverts the other. The calendrical aspect of the story of the wingless gosling is presented with uncommon clarity, for the story deals specifically with seasonal migrating waterfowl (compare also the arrival of ducks-grebes). Thus a direct examination of this series of mythological variants, which make up a kind of cycle, completely confirms the calendrical aspect of the story of Yiñea-ñeut's departure for the sky in certain Itel'men myths, and at the same time it clarifies a number of puzzling details in these myths. When the Koryak text (IK, 114) is compared to a number of Itel'men texts (II, 1, 32, 33, 14, 6), one gets the impression that the Koryak text has, as it were, collected significant features scattered throughout different Itel'men variants. This may possibly indicate that the original Koryak text is relatively archaic. To make this clear we cite a table of the principal correspondences and transformations (see Diagram 3 on pp. 181-82).

It is not hard to see that the first column deals with a heroine (in II, 6, a hero) who has been badly treated and abandoned by her father (IK, 114; II, 6) or her husband (II, 1, 8, 14, 32, 33; in II, 8, 33, she leaves him). The second column tells of the saving of the hero in heaven (IK, 114; II, 1, 32) if the hero is terrestrial, or on earth (I, 6) if he is "heavenly" (in II, 8, 33, it is the sea instead of the sky). The third column expresses the shortage of food in winter as the temporary absence, the disappearance of animals for the hunt. Here the calendrical aspect is expressed quite clearly. The fourth column reverses the situation in the first and solves it (reconciliation with father or husband), as it does with the second (reunification with kinfolk) and the third (calendrical return of game in the spring). The action develops on two levels — the family and the calendrical — and the sep-

Diagram 3

IK, 114	Yiñea-ñeut is mistreated by her father, abandoned for the winter alone without food and crippled	Makes herself a goose wing and flies off into the sky, where she marries a cloud-man	Takes animals with her into the sky, producing famine on earth	Is reconciled with her father, returns animals to earth. Ememqut marries a cloud-woman
II, 8, 33	Sinanewt and her sister are mistreated by their father	Make a wooden whale and sail into the sea to Kutq	Overseas they acquire animal meat and hides	Are reconciled with father and bring home meat and hides in the spring. Themselves appear in the skins of animals and marry hunters
II, 1, 32	Sinanewt is abandoned by her husband (the action takes place in the autumn)	Departs for the sky up a mountain with a female spider	Takes animals with her into sky, producing famine on earth	Is reconciled with her husband. He follows her into the sky, where there are animals to hunt

181

II, 14	Maroklnawt is abandoned by her husband without food. Killed, but resurrected by her son	Goose flies in. She marries Goose	Goose temporarily flies away for the winter	Goose returns in the spring and becomes an object of the hunt. Reconciliation with husband
II, 6	Gosling is abandoned by his parents in winter, without food or wings	Sinanewt feeds him and makes wings for him		Gosling's parents return. Their elder son marries Sinanewt

aration from parents or husband leads to oppositions of poles in the cosmos (earth and sky, land and sea) and calendrical disappearance of game, which also departs for another element of the cosmos, with the heroine or without her. Mediation of the poles leads to the return of the game and the reunification of kinfolk.

This analysis of the "raven" myths of the Koryaks and Kamchadals serves as an example of how plots which at first glance have little connection with each other may prove to be elements of a highly ordered system, thanks to the uncovering of their underlying structure. Study of the unique and highly archaic folklore of the Paleo-Asiatics of the Chukotka-Kamchatka group is of fundamental importance in developing the theory of the myth.

Key to Identification of Sources
(Paleo-Asiatic Texts)

Baboshina: O. E. Baboshina, Skazki Chukotki, Moscow, 1958.
Stebnitskii: S. N. Stebnitskii, Nymylanskie (koriakskie) skazki, Leningrad, 1938.
BK: W. Bogoras, Koryak Texts, Publications of the American Ethnological Society edited by Franz Boas, Vol. V, New York, 1917.
IK: W. Jochelson, The Koryak, Vol. 1, Religion and Myths, chapters VIII-XIV, Jesup North Pacific Expedition. Memoirs of the American Museum of Natural History, Vol. VI, Part 1, New York, 1905 (texts 1 to 30 are Koryak; 131-39 are Itel'men).
II: D. S. Worth, Kamchadal Texts Collected by W. Jochelson, S'Gravenhage, 1961.

Notes

1) On this, see E. M. Meletinskii, "Skazaniia o Vorone u narodov Krainego Severa. O drevnikh sviaziakh Azii i Ameriki," Vestnik istorii mirovoi kul'tury, 1959, No. 1.
2) See the end of the article for source abbreviation key.

Toward the Origin of Certain Poetic Symbols: The Paleolithic Period

V. N. TOPOROV

Titles like this one, for all their seeming simplicity, require clarification. Without it they lose, strictly speaking, the most important part of their meaning. The temptation of purely speculative solutions arises. And the worst of these is the one that, by virtue of its seeming naturalness, appears most plausible. Such, as a rule, turn out to be solutions arrived at by an external identification of some facts of archaic cultures with some facts of substantially later cultures taken in isolation, and by subsequent extrapolation of the conclusions thus obtained to areas having no obvious correspondences with each other in the present state of affairs.

In the present article (if we are to speak of the most necessary refinements and limitations) the term "poetic symbols" means those initial elements (linguistic, painting, plastic, ritual, etc.) that in the presence of the oppositions poetic (aesthetically marked) and nonpoetic (aesthetically unmarked) and symbolic (marked by signs) and nonsymbolic (unmarked by signs), even if the formation of these initial elements and named oppositions is separated in time, might have served as representatives of the first terms in these two oppositions. With this approach it is possible to avoid the principal danger threatening those interested in the question of the origin of poetic (in the broad

The Origin of Poetic Symbols

meaning of the term) forms, that is, the danger of speaking about art when it was not yet an independent sign system but only one of the variants of the level of expression for considerably broader concepts of universal character. Moreover, it would be a mistake to begin the history of art with that late epoch in which it becomes a self-sufficient whole. From this it follows that, when studying the earliest period in the development of art (or poetry), it would be appropriate to employ the very word "art" in a limited sense, bearing in mind that Paleolithic rock painting, sculptured figures, or ornaments are related to art to the same degree as an incantation, ritual act, funeral rite, the gathering of bone remains, or meditation. Therefore, with respect to the most ancient period it is more correct to speak of "markedness" than of "the poetic," "artistic," "aesthetic," and so forth.

The word "origin" (of poetic symbols) in the title of the article should be understood as <u>identification of a text</u> or <u>class of texts</u> (in the semiotic meaning of the word) in which there <u>might</u> have appeared elements later interpreted as poetic symbols and <u>identification of the place</u> (determined by formal means) <u>of these elements</u> in texts.

Consequently, the task resolves to reconstruction of texts and their internal structure, in particular links of which future poetic symbols could have appeared. It is important to emphasize that the texts being reconstructed do not absolutely have to be brought to verbal form, although there is no doubt that each of these texts could be translated into verbal form. In reconstruction it is sufficient to establish certain basic, semantic (in the supralinguistic meaning) units of text realizable both in linguistic and in nonlinguistic forms and the rules for combining them. A text regarded in this way should possess certain properties that appear independent of the level of expression. These include, first of all, a common semantic set and certain rules of organization of the text, which the user of the text is able to recognize from the given fragment. Reference is to <u>rhythm</u> or "correct" repetition of elements, which assumes the ability to achieve <u>identification of them</u> and knowledge of a number of

Semiotics and Structuralism

syntactic (distributive) structures. The reproduction of these structures and the repetition of elements under the conditions of the mythopoeic consciousness were meant both to bare and emphasize the very structure of its elements and, consequently, to affirm the discrete (as linked to culture), its triumph over the continuous (as a reflection of the chaotic principles of nature). Under these conditions repetition in texts could not but be correlated with repetition in rituals and in meditation, not to speak of repetition of events in nature. This correlation of texts with the mystery of the change and recurrence of natural cycles determined the sacralization of the texts themselves and the moment at which they were generated (similarly, at later stages of development, silence, the antithesis of external texts, became sacralized in a number of confessional traditions).

On the basis of what has been said, it is desirable to attempt to define all the "correct" sequences among a given number of elements. For example, it is not difficult to see that, given two elements "a" and "b" forming a four-term sequence, the following combinations are "marked": (1) aabb, (2) bbaa, (3) abba, (4) abab, (5) baab, and (6) baba. (1) Given two elements "A" and "B" forming a seven-term sequence, the following types of organization are "marked": (1) ABBBBBA, (2) AABABAA, (3) ABAAABA, (4) AABBBAA, (5) AAABAAA, (6) ABBABBA, (7) ABABABA, (8) BAAAAAB, (9) BBABABB, (10) BABBBAB, (11) BBAAABB, (12) BBBABBB, (13) BAABAAB, and (14) BABABAB. (2) Such sequences serve as an entirely suitable means for describing correlations of elements both in linguistic texts (at various levels: sound organization of the text, morphological forms, syntactic structures, semantic units, stylistic figures) and in pictorial texts ("mimetic" and "nonmimetic") (3), sculptural, musical, choreographic, in architecture, in ritual, and so forth. "Correctly" organized sequences are also reproduced on the content level. Therefore, for a whole series of traditions (as a rule, typologically archaic) the appearance of a "correct" sequence in any text always proves to be "marked" (unlike later traditions). For archaic cultures this property of "correct" sequences cannot be regarded as trivial, the more

The Origin of Poetic Symbols

so as it also extends to the extratextual realm (compare the sacralization of similar sequences or the number of elements in them in life, the seven stars of the Big Dipper, of any seven homogeneous objects, the seven-day cycle, etc.).

Nevertheless, an enumeration of the types of organization of textual elements used is absent in corresponding descriptions. Moreover, one usually does not find traces of understanding of the limitation and enumerability of the number of possible types of text organization with given elements and distributive structures. This misunderstanding has caused the lack of development of the language of description of such texts, and this in turn is the source of difficulty in identifying variants of one and the same type of organization and, consequently, in cataloging structures of a similar kind. (4)

This article will analyze certain features of the most archaic stage in the development of initial forms later serving as the basis for poetic symbolism — the Upper Paleolithic. The extremely limited nature of the material does not permit us to point out, with the desired completeness and reliability, all the "marked" elements characteristic of Paleolithic painting and sculpture. Nevertheless, some observations follow whose reliability significantly increases when one considers the data pertaining to the investigation of art and the verbal creation of one of the most integral and significant epochs in the development of mythological and cosmological conceptions and artistic images — the epoch of the "world tree." The second article in the series, devoted to the origin of poetic symbols, is associated specifically with this epoch. The results achieved in this second article, published elsewhere, retrospectively emphasize some of the observations in the present article. This must constantly be borne in mind.

Upper Paleolithic relics, comprising the first page in the history of art, embrace a period of about 20,000 years (apparently from 30,000 to 10,000 B.C.). (5) Despite the incompleteness of our knowledge, it is possible (albeit in general outline) to establish a chronological differentiation by periods, which is usually done in the best works on Paleolithic art and religion.

Semiotics and Structuralism

Identically, the territorial differentiation of Upper Paleolithic relics is also often noted, with the isolation of certain local features (compare, for example, Kühn, 1957). But if one is to speak of the most characteristic part of Paleolithic art from the standpoint of conceptions of the "world tree" period, it is useful to further distinguish rock (or wall) painting (l'art pariétal) from representations of objects of everyday life, sculptural figures, and the like (l'art mobilier). For our further purposes, differentiation between these two varieties of Paleolithic art and preferential attention to wall painting is significant insofar as topographic context is characteristic specifically of wall painting (compare Leroi-Gourhan, 1964, pp. 81-82). In other words, the siting of a depiction in a particular place and the position of one picture relative to another is relevant for it alone. This feature makes it possible to compensate for the shortage of direct means for establishing the chronology of styles (unlike l'art mobilier) by revealing additional links between depictions (their syntax), on the one hand, and between them and the reality lying outside art, on the other hand. A second, no less important, feature of Paleolithic art derives from the need to distinguish works of art in underground sanctuaries and those in the open air (les oeuvres de plain air), accessible to the viewer at all times (compare Laming-Emperaire, 1962, pp. 291 ff.). What is significant in this difference is the technical aspect (aside from the geographic): painting and engraving in underground sanctuaries, sculpture generally in the open air. Inasmuch as painting, even in the Paleolithic period, had a greater capacity for solutions than sculpture and was consequently a more powerful model of the general conceptions of Paleolithic man, it is the works of art in underground sanctuaries that are of primary interest. Scholars also note differences in themes and content between these two varieties of art: Signs (particularly the so-called tectiformes) are considerably more numerous in underground sanctuaries, as are representations of fantastic animals, beings of semianimal-semihuman character, and schematic depictions of people. On the other hand, in works in the open air, depictions predominate over signs, "realistic" treatment over schematic, depictions of well-known animals over fantastic

The Origin of Poetic Symbols

ones, and female images over masculine ones (ibid., p. 293).

By virtue of these features, the wall paintings of underground sanctuaries should be regarded as the most representative example of Paleolithic art. Sacralized (in any case, to a greater degree than the relics of l'art mobilier and those in the open air) and linked with rituals, the paintings of the underground sanctuaries at the same time possessed greater independence from the world of tangible denotata, greater freedom for modeling the general conceptions of Paleolithic man, greater pragmatism (focus on attainment of an objective, orientation toward the future, etc.), and greater explanatory force. In speaking of the origin of particular elements of art, it makes sense to direct attention primarily toward such sacralized forms of art in which the freedom of what is depicted is limited only by the confines of the general conceptions, within which the selectional possibilities of art are maximally free.

One of the most suggestive features of Paleolithic painting is the "openness" of depictions, which appears, naturally, not only in the lack of a frame as a formal device (6) but also in the inability of what is depicted to indicate the limits of the depiction, its center, top, bottom, direction of the action, and so forth. (7) This is the origin of instances in which given depictions were supplemented by others that could be put either in unoccupied space or on top of an existing depiction (the palimpsest technique). (8) The "openness" of Paleolithic works of art is directly associated with the absence or extremely weak expression of composition and, consequently, of internal connections between the depicted objects and, to an even greater degree, of the hierarchy of these connections. In principle each image is separate (see qualifying remarks on this subject below). Multifigure compositions are quite rare, and apparently there are no grounds for insisting that any connection existed within them other than the "additive." Exceptions are either minimal in number (see the picture of a herd on the stone from Limeuil [9] or of deer in the bone-carving from Lorthet) or are themselves illusory. In any case, one is struck by the fact that depictions with the rudiments of composition (for example, diminishing

Semiotics and Structuralism

in accordance with perspective) are related to l'art mobilier or works in the open air. The presence of the "additive" link is most clearly traceable in cases of the appearance of the so-called "third animal" on the periphery of the picture. Thus figures of the mountain sheep (Niaux, Ebbou) or mammoth (Font-de-Gaume, Les Combarelles, Rouffignac) or reindeer (Lascaux, Pindal) or fallow deer (Altamira) are usually associated with those of the horse and bison. Less often one notes the appearance of a "fourth" and "fifth" animal at the edges of the composition. Of particular interest are instances, to be seen at Les Combarelles or Gabillou, where each twist in the cave or narrowing between the underground chambers is accompanied by the appearance of an animal new in comparison with the basic composition (see Leroi-Gourhan, 1964, pp. 109 ff.). It is not out of the question that numerous folkloric texts in which animals take part (such as "The Little Tower" [Teremok]), based on sequential addition of a successive animal to the existing set (the total number of animals in such a set is usually between six and ten, most often six or seven), are associated with these pictorial texts or with their sequences. It is quite probable that the same group of verbal texts includes such incantations built on sequential addition or removal of objects as: "Black raven, do you have many worms? — Nine, and of nine there are eight, and of eight there are seven, and of seven there are six, and of six there are five, and of five there are four, and of four there are three, and of three there are two, and of two there is one, and of one there is none" (Romanov, 1891, p. 58; Ivanov and Toporov, 1965, p. 87; Toporov, 1969). Later, in connection with examples from the period of the "world tree," a few words will be said about numerical constants, particularly the number seven. But it is characteristic that even in the preceding era (both in the Neolithic and in the Paleolithic) this number could already acquire particular meaning in magic operations. Compare the picture of the horse with seven arrows at Lascaux (see Laming, 1962, p. 56 and Fig. 10); in the same place there are depictions of felines, one of which has been pierced by seven arrows (see Laming-Emperaire, 1962,

The Origin of Poetic Symbols

p. 248 and Plate XIV); seven mammoths in Kapovaia Cave in the Urals (see Bader, 1962, 1965; compare also Garutt, 1960); seven lines on an incised fragment from the Gvardjilas-Klde Cave in the Caucasus (arrowhead with ornamentation) (see Abramova, 1962, Plate XLII, p. 9); the necklace of shells and animal teeth from Kostienki, where every seventh element on the string is a tooth (ibid., Plate XXI, p. 5) (10), etc. An "additive" connection of the $(A + A) + (B + B) + (C + C) + \ldots$ type can be seen in one of the most archaic incantatory texts, which, by a number of indications, dates to the Stone Age. (11) Compare: "May body and body, bone and bone, sinew and sinew knit, grow together...." (Maikov, 1869, No. 168), the Lettish: "griežās miesa pie miesas, spiežās kauls pie kaula, griežās veselība pie veselības..." (Treiland, 1881, No. 235), the Old High German: "ben zi bena, bluotzi bluoda, lid zi geliden, sose gelimida sin" (second Merzeburg incantation), and the Old Hindi: "sam te majjā, majjñā bhavatu smu te parusā paruh... carmanā carma... māmsam māmsena..." (Atharvaveda, IV, 12, 3-5), etc. (for fuller detail, see Toporov, 1969). It is curious that here, too, if we disregard obviously corrupt cases, seven is the limit for the number of elements in a set. Compare: "Body to body, flesh to flesh, sinew to sinew, bone to bone... joint to joint, heart to heart, liver to liver" (Vinogradov, 1908, No. 30; compare the seven elements in the partially quoted formula above from the Atharvaveda, etc.). Approximately the same picture is repeated in incantations whose purpose is to drive out disease, to draw it out from parts of the body. To these incantations correspond two types of formulas: $(A \rightarrow B) + (B \rightarrow C) + (C \rightarrow D) + \ldots$ and $A + B + C + \ldots$. An example of the first type is the German "Ich bitte dich aus Gottes Kraft, dass du hinausgehst aus dem Mark ins Bein, aus dem Bein ins Fleisch, aus dem Fleisch in die Haut, aus der Haut ins Haar, aus dem Haar in den wilden Wald..." (Eis, 1964, p. 12). An example of the second type is the Belorussian "z zhil s pazhil... s kos'tsei, z mozhchei, s pal'chikov, s sustavchikov, z nokhtsikov" (Romanov, 1891, No. 96; seven terms!).

On the basis of the foregoing it is logical to suppose that the

Semiotics and Structuralism

"additive" connection is the only method of organization of Paleolithic texts (pictorial and verbal) that can be more or less dependably reconstructed. (12) This does not conflict with very rare instances of more subtle organization of the text, resting on more complex types of rhythmical repetitiveness, with the use of symmetrical repetitions. Such is the depiction of the bull and horse (Lascaux), tail to tail, forming a symmetrical figure and looking at signs in the shape of tridents placed symmetrically along the edges (see Laming-Empiraire, 1962, Fig. 36) (see Fig. 1). Therefore, the hypothesis may be offered that the abil-

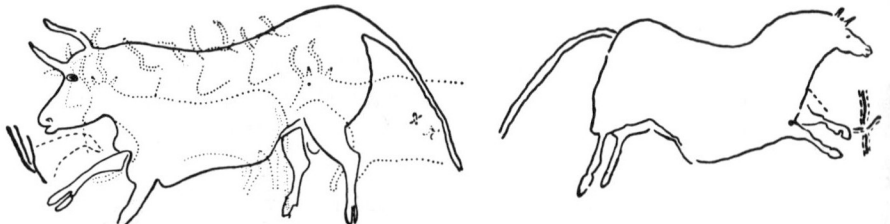

Figure 1

ity to transmit the "additive connection" was the highest formal achievement of the Upper Paleolithic period (in any case, during the Magdalenian), although this ability was still highly relative and, naturally, did not become a stereotype readily transmittable in time and space. So significant a limitation on the level of expression made impossible (at least, in representational art) the transmission of plot. Certain facts indicating the relation of Paleolithic man to wall painting also make one think that the most ancient examples of representational art did not even pursue the object of transmitting a plot. (13) It is more likely that in them certain stereotypes were merely prepared that pointed to some set of objects and the relationships between them, which might later be molded into a plot. The general notions of the subsequent epoch served as a kind of magnetic field in which the poetic drafts of the Stone Age took their special place in the total picture and finally attained their real meaning. (14) This circumstance should not, however, discourage the researcher seek-

The Origin of Poetic Symbols

Figure 2

ing sources for various kinds of mythopoeic images. Comparison of the use of the image of a horn in incantations and rituals aimed at restoring child-bearing capacities and — more broadly — at increasing fertility with such images as a woman with hypertrophied shapes, holding a horn in the right hand, from Laussel (the picture retains traces of red coloring) (15) (see Fig. 3), is quite promising. If we bear in mind that the figure of a man who is apparently throwing an arrow (see arrow in the corresponding incantations and in the deep tradition of various peoples, for example, the arrows of love) and the representation of a scene some interpret as childbirth and others as coitus (16) are also present there, then the general context confirms even more strongly the hypothesis that we are at the sources of the poetic image of the horn of plenty that is so widespread later on. Here it turns out that texts such as the images from Laussel or ritual-incantational formulas reflect a considerably more primitive stage of development of this image than does the symbolism that has come down to us in ancient myths and fine art.

Proceeding to a characterization of the content level of Paleolithic relics, we must note above all the nonhomogeneity of pic-

Semiotics and Structuralism

Figure 3

torial space with respect to the objects depicted within the confines of one and the same sanctuary. This is exceptionally important on the most general level, inasmuch as it is precisely the mythopoeic consciousness (not to speak of certain modern scientific theories and artistic conceptions) that typifies such an understanding of space and time. The nonhomogeneity of pictorial space in Paleolithic sanctuaries appears in the presence of seven different zones that are defined both by the contours of the cave itself and by the choice of various depictions in given zones. As was established by Leroi-Gourhan (17) on the basis of analysis of 63 grottoes, the following zones or situations must be distinguished: I — the entry (first appearance of figures); II — turns, passages, constrictions between underground chambers; III — entry into corners of the alcove type and the like; IV — the last (final) place where figures appear; V — the central part of the wall in the chambers or at widenings; VI — the periphery of the central part of the wall; and VII — space within corners of the alcove type. It turns out that signs of the male type (elongated objects: sticks, "herringbones," points along a straight line, etc.) are distributed so that 60 percent fall into zones I, II, III, IV, and VI, and 31 percent in zones V and VII.

The Origin of Poetic Symbols

Even more striking is the distribution of signs of the female type (oval forms, rectangles, "little houses," etc.): only 9 percent of these signs are found in the same zones I, II, III, IV, and VI; 91 percent of them are in zones V and VII. Consequently, the distribution of male and female signs gravitates toward mutual complementarity. Another important feature of the distribution lies in the fact that the female signs are distributed chiefly in the most sacralized parts of the sanctuary (the central wall of a chamber, an alcove), while the male signs gravitate rather to the less sacralized transitional parts of the cave. The data pertaining to the distribution of the depictions (animal and human) are equally interesting: 100 percent of the female figures, 96 percent of the depictions of the aurochs, 94 percent of the pictures of bisons, and 88 percent of the horses are in zone V, while the overwhelming majority of pictures of other animals and of male figures fall in zones I, II, III, and VI (deer — 88 percent, ibex — 86 percent, bear — 82 percent, fallow deer — 79 percent, reindeer — 72 percent, mammoth — 70 percent, male human — 76 percent, and so forth). From these counts follow the statistical regularities of the combinability of one of the two types of signs with particular kinds of animals within the bounds of a given zone (see Fig. 4)

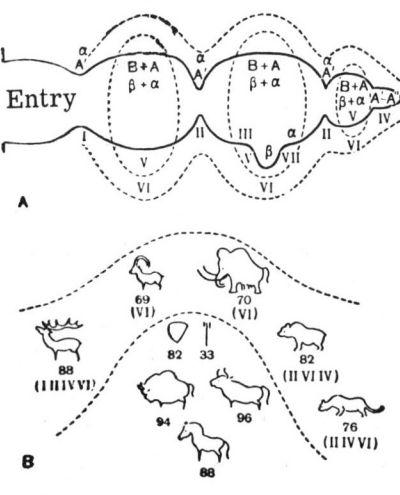

Figure 4

Semiotics and Structuralism

Thus the impression is created that in Paleolithic relics the organizing principle (associated with composition) is concentrated not so much within the bounds of the given individual depiction as in the totality of images following one after the other and, accordingly, the topographic zones. In other words, if we confine ourselves to an individual depiction ("picture"), as is usually done in the analysis of European painting, the composition is, so to speak, "factored out" of this depiction, lies outside it, similar to such a factoring out of plot (see above). The task of subsequent periods in the development of representational art consisted, in part, of bringing composition and plot in from the nonsemiotic realm, of putting them within brackets, within the pictorial space, the semiotic realm of art, and then, after the empirical reality has been interiorized in the work of art, of finding means for constructing new devices, not derived necessarily from empirical reality, for compositional and plot development. With the help of these devices the "intensification" effect in art is achieved.

The things depicted in Paleolithic painting are well known: there exist corresponding indices to (compare Laming-Emperaire, 1962, pp. 403 ff.; Leroi-Gourhan, 1965), and statistical data on, objects depicted. (18) The question of the meaning of these images and of ways to assure the establishment of their meanings is more complicated. A number of complexities are explained if one turns one's attention to the fact that more than half of all the depictions in the Upper Paleolithic monuments fall into three classes of objects — the horse, the bison, and signs. There are weighty reasons to assume that the signs represent male and female symbols (see Fig. 5). (19) Confirmation of this can be found specifically in the evolution of Upper Paleolithic styles, starting in Aurignacian times, when abstractly rendered (and by no means always identifiable) figures of animals were accompanied by entirely naturalistic depictions of genitalia, up to Middle and Late Magdalenian times, characterized by naturalistic depictions of animals and entirely stylized signs (not always recognizable without retrospective historical examination).

The Origin of Poetic Symbols

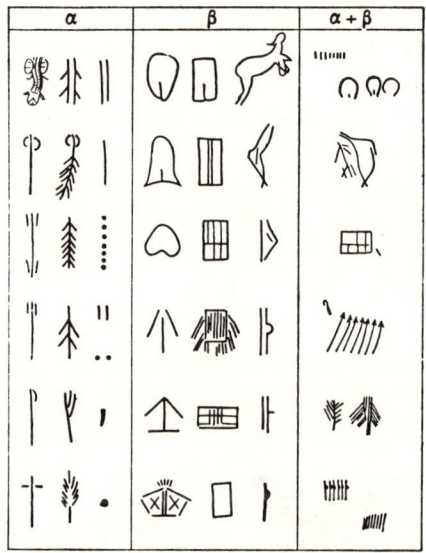

Figure 5

With this approach the signs prove to be something analogous to semantic multipliers. A significant argument in favor of this hypothesis could be those forms of notation that are characteristic of Paleolithic pictures. In this connection, particularly characteristic are cases of paired combination of male and female signs ($\alpha + \beta$), which are very widely represented in the monuments; cases of combinations of the same signs in depicting pairs of animals of opposite sex (for example, bison and horse), while the animals, as is often found in Paleolithic relics (see Leroi-Gourhan, 1964, p. 94), are depicted deprived of sex characteristics; cases of combinations of representations of female animals with male signs (α) and male animals along with female signs (β); cases of representation of a male and a female individual. If we denote a male animal as M and a female as F, we obtain: (1) $\alpha + \beta$; (2) ($\alpha + \beta$) (M + F); (3) α + F, β + M; (4) M + F (see Fig. 6). Consequently, the signs are elements of the formal notation of Paleolithic images. This notation can appear both in the pure form ($\alpha + \beta$) and in a mixed one (with drawings).

In the latter case, particularly when animals are depicted without sex characteristics, the sign notation is equivalent to factoring out the semantic multipliers (the sex of the animal) (an operation that has been noted more than once above in connection with analysis of Paleolithic art). If what has been said about the semantic of signs is true, then the placement of the combinations $\alpha + \beta$ precisely in zone V indicates that this formula is used to describe the principal theme of the Paleolithic monuments, the conceptual nucleus of the world-view of men of the Old Stone Age. Through signs identification and differentiation between objects took place (20), i.e., certain rules were offered for the reading of the meaning of the text, which entered, in transformed form, into the hieroglyphic systems of a later period.

Figure 6

In the study of the semantics of Paleolithic images, one's attention is drawn by yet another feature, which is quite significant both from the standpoint of the internal characteristics of the world of Paleolithic man and from the standpoint of the origin of the most ancient mythopoeic symbols. We refer to the predominance (in all variants of Paleolithic representational art) of animal over human depictions (on this see Saccasyn-della Santa, 1947), female pictures and figurines over male (21), and (if we speak of a later period when opportunities for interpretation become relatively greater) depictions of aliens (22) over one's own. For the Upper Paleolithic these oppositions could, apparently, be reconstructed even on the basis of statistical

The Origin of Poetic Symbols

data. The relationships between elements of these oppositions determined themes that later formed themselves into plots (compare Stoliar, 1964, pp. 8 ff.) and the structure of oppositions of later date related to them.

It is interesting that for Paleolithic art we can reliably reconstruct a tendency to avoid depictions of those members of an opposition later definitely qualified as positive, i.e., as <u>human</u> rather than animal, <u>male</u> rather than female, <u>one's own</u> rather than alien. This tendency, apparently, can be correlated (at least for certain periods in the development of Paleolithic art) with a more general tendency to prefer schematic depiction (including here the <u>torso</u>, the outline [23], the absence of modeling of the face [24], and so forth) to the so-called realistic. The presence in Paleolithic sites of a large number of hybrid human-animal figurines and depictions (with precisely the head usually being animal; human figures in masks and femal figurines with tails fall into the same category)(<u>25</u>) would also, evidently, be linked to a system of emerging general semantic oppositions and to the relationship between their terms and the principles of taboo. (<u>26</u>)

Special interest attaches to clarification of the question of semantic interpretation of the colors red and black in Paleolithic relics. Unfortunately, it seems difficult thus far to speak of any regularities in the distribution of colors in the pictures: as early as at La Ferrassie there appear red-black animal figures (compare the large red horse with black head, tail, and legs from Lascaux or the multicolored bison from Altamira). Further, along with the very frequent red-colored pictures of animals, we know of black depictions of bulls at Font-de-Gaume and Lascaux. The connection of the color red with blood, life, breathing (<u>27</u>), postulated on the basis of a few not very reliable examples (compare the red line coming from the nose and the mouth in the Cavillon burial in Grimaldi), requires further substantiation. Basic here would be establishing the semantics of the color black. It is not out of the question that the key to the solution should be sought in compositions similar to that found in the Great Hall of the Bulls at Lascaux, where, apparently, one can speak of at least an approximate distribution of colors —

Semiotics and Structuralism

black bulls and a large red horse. (28) Particularly profitable here could be analysis of such depictions as those discovered at El Castillo (Santander), where female signs are done in red and the associated male sign (in the form of a whisk or beard or, more precisely, a tree) is in black (see Leroi-Gourhan, 1965, pp. 101 ff., Fig. 63). Whatever the case may be, it is difficult to rid oneself of the thought that in Upper Paleolithic art there were no attempts at semanticization of the oppositions of the colors red and black. (29)

Figure 7

Finally, there is one more question associated with the possibility of semantic differentiation of Paleolithic pictures. Above we spoke of the opposition of the male principle to the female in connection with depictions of animals. In such cases reference is always to hooved animals, which make up about two-thirds of all depictions in Paleolithic monuments. However, two groups of depictions exist in which this opposition is not expressed at all: birds (about 3 percent of all the pictures) and amphibians (snakes, fish [30], also totaling about 3 percent of the pictures). If we do not consider depictions of the bear and members of the feline family (totaling up to 5 percent of all pictures in the Franco-Cantabrian Paleolithic region) or the extremely rare and frequently dubious depictions of the wolf, hyena,

The Origin of Poetic Symbols

seal, and the like, then it turns out that precisely birds and fish-snakes could be opposed to the basic mass of pictures — hooved animals. In the light of the further development of art, the presence of these three groups, later correlated with the three cosmic zones, is quite curious, although it remains far from clear in what way the differences between these three groups of animals were semanticized in the Paleolithic (we are not discussing the semantics of natural language). The lack of clarity can be explained by the paucity of depictions or figurines of birds and fishes or snakes, and a number of examples yield with difficulty to any reliable interpretation (for example, the scene with the bird and man with the head of a bird in Lascaux; see Fig. 7). (31) Nevertheless, some features, particularly in the depiction of birds, may prove to be symptomatic in the highest degree. One's attention is drawn by the fact that birds are usually depicted in connection with some elongated object on which they are situated. Compare the bird from Lascaux perched on a long stick (or pole); the fragment of a bird on a fragment of a spear-thrower from Le Mas d'Azil (see Vayson de Pradenne, 1934, pp. 3 ff.); the head and long neck of a bird on a rod found in Laugerie Basse (Magdalenian) (ibid., Fig. 8); the depiction of birds on tusks, etc. (perhaps the renditions of wading birds from the cave of Labastide fall into the same category: see Simonnet, 1947, pp. 55 ff). It seems that the materials from the Paleolithic sites in Eastern Europe (Kostienki, Mezin) and in Siberia (Mal'ta and Buret') display greater interest in themes associated with birds (32) and, perhaps, indicate a more advanced semantic interpretation of these images than in Western Europe. (33) It is indicative that in the Neolithic the number of bird figurines and pictures rises sharply (34), and entire corteges of birds or symmetrical "bird" compositions appear. (35) From the semantic point of view it is significant that birds are most often depicted with long necks and often in combination with solar symbols above them.

As far as the depictions of snakes are concerned, they are virtually absent from the rock paintings of the Western European Paleolithic sites (36) (true, there are a number of cases in which wavy lines can be interpreted as schematic depictions of snakes).

However, relics of l'art mobilier contain a certain number of depictions of serpents. In general form it can probably be asserted that these images are usually arranged parallel to the longer (broader) edge of the object (a characteristic example is the pictures of three snakes on a trapezoidal slab from Mal'ta; see Abramova, 1962, Plate L, 2 and L 1, 2), and this edge most often presumes its horizontal position. Frequently such a position is emphasized by the parallel location of two or several snakes. (37) At the same time, one must also not forget such images as those that decorate the staff from Montgaudier (two snakes stretching along the staff [38], while the normal position of the staff was, naturally, vertical). It is possible that the depiction of the serpent on the staff is not merely the result of adaptation to the shape of the object. In any case, in a later epoch the link between snake and staff and their consequent vertical position find a convincing explanation: the staff or its variant — a thyrsus, crowned by a knob and garlanded with ivy — is equivalent to the world tree or a variant of it; a female snake (or male one) could also serve as a variant of the world tree, at least in a number of traditions (39) (compare the staff with orblike head from the Kostienki I site, top layer, in which some see a conventional depiction of a human figure — see Efimenko, 1958, p. 301, Fig. 111.1; Abramova, 1962, p. 15, Plate XI, 1). Thus mythological conceptions of a later time explain well the connection between the snake and the world tree, and therefore its vertical position. (40)

Figure 8

Another analogy with mythological and cosmological conceptions suggests itself upon comparison of the depiction of snakes on a staff with the depiction of a bird on a staff, already mentioned, from the Magdalenian layer in Laugerie Basse: we are

The Origin of Poetic Symbols

dealing with a motif of a tree with a bird on it and a snake under it, which is extraordinarily widely distributed both in fine art and in corresponding verbal texts (compare the ancient cultures of Asia Minor, Iran, India, Southeast Asia, the shamanistic traditions of Eurasia, and so forth). Evidence of the presence of connections between the images of a bird and a snake in Upper Paleolithic depictions and the semantic oppositions hidden behind these connections can be seen not only in the approximately identical statistical distribution of the pictures of these two classes of animals in Paleolithic monuments but also in the sharp rise in such depictions in the Neolithic and in an even later period. (41) Depictions of the fish in the Paleolithic monuments of Western Europe are, in a certain sense, similar to snake images (horizontal orientation, sometimes pictures of snakes and fish are linked with each other; compare La Madeleine, Magdalenian layer III-IV). It is possible that, on the basis of the well-known depiction of a fish at Gorge d'Enfer (Dordogne), the conclusion can be drawn that there was an effort to place such images at the bottom, for above the fish there is an unclear picture in which some see the head of a bird (compare above about snakes and birds) and others the head of a rhinoceros (42) (see Fig. 8). However, thus far such observations can be neither checked nor confirmed.

* * *

In conclusion a few comments on the way in which some of the elements of Paleolithic art we have traced fall into a general picture described in a broad class of texts devoted to the world tree.

The world (or cosmic) tree is an image of a certain universal conception that defined, for a long time, the model of the world of human societies in the Old and New Worlds. At the same time, it is the leading (and in some traditions the only) theme of art right up to the beginning of the Buddhist and Christian stages in the development of art. (43) In a number of cases the world tree continues even today to be the principal theme in

Semiotics and Structuralism

some cultural traditions (compare certain peoples of Siberia). Moreover, Christian art until the Renaissance, like Buddhist art in the first centuries of its existence, also clearly reveals a successive continuity with the art of the epoch of the "world tree." The art of ancient Egypt, Asia Minor, Iran, India, China, Southeast Asia, the old cultures of the New World, and the like can be regarded as creolized, having arisen at the transition from the epoch of the "world tree" to the era of anthropomorphic art (in the broad sense, not presuming invariable depiction of man).

The fate of Paleolithic "drafts" in the art of the epoch of the "world tree" can be briefly described as follows. Unclear relationships between depictions of hooved animals, birds, and snakes-fish become transformed into a precise, three-term, vertically projected system: birds — hooved animals — snakes-fish (more broadly, the class of chthonic animals), in which the birds are associated with the top of the composition, the sky, the hooved animals with its middle portion, with the earth, and snakes-fish with the bottom, with the subterranean realm. These associations were so stable that peripheral elements of the vertical structure became symbols of the sky (birds) and of the subterranean realm (snakes-fish), retaining their significance independently of the position of their depiction in pictorial space. (44) The world tree or its alloelements (mountain, temple, pillar, anthropomorphic being, etc.) became means for expressing the idea of vertical structure. (45) Therefore, birds, in both verbal texts and representational art, are usually localized in the branches of a tree; snakes, at its roots; and hooved animals, on both sides of its trunk. The trinitarian division of the world tree along the vertical corresponds ideally to the idea of dynamic integrity and, by virtue of this, can be regarded as a model for any dynamic process presuming appearance, development, and decline. In the corresponding texts these three parts of the world tree were semanticized in such a way that the upper portion was related to the positively marked feature and the lower to the negatively marked feature. The further refinement of the semantics was based on examination of the parts of the tree in

The Origin of Poetic Symbols

connection with spatial, temporal, ethical, etiological, and similar structures.

The timid attempts of Paelolithic painting to organize space along the horizontal axis (processions of animals, some instances of symmetry, alternation of signs and pictures, etc.) culminated in the art of the epoch of the "world tree" in the creation of a multipositional horizontal composition. Its most important feature was the singling out of the central position occupied by the world tree, the two adjacent positions — one to the right and the other to the left — usually being occupied by depictions of hooved animals or human beings. In principle, however, the horizontal composition was open, as shown by, for example, archaic friezes in Mesopotamia or India. The semantics of the central element in the horizontal composition was determined by the opposition to two adjacent elements: the object of worship (the goal of ritual activity) and the participants in the ritual. While by means of the vertical axis pictorial space acquired the potential to discriminate between top, center, and bottom, by means of the horizontal axis the left side, middle, and right side were distinguished. (46) In addition to the indicated semantics of these three parts and with the introduction of the idea of motion along the horizontal, the right side was counterposed to the left as the positive to the negative. It is characteristic that of the nonmimetic elements, the semantics of the positive and negative, along both the vertical and the horizontal, was often expressed by the opposition between the colors red (less often — white) and black, which was also used in Paleolithic painting, although in it their semantics (see above) was less clear or, in any case, difficult to reconstruct. Compare, for example, the device, commonly used in shamanistic drawings in Siberia, of coloring the upper and right-hand part of the "picture" in red and the lower and left-hand part in black. With the introduction of the idea of circular motion, the composition of the world tree acquired yet another dimension — depth. The most suggestive examples of this kind are associated with verbal and, sometimes, with pictorial texts (compare the corresponding pre-Columbian monuments, describing the organization of the horizontal plane, in

Semiotics and Structuralism

the center of which one finds the world tree, pointing out the four corners of the world, directions, winds, seasons of the year, the elements. Compare also gods in groups of four or gods in four hypostases, etc.). Unlike three, four forms a <u>static</u> whole and ideally stable structure (see Edinger, 1964, pp. 16 ff.; Jung, 1948; and others). It is characteristic that symmetrical relationships are realized (both in the art of the "world tree" era and in other periods of the development of art) along a horizontal axis or in the horizontal plane but not along the vertical. Compare the difference between meditations of the symmetrical type, based on periodic repetition of elements, and meditations built on the principle of gradual ascent or descent, which can be done through a series of antithetical pairs of elements. Moreover, the greater part of typologically archaic texts was built on these principles, which are used even today but for different purposes.

Thus the representational space in the art and mythology of the "world tree" epoch was organized in the form of the following two figures:

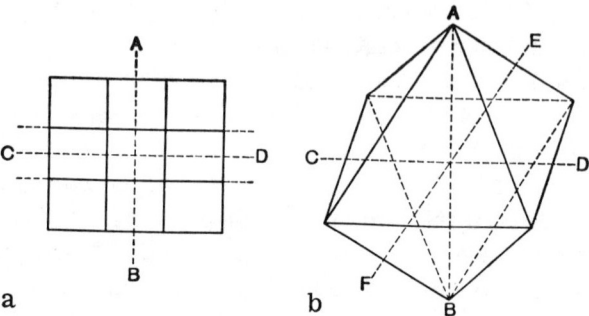

From diagram <u>b</u> derived the existence of the <u>seven</u> principal coordinates of the world tree and the cosmological space it symbolizes: (1) top, (2) center, (3) bottom, (4) north, (5) east, (6) south, and (7) west, (compare the precisely identical coordinates of the universe in a number of historical-cultural traditions, for example, that of the Zuñi Indians). The number <u>seven</u> returns us to what was said about it in connection with

The Origin of Poetic Symbols

Paleolithic art. This numerical constant, which is not entirely evident for the most ancient epoch, became in the art and the mythology of the "world tree" epoch one of its most vivid and frequently repeated characteristics (compare the very frequent filling of the seven positions along the CD axis in diagram a or the existence of seven branches of the world tree — correspondingly, seven heavens, hence seven levels of the subterranean realm, etc.).

From these brief considerations alone it is possible to conclude that the basic difference between the "art" of the Paleolithic epoch and the art of the era of the "world tree" lay in the following. If in Paleolithic painting the lack of organization within each individual picture (or very weak organization; this applies to both the syntactic and the semantic levels) was compensated by the organization of the given totality of pictures, determined by the structure of the underground sanctuary (seven zones), then in the art of the "world tree" era organization from without is introduced into representational space (this applies both to syntax and to semantics). It takes on the features of an ideally organized system that models both the static and the dynamic aspects of existence, while the elements outside lose all traces of organization and are surrendered to the power of chaos. Numerous pieces of evidence support what has been presented: the elevation of the world tree (or an image of it, the shamanic tree) signifies the establishment of all conceivable connections between the parts of the universe and the cessation of the state of chaos.

Above we spoke of the fact that in Paleolithic art the plot was, so to speak, factored out of representational space and was external to the monument. Identically, the ritual aspect of the paintings in the underground sanctuaries did not, strictly speaking, enter into the depiction itself. In the art of the "world tree" era, plot was introduced into the depiction; and the art of this epoch thus acquired a more autonomous character. The introduction of plot into the picture became possible thanks to the organization of representational space, which determined, as it were, the "grammar" of this space and distributed the weight among its various parts. When objects were introduced into space organized in this way, they more or less automatically acquired certain predicates, names of actions or operations (which could be reduced to attributes), constituting the basis for the appearance of plot. It is no accident, therefore, that the "world tree" era knows essentially but a single common plot: the ultimately successful struggle of the positive, light principle — the principle associated with heaven — against the negative, dark principle — associated with the nether regions (usually a snake or dragon). All other motifs (47), sometimes forming secondary plots, enter as component parts into this common, universal motif. A ritual aspect was also introduced into depiction in the art of the "world tree" era.

It is necessary, however, to observe that ritual motifs usually fill the periphery of representational space, which is compositionally and by content readily identifiable and separable from what is placed in the center. Strictly speaking, this peripheral portion and the depictions located in it are correlated with the center in a manner quite different from the way in which the pictures of the central portion are correlated with each other. The latter reveal incomparably closer ties — formal, compositional, and in content (up to plot), presupposing a network of interdependences and, consequently, a definite semantics of the whole and its parts. Therefore, the function of the periphery in schemas of this type lies in combining two levels: the purely depictive (autonomous) and the ritual-evaluative, lying outside the depiction itself. In this sense the periphery forms a transition between what forms the essence of the picture (a certain totality of objects ordered in accordance with a known conception) and the user of this depiction, the one for whom what is depicted has a pragmatic function (worship of sacrally marked objects). Thereby the periphery contains references to what lies outside the depiction and what is only conventionally duplicated on the periphery of representational space. In this sense schemas of this kind find typological parallels both in Paleolithic monuments, in which the meaning was re-created not only by the pictures themselves but by their sequence and the corre-

The Origin of Poetic Symbols

sponding topographical zones, and in many specimens of a later time. Compare the introduction of self-portraiture: timidly by Van Eyck in the portrait of the Arnolfini couple, somewhat more forthrightly in Botticelli's paintings (see <u>Adoration of the Magi</u> or <u>The Punishment of Korah</u>), and with unusual fullness and boldness in Velasquez's <u>Las Meninas</u> (moreover, while in the case of Van Eyck the artist's picture is given in a small mirror and requires his explanatory inscription: "I was here," in <u>Las Meninas</u> a hazy depiction of the royal pair has migrated into the mirror, and the picture of the artist becomes one of the central elements). In the final analysis, the practice of art in the first half of the twentieth century (a hybridization of forms of art like "sculpture-painting," some experiments of Cubist painting and of artists of a school like MERZism, which incorporates concrete indicators of an extra-artistic world) reflects, in a whole series of instances, similar strivings. If one were to speak of the chronological bounds of destruction of composition still revealing clear features of connection with the world tree pattern, then one would have first to name Giotto, with his pronounced effort to destroy the picture as a supplicatory image, presupposing a link with the viewer-adept (i.e., to eliminate the opposition <u>adept</u> — <u>object of worship</u>) at the expense of profile orientation of the persons depicted and of incorporating them into a network of internal links (often of a dialogic nature). (48) The adept (or adepts) is included in the core of the depiction, and the picture acquires an independent, autonomous plot, as a consequence of which the ritual significance of the depiction is minimized: it changes its semiotic topos.

It is quite revealing that to both of these parts of the world tree schema (the center and periphery) correspond verbal texts that make up an entire class of them. Here we are dealing not just with texts of a pronouncedly mythopoeic character, which we have discussed elsewhere and which are of particular value precisely by virtue of the fact that the system of images they contain is comparable to the images of representational art and, consequently, provides grounds for posing the question of the origin of the entire set of poetic symbols. There exist what

Semiotics and Structuralism

might be called "substitutional" texts that are secondarily correlatable with the world tree schema. It suffices to cite a few examples. Compare, first, the subject of the Etruscan mural of the Sarcophagus of the Bulls (sixth century B.C.), which originates quite directly from the composition of the world tree but which is also connected to a motif from the ancient Greek epic: Achilles warning Troilus. Compare, secondly, an early specimen of Roman art, the depiction of God setting the moon in the sky (with the world tree alongside), from Saint-Savin (about 1100 A.D.), which may be correlated with the Christian version of a Biblical motif. Compare, thirdly, one of the early incarnations of the image of St. Francis as depicted by Bonaventura Berlingueri (St. Francis Preaching to the Birds, Pescia, 1235), which may be correlated both with the "Cantico di frate sole o delle creature" (Altissimu, onnipotente, bon Signore...) by St. Francis himself, reflecting the schema of the world tree, and with motifs from "Fioretti" (in this sense the image of the saint as portrayed by Berlingueri, as well as in Giotto's St. Francis Gives Away His Cloak, proves to be equivalent to the image of the world tree, the only component of the model not named in the "Cantico"). Compare, finally, the depiction of the tree of love at the beginning of the thirteenth-century Provençal "Breviari d'amor," by Matfre Ermengaut, in connection with the text of the poem itself. Despite all this, one must remember that the very schema presumes a set of fundamental semantic oppositions that, in their remote sources, were rooted in Paleolithic depictions (see above), but — unlike in a somewhat later period — had not yet fully crystallized.

Yet another highly significant difference between the conceptions of the two eras under examination lies in the fact that in the art of the "world tree" epoch, the identifying signs of Paleolithic painting proved to be either excluded (partially, becoming an ornament, usually associated with the frame, or completely excluded) or, on the other hand, sublimated to the level of images provided with predicates and introduced into the circle of "personages." There are reasons (formal, distributive, and conceptual) to suppose that the Upper Paleolithic female and male

The Origin of Poetic Symbols

signs could have provided the origins of, respectively, the lunar and solar signs so widely represented in Neolithic painting and, later, also in the depictions of moon and sun in the art of the "world tree" era. (49) The universally known theme of the marital relations between the moon (usually a man) and the sun (usually a woman) permits us to think that it may be correlated with the same semantics embodied in combinations of signs α and β in Paleolithic monuments (may one not hypothetically associate Dawn in the plot of the Moon and Sun with the theme of the "third" animal in Late-Stone-Age painting?). At the same time, the story of the moon and sun is in many respects reminiscent of parables, common in archaic traditions, which reflect the rules of marital relations with regard for the existing matrimonial classes, and, if one were to go somewhat further, the schemas of generation of elements of the universe — be they divine personages or material components of the universe (50) in early historical traditions. If our speculations with respect to the fate of Paleolithic signs are correct, it is possible to pose the question of the point at which painting and pictography split. (51)

The list of transformations of "marked" elements of the Paleolithic epoch in later times would, naturally, not be difficult to extend. But here it is more important to emphasize common factors: both in the Paleolithic and in any of the subsequent periods, man possessed the capacity to translate his environment into symbols and to build from them a world of symbols parallel to the material world. The principles and purposes of the construction of this world of symbols can explain much concerning the problem of the origin of poetic forms and can place it in an appropriate context.

Notes

1) Compare also the "monotone" sequences aaaa and bbbb.

2) Seven-term sequences are particularly characteristic of a number of archaic traditions that have left their mark on considerably later cultures as well. These seven-term sets are known both in paradigmatics (the seven musical tones, the seven

colors of the spectrum, the seven levels along the vertical; compare the maximum number of stories in Mesopotamian ziggurats or the seven-story structure of the celestial world, the seven elements of the Pantheon, the seven branches of the world tree, the seven coordinates of the Universe, and derived from it, seven as the expression of the idea of the Universe, the seven categories of grammatical semantics, etc.) and in syntagmatics, in which the number seven defines the capacity of the active memory of the user of texts.

3) An abundance of such examples is cited in Boas, 1927 (see the chapter "The Formal Element in Art").

4) One may offer the hypothesis that many texts belonging to very different cultural-historical traditions (and all texts in a number of traditions) are satisfactorily described by means of models developed in the mathematical theory of symmetry (here symmetry is regarded as a special kind of geometrical regularity). The differentiation between symmetry, antisymmetry (by which is usually understood opposite symmetry, an example of which is the symmetry of three-dimensional figures in four-dimensional space), and dyssymmetry (the dropping of some elements of symmetry from the given group), the establishment of four kinds of symmetrical transformations (motion, antimotion, mirror motion, and mirror antimotion), and the incorporation of the problem of time in this range of questions probably make it possible to presume the possibility of using the apparatus of the theory of symmetry to describe many relatively simple texts that have drawn the attention of investigators of archaic forms of art and verbal creation. See Weyl, 1952; Shubnikov, 1940, 1951, 1961, 1966; and others. Some of these works contain a number of analyses of works of applied art (for example, of ornaments, friezes, borders, designs on rugs and wallpaper, etc.) and even modern graphic art (compare "Day and Night" in the well-known album by Esher).

5) This is valid at least for the classic Paleolithic monuments in southern France and Spain. The lower limit might perhaps be moved back somewhat if one included the "prefigurative" period (periode prefigurative), when decorations were already

The Origin of Poetic Symbols

identifiable, certain objects marked in some respect were collected, supplies of ocher were accumulated for use, particularly in painting the human body, and so forth.

6) Here we are not discussing the natural framing of images inscribed in objects of canonical form (a horn, bone implements, staffs, etc.).

7) Compare the depictions of animals with the legs up, differing fundamentally from depictions or descriptions of the "upsidedown" tree in the period that followed. Compare Kagarow, 1929; Coomaraswamy, 1938; and others. For that matter, a differentiation between top and bottom could be assumed in cases like the two-tier depiction of two herds of horses on a stone from the grotto of Chaffaud.

8) However, the use of the palimpsest technique admits of other explanations. In particular, one can imagine that it was based on the same psychological premises noted in connection with Zen Buddhist art.

9) Capitan and Bouyssonie, 1924; also the herd of reindeer (chiefly the horns) depicted on bone: Mairie Cave (near Teyjaf).

10) It may perhaps be no accident that in a limited space near two hearths at Kostienki I, precisely seven anthropomorphic heads were found, each of which also reproduces the features of some animal. See Abramova, 1962, pp. 15-16.

11) Compare Genzmer, 1950, pp. 21 ff., 1949, pp. 37 ff., and 1952, p. 5; Burger, 1952, p. 5 (on the reflection of steinzeitlichen Urformeln). Compare the use in incantations of this type of the word stone as a "universal" epithet, stone arrow, stone, etc. Finally, it is possible that concepts of a stone sky, which were retained even among the Indo-Europeans, may date back to the Stone Age. Aside from etymological concepts and fairy tales about the stone sky, compare the ritual formula combining the motifs of wood, stone, wool, etc., which has been given a probable explanation in the light of the ritual of summoning rain among the Australian Dieri (where stone = sky, down = clouds, etc.). Also compare the myth of the cosmic egg (stone) from which earth and sky emerge.

12) In any case, pictorial space is organized almost exclusive-

Semiotics and Structuralism

ly within bounds established by "additive" connection.

13) This does not, however, rule out Paleolithic depictions in which a plot is obviously present, although its details may be unclear. Compare the picture in Les Trois Frères Cave, in which a man with a bison's head pursues an animal with the head of a bison but the body of a fallow deer, and a reindeer with webbed front paws. Over the croup of the fallow deer are two human silhouettes (see Fig. 2 on p. 122). Also compare the incised drawing on a piece of horn from Laugerie Basse depicting a hunter crawling up from behind on two grazing bison.

14) Compare, in O. E. Mandel'shtam:
Perhaps before lips the whisper was already born,
And in treelessness the leaves whirled,
And those to whom we dedicate the experiment,
Took shape before the experiment.

15) See Lalanne, 1911-1912, 1912; Lalanne and Bouyssonie 1941-1946; Déonna, 1913; Breuil, 1952, pp. 279-81, and others.

16) As we know, scenes of this kind are absent from Paleolithic monuments and, on the other hand, are not rare in a later period. Compare, for example, the petroglyphs of Lake Onega and the White Sea (including scenes of supernatural impregnation). Analysis of similar pictures can be found in Laushkin, 1962, pp. 241 ff. Also compare a scene depicting coitus from Bardal, Norway: see Hallström, 1938, pp. 303-5, 318 ff. However, such examples as the erotic scene in Les Combarelles Cave (compare Breuil and also Brown, 1928, p. 242), the phallic figure from Mas d'Azil (see Piette, 1902, Fig. I), and certain others (see Saint-Périer, 1932, Plate XLIX, and others) do not rule out the hypothesis that the depiction from Laussel is devoted to the same theme.

17) Leroi-Gourhan, 1964, pp. 95 ff.; compare also his other works: Leroi-Gourhan, 1958a, b, c, 1965, pp. 113 ff., and others.

18) Compare the data in Leroi-Gourhan, 1964, p. 91. According to these data, pertaining both to wall paintings and to l'art mobilier, 24 percent of all Paleolithic depictions are of horses; 15 percent, bison; 15 percent, signs; 7 percent, mountain sheep; 6.5 percent, reindeer; 5 percent, aurochs; 4.5 percent, deer and

The Origin of Poetic Symbols

fallow deer; 4 percent, human males; 3 percent, bears; 3 percent, fish; 2.5 percent, human females; 2 percent, felines; 1 percent, birds; 1 percent, mammoth; 1 percent, rhinoceros; and less than 1 percent each (including dubious identifications), camels, saiga antelope, musk ox, wolf, hyena, snakes, and monsters. Characteristic instances of distributions should be borne in mind: less than 1 percent of the depictions of the reindeer fall into the wall-painting category, and 15 percent are in the class of l'art mobilier. Representations of fish are virtually absent from the paintings in the underground sanctuaries, while they make up 7.5 percent of l'art mobilier works.

19) With respect to these, see Leroi-Gourhan, 1965, pp. 94 ff., 105 ff., and numerous illustrations, including depictions of paired signs: see Fig. 782 and others.

20) Compare the establishment of identity of elements in the series: the sign β, a wound, an arm, vulva, etc. Compare Leroi-Gourhan, 1964, pp. 101 ff. On the reflection of this theme in objects made to be suspended, see Leroi-Gourhan, 1965, pp. 57 ff., particularly Figs. 228 and 229 (Isturitz).

21) Compare, for example, the absence of male Paleolithic images in USSR territory while there is a large number of female depictions. See Abramova, 1962, pp. 55 ff., and also pp. 9-15, 28-30, 44-47, 51-52. A special case is the depiction of an androgyne (see Zotz, 1951).

22) Different variants — an enemy, a corpse, etc. (compare depictions of boats of the dead).

23) Compare the first minor specimens of Paleolithic painting from La Ferrassie.

24) Devices of distinct modeling of the face are quite rare. Compare the head from Dolní Věstonice (see Absolon, 1949, p. 210, Fig. 8) and, in part, the Negroid head from Grimaldi (see Piette, 1902, p. 7, Fig. 3) and the head in a hood, with only the scantiest modeling (Brassempouy) (see Piette, 1895, pp. 149 ff., Fig. V, 2, 2a). True, in Siberian Paleolithic statuettes the chin, eyebrows, nose, and even mouth and eyes were usually modeled (see Abramova, 1962, pp. 55 ff., and also Formozov, 1966, pp. 20-22).

25) About them, see Déonna, 1914, pp. 107 ff. and 597; Breuil,

Semiotics and Structuralism

1914a, pp. 420 ff., 1914b, p. 300; Bégouen and Breuil, 1934, pp. 115 ff.; and also corresponding sections in general works.

26) Compare the strong development of zoo-anthropomorphic transformism among the Australian aborigines and the corresponding terminology (compare the Murinbatan demniŋoi — "to change body" and "to transform oneself from a man into an animal"; compare also one of the verbal clichés at the beginning of the tale, "when animals were still people...").

27) Compare evidence about painting the body with red paint, on the one hand, and on its use in funeral rituals, on the other. On the interpretation of the color red as sacralized, see Gobert, 1950, pp. 18 ff., 1953, pp. 177 ff. Also deserving of attention are large, red-colored symbols in finds of Solutrian-Magdalenian time.

28) Compare Laming, 1962, pp. 48 ff., Fig. 1. It is curious that the color black is used more often in crosshatching, drawing outlines, or depicting peripheral parts of an animal.

29) On the entire set of colors, see Franchet, 1924, pp. 381 ff.

30) This does not contradict the fact that the most frequent subject on staffs with apertures is a fish in the form of a phallus; it should be remembered that the aperture may have been equivalent to a symbol for the female (see Leroi-Gourhan, 1965, pp. 49 ff.). It is suggestive that of 41 staffs studied by Leroi-Gourhan, 35 bore "male" depictions, and 4 had "male" and "female" in association with each other.

31) Yet it is precisely this scene that offers the greatest potential for research. The black color of the contour lines, the figure of the paralyzed man (four-fingered), who seems to be falling on his back, the black horse's head, the bison threatening the man, and so forth, evoke associations with the theme of death (in any case, when one takes into account the symbolism of death and the kingdom of the dead in later periods). It is significant that the representation is found in the well of a dead man. On this scene, see Laming, 1962, pp. 76-77 and Fig. 35; Laming-Emperaire, 1962, pp. 33, 223-24, 250, and Plate IVc.

32) See detailed presentation in Abramova, 1962, pp. 63-64. and also 33-34, 47-48, 52, and the corresponding plates.

The Origin of Poetic Symbols

33) It is possible that the simultaneous presence in Mal'ta of depictions of birds (nine figurines) and snakes indicates the existence of a specific concept or even plot combining the two.

34) Breuil, 1925, pp. 47 ff.; Ravdonikas, 1936, 1938, 1937, pp. 20 ff.; Laushkin, 1962, pp. 231 ff.; Hallström, 1938, pp. 271 ff.; and others. Also see Formozov, 1966, pp. 14 and 117.

35) Compare numerous examples among the petroglyphs of Lake Onega and the White Sea. Considerably later, images of birds perched on the world tree underlay ornamentation (see, for example, Shneider, 1927, pp. 150 ff., Fig. 1-3, Fig. 4-6).

36) The same may also be said of sculptured depictions from the same period. An exception is the snake figurine of Mas d'Azil (see Piette, 1907, Plate XLIII, 1, 1a).

37) Compare finds at Laugerie Haute (see Breuil and Saint-Périer, 1927, p. 148, Fig. 70, 7), Laugerie Basse (see Lartet and Christy, 1875, Plate B, VIII, Fig. 5a), Isturitz (see Passemard, 1925, pp. 135 ff.), Lespugue (see Saint-Périer, 1924, p. 11, Fig. 4), Mal'ta, and some other places.

38) See Breuil and Saint-Périer, 1927, p. 145, Fig. 68, 2. Also compare shamanic staffs with depictions of snakes.

39) Compare a serpent raising the sky, fallen upon the earth. See Métraux, 1942, p. 26 (compare the concept held by these same tribes according to which a serpent continues to keep sky and earth separated, while itself playing the role of the connecting link), or the identification of serpent and lightning joining sky and earth (see Shternberg, 1933, p. 572), serpent and rainbow (see Radcliffe-Brown, 1926; Nevskii, 1934; Ellis, 1890, pp. 47 ff.; Baumann, 1936, p. 197; Chaseling, 1957; and others. Among recent works, see Ivanov and Toporov, 1970).

40) Compare the vertically organized depictions of man and snake (below him) in Ligurian rock painting in the Alps; compare also Leroi-Gourhan, 1965, pp. 57 ff., and Fig. 230 (Lespugue: snakes along a staff-member).

41) See, for example, Almgren, 1934, pp. 130 ff. One of the pictures at North Cape of Besov Nos on Lake Onega (see Ravdonikas, 1936, pp. 84-85, Plates 22, 64, 65) is of exceptional interest from the standpoint of chronology. It shows a person with

an animal mask on his head and wearing a tail, who holds in his hands (which are, it is true, lowered) solar and lunar signs, while standing on a snake (the probable interpretation of the wavy line). Compare also certain other depictions resembling this; for example, the man with arms upraised, accompanied by the sun and a snake on a cliff (Hvitlycke, Tanum); compare the image of a man with the sun sign in his hand (Bohuslän, Sweden); a priest before objects representing the sun and moon (Babylonian cylindrical seal); two men holding a winged sun in their upraised arms (in a North Syrian stone carving of the Second Millennium B.C.); and the common depictions of the winged sun with uraeuses in ancient Egyptian art, etc. This composition corresponds to the schema of the world tree with sun and moon above and snake beneath. Furthermore, as often occurs in Buddhist iconography, the depiction of the tree is replaced by an anthropomorphic image (compare Toporov, 1964).

42) Laming-Emperaire, 1962, pp. 50-51, 215-16, and Fig. X. On depictions of fish in Paleolithic monuments, see Breuil and Saint-Périer, 1927; Hardy, 1889 (particularly about depictions of two fish at Laugerie Basse); and others. The extremely cleverly done depiction of birds and fish to form the swastika is known from the painting on a bowl from Samarra (Mesopotamia, late Fifth or early Fourth Millennium B.C.). Depictions of fish in association with deer are widely present in Scandinavian petroglyphs (compare Hallström, 1938, pp. 43, 117, 344 ff., 350-51, 518 ff., and others).

43) The contribution of images of the art of the "world tree" epoch to the symbolism of succeeding periods is exceptionally large. Research that has now been done in the realm of the symbolism of Buddhism (compare Kirfel, 1959) and Christianity (compare Ferguson, 1961) permits us to determine the extent of this contribution.

44) On the universal connection of birds and snakes in ancient art, see Bobrinskii, 1902, pp. 66-75. Attention was directed to the significance of this work in an article by Ivanov, 1968, p. 236.

45) It is possible that attention should be paid to American Indian totem poles, which depict in some examples a combina-

The Origin of Poetic Symbols

tion of three heads distributed vertically and symbolizing totemic animals (compare Boas, 1927, p. 217, Fig. 206). Also perhaps of interest are the door frames of the Bamum in the Cameroon (see Adam, 1949, Fig. 3), where, specifically, vertical posts consist of figures of a person and animals.

46) See a number of interesting thoughts on this score in the article by Shapiro, 1966 (paper at a symposim on semiotics in Poland, 1966).

47) Compare: eagle and snake, eagle and sun, eagle and deer (horse, cow, etc.), moon and snake, moon and corpse, a journey to the world above, a descent to the nether regions, etc.

48) It is significant that images of the world tree or variants and continuations of it in subsequent European painting (Bosch, Callot [The Gallows Tree], etc., down to Van Gogh, Klee, Miro, or Zadkine) consistently ignore this aspect, reflected by the periphery.

49) The word denoting vulva in some languages also expresses the notion of a sacrificial "table" (often in the shape of the sun) or hearth (compare Almgren, 1934, p. 352).

50) Compare, for instance, numerous examples of texts describing the generation of the elements in terms of life and death (Heraclitus, Anaximander, the Upanishads, Po Hu-t'ung, etc.)

51) On the evolution of male and female signs in the art of subsequent periods, see the author's articles, "Mirovoe derevo" and "Neskol'ko parallelei k odnoi drevneegipetskoi mifologeme," 1967.

Literature

ABRAMOVA 1962: Z. A. Abramova, Paleoliticheskoe iskusstvo na territorii SSSR, Moscow and Leningrad, 1962.

ABSOLON 1949: K. Absolon, "The Diluvial Anthropomorphic Statuettes and Drawings, Especially the So-Called Venus Statuettes Discovered in Moravia," Artibus Asiae, Vol. XII, New York, 1949, No. 3.

ADAM 1949: L. Adam, Primitive Art, Harmondsworth, 1949.

ALMGREN 1934: O. Almgren, Nordische Felszeichnungen als religiöse Urkunden, Frankfurt on Main, 1934.
BADER 1962: O. N. Bader, "Sledy paleolita na Iuzhnom Urale," Arkheologo-etnograficheskii sbornik Bashkirskogo filiala Akademii nauk, Ufa, 1962.
BADER 1965: O. N. Bader, Kapovaia peshchera. Paleoliticheskaia zhivopis', Moscow, 1965.
BAUMANN 1936: H. Baumann, Schöpfung und Urzeit des Menschen im Mythus der afrikanischen Völker, Berlin, 1936.
BÉGOUEN AND BREUIL 1934: H. Bégouen and H. Breuil, "De quelques figures hybrides (mi-humaines, mi-animales) de la caverne des Trois-Frères (Ariège)," Revue anthropologique, Vol. XLIV, Paris, 1934.
BOAS 1927: F. Boas, Primitive Art, Oslo, 1927.
BOBRINSKII 1902: A. A. Bobrinskii, "O nekotorykh simvolicheskikh znakakh, obshchikh pervobytnoi ornamentike vsekh narodov Evropy i Azii," Trudy Iaroslavskogo oblastnogo s"ezda (issledovatelei istorii i drevnostei Rostovo-Suzdal'skoi oblasti), Moscow, 1902.
BREUIL 1914a: H. Breuil, "À propos des masques quaternaires," L'Anthropologie, Vol. XXV, Paris, 1914, No. 3-4.
BREUIL 1914b: H. Breuil, "Observations sur les masques paléolithiques," Revue archéologique, 4th series, Vol. XXIV, Paris, 1914.
BREUIL 1925: H. Breuil, "Oiseaux peints à l'époque néolithique sur des roches de la province de Cadiz," Jahrbuch für prähistorische und ethnographische Kunst, 1925.
BREUIL 1952: H. Breuil, Quatre cents siècles d'art pariétal, Montignac, Dordogne, 1952.
BREUIL AND SAINT-PÉRIER 1927: H. Breuil and R. De Saint-Périer, "Les poissons, les batraciens et les reptiles dans l'art quaternaire," Archives de l'Institut de paléontologie humaine, Book 2, 1927.
BROWN 1928: B. Brown, The Art of the Cave Dweller, London, 1928.
BURGER 1952: H. O. Burger, Annalen der deutschen Literatur, 1952.

The Origin of Poetic Symbols

CAPITAN AND BOUYSSONIE 1924: L. Capitan and J. Bouyssonie, Limeuil. Un atelier d'art préhistorique, Paris, 1924.
CHASELING 1957: S. Chaseling, Julengor, Nomads of Arnhem Land, London, 1957.
COOMARASWAMY 1938: A. Coomaraswamy, "The Inverted Tree," The Quarterly Journal of the Mythic Society, Vol. 29, 1938.
DÉONNA 1913: W. Déonna, "À propos d'un bas-relief de Laussel," Revue archéologique, Vol. 22, Paris, 1913.
DÉONNA 1914: W. Déonna, "Les masques quaternaires," L'Anthropologie, Vol. XXV, Paris, 1914, No. 1-2.
EDINGER 1964: E. F. Edinger, "Trinity and Quaternity," Der Archetyp, Basel and New York, 1964.
EFIMENKO 1958: P. P. Efimenko, Kostenki I, Moscow and Leningrad, 1958.
EIS 1964: G. Eis, Altdeutsche Zaubersprüche, Berlin, 1964.
ELLIS 1890: A. B. Ellis, The Ewe-Speaking Peoples of the Slave Coast of West Africa, London, 1890.
FERGUSON 1961: G. Ferguson, Signs and Symbols in Christian Art, New York, 1961.
FORMOZOV 1966: A. A. Formozov, Pamiatniki pervobytnogo iskusstva na territorii SSSR, Moscow, 1966.
FRANCHET 1924: L. Franchet, "Les couleurs employées aux temps préhistoriques," Congrès International d'anthropologie et d'archéologie préhistorique, 1924.
GARUTT 1960: V. E. Garutt, "Mamont v izobrazhenii cheloveka verkhnego paleolita," Materialy i issledovaniia po arkheologii SSSR, 1960, No. 79.
GENZMER 1949: E. Genzmer, "Da signed Krist-thu biguol en Wuodan," ARV 5, Stockholm and Copenhagen, 1949.
GENZMER 1950: F. Genzmer, "Germanische Zaubersprüche," Germanisch romanische Monatsschrift, N. F. 1, 1950.
GENZMER 1952: F. Genzmer, "Vorgeschichtliche und frühgeschichtliche Zeit," in H. O. Burger, Annalen der deutschen Literatur, 1952.
GOBERT 1950: E.-G. Gobert, "La valeur magique de l'ocre," Bulletin de la Société des Sciences naturelles, Vol. III, 1950.

GOBERT 1953: E.-G. Gobert, Seizième Semaine de Synthèse à la recherche de la mentalité préhistorique, Paris, 1953.
HALLSTRÖM 1938: G. Hallström, Monumental Art of Northern Europe from the Stone Age. I. The Norwegian Localities, Stockholm, 1938.
HARDY 1889: M. Hardy, Gravures de l'âge du renne trouvées à Laugerie-Basse, Paris, 1889.
IVANOV 1968: V. V. Ivanov, "Lingvistika i gumanitarnye problemy semiotiki," Izvestia AN SSSR. Seriia literatury i iazyka, Vol. XXVII, No. 3 (May-June), Moscow, 1968.
IVANOV and TOPOROV 1965: V. V. Ivanov and V. N. Toporov, Slavianskie iazykovye modeliruiushchie semioticheskie sistemy, Moscow, 1965.
IVANOV and TOPOROV 1970: V. V. Ivanov and V. N. Toporov, "Le mythe indoeuropéen du dieu de l'orage poursuivant le serpent: reconstruction du schéma," Échanges et communications. Mélanges offerts a C. Lévi-Strauss, Paris, 1970.
JUNG 1948: G. G. Jung, "A Psychological Approach to the Dogma of Trinity," Collected Works, Vol. II, New York, 1948.
KAGAROW 1929: E. Kagarow, "Der umgekehrte Schamanenbaum," Archiv für Religionsgeschichte, Vol. 27, 1929.
KIRFEL 1959: W. Kirfel, Symbolik der Buddhismus, Stuttgart, 1959.
KÜHN 1957: H. Kühn, Die Felsbilder Europas, Zurich and Vienna, 1957.
LALANNE 1911-1912: G. Lalanne, Découverte d'un bas-relief à représentations humaines à Laussel, Paris, 1911-1912.
LALANNE 1912: G. Lalanne, "Bas-relief à figurations humaines de l'abri sous roche de Laussel," Congrès International d'anthropologie et d'archéologie préhistorique, Vol. I, Geneva, 1912.
LALANNE AND BOUYSSONIE 1941-1946: J. G. Lalanne and J. Bouyssonie, "Le gisement paléolithique de Laussel," L'Anthropologie, Vol. L, Paris, 1941-1946, No. 1-2.
LAMING 1962: A. Laming, Lascaux. Am Ursprung der Kunst, Dresden, 1962.
LAMING-EMPERAIRE 1962: A. Laming-Emperaire, Le signification de l'art rupestre paléolithique. Méthode et applications, Paris, 1962.

The Origin of Poetic Symbols

LARTET AND CHRISTY 1875: E. Lartet and H. Christy, Reliquial Aquitanicae, Paris, 1875.
LAUSHKIN 1962: K. D. Laushkin, "Onezhskoe sviatilishche, ch. II (Opyt novoi rasshifrovki nekotorykh petroglifov Karelii)," Skandinavskii sbornik, V, Tallinn, 1962.
LEROI-GOURHAN 1958a: A. Leroi-Gourhan, "La fonction des signes dans des sanctuaires paléolithiques," Bulletin de la Société Préhistorique Française, Vol. LV, Paris, 1958, No. 5-6.
LEROI-GOURHAN 1958b: A. Leroi-Gourhan, "Le symbolisme des grandes signes dans l'art pariétal paléolithique," Bulletin de la Société Préhistorique Française, Vol. LV, Paris, 1958, No. 7-8.
LEROI-GOURHAN 1961: A. Leroi-Gourhan, "Sur une méthode d'étude de l'art pariétal paléolithique," Bericht über den V. Internationalen Kongress für Vor- und Frühgeschichte, Hamburg, 1958, Berlin, 1961.
LEROI-GOURHAN 1964: A. Leroi-Gourhan, Les religions de la préhistoire. (Paléolithique), Paris, 1964.
LEROI-GOURHAN 1965: A. Leroi-Gourhan, Préhistoire de l'art occidental, Paris, 1965.
MAIKOV 1869: L. Maikov, Velikorusskie zaklinaniia, St. Petersburg, 1869.
MÉTRAUX 1942: A. Métraux, The Native Tribes of Eastern Bolivia and Western Matto Grosso, Washington, 1942.
NEVSKII 1934: N. A. Nevskii, "Predstavlenie o raduge kak o 'nebesnoi zmee,'" S. F. Ol'denburgu. Sbornik statei, Leningrad, 1934.
PASSEMARD 1925: L. Passemard, "Dessins sinueux sur bois de renne dans la caverne d'Isturitz (Basses-Pyrénées)," Bulletin de la Société Préhistorique Française, Vol. XXII, Paris, 1925.
PIETTE 1895: E. Piette, "La station de Brassempouy et les statuettes humaines de la période glyptique," L'Anthropologie, Vol. VI, Paris, 1895, No. 2.
PIETTE 1902: E. Piette, "Gravure du Mas d'Azil et Statuettes de Menton," Bulletin et Mémoires de la Société d'Anthropologie de Paris, 2nd series, Vol. III, 1902.

PIETTE 1907: E. Piette, L'art pendant l'âge du renne, Paris, 1907.
RADCLIFFE-BROWN 1926: A. B. Radcliffe-Brown, "The Rainbow Serpent Myth in Australia," Journal of the Royal Anthropological Institute of Great Britain and Ireland, Vol. 56, London, 1926.
RAVDONIKAS 1936: V. I. Ravdonikas, Naskal'nye izobrazheniia Onezhskogo ozera, Moscow and Leningrad, 1936.
RAVDONIKAS 1937: V. I. Ravdonikas, "Elementy kosmicheskikh predstavlenii v obrazakh naskal'nykh izobrazhenii," Sovetskaia arkheologiia, 1937, No. 4.
RAVDONIKAS 1938: V. I. Ravdonikas, Naskal'nye izobrazheniia Belogo moria, Moscow and Leningrad, 1938.
ROMANOV 1891: E. R. Romanov, Belorusskii sbornik, Issue V, Vitebsk, 1891.
SACCASYN-DELLA SANTA 1947: E. Saccasyn-della Santa, Les figures humaines du paléolithique supérieur Eurasiatique, Anvers, 1947.
SAINT-PÉRIER 1924: R. De Saint-Périer, "Les fouilles de 1923 dans la grotte des Rideaux, â Lespugue," L'Anthropologie, Vol. XXXIV, Paris, 1924, No. 1-2.
SAINT-PÉRIER 1932: R. de Saint-Périer, L'art préhistorique, Paris, 1932.
SHAPIRO 1966: M. Shapiro, "On Some Problems of the Semiotics of Visual Art: Field and Vehicle in Image-Signs" (paper read at a semiotics symposium in Poland in 1966).
SHNEIDER 1927: E. R. Shneider, "Kazakskaia ornamentika," Kazaki. Antropologicheskie ocherki, Moscow, 1927.
SHTERNBERG 1933: L. Ia. Shternberg, "Ainskaia problema," Giliaki, orochi, gol'dy, negidal'tsy, ainy, Khabarovsk, 1933.
SHUBNIKOV 1940: A. V. Shubnikov, Simmetriia, Moscow and Leningrad, 1940.
SHUBNIKOV 1951: A. V. Shubnikov, Simmetriia i antisimmetriia konechnykh figur, Moscow, 1951.
SHUBNIKOV 1961: A. V. Shubnikov, Problema disimmetrii material'nykh ob"ektov, Moscow, 1961.
SHUBNIKOV 1966: A. V. Shubnikov, Antisimmetriia, Moscow, 1966.

The Origin of Poetic Symbols

SIMONNET 1947: G. Simonnet, "Une nouvelle plaquette de pierre gravée magdalénien de la grande grotte de Labastide," Bulletin de la Société Préhistorique Française," Vol. XLIV, Paris, 1947.
STOLIAR 1964: A. D. Stoliar, "Problemy proiskhozhdeniia siuzhetnogo izobrazitel'nogo iskusstva verkhnego paleolita Evrazii," Tezisy dokladov na nauchnoi sessii Gos. Ermitazha (2. Sektsionnye zasedaniia), Leningrad, 1964.
TOPOROV 1964: V. N. Toporov, "K rekonstruktsii nekotorykh mifologicheskikh predstavlenii (na materiale buddiiskogo izobrazitel'nogo iskusstva)," Narody Azii i Afriki, 1964, No. 3.
TOPOROV 1969: V. N. Toporov, "K rekonstruktsii indo-evropeiskogo rituala i ritual'no-poeticheskikh formul (na materiale zagovorov)," Trudy po znakovym sistemam, IV (Uchenye zapiski Tartuskogo gosudarstvennogo universiteta, Issue 236), Tartu, 1969.
TREILAND 1881: F. Ia. Treiland, "Materialy po etnografii latyshskogo plemeni," Trudy etnograficheskogo otdeleniia pri Moskovskom universitete, Vol. XL, Moscow, 1881.
VAYSON DE PRADENNE 1934: A. Vayson de Pradenne, "Les figurations d'oiseaux dans l'art quaternaire," Jahrbuch für prähistorische und ethnographische Kunst, 1934.
VINOGRADOV 1908: N. N. Vinogradov, "Zagovory, oberegi i spasitel'nye molitvy," Zhivaia starina, Issue 2, 1908.
WEYL 1952: H. Weyl, Symmetry, Princeton, 1952 (Russian translation: G. Veil', Simmetriia, Moscow, 1968).
ZOTZ 1951: L. F. Zotz, "Idoles Paléolithiques de l'Être Androgyne," Bulletin de la Société Préhistorique Française, Vol. XLVIII, Paris, 1951, No. 7-8.

Restoration of the Original Text of the Ket Myth about the Destroyer of Eagles' Nests

Viach. Vs. Ivanov

Dedicated to the memory of A. P. Dul'zon

The Ket myth of the destroyer of eagles' nests is known in two variants.* The shorter, M_a, was recorded by A. P. Dul'zon (A. P. Dul'zon, Skazki narodov Sibirskogo Severa, Vol. I, Tomsk, 1972; abbreviated SS, No. 113) in Sulomai, according to his communication in a letter to the author, "from the words of an old woman, Anna Iosifovna Liamich (her name was siYo of the clan of bogde), who spoke Russian very badly and spoke unclearly in Ket, constantly forgetting what she had already said or wanted to say." A considerably longer variant, M_b, was also recorded by him in the same place (A. P. Dul'zon, "Ketskie skazki i drugie teksty," in Ketskii sbornik. Mifologiia. Etnografiia. Teksty, Moscow, 1969; cited hereafter as KS, No. 57) from the words of O. V. Tyganova (born 1917, native language Yug, from

---

*Full texts of the two variants of the myth are provided at the end of this article. See pp. 239-243.

Restoration of a Ket Myth

which she switched to Ket at age three), who is not a storyteller of the old type.

M_b retains significant characters, particularly the mammoth, which is present in M_a only in the title (tēl'aska, "Story about the Mammoth"). But M_b omits such figures as the old woman, wife of the old man and a she-dog in the opening episode; while certain motifs and functions (the tree, the eagle, the stone tool) are replicated, the initial order of transformations of certain characters into others is mixed up, and episodes are inserted that are common to other specimens of Ket folklore or texts from other literatures (drunken devils drinking from horns). With the removal of these later stratifications, it becomes possible, on the basis of comparison of both variants with each other and with other Ket myths and fairy tales, to determine the initial schema of the myth and to restore in part the original Ket text. The myth begins with an episode in which the old man Ydat (M_a), or Yrohot (M_b), and the old woman raise (d-ū-tos "brings up"; d-i-Y-u-tos-in "we will bring up," past tense d-o-l'-tus-n) the hero of the myth, Fox Cub (KyYyn'-get in M_a and M_b) or Kas-ket (M_c, SS, No. 73): Compare the combining of the two names of the hero in M_b, which is named after Kasket. The connection between Kasket and Ydat can be seen in M_d (A. P. Dul'zon, Ketskie skazki, Tomsk, 1966, No. 5), in which Kasket upbraids Dootem-Baba-Yaga because she "ate Ydats." Kasket emerges not as having been raised by Yrahat but as murderer of his son in M_e (SS, No. 86); in M_b he appears first as the enemy of Fox Cub, but later he allies with him. In M_f ("Old Man Yrahat," in G. K. Verner, "O realizatsii eniseiskikh slogovykh tonov v potoke rechi," Voprosy filologii. Uchenye zapiski Omskogo Gosudarstvennogo pedagogicheskogo instituta im. Gor'kogo, Issue 62, Omsk, 1971; cited hereafter as VF, pp. 148-52), which represents a variant of M_c (both myths taken down from the words of the same O. V. Tyganova), the hero is Man of Fire (Bog-de-s'-ket), later also called Kasket, who transforms himself into an ermine and who steals (as does Fox Cub in M_a and M_b) food from a storage platform (i). The theft of fish in M_a and M_b is preceded by the departure of Fox Cub, who crosses the river, from the old man who brought him up and from the old woman (nang-al' o-Y-o-n' "from them he — left," also used in M_b, in which the old woman has not been mentioned up to that point). Fox Cub, who steals fish for Ydat from the platform, is stalked by In'-get. Judging on the basis of M_a, in which one encounters a combination of this word with hang-get "a little she-dog," In'-get may be the diminutive for dog. Compare, in an Evenki dialect, in-a "dog" (Japanese inu), ŋina- particularly in the tale in which a dog hunts a fox — hulakī (Sbornik materialov po evenkiiskomu (tungusskomu) fol'kloru, compiled by G. M. Vasilevich, Leningrad, 1936, No. 1). Compare M_b, in which In'-get, as a dog, chases Fox Cub, having found his track. In M_a and M_b the critical point in development of the plot is marked by a verb of phonation, tut ær' æj = (g'æs') "to fall down heavily." Having heard the noise caused by the dropping of the stolen salmon trout on the ground, In'- get appeals to the people to pursue Fox Cub: alaragan "Come out!" (this also appears in M_b, in which people are not explicitly named). The role of hang-get "the little she-dog" in M_a is similar to the function of the she-dog (hang), from which one finds out about the daughter (not about the ward, as in M_a) of Yrahat, in M_b (SS, No. 112). In the following part of M_a, Fox Cub, seeking to escape the chase (and, in M_b, Kasket, who is pursuing him) and therefore moving upriver, undergoes a number of consecutive transformations: into an ermine (as does the hero of M_f, Man of Fire, and as does Kasket in M_c), and then into a man, in whose shape he mounts a three-legged horse (dong-bul-eng) and rides on. The next turning point in the development of the plot in M_a and M_b is marked by another verb of phonation, huYæj-væta "rings, sings," which is applied to the sound of the shamanic tree — a staff with beads, on which the hero finds a cradle (uj) hung. A comparison with M_i (VF, pp. 145-48), in which childless old man Ydat makes a son out of clay and puts him in the cradle, after which he rocks it (d-an- gō-bl'-o-k; compare b-u-gō-bl'-ū-k in M_a and M_b), makes it possible to determine the function of the cradle and its rocking. Later Ydat's son was compelled to climb to heaven, to God (Es')

Restoration of a Ket Myth

because he had been persecuted by a woodspirit whom he had tried to kill. This trip to heaven in M_i can be compared with the trip to the God of Warmth (Us-es') in M_k (KS, No. 61) made by Yrohot's daughter, whom the divinity takes to wife. Compare Yrohot's daughter's trip back to the lower world, where she is taken to wife by a water spirit described as a man burning like a fire (bok) in M_l (SS, No. 114). A similar trip to the upper world is made by the man Fox Cub (or Kasket), the ward of Ydat in M_a and M_b, who ascends along the Celestial Tree (es'-oks) after he had been rocked in the cradle (i.e., had experienced a second birth). In M_a and in M_b it is said that the hero went up "in the mask (literally, 'in a casing, in a cavity,' the auxiliary morpheme being ol') of a deer" (compare qoj-ol' "in a bear mask" in M_e, with respect to Kasket, who in a bear mask kills the son of old man Yrahat). In both variants of the myth there is preserved the archaic formula "There above is an eagle's nest on the Celestial (Divine) Tree" (toj kas'eŋ daY-aj es'-oks-daŋtæn, a combining of two compound words). The third turning point in development of the plot is marked by a third verb of phonation, sikæj "to cheep," pertaining to the cheeping of the eaglets whose nest the hero of the myth had begun to tug (or shake). In response to the cheeping of the eaglets there flew up qe da:(Y) "a large female eagle," from whom the hero requested "a sack for flint," literally a "fire casing" (bog-d-ol'). The she-eagle agrees to give the sack with fire-making implements on the sole condition that the hero of the myth obtains for her a talon — the spine — of a ruff-fish (Ket in "talon," "spine"). The next chain of episodes is absent from M_a, while in M_b it appears with a replication of the motif of the tree and the eagle by the tree: after the hero descends, the tree motif appears again (this time it is a larch with Tyl'get [bole]) as does the eagle that has flown to this tree. The same mythological personage — Kasket, who is presented in this episode of M_b — is associated with the larch in the myth M_d, in which Kasket, saving himself from persecution by Dootem (Baba-Yaga), hides in seven larches that have miraculously grown up at his request. At this point in M_d the motif of seeing and not-seeing appears. Kasket proposes to Dootem that she keep her eyes open by means of little sticks. When she obeys him, he fills her eyes with fragments of stones and then kills her. In a transformed form the motif of loss (and return) of the eye of a mythological being appears in M_b, in which the eagle loses an eye and then gets it back in exchange for having helped the hero to return to the top of the Celestial Tree.

    The eagle, who wants to catch Tyl'get, loses the eye that Tyl'get had seized, just as it is subsequently said of the she-eagle that she lost her talon because she wanted to catch the mammoth with whom her talon had been left. In order to obtain this talon from the mammoth, the hero had to return to the mammoth its "horns" (kong), i.e., the tusks that had frozen to the ice in winter (reflected here is the idea of the mammoth as a fish whose horns freeze in winter to the ice of the sea). The plot of M_b thereafter is built on a series of consecutive exchanges. Having found the "horns" in the possession of the drunken devils, the hero returns them to the mammoth, for which he obtains the talon of the she-eagle. At the end of this series of episodes, Tyl'get again appears, playing on a harmonica (kāt kitevit). The sea, rising (apparently in response to the sound of his playing), carries off a whetstone (sal'tys) that the hero places on a branch of the larch. The same harmonica music attracts the eagle. At the end of the myth a concluding series of exchanges takes place: the eagle's eye is returned to him, after which he carries the hero of the myth up to the she-eagle. In both M_a and M_b the she-eagle, in exchange for its talon, which it puts onto its toe, gives the hero a sack with tools for making fire and instructs him to descend to old man Yrahat. The hero returns home (past tense s'uY-æ-o-n'-den) to Ydat. The present study would have been impossible if Dul'zon, to whom the author is obliged for a number of explanations of the texts of myths, had not pointed out, in a letter to the author, the parallelism of the M_a and M_b variants. The author is grateful to G. K. Verner and E. A. Kreinovich for valuable advice used in analysis of the texts.

Restoration of a Ket Myth

Structure of the Ket Myth on the Destroyer of Eagles' Nests

The original text of the myth, which is restored on the basis of comparison of M_a and M_b (and use of other myths), divides into four principal parts. The first part, more completely represented in M_a, consists of the story of Fox Cub, who steals the fish; and it has analogies in the animal fairy tales and in the animal epic of Siberia and the Far East (compare, for example, the Ainu myth about the punishment of the Fox-God who has stolen fish: N. A. Nevskii, Ainskii fol'klor, Moscow, 1972, pp. 102 ff.). In the second part, which coincides in M_a and M_b, the hero appears as the destroyer of eagles' nests with the Ket myth distinctly showing the transparent connection between the destruction of the nest and obtaining implements with which to kindle fire: having made the eaglets cheep, the hero forces the she-eagle to negotiate with him (compare the similar motif of the kidnapping of a baby from the animal fire guardian by Raven, in exchange for which he obtains fire, in the North American Indian myths about Raven; with respect to these myths E. M. Meletinskii, in his cycle of works about Raven as culture hero, pointed out a series of Paleosiberian parallels). In the third part, preserved (and, apparently, enlarged) in M_b, a number of episodes are described that are associated with obtaining the "claw" ("spine" — in:) from the ruff-fish and the mammoth (tēl'). In the fourth part, which coincides in M_a and M_b, an exchange occurs: the "talon" that has been obtained for a sack of implements for making fire. All in all, the myth may be regarded as one about the obtaining of fire. Exceptionally interesting is the fact that M_a was told to us by an old woman of the bog(di)deng "People of Fire" phratry (M_b, however, was told by a representative of the opposite phratry). Compare "man of Fire" (Bog-de-s'-ket) as hero in M_f, in which one might see a myth explaining the origin of the phratry of the people of Fire, inasmuch as the end of the myth tells how the man of Fire married an "old woman" after he settled accounts with "the old man," her husband, by pushing him into the water — ul', as also in the M_c variant of the same myth. Compare the opposite plot scheme in M_1, in which the old man's daughter marries a water spirit who "flames like fire." The phratry of the people of Fire, associated with certain birds, was opposed among the Kets to the "Half (qolæp) of the water (ul')" (or a phratry whose totemic designation is based on the name of a fish). A similar binary opposition of fire-water, bird-fish determines the structure of the myth of the destroyer of eagles' nests. In the first part of the myth the principal theme is set by fish (salmon trout), stolen by Fox Cub, and a river (channel) that he crosses at the beginning of the myth and along whose shore he flees to safety from pursuit in the following episode. The second part of the myth, in which the theme of the treetop and birds (eagles) associated with fire appears, is followed by a third part, in which there is repeated again the theme of water — this time not the river but the sea — and of a water animal — this time not an ordinary fish but a mythological one, a mammoth. The common Siberian ideas of the mammoth as a fish — an animal of the lower (underground or underwater) world (see S. V. Ivanov, "Mamont v iskusstve narodov Sibiri," Sbornik Muzeia antropologii i etnografii, XI, Moscow and Leningrad, 1949, pp. 133-61) — are reflected among the Kets: The Kets' very term for "mammoth," tēl', is close to the common Siberian kheli-seli (see G. M. Vasilevich, "Iazykovye dannye po terminu khel~kel," ibid., p. 154). Compare also the Ket s'el' "deer" (with reference to the common Siberian mythological concept of a horned mammoth-elk) and the combination "mammoth-pike" (Ket qôt-tēl', for which O. V. Tyganova offered the translated equivalent "crocodile," "the animal of which the shamans sing": compare to the makāras in Indian mythology; data from G. K. Verner, who has communicated in a letter to the author a number of other testimonies to the understanding of the mammoth as a mythological being: Ket tēl', Yug čel) similar to the Sel'kup koshchar pichchi. In the third part of M_b the mammoth appears as the principal animal of the lower world, associated with water (the sea), just as the eagle in the myth represents the principal animal of the upper world, associated with heavenly fire (reindeer — s'el', in whose mask the

Restoration of a Ket Myth

hero climbs to the top of the tree, is in the given context a
mediator between the terrestrial and celestial world as a
shamanic animal: compare reindeer next to the cosmic tree
in other traditions).

The opposition eagle-mammoth in this myth proves to be a
variant of the opposition bird-fish, which in turn is linked with
the opposition fire-water.

It appears that the myth as a whole is built on the opposition top-bottom, correlated with other oppositions listed above, as well as celestial fire- (of Es' the thunder god; compare eś-oks "Celestial-Divine-Tree" in the second part of the myth) terrestrial fire, sky-sea. The adverbial indications "upward"-"up" (tos'o), pertaining to motion up along the Celestial Tree, and "downward" (hyta), pertaining to return from the top of the Celestial Tree to earth, are contained in the text of the myth itself. In accordance with the Ket spatial model of the world, in which the oppositions top-bottom, pertaining to the headwaters and downstream portions of a river, and top-bottom vertically understood (sky-ground) are combined, it is possible to assume a unitary structure of the entire myth. Compare the role of derivatives from the root et- "top" in the text of the myth. In the first part the persecution of Fox Cub compels him (and Kasket in M_b) to move upward along the course of the river (kat d-et-u-j-d-aq "by the shore upward he went along the river"). Continuation of this motion upward along the vertical leads the hero to the top of the Celestial Tree. Associating himself with this interpretation of the Ket myth, C. Lévi-Strauss observes, in a letter to the author: "Petit-Renard est exposé à un danger: l'un sur l'axe vertical, prisonnier en haut d'un arbre, l'autre sur l'axe horizontal, poursuivi par les chiens." The "acoustic code" of the myth, formed by verbs of phonation, which in Ket constitute a distinct morphological class, is associated with the same top-bottom opposition. The first verb of phonation denotes the sound of the fall of the fish that Fox Cub casts down from the platform. The second verb of phonation denotes the sound emitted by the shamanic tree from which hangs the cradle — the means for the hero's ascent up the Celestial Tree; the third verb of phonation denotes the cheeping of eaglets in the nest at the top of the Tree; the verb denoting playing on "a harmonica" is associated with the arrival of the eagle carrying the hero back upwards. In M_c and M_f the principal plot function is borne by the verb denoting the whistle of Kasket — the man of Fire.

Therefore, analysis of the myth leads to the conclusion that there is a structural unity of all its parts, including the first. In its first part, in opposition to the second, one can see reflection of two ways of preparing food: fish was either dried in the light of the sun (using the fire of heaven), or was prepared by means of earthly fire. A fish that had been put out to dry on the top of the platform is stolen by the hero, who later obtains fire-making implements for his (adoptive) parents, for whom he had stolen fish. Agreeing with this interpretation, Lévi-Strauss points out in the cited letter: "S'il s'agit chez les Ket, comme il semble, d'un mythe sur l'origine du feu, il faut admettre que la situation initiale expose Petit-Renard et les siens à un double état de manque (au sens de Propp); ils n'ont pas le feu (par hypothèse) et ils n'ont pas non plus de nourriture, puisque Petit-Renard doit aller voler les poissons. Ces poissons sont le monopole des Chiens, animaux domestiques donc à mi-chemin entre l'humanité et l'animalité, qui, n'ayant pas le feu, sont seulement capables d'amener la nourriture à mi-chemin entre la crudité et la cuisson: poissons séchés au soleil, mais qu'il faut consommer tels quels." M_c, in which Kasket does not catch animals at all (which is why his adoptive parents — Yrohot and the old woman — want to separate from him) testifies in favor of this interpretation of the hero of the myth in his relationship to food. At the same time, the hero's link to fire is shown by the fact that he sits at the fire (bog-dotke) instead of hunting. The structural unity of the second and third parts of M_b is revealed particularly explicitly in the fact that the motifs of larch, eagle, and whetstone in the third part of the myth reproduce, respectively, the motifs of the Celestial Tree, the she-eagle, and the sack with fire-making tools in the second part. In the third part of M_b the sea takes the whetstone away from the hero, but in the fourth part of M_a and M_b the hero succeeds in obtaining another stone tool — a means for kindling fire, while grateful animals associated with the sea give him indirect help in the third part.

The author takes the opportunity to express his gratitude to G. K. Verner and C. Lévi-Strauss for their detailed discussion of his hypotheses in letters.

Parallelism between American Indian and Ket Myths about the Destroyer of Eagles' Nests

The Ket myth about the destroyer of eagles' nests displays striking features of coincidence with those South American and North American myths that Lévi-Strauss derives from an archaic common source. The following basic parts and motifs in the myths coincide: (1) At the beginning the hero of the myth leaves his father (separates from him), for which the acquisition of food is often given as the motivation (specifically, in the Ket myth M_j). (2) The hero of the myth ascends a tree growing up to the sky to an eagle's nest at its top. (3) The hero destroys the nest of eaglets. (4) Fire is acquired thanks to the hero (at the end of the myth the hero obtains the means of making fire). In addition to these fundamental coincidences there are certain more particular coincidences, specifically with Salish myths, which, according to Lévi-Strauss, are particularly archaic and at the same time most complete (C. Lévi-Strauss, L'homme nu, Mythologiques IV, Paris, 1971; cited below as HN, p. 451). The fact that the hero of the myth, Fox Cub, in M_a and M_b, like the orphan Kasket in M_c, "is brought up" by the old man Ydat/Yrahat, and that in M_j Ydat makes himself a son of clay, is analogous to the motif of "making... an artificial son" Coyote (including making one of clay) in M_{667} and M_{738} (here and below the numeration of American Indian myths is that of Lévi-Strauss in HN).

It would appear possible that the absence of the incest motif in M_a, M_b, and M_j is associated with the special (not blood-kin) character of the relation between Ydat and his adoptive son or ward (among Ket myths of this cycle, it is only in M_c and its variant M_f that there is open rivalry over a woman between old man Yrahat and the hero of the myth — Fire Man or Kasket; these myths are, however, characterized in general by the complete absence of any family relationships among male characters). Lévi-Strauss, not agreeing with the explanation offered by the present author for the absence of the incest motif in the Ket myth, suggests in a letter to the author that direct incest is replaced by the stealing of food: "Je ne crois pas qu'on puisse expliquer cette lacune par le fait que le héros est un enfant adoptif; il aurait pu mal se conduire avec la femme du vieil Ydat. Voyez par exemple M_{805}, HN, p. 524-525, où Vison (un 'petit renard'!) se rend coupable d'indiscrétion sexuelle envers sa marâtre. Curieusement, on retrouve dans ce mythe deux éléments du mythe ket: vol (sexuel au lieu d'alimentaire) commis en grimpant sur le toit, et (avant au lieu d'après), bruit anormal associé au tonnerre (puisque la marâtre est le tonnerre dans le mythe Stseelis, dont il existe d'ailleurs d'autres versions sur le côte nord-ouest du Pacifique). Je crois donc que l'inceste des mythes américains est remplacé dans le mythe ket par le vol de nourriture (ce qu'est, métaphoriquement, l'incest, en raison de l'equation sur laquelle j'ai maintes fois insisté: copulation = consommation alimentaire). Le vol commis par un Renard au préjudice de Chiens, animaux très proches dans le rapport zoologique, n'a-t-il pas, d'ailleurs, un aspect 'incestueux'?"

The significant similarity between the American myths examined in Lévi-Strauss's Mythologiques and the Ket myths lies in the fact that the origin of the distinguishing feature of a bird (the eagle's talon in the Ket myth) is also associated with myths about the origin of fire. At the same time, the role of the prickle-spine (thorn) of a fish (ruff) in the Ket myth is reminiscent of "the common origin of fire and fish" in American Indian myths (HN, p. 411). The transformation of the persecuted hero of the Ket myth into an ermine is similar to the role of the ermine in the episode of rescue of the hero in M_{766}, M_{767a} (HN, p. 468),

Restoration of a Ket Myth

in which, as in the Ket myth, the persecution is associated with dogs and with the sound heard by the hero's enemies (possibly comprising, in the Ket myth, the pair man-dog: compare HN, pp. 433-34, 516). In his letter regarding the analysis of the Ket myth proposed by the author, Lévi-Strauss observes: "Dans le registre des animaux sauvages, le Renard est analogue au Chien dans celui des animaux domestiques. Le chien occupe une position passive entre humanité et animalité, entre culture et nature. Le Renard va jouer un rôle actif entre animal céleste et animal aquatique (lui-même étant, bien entendu, le prototype de l'animal terrestre), entre haut et bas:

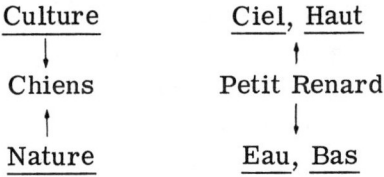

Petit-Renard vole les chiens (conduite anticulturelle); avec l'aigle, il échange (conduite culturelle)."

The third part of the Ket myth reveals a striking similarity to those myths of the North American Indians (particularly to "transformation of the Putiphar type" of the basic myth about the destroyer of eagles' nests) in which the sea and a large sea animal, the whale, appear (HN, pp. 202, 228, 342, 508, 505, 511; M_{594a}, M_{604a}, M_{796}). Compare the conventional Russian translated equivalent "whale" (or "shark") of the Ket tēl' "mammoth" (compare above, "crocodile" for q̂ot-tēl') in the words of O. V. Tyganova, who, as Dul'zon observed in a letter to the author, had an idea about whales and sharks thanks to a school education. Particularly interesting for comparison with part three of M_b are such North American Indian myths of the origin of fire as M_{604a}, in which a whale participates, and also the Tlingit myth M_{594b}, which tells about various sea animals on sand (compare the seven devils on sand in M_b) and about how the demiurge Raven inserts points into the body of the mistress of the marshes (compare the spine of the ruff-fish in M_a and M_b). In American Indian myths, equivalents are also found for the motif of the eye of the mythological being (eagle), which is exchanged in the course of the development of the myth (compare Coyote's loss of an eye, HN, pp. 251 and 355, and parallels in the mythologies of the Old World — Egyptian, Hittite, etc.)

The theme of a musical instrument (a "harmonica" in M_B), the sound of which is associated with a journey and return, coincides with the principal myth (M_1) in the mythology of the American Indians.

A possible parallel with American Indian myths, in which, as in the myth of the Yan M_{548} (with participation of the Eagle), the ascent to Heaven is accomplished by means of a "basket," lies in the use of the "cradle" (uj, which among the Kets is like a basket) as a means of reaching heaven (the top of the Celestial Tree) in the Ket myth. As Lévi-Strauss observes in his letter pertaining to the analysis by the author of this function of the cradle in the Ket myth: "le rôle conjoncteur qui lui est dévolu coincide avec celui que je lui avais attribué dan les mythes américains, cf. M_{374b} et mon commentaire, Origine des manières de table, pp. 48-50; HN, p. 371, n. 1."

With this Lévi-Strauss directs attention to the significant similarity of means of escaping dangers in the American and Ket myths. The heroes of these myths escape danger "l'un en redescendant grace à un animal secourable maître du feu (le jaguar gé, cf. M_{7-12}), l'autre, au contraire, en montant en haut de l'arbre où il est accueilli par l'aigle, maîtresse des moyens de faire le feu. Dans les deux cas, le héros obtient le feu en échange soit de la nourriture crue (les oisillons que le héros gé offre au jaguar), soit du moyen de se procurer la nourriture crue (la griffe qui manque à l'aigle et sans laquelle, peut-on-penser, elle ne peut pas chasser)."

Some of the similarities between the Ket and the North and South American Indian myths noted by the author (and by Lévi-Strauss, who agrees, on the whole, with his conclusions) can be explained typologically (specifically the connection between heavenly fire and the top of the World Tree and the bird, particularly an eagle, associated with this top, bears the character of a universal, to which compare Old Indian and other Eurasian

Restoration of a Ket Myth

parallels). But the similarity of a large number of details and combinations thereof into motifs, particularly the very motif of destruction of an eagle's nest, is of a different character and suggests a common origin. The simultaneous similarity of the surface and deep structures of the myths permits one to derive them from a common source. Lévi-Strauss (HN) commented on the relict character of the myth in America, manifested in its geographical identification with isolated areas. The same may also hold with respect to Siberia. In this case one might see in these correspondences a confirmation of the hypothesis of the archaic character of the American myth, dated to the period of the initial populating of America by Lévi-Strauss even before the discovery of the Eurasian example of this myth (thus far the only one found there), which we examined above.

Texts of the Ket Myth

M_a (SS, No. 113): Story about a Mammoth

Old Man Ydat lives with his old woman. They brought up a vixen who later left them.

In order to hunt foxes the vixen crossed the Podkamennaia Tunguska River, then climbed onto a storage platform, and made away with fish. In'get (name) said, "The vixen has gone away, has made away with fish, has taken it to old man Ydat."

In the morning Ydat woke up: "Look (again), fish is lying there! Probably, our man (the vixen) has brought it!"

Then it went off again. In'get and the little she-dog were waiting. The vixen again (came), climbed onto the storage platform, took the salmon trout, and threw this fish down.

In'get and the little she-dog heard the sound (of the fall): "Come outside!" (they say). The people looked — the vixen has again made away with fish, taken it to old man Ydat. The people chased after it: "It is eating our fish!"

It (the vixen) struck itself against the ground and became an ermine. Then it left, walked, walked, walked up along the shore

Semiotics and Structuralism

of the Podkammenaia Tunguska River.

Was it long, was it far that it went up; it looks — a three-legged little horse is going up (river). It (the ermine) struck itself against the ground and became a man. He mounted the horse. The horse ran off.

He rode, rode, (hears) — a shamanic staff with beads is ringing, a cradle hangs from it. He went up into it and began to rock it. Now he went up in the mask of an eagle, up, and went away. There above is an eagle's nest on the celestial tree. He began to jostle the eaglets (so that they would cheep). A large she-eagle flew in. He told the she-eagle: "Give me the sack for fire!"

The old woman, this female eagle, says: "Bring me my talon. In the sea lurks the ruff-fish. If you bring me my talon, then I will give you the sack with the flint."

He (then) went from there. A tree stump stands, he sat on it, and began to search (with his eyes) for the man. On the back (on the reverse side) there is a needle stuck in. He pulled it out and put it in his pocket.

Then he again went off, walked, walked — again returned to the she-eagle, and brought her her talon. "Grandmother," he says, "put your finger here!" He put (the talon) into the finger. She gave him the sack with flint. Afterwards, he went home, and again returned to old man Ydat.

M_b (KS, No. 57): Kasket

1. Old man Yrohot lived on the shore of a pebbled channel, he is raising a vixen.
2. Then it left them, crossed the pebbled channel, found In'get's storage platform, climbed onto the platform, took some fish, and took them to old man Yrohot.
3. The people passed the night, morning came, it (the vixen) again went to that storage platform, climbed onto it, and threw down the salmon trout — the earth trembled.
4. Among the Inits lives Kasket. 5. Init tells Kasket: "Go outside!"

Restoration of a Ket Myth

6. Kasket answers: "No, there is no one there."
7. The vixen again took salmon trout for old man Yrohot, and brought it to him.
8. Init went outside, found the vixen's trail, chased after it, chased, chased.
9. Was it long, was it short that he chased — the vixen struck itself against the ground and became a three-legged horse, while Init changed into Kasket.
10. Kasket mounted the horse and galloped ahead on it, galloped and galloped.
11. Kasket listens — a shamanic tree cries (sings) like a black grouse. 12. He looked there — a cradle is tied to it.
13. He jumped into it, began to rock, rocked, rocked — it lifted him up.
14. Then he went upward in the mask of a deer.
15. There above an eagle's nest hangs on the divine tree. He began to shake the eaglets. The eaglets started to cheep. 16. The she-eagle came to her fledglings (children).
17. Kasket said to the she-eagle: "Give me the sack for flint!"
18. The she-eagle answered: "Go to the sea, bring my talon from the ruff, then I shall give you the sack."
19. Kasket [then] left that place, was it long, was it short that he walked. 20. Kasket (the vixen) is walking, is walking, struck himself against the ground — became Tyl'get with a little larch tree.
21. Tyl'get sits on the larch. 22. An eagle flew in from somewhere.
23. The eagle wanted to seize him, but Tyl'get somehow snatched one of his eyes.
24. Tyl'get, with the little larch tree, again became Kasket.
25. He walked, walked, came to the seashore.
26. Kasket took a look: "And where has the ruff-fish hidden?"
27. Kasket talks with himself: "They have sent me somewhere to some ruff-fish!"
28. Shortly afterwards, either a shark or a whale (the narrator's translation) stuck its nose up from the sea. 29. "Grandson," it says, "What are you looking for?"

30. "Grandmother, the she-eagle has sent for her talon, the she-eagle has said that a ruff-fish has carried it away."
31. The shark said: "Grandson, grandson, the she-eagle wanted to seize me with her foot, I have her talon. 32. Grandson, I will not return it. My head horns froze in the winter to the ice. 33. If you bring me my horns, then I shall give it to you."
34. Kasket left, searches the sand on the seashore.
35. Whether a lot or a little time passed, even he did not know, he glanced forward — men are sitting on the sand. 36. They are really getting drunk!
37. Kasket looked at them closely — devils are sitting there.
38. Kasket covered himself in soot, became like the devils, walked up, and sat next to them.
39. The devils were drinking so much! 40. They pour Kasket vodka, a full horn of it.
41. Kasket pretended that he drank it, he spilled it to the side, and hid the empty in his bosom.
42. They drank, drank, and the devils got all sandy. 43. Kasket again and again poured to the side and hid in his bosom. In this way they gave him seven horns.
44. The drinking ended, the devils cannot see a thing [don't recognize].
45. In the meantime Kasket went to the shark.
46. And the devils guessed later: "This," they said, "was again a man from the other world, he was drinking with us, and now he has disappeared somewhere."
47. Kasket walked, walked, and came to the place where earlier the shark lay in the water (is lying).
48. Kasket looks around the place, and the shark has poked out of the sea.
49. Kasket said: "Grandmother, I have brought your horns."
50. The shark answered: "Well, well, very good!"
51. The shark returned the sea-eagle's talon, and he gave it the horns. 52. Kasket set off on the return trip.
53. Was it long, was it short that he walked, walked — he again found the place where there was Tyl'get and the little larch tree. 54. Tyl'get is playing the harmonica and does not pay attention to anyone.

Restoration of a Ket Myth

55. He looked down — a whetstone is lying at the bole of the larch tree. 56. He stuck it in his bosom and again climbed the little larch tree. 57. And it, as it played (plays) the harmonica, so it continues playing.

58. The sea rose.

59. Kasket pulled the whetstone out of his bosom, and tramped down on the bough of the little larch tree [here he put the whetstone], 60. and the seawater reached the whetstone and took it.

61. Kasket continues playing on the harmonica, and from somewhere an eagle flew in and sat on top of the little larch tree.

62. Tyl'get gave back the eagle's eye. Kasket said to the eagle: "I will not return the she-eagle's."

63. The eagle took hold of Kasket. 64. Was it long, was it short that they flew, they came to the eagles' nest.

65. Kasket said to the she-eagle: "Here is your talon."

66. The she-eagle took it, put it on her finger.

67. The she-eagle gave the flint. 68. "Now," she says, "go down to old man Yrohot."

Toward Formal Analysis of Plot Construction

O. G. REVZINA and I. I. REVZIN

Introductory remarks. The foundations of the formal theory of plot construction were laid in the writings of Russian formalists, primarily V. Shklovskii and B. Eikhenbaum. The morphological analysis of the fairy tale undertaken by V. Propp (1) was the next significant step in the construction of this theory. Propp's methods gained further development in the writings of Viacheslav Ivanov and V. Toporov, on the one hand, and of Iu. Meletinskii, S. Nekliudov, N. Novik, and D. Segal (2), on the other. In this connection a need developed and an opportunity arose for a more general and formal approach, applied to a broader class of texts. (3) In this article some examples of the application of this theory to analysis of specific material are provided.

Certain concepts of the theory of relations. Below we shall treat the plot of a work under analysis as an n graph, i.e., as a set M on which a number of relations are defined that are valid either for the entire text or for some specific portion of the text. The elements of set M are the characters, and the relations may be of utmost diversity, for example, coencounter, kinship, betrothal, intimacy, friendship, enmity, etc. Let us note that Propp's functions can also be interpreted as relations, and specifically such relations as are particularly essential for

Formal Analysis of Plot Construction

the development of action in a given type of texts.

Depending on the relations a character enters, the whole set of characters is divided into classes. Thus Propp identifies seven classes of characters: the antagonist, the giver, the helper, the princess, the sender, the hero, the false hero. (4) Analysis of detective stories revealed eight classes (5): a person interested in a murder, the initiator of the murder, the murderer, the detective, the detective's assistant, a sympathetic young thing, a kindly old thing, the victim. In drama six classes were identified (6): the representative of the thematic strength, the representative of a value, the recipient, the antagonist, the arbiter, the mediator. Our task here does not include demonstrating the fact that the matter at issue pertains to diverse embodiments of one and the same (only more or less fractionated) division into classes, which is apparently universal. We are concerned only with the fact that there exists a set of characters, a certain division of it into classes, and a totality of relations defined on the set of characters (or on the set of corresponding classes).

Relations of coencounter. Relations of coencounter are a class of relations defined on a set of characters, which is the simplest and most easily formalizable. For their analysis we use in part the apparatus proposed by S. Marcus (7) for the formalization of dramaturgical poetics. We, too, shall illustrate these relations on the basis of the example of dramatic works, for here these relations lie at the surface, and no need exists for special, supplemental means for extracting them from the text. Let us picture a description of the drama by an observer who does not understand a text (i.e., at this level we disregard contentual relations) but who can identify characters in the various scenes (i.e., can establish the fact that a certain character has already appeared) and can clearly identify the appearance and exit of each figure. We note that for him the play is unambiguously divided into scenes, for each new event in the play is marked by a change in the dramatis personae present on stage. Let him in the course of the action compile "minutes" of the action, a record-table of the following type: the columns

Semiotics and Structuralism

Scene	Queen Anne	Duchess of Marl-borough	Viscount Boling-broke	Masham	Abigail	Marquis de Torcy	Thompson
1	O	O	I	I	O	I	O
2	O	O	I	I	O	O	O
3	O	O	I	I	I	O	O
4	O	O	I	O	I	O	O
5	O	I	I	O	I	O	O
6	O	O	I	O	I	O	O
7	O	O	O	I	I	O	O
8	I	O	O	O	O	O	I
9	I	I	O	O	O	O	O
10	I	I	O	O	I	O	I
11	O	O	O	O	I	O	O
12	O	O	I	O	I	O	O
13	I	I	I	O	I	O	O
14	O	O	I	O	I	O	O
15	O	O	I	I	I	O	O
16	O	O	I	O	O	O	O
17	O	I	I	O	I	O	O
18	I	O	O	O	I	O	O
19	O	I	O	O	I	O	O
20	O	O	O	I	I	O	O
21	I	O	O	I	O	O	O
22	I	O	O	I	I	O	O
23	I	O	I	O	O	O	O
24	I	I	I	O	I	O	O
25	O	I	O	O	O	O	O
26	O	I	O	O	O	O	O
27	O	I	O	I	I	O	O
28	O	O	O	I	I	O	O
29	O	O	O	I	I	O	O
30	O	O	I	O	I	O	O
31	O	I	I	O	O	O	O
32	I	I	I	O	I	I	O
33	O	O	I	I	O	O	O
34	O	O	I	O	I	O	O
35	O	I	I	O	O	O	O
36	I	O	I	O	I	O	I
37	I	O	I	O	O	O	O
38	I	O	O	O	I	O	O
39	I	O	O	I	I	O	O
40	I	I	I	I	I	O	O

Formal Analysis of Plot Construction

in the table represent the characters while the lines represent the successively changing scenes in the play. We enter an O in a given square if the character was absent in a given scene, and an I if he was present. Above, by way of illustration, we present a table drawn up for Scribe's play <u>The Glass of Water</u>.

What information can be extracted from such tables? (8)

Each character, P_i, is correlated with a set $f(P_i)$, which is the set of scenes in which he participates. If we find $f(P_1)$ cf (P_2), we say that character P_1 is predicted by character P_2. Thus in our table the appearance of Thompson is predicted by the appearance of the queen (this is natural to the audience, which knows that Thompson is her personal servant, but our observer gains this information by formal means). The appearance of the Marquis de Torcy is predicted by the appearance of Bolingbroke (which is also natural, for the association of Marquis de Torcy with the intrigue is carried out entirely through Bolingbroke). Because of their clearly secondary role, we shall not deal further with the predicted characters. A situation not occurring in our table is possible in which two characters mutually predict each other. This is the case, for example, with Bobchinskii and Dobchinskii in Gogol's <u>The Inspector General</u>, i.e., when one is dealing with the doubling of a single character.

Now let us take for each P_i the power of a set $f(P_i)$, i.e., the number of scenes in which he participates. This makes it possible to establish a definite hierarchy of characters. We shall call their place in the hierarchy their rank. For our table we obtain:

Rank:	Character:	No. of scenes:
1	Abigail	27
2	Bolingbroke	23
3	Queen	16
4-5	Duchess of Marlborough Masham	14

We see that even this simple characterization is significant, for the two persons conducting the intrigue have the highest rank. True, such an indicativeness of rank is characteristic only of simple comedies of intrigue. For purposes of comparison let us present (without a table, which could be easily reconstructed from the text of the comedy), the hierarchy by rank in Molière's Tartuffe:

Rank:	Character:	No. of scenes:
1	Orgon	21
2	Elmire	18
3-4	Cléante, Dorine	17
5-6	Mariane, Damis	14
7	Tartuffe	10
8	Mme. Pernelle	7
9	Valère	4

It is obvious that the weight of these characters in the action and their influence on the development of the intrigue are reflected only obliquely. Particularly amazing is Tartuffe's excessively low rank and the excessively high rank of Orgon.
Nor is the leading role of the women, Elmire and, particularly, Dorine, in the development of the intrigue accurately reflected. Now we want to demonstrate that other information as well can be extracted from the table.

Let us term the mobility of a characer the number of his appearances on the stage irrespective of the change of other characters. Now the hierarchy looks somewhat different:

The Glass of Water		Tartuffe	
1 Abigail	10	1-3 Elmire, Dorine, Mariane	5
2 Duchess of Marlborough	9	4-5 Tartuffe, Damis	4
3 Masham	7	6-7 Orgon, Cléante	3
4 Queen Anne	6	8-9 Mme Pernelle, Valère	2
5 Bolingbroke	5		

Here the hierarchy in Tartuffe has changed somewhat, but

Formal Analysis of Plot Construction

the characteristics obtained are excessively brief: in fact, all that is of interest is the greater mobility of the women engaging in the intrigue. This is confirmed by the data for The Glass of Water, in which the greatest mobility was displayed by the two competitors, Abigail and the Duchess of Marlborough, while the organizer of the intrigue has the least mobility of all.

Marcus, in the work cited, examines a number of other characteristics, but he takes as premise that a character participating in scenes involving larger numbers on stage at once carries a greater weight. This may be true of the plays with political plots that he analyzed. We take the opposite premise as point of departure: a character is all the more important to the plot the smaller the number of persons, on the average, appearing with him. To establish the degree of individuality of the character, we use the index $\frac{\Sigma n \alpha_i}{n}$, where α_i is the number of characters in the i-th scene in which the particular character participates, and n is the number of scenes in which he participates. By individuality, for which we will identify rank in inverse order, we obtain:

The Glass of Water		Tartuffe	
1 Bolingbroke	2.6	1 Tartuffe	3.4
2 Abigail	2.8	2 Orgon	4
3 Masham	3	3 Dorine	4.3
4 Duchess of Marlborough	3.1	4-5 Cléante, Elmire	5
5 Queen Anne	3.2	6-7 Damis, Mariane	5.5

These characterizations sufficiently reflect the influence of a character on the course of the intrigue. And the totality of characteristics provides quite an interesting picture.

Relations of coencounter can be used to identify new relations, such as the relation (ternary): character P_1 is closer to character P_2 than to character P_3. This relation is obtained as follows. Let us denote the distance between two characters, P_1 and P_2, by the number $S(P_1,P_2) = \frac{A(P_1,P_2)}{B(P_1,P_2)}$, where $A(P_1,P_2)$

is the number of scenes in which only one of these two characters appears, and $B(P_1, P_2)$ is the number in which at least one of them appears. Below we present a diagram of distances for four protagonists from <u>The Glass of Water</u> (excluding Masham, whose role was more passive):

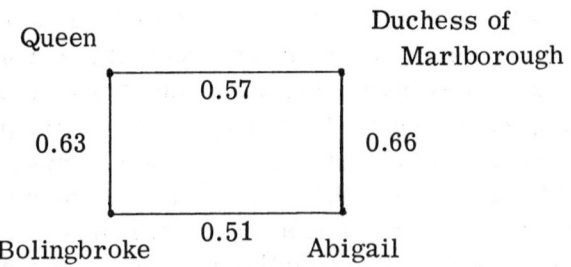

Here are reflected both the struggle of Bolingbroke and the Duchess of Marlborough (the political intrigue) and the rivalry of Abigail and Queen Anne (the love intrigue). Moreover, the distribution of forces is clearly outlined. As we see, our observer could have established a great deal without knowing the meaning of what was going on. His position is analogous to the position of a descriptive linguist or the position of a decoder. As we know, the apparatus of linguistics has been greatly enriched thanks to decoding procedures, but modern linguistics is not confined to them. Identically, the poetics of plot construction, while making use of relations of coencounter, cannot be confined to them. Below we proceed to other types of relations.

<u>Relations of coincidence or pasting</u>. Propp, in the work cited above (p. 74), had already examined a case of coincidence of functions, i.e., a character's membership simultaneously in two classes of dramatis personae. The relations of pasting are particularly important to the poetics of the detective story, in which some kind of pasting always occurs, in particular, the pasting of the role of murderer with some other category. Let us cite examples of nontrivial pastings from the novels of Agatha Christie. In the novel <u>Death in the Air</u>, the

Formal Analysis of Plot Construction

murderer proves to be a sweet young thing, whereas in the novel Murder on the Links there is coincidence between the victim and the person who has thought up the murder; and in the renowned novel The Murder of Roger Ackroyd, the detective's assistant (the narrator) and the murderer coincide, i.e., the story is told by the murderer, but in such a way that the reader cannot guess this. The choice of linguistic means in the latter case is characteristic: "I did everything that remained to be done," says the narrator, actually referring to the murder.

It is necessary to distinguish coincidence that actually takes place and coincidence as other characters conceive of it to themselves, since the latter can influence their behavior (thus for Bella Duveen in the novel Murder on the Links the murderer and the sweet young thing are pasted together, and this explains her false testimony; the conduct of Jack Renauld is explained similarly).

"Homeostatic" plots. In most plots it is possible to identify certain disturbances and the liquidation of the consequences of these disturbances (compare "lack" and "liquidation of the lack" in Propp's schema). However, one can identify a class of plots whose motion can be entirely reduced to a disturbance of the initial system and subsequent acquisition of a new stability. Such plots, which, as we shall see, the theory of relations particularly suits, we shall tentatively term homeostatic. Below we shall examine two types of such plots: the first pertains to the simplest type, in which the system returns in some sense to its initial state; and the second to a more complex type, in which the system changes from an initial state of stability to a labile state and then enters a new state of stability not identical with the initial one.

As our first example, we also take a detective novel, Georgette Heyer's Death in the Stocks, first published in 1935.

The initial situation involves five characters, among whom the following relations are identified: R_1 — hostility; R_2 — betrothal; R_3 — friendship; R_4 — kinship through the father; and R_5 — kinship through the mother.

There is yet another character who personifies the relationship of the family and the author to the other characters. We shall denote by plus or minus signs the corresponding evaluations (in theory this is yet another type of relation).

The initial state is reconstructed in the form of a graph:

(1)

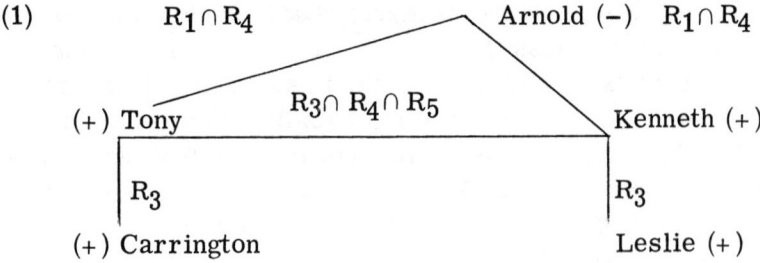

The next stage might be pictured by the following graph:

(2)

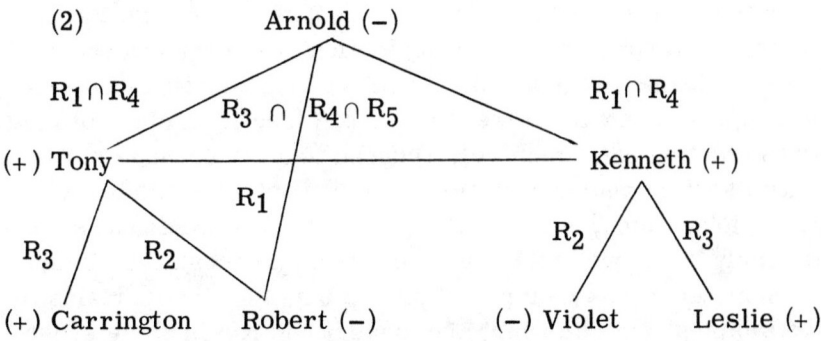

Unlike graph 1, graph 2 is asymmetrical; and this already reflects the instability of the system, caused by the two "disturbing" (from the standpoint of the family) betrothals. The murder of Arnold and the suspicion falling, first, on those associated with him by relation R_1 introduce new disturbances into the system. Next appears Arnold's brother Roger, who takes his place; and since the inheritance goes to him, there arises a new asymmetrical relation, R_6: potential disappointment because of the lost inheritance. Therefore, the model takes on a form nonisomorphic to Diagram 2:

Formal Analysis of Plot Construction

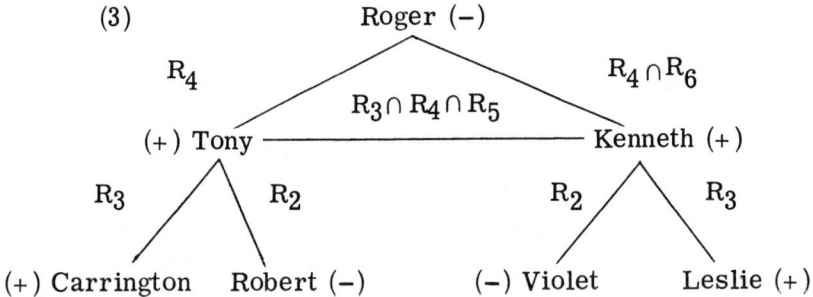

(3)

Comparison of diagrams 2 and 3 shows that if we are dealing with a homeostatic plot, Roger has to be murdered, if only "because of considerations of symmetry." And in fact a second murder occurs, with suspicion falling only on those who are in the R_6 relation with him. Next comes a structurally very important breakup of the betrothal of Tony to Robert and her engagement to Carrington. Robert becomes unnecessary not only because he disturbs tranquility but also because he is not in an R_6 relation with Roger and cannot be suspected of the second murder (by the laws of the detective story, the first and second murders must be committed by the same character). The diagram of relations assumes the form:

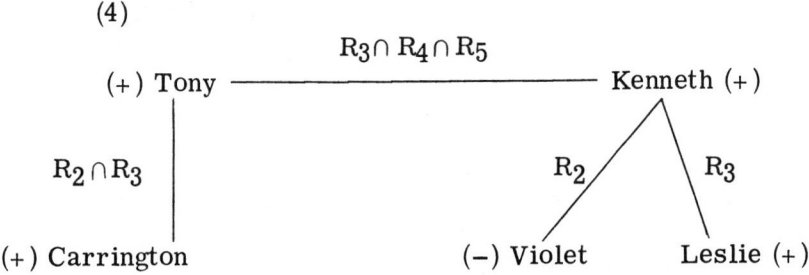

(4)

The moment when diagram 4 is established coincides with the culmination of the plot. Kenneth, who has the sympathy of his family, is jailed, accused of the two murders. It is necessary to save him and find the real murderer. For structural considerations it is easiest of all to conceive of Violet as the murderer, for then only characters with (+) valuations will remain, and the diagram will again become symmetrical. Carrington assumes the role of detective, i.e., there takes place one of the pastings we discussed in an earlier section. Carrington's actions as detective are explainable by graph theoretic operation of composition of relations. Specifically, the composition $R_1 \oplus R_2$ and $R_6 \oplus R_2$ immediately associates Violet with both victims (let us note that the length of this chain determines the degree of complexity of the author's design). Violet is exposed by Carrington, symmetry is restored, and the plus portion of diagram 1 is again attained. The "homeostat" has returned to its initial state. Such homeostatic plots have a reassuring effect on the mass audience: it is pleasant to know that the world is ruled by laws that preserve the bulwarks of our existence. (As A. M. Piatigorskii has observed, homeostatic plots are particularly typical of English literature and can be related to the national psychology.)

This example shows the similarity of the homeostatic plot to the happy-end plot. But for more complex homeostatic plots, this similarity is no longer essential.

As an example of a more complicated homeostatic plot we employ Iris Murdoch's novel A Severed Head. The initial situation in the novel is the usual triangle: the narrator, his wife, Antonia, and his mistress, Georgie. This situation is described not as transitory but specifically as stable and long-lasting. The disturbance of the system is connected with the appearance of two additional characters: a psychoanalyst who uses the "spouses," and then his sister Honor. As disturbers of tranquility these characters could be given minus evaluations; but in the psychological novel, unlike the detective story, such an approach is regarded as too primitive.

The narrator also has a brother, Alexander. Thus along with the relation of intimacy R_7, which links the narrator and Antonia, as well as the narrator and Georgie, the relation of direct kinship R_8 is also of significance. It turns out that the initial relation between the doctor and Honor has to be described as an intersection $R_7 \cap R_8$.

Formal Analysis of Plot Construction

And thus we have two mutually unconnected graphs:

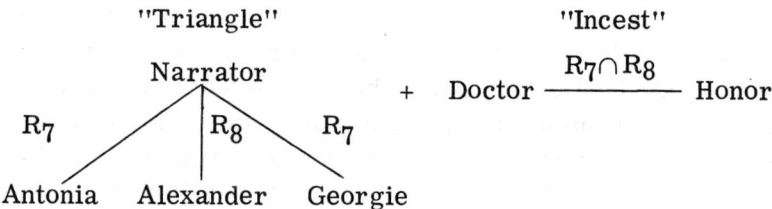

The movement of the plot is advanced by a means that can be characterized as a transmission of a relation, specifically, it is as though a new relation, R_9, were introduced. This relation can be characterized as follows:

$$xR_9y \underset{Df}{\equiv} (\forall z)(xR_7z - yR_7z).$$

As a result of the establishment of relation R_9 between the narrator and Alexander, and between the narrator and the doctor, the following relations come into being:

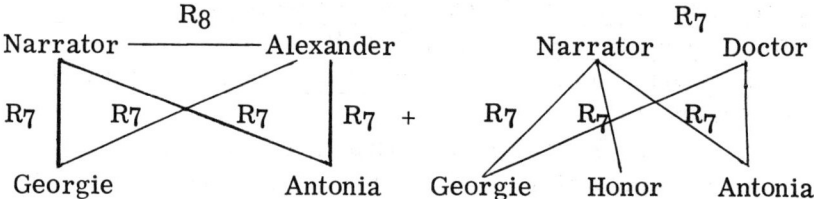

The final stable state is attained, however, by complete liquidation of the narrator, for whom all connections are broken. What remains is a world brought into a stage of stable equilibrium, in which there is no room for the narrator:

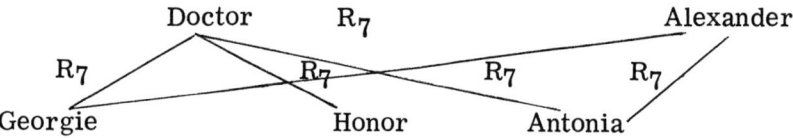

(The connection Alexander R_7 Honor, the only one not described in the novel, is easily hypothesized "for reasons of symmetry.")

As may be seen from the plot described, the "homeostatic" diagram can also be associated with a claim to a tragic world view. Nevertheless, it seems that plots that are too easily described in this fashion can hardly be the basis of great works of art. But analysis of such plots provides an easier point of departure for the study of plot construction, while one can attempt to describe a genuinely artistic work and its plot as a departure from similar, too obvious patterns.

Notes

1) V. Propp, Morfologiia skazki, 2nd ed., Moscow, 1969.
2) Trudy po znakovym sistemam, IV, Tartu, 1969.
3) This was done in V. V. Ivanov and V. N. Toporov, "K rekonstruktsii praslavianskogo teksta," Slavianskoe iazykoznanie, Moscow, 1963.
4) Ibid., pp. 72-73.
5) I. I. Revzin, "K semioticheskomu analizu detektivov," Programma i tezisy dokladov v letnei shkole po vtorichnym modeliruiushchim sistemam, Tartu, 1964.
6) E. Souriau, Les deux cent mille situations dramatiques, Flammarion, 1950.
7) S. Marcus, Poetica matematică, Bucharest, 1970.
8) L. Varpakhovskii, director at the Vakhtangov Theater, has kindly communicated to us the fact that he always begins his work of staging a play by drawing up such a table.

O. M. Freidenberg as a Student of Culture

Iu. M. LOTMAN

The name of O. M. Freidenberg is rarely cited today in surveys of works on the theory of literature. Yet it is enough merely to glance through the titles of Freidenberg's books and articles to be persuaded of the extraordinary breadth and diversity of her scholarly interests. Even if one leaves aside problems in classical philology, there remains a broad range of topics illuminating various facets of theoretical poetics. The structure of genre, plot, the relationship between mythology and literature, the origin of rhythmics and poetic language, the essence of art and the laws of its evolution — this is an incomplete list of the subjects investigated by Freidenberg.

What is the reason for this silence? The history of philology as a discipline is basically undeveloped and undocumented (with the result that the level of contemporary scholarship, which sometimes carelessly commits to oblivion achievements of the past and disregards the level previously attained, has been lowered). Aside from this, we must note a more basic reason: The broad, contradictory, and complex legacy in literary scholarship, ethnography, and folkloristics left by scholars who in the late 1920s and 1930s were grouped around Academician N. Ia. Marr has not yet received calm and objective evaluation. The point is not merely that the discussion on linguistics at the

Semiotics and Structuralism

beginning of the 1950s occurred in an atmosphere remote from scholarly objectivity. Another factor is more important: It very quickly became clear to what degree "the new teaching on language" lagged behind the level attained by world linguistics. Further advance of the discipline required neither discussion nor refutation — it simply followed a different path. As a consequence, while, on the one hand, the work of the scholars who now interest us was erased purely by fiat, on the other hand, the scholars who most seriously studied, in the latter half of the 1950s and during the 1960s, problems of the theory of art and the theory of culture did not sense any organic need to turn to this scholarly tradition.

However, entirely aside from general evaluation of Marrism as a scholarly stage, at least two other questions remain: To what degree is it valid to subsume under its general evaluation the activity of a particular scholar ? and, what is particularly significant for us, Is the evaluation of what was done under Marr's aegis in linguistics and in the study of culture identical?

The historical paradox lay in the fact that it was precisely in linguistics that the weakest sides of the "new teaching on language" emerged. The direction of scholarly thought within the framework of this school was directly opposed to one of the principal trends characterizing the humanities in the twentieth century. This tendency may be defined as an intrusion of linguistic methods into the nonlinguistic disciplines. Marrism, on the other hand, is distinguished by the intrusion of nonlinguistic methods into the realm of linguistics. This trend proved to be historically sterile. The complete identification of language and thought deprived linguistics of its own content, and the humanities of a method. However, the task of studying consciousness as a system was posed at the same time, primarily with respect to archaic thought. The study of language was sacrificed to research on secondary models of a culturological type. But what was done in the latter field merits serious attention.

As early as 1964, in the first issue of Works on Semiotics [Trudy po znakovym sistemam], in speaking of the historical roots of structural-semiotic studies we felt it necessary

O. M. Freidenberg as a Student of Culture

...to recall that the structural method studies, above all, the meaning, the semantics of literature, folklore, and myth. Therefore, it would be of interest to trace its contact with those trends in Soviet literary scholarship that sought to investigate historical semantics and, to some degree, reflected the most fruitful sides of N. Ia. Marr's linguistic teaching (see O. M. Freidenberg's The Poetics of Plot and Genre [Poetika siuzheta i zhanra] and the articles of I. G. Frank-Kamenetskii, I. M. Tronskii, and others). (1)

Adopting a view of the prehistory of structural poetics somewhat different from that sketched by A. K. Zholkovskii and Iu. K. Shcheglov, we would consider it useful to direct attention to the way structural-semiotic methods formed and blazed a path for themselves within the framework of different and sometimes conflicting trends in scholarly thought.

The method that its own creators sometimes defined as "semantic," and elsewhere as "semantic-paleological," counterposed itself to formalism. In the programmatic work "The Aim of the Collective Study of the Plot of Tristan and Isolde" [Tselevaia ustanovka kollektivnoi raboty nad siuzhetom "Tristana i Isol'dy"], O. M. Freidenberg devoted a special section (the second) to a polemic against the formalist schools and to opposing to it "paleontological analysis as advanced by japhetology":

> Paleontological analysis (genetic-sociological analysis) proceeds from the "finished" phenomenon into the depths and reveals, step by step, the multistage character of the development of the phenomenon. Unlike formalism, it shows that "artistic forms given once and for all" are historically labile and that their qualitative variability is produced by society's view of the world, conditioned by the base; on the other hand, what the formalist ascribes to the individual author, the paleontologist can find in folklore and mythology. (2)

What is essential for us now is not the author's polemical ardor or even less her presentation — clearly tendentious — of her opponents' views. Of interest is something else — the parties to the dispute, as often happens, split up a single scientific problem between them and consequently were collaborators in a broad historical context. The formal school singled out study of the syntagmatic structure of a text as an independent and fundamental scientific problem. Immanent-relational meanings overshadowed the semantic. The reaction to this was an attempt to concentrate attention on semantics — sociological, cultural, and religious-mythological. The fact that this entailed loss of comprehension of the structural unity of the text, of the syntagmatic interrelationship of its elements, may be seen as a serious scholarly loss. The unity of any work, and consequently its meaning as a whole, could hardly have interested the "japhetologists" less. Even in such brilliant works as "Three Plots or the Semantics of One" (3) or "A Blind Man at the Precipice" (4), Freidenberg was primarily interested in the texts of relics, fragments of preceding textual formations — myths and rituals — which are meaningless in this new environment, often incomprehensible to both author and audience, and meaningful only when transferred into actual or hypothetical contexts of profound antiquity.

However, if a text as a whole invariably decays (paradoxically, precisely that which led to understanding of the meaning of the text as a whole is discarded from the legacy of the Formalists!), alongside it another whole is created: the structure of the archaic consciousness. Therein lies the undeniable service of the scholarly school that interests us. Basing themselves not on linguistics (yet another paradox in a school that proclaimed itself herald of a linguistic conception), but on the ethnology of their day, the "japhetologists" tried to reconstruct the universal structure of the archaic consciousness. Language attracted them merely as object, and their techniques were borrowed from the sociological disciplines. And although the edifice erected in this way could not be successfully completed, the broadly conceived attempt to create a model that would cover all the early forms of human consciousness is in itself noteworthy.

Of great interest in this connection is a work by I. Frank-

O. M. Freidenberg as a Student of Culture

Kamenetskii, "Primitive Thought in the Light of Japhetic Theory and Philosophy." (5) Basing himself on the writings of E. Cassirer (particularly Language and Myth, The Philosophy of Symbolic Forms, and Mythical Thought), seeking to combine them with Marr's methodology, and also employing a broad range of ethnological sources, Frank-Kamenetskii built a model of "prelogical thought." His view of the "diffuseness of the primitive mind" and its distinctive "prelogical" nature was no discovery at the time. Something else is interesting here: the idea that archaic thought was systemic, reference to the sign nature of the system, and the idea that neither modern language nor modern logic can give us a metalanguage with which to describe it.

Differentiating between the mythological, scientific-logical, quotidian, and poetic consciousness, the author directly confronted problems that also concern modern culture studies. It is curious that the term he used to define the realization of such systems — "picture of the world" (6) — has also proved to be convenient for modern typological constructs. While in the usual Marrist constructs the complete identification of language and thought eliminated the problem of the modeling influence of the former on the latter, in this work Frank-Kamenetskii, associating himself with Cassirer, emphasized the role of "language as the shaping and organizing principle thanks to which a one-dimensional flow of impressions first acquires definite contours, merging into a structured, internally organized world." (7)

The striving to penetrate into the "special structure of primitive thought" (8) led, however, to contradiction with an important shortcoming of the method: In examining the evolution of semantic linkages tying the modern consciousness to its archaic foundation, Frank-Kamenetskii (who moves along this chain retrospectively: see the demonstrative subtitle of the collection Tristan and Isolde) disdained descriptions of synchronic cross sections of culture and consciousness. No description of structure resulted, despite the fact that he oriented his research toward it.

Disregarding the apparatus that structural linguistics possessed at that time, these scholars deprived themselves of the opportunity to attain the goal for which they strove. All the more interesting are the gropings, if only empirically, for the synchronic mechanism of archaic culture. Very profound in this regard is the persistent view in Freidenberg's works of ritual as the plot- and myth-generating mechanism of culture. The appropriateness of such a change was evident in the fact that it was at approximately the same time that B. M. Eikhenbaum and Iu. N. Tynianov were groping for analogous cultural functions in the ritualization of writer's existence, and V. Ia. Propp tried to interpret initiation rites as the generative mechanism of the magical tale. It was precisely the unity of the ritual function that permitted Freidenberg, with extraordinary scholarly perception, to identify seemingly remote plots, reducing them to invariant patterns; to identify remote characters; to see in antonyms variants of the identical. On this basis a bold attempt was made to see in all folklore plots variants of a single, invariant semantic model: "All folklore plots and genres are variant paraphrases of one and the same semantic meaning, which has regular morphology." The primitive consciousness "perceives the world in identities and repetitions; however, images are heteromorphous from the very outset, differing from each other in structure while having complete semantic identity." (9) On this foundation a system of analysis of the ritual ambivalence of genres and characters is constructed that reveals the dialectical transformation of antonyms into synonyms. (10)

Thus whereas Propp brought up the task of syntagmatic description of fairy-tale and mythological texts, Freidenberg, seeing in various myths variants of a single invariant plot, posed the problem of the paradigmatics of folklore texts, a problem whose timeliness we feel particularly clearly at present.

Freidenberg's thoughts about the role of the "double," the twin, in plots are very profound and still await interpretation and evaluation.

Interest in the problem of the plot double, the comic or

O. M. Freidenberg as a Student of Culture

parodic double of the "lofty" hero, and in the parodic ritual that is a reflection of sacral ritual, and the idea that these cultural doubles are mutually connected and that ridicule plays an ambivalent role bring the scientific constructs of O. M. Freidenberg close to a number of fruitful ideas first advanced by M. M. Bakhtin.

We have stated that interest in archaic relict interjections in later texts destroyed synchronic-structural analysis of the work. However, this same feature simultaneously makes the scientific thinking of our researcher quite timely, for we are witnesses to a steady growth of interest in the mythological, the fairy-tale, and more broadly, the archaic elements in modern culture. They are presently treated not as regrettable and useless fragments but as organic forms assuring the wholeness of human culture as such. However, the search for such elements is sometimes carried on without the necessary methodological rigor; and here it is more than appropriate to recall the scholarly heritage left by Marr, Freidenberg, Frank-Kamenetskii, Tronskii, and other scholars of this school.

When speaking of the fate of the scientific ideas advanced by this group, one must recall the influence of the concept of stages in the literary process developed by G. A. Gukovskii. It would be a very interesting undertaking from the standpoint of the history of science to show how fruitfully philologists, differing in scholarly positions but equally brilliant in talent and erudition, whom fate brought together with unique generosity within the walls of Leningrad University in the 1930s and 1940s, influenced each other.

We should like to complete this brief and by no means systematic survey by pointing to one feature of the positions taken by the scholars of this group that we feel is quite pertinent at present: The object of their study was culture as such, not some particular side of it. It is precisely here, within the framework of our native scholarship, that it has most clearly and consistently been shown that linguistics or the study of literature is merely part of the theory of culture. In the 1920s and 1930s this position had a weak spot because the development of a method for culture studies could be carried out only by temporal narrowing of the task. Only synchronic description of certain sign systems, natural languages above all, could open the way to semiotic study of culture as a whole. Thus a problem was posed for whose solution no methods then existed. The separation of goal from method was the weak side of Marrist culture study. But the breadth of the scientific formulation of this question was its indubitable achievement.

It is difficult now to evaluate the overall significance of Freidenberg's works for the very simple reason that the overwhelming majority of her studies are still in manuscript form. Their publication would bring to light riches of scientific thought that have been hidden to this day.

O. M. Freidenberg is also entitled to our interest as a cultural figure of our era: a scholar of extraordinary erudition, the first woman in the USSR to hold the degree of doctor of philological sciences, she was an individual with a complex and rich intellectual life. Her correspondence with her cousin, the poet Boris L. Pasternak, is a cultural monument that will draw the attention of scholars. (11) In her fate and human makeup she belongs not only to the history of science but also to the history of culture.

* * *

The manuscripts of O. M. Freidenberg are presently kept by her heir, R. Orbeli, who graciously granted us an opportunity to familiarize ourselves with them. The list of Freidenberg's scholarly works published below will provide the reader with a preliminary orientation in this matter.

The works of Freidenberg we have selected for publication cannot even pretend to provide a representative picture of her scholarly legacy. We only wanted to familiarize the reader with works from various periods, and have chosen some that have the form of theses and at the same time deal with key scholarly problems.

Publication of the selected works of O. M. Freidenberg is a

O. M. Freidenberg as a Student of Culture

scientific necessity. It is the duty of the scholarly institutions in which she worked actively and fruitfully for long years to prepare them.

Notes

1) Uch. zap. Tartuskogo un-ta, Issue 160, Tartu, 1964, p. 13.
2) "Tristan i Isol'da." Ot geroini liubvi feodal'noi Evropy do bogini matriarkhal'noi Afrevrazii, a team work of the Sector of the Semantics of Myth and Folklore, edited by Academician N. Ia. Marr, Leningrad, 1932, p. 5.
3) O. M. Freidenberg, "Tri siuzheta ili semantika odnogo," Iazyk i literatura, RANION, Research Institute for the Comparative History of the Literatures and Languages of West and East, Vol. V, Leningrad, 1930.
4) O. M. Freidenberg, "Slepets nad obryvom," Iazyk i literatura, Vol. VIII, Leningrad, 1932.
5) I. Frank-Kamenetskii, "Pervobytnoe myshlenie v svete iapheticheskoi teorii i filosofii," Iazyk i literatura, Vol. III, Leningrad, 1929.
6) Ibid., p. 106.
7) Ibid., pp. 117-18.
8) Ibid., p. 119.
9) O. M. Freidenberg, Poetika siuzheta i zhanra. Period antichnoi literatury (theses from doctoral dissertation), Leningrad, 1935, p. 4.
10) "Along with liturgical ritual there appears farcical ritual, as its phasic aspect," ibid., p. 7.
11) We are indebted to E. B. Pasternak for our information on the existence of this correspondence and on its character.

Bibliography

List of O. M. Freidenberg's Published Works and Those Mentioned in Print

1. «Деяния Павла и Феклы», 1919—21. См.: С. А. Жебелев. Апостол Павел и его послания. Пг., 1922, с. 51, пр. 1.
2. Идея пародии. Машинописный сборник в честь С. А. Жебелева. 1926, с. 378 и сл. См.: Recueil G é b é l e v. Leningrad, 1926, p. 8. Издание Госу-

дарственной Академии Истории Материальной Культуры.
3. **Thamyris**. Яфетический сборник. V. 1927, сс. 72—81.
4. Сюжетная семантика «Одиссеи». Язык и литература. IV, 1929, сс. 59—74.
5. Три сюжета или семантика одного. Там же, V, 1929, сс. 33—60. Перепечатано в приложении к «Поэтике сюжета и жанра», 1936, с. 335—361. См. № 18.
6. Прокрида (автореферат «Семантики сюжета»), см.: Отчет Коммунистической Академии за 1929 г., М., 1930.
7. Терсит. Яфетический Сборник. VI. 1930, сс. 231—253.
8. Евангелия — один из видов греческого романа. Атеист. XII. 1930, сс. 129—147 (№ 59).
9. Миф об Иосифе Прекрасном. Язык и Литература. VIII. 1932, сс. 137—158.
10. Слепец над обрывом. Там же, сс. 229—244.
11. Целевая установка коллективной работы над сюжетом «Тристана и Исольды». АН СССР. Труды Института Языка и Мышления, II. «Тристан и Исольда». Л., 1932, сс. 1—6.
12. Сюжет «Тристана и Исольды» в мифологемах эгейского отрезка Средиземноморья. Там же, сс. 91—114.
13. Фольклор у Аристофана («Тесмофориазусы»). Сергею Федоровичу Ольденбургу. Сб. статей. Л., Изд. АН СССР, 1934, сс. 549—560.
14. Поэтика сюжета и жанра (тезисы к докторской диссертации), Л., 1935. Изд. Ленинградского Института Истории, Философии, Литературы и Лингвистики.
15. Из до-гомеровской семантики. Академия Наук СССР академику Н. Я. Марру, М., 1935, сс. 381—392.
16. Проблема греческого литературного языка. Советское Языкознание. Т. I, 1935, сс. 5—31.
17. Античные теории языка и стиля (общая редакция и предисловие), М.—Л., 1935.
18. Поэтика сюжета и жанра. Период античной литературы, Л., 1936.
19. К семантике фольклорных собственных имен. Makkus и Maria. Советское Языкознание. II, 1936, сс. 3—30.
20. Что такое фольклор? См.: Ю. Соколов. Русский фольклор. 1938.
21. Об основном характере греческой литературы. См.: Ленинградский гос. ун-т. Научная сессия. 1939, с. 7.
22. То же. 120 лет Ленинградского государственного университета, Тезисы докладов на юбилейной научной сессии, Л., 1939, сс. 124—125.
23. То же. Уч. зап. ЛГУ, 1940, серия филологических наук, № 6, сс. 32—50.
24. Проблема греческого фольклорного языка. Уч. зап. ЛГУ. 1941, серия филологических наук, № 7, сс. 41—69.
25. Характеры «Теофраста». Там же, сс. 129—141.
26. Сборник статей по классической филологии (редакция и предисловие). См. № 24, сс. 1—175.
27. Кафедра классической филологии. Ленинградский гос. ун-т, отчет о деятельности за 1940 г. Изд. ЛГУ. 1941, сс. 157—158.
28. Происхождение сравнения. См.: Программа юбилейной научной сессии Ленинградского университета. Л., 1944, с. 19.
29. Происхождение литературной интриги. См.: Программа научной сессии Ленинградского университета. Л., 1945, с. 11.
30. То же, тезисы, Научная сессия 1945 г., Ленинградский гос. ун-т, Л., 1945, с. 28.
31. Орестейя в Одиссее. Научный Бюллетень ЛГОЛУ. № 6. 1946, сс. 18—21.
32. О жанре древней аттической комедии. Там же, № 9, 1946, сс. 33—35.
33. Происхождение эпического сравнения (на материале Илиады). ЛГУ. Труды юбилейной научной сессии. Л., 1946, сс. 101—113.
34. Происхождение греческой лирики. См.: Программа научной сессии Ленинградского университета. Л., 1946, с. 22; и: Вестник Древней Истории. 4. 1947, 140.
35. То же, ЛГУ. Научная сессия 1946 г. Тезисы докладов на секции филологических наук. Л., 1946, сс. 21—23.
36. *Редактирование* проф. И. М. Тронский. История античной литературы, Л., 1946.
37. Над бумагами. Проф. Р. А. Орбели. Исследования и изыскания. Подводная археология. Материалы по истории подводного труда. М.—Л., 1947.
38. О ближайших задачах кафедры классической филологии Ленинградского университета, см.: Вестник Древней Истории, 2, 1947, с. 215.
39. Лирика Сафо. См. ЛГОЛУ, Научная сессия 1947 г., Программа научной

O. M. Freidenberg as a Student of Culture

      сессии Ленинградского университета, Л., 1947, с. 18.
40. Пятнадцать лет советской классической филологии в Ленинградском университете. См.: Вестник Древней Истории. 4. 1947, с. 140.
41. Фрагмент 2 Сафо. См.: там же, стр. 141.
42. О социальном факторе в образовании греческой литературы, см.: Программа 5-й научной сессии ЛГУ, Л., 1948, с. 42.
43. То же, тезисы, ЛГОЛУ им. Жданова. Научная сессия 1948 г. Тезисы докладов по секции филологических наук, Л., 1948, сс. 51—53.
44. К вопросу о происхождении греческой метрики. Уч. зап. ЛГУ, 1948, № 90, серия филологических наук № 13, сс. 291—320.
45. Сафо. Доклады и сообщения Филологического института, ЛГОЛУ им. Жданова. 1949. Вып. 1, сс. 190—198.

A. Unpublished Articles

1. Былина о женитьбе Добрыни Никитича, 1918 (рукопись).
2. «Электра» у трех трагиков, 1919 (рукопись).
3. «Вступление к греческому роману», 1922, сс. 1—8.
4. Происхождение пародии (1923), сс. 1—16.
5. «Крест в могиле», 1925, сс. 1—6.
6. Методология одного мотива, 1925, сс. 1—14.
7. Система литературного сюжета, 1925, сс. 1—34.
8. Семантика постройки кукольного театра, 1926, сс. 1—26.
9. Учение греков о перевороте (тезисы), 1928, сс. 1—2.
10. Въезд в Иерусалим на осле, 1930, сс. 1—45 + 11 с. примечаний.
11. О неподвижных сюжетах и бродячих теоретиках, 1931, сс. 1—32.
12. Что такое фольклор? 1931, сс. 1—12.
13. Из до-аристофановской семантики. Сюжет «Птиц», 1933, сс. 1—3.
14. Игра в кости, 1933, сс. 1—11.
15. Марр и классические языки, 1933, сс. 1—21.
16. *Παρακλαυσίθυρον*, 1935, сс. 1—7.
17. Настоящий учитель, 1936, сс. 1—6.
18. Воспоминания о Н. Я. Марре, 1936, сс. 1—25.
19. Проблема фольклорного языка, 1936, сс. 61—82. (I печ. ред., в верстке).
20. Кафедра классической филологии, 1937/1938 уч. г., сс. 1—12.
21. Расовая теория в свете нового учения о языке, 1943, сс. 1—18.
22. Отзыв о диссертации С. В. Поляковой, 1944, сс. 1—4.
23. Происхождение литературной интриги, 1945, сс. 1—33.
24. «Повесть об Аполлонии Тирском», 1946, сс. 1—6.
25. Происхождение греческой лирики, 1946, сс. 1—23.
26. Из наблюдений над паллиатой, 1946, сс. 1—5.
27. Что такое эсхатология? 1947, сс. 1—6.
28. Пятнадцать лет, 1947, сс. 1—5.
29. Баховен, 1947, сс. 1—7.
30. Фрагмент I Сафо, 1947, сс. 1—8.
31. Программа по введению в агиографию, 1948, сс. 1—5.
32. Литература как особая форма освоения мира, 1949, сс. 1—9.
33. По поводу языковедческой дискуссии, 1950, сс. 1—8.

B. Unpublished Monographs

I. Этюды к «Деяниям Павла и Феклы»

    Часть I

1. Церковная история, сказания о св. Фекле, 1920, сс. 1—4.
2. Введение к славянским переводам, 1920, сс. 1—8.
3. Мучение святой первомученицы Феклы Прехвальной. Пер. с церк.-слав., 1920, сс. 1—24 (рукопись с поправками С. А. Жебелева).
4. План работы, 1920, сс. 1—4.
5. Литература вопроса, 1920, №№ 37.

Semiotics and Structuralism

   6. Θεκλα τις παρϑενος, 1920, сс. 1—8.
   7. Деяния Павла и Феклы. Пер. с герч., 1921, сс. 1—33 (рукопись с поправками С. А. Жебелева).
   8. О месте зарождения апокрифа, 1921, сс. 1—9.
   9. Хронология, 1921, сс. 1—9.
   10. Свидетельство Тертуллиана, 1921, сс. 1—8.
   11. Деяния Павла и Феклы (без начала и окончания), 1921, сс. 1—72.
   12. Комментарий, 1921, сс. 1—10.

   Часть II

   13. Die Genesis der Griechischen Romans, 1925, сс. 1—22.
   14. Die Handlung—Personen, 1927, сс. 1—10 + 11 сс. примечаний.
   15. Studien zur Acta, 927, сс. 1—15.
   16. Из истории греческого литературного языка, 1936, сс. 1—13.

II. **Проблема греческого романа**, 1929, сс. 1—192 + 14 с. примечаний + варианты, резюме, аннотация (II ред. диссертации «Происхождение греческого романа», 1923 г.).

III. **Хрестоматия** по антирелигиозным мотивам в художественной литературе, 1931, сс. 1—191. Для ГИЗ'а (не напечатано).

IV. **Семантика композиции «Трудов и дней» Гезиода»**, 1933—1939, 3 папки, с. 1—601 + 5 этюдов: 1. «Эйрена» Аристофана + примечания, 1935, сс. 1—22. 2. К происхождению буколики, 1938, сс. 1—16. 3. Сюжет «Одиссеи», 1939, сс. 1—20. 4. К генезису греческой элегии, 1938, сс. 1—8. Metabolê 1928, сс. 1—16 + 6. Указатель, аннотация и предисловие (всего 700 с.).

V. **Лекции** по введению в теорию античного фольклора, 1939—1943.

VI. **Гомеровские этюды:**
   1. Гомеровские сравнения, 1941, сс. 1—87.
   2. Комическое до комедии, 1942—1944, сс. 1—82.
   3. Гомеровский «пример», 1949, сс. 1—18.

VII. **Паллиата**, 1945—1946, сс. 1—212.

VIII. **Сафо**, 1946—1947, сс. 1—238.

IX. **Образ и понятие**, 1945—1954, сс. 1—618.

The Origin of Parody

O. M. FREIDENBERG

1.

We are all quite familiar with the fact that parody is the term for imitation in which a sublime form is filled with a paltry content. Parody is the imitation of the lofty by means of the pitiful, disparity of content and form, mimicry, a translation from the tragic to the comic. We all know this quite well.

However, the Batrachomyomachia, with its schoollike persuasiveness, remains the Batrachomyomachia: here the parody of an epic and the replacement of great passions and great heroes by those of mice and frogs evidences comic intent. Here, I repeat, everything is well. After all, in literature we have become accustomed to explaining every phenomenon in terms of the author's design and the inventiveness of his fantasy. Scholarship also has a realm in which its criterion changes sharply and in which it is permissible to introduce more

---

*Draft of my first published article (titled "Ideia parodii," it appeared in a typewritten collection in honor of S. A. Zhebelev in 1926). It was preceded by an essay, written as early as 1923, "Smekh komedii," which I presented while a student in Professor Zhebelev's seminar. (Note by O. M. Freidenberg — Iu. L.)

objective methods. This is the realm of ritual. Just as in "words" [slovesa] we do not have the right to go outside the bounds of the author's fantasy, so in the practice of ritual we are, contrariwise, required to look for some phenomenon detached from the words themselves, with a substrate of impersonal psychology. I should like to use this imposed freedom. And then I pose the question thus: How is one to explain the presence in ritual of the parodic principle, if ritual is not created by the random will of some individual author, and if its essence is comic mimicry of the lofty?

2.

I mentally review certain medieval rituals that come to mind. Of course, one first recalls the most amazing and the most inexplicable: the famous parodies of church services, of the liturgy. And what is it, in fact, that we say about church imitation, in church surroundings, of the story of the Virgin Mary, in which the central figure is an ass, and the role of the Mother of God is played by a drunken maiden? Can we understand or can we forget the fantastic procession of ragamuffins who, with great ceremony, would lead an ass cloaked in golden vestments into a church, would dress it in a rich chasuble, and would conduct a solemn divine service over it? Can we explain the conduct of the higher clergy who, when this went on, would sing hymns and imitate the brayings of a jackass? Or what can we say about the church parody of the flight of the Virgin Mary to Egypt, again one in which the entire clergy participated? Or about the triumphal entry of a jolly maiden into church astride an ass? Accompanied by a vast mob and the entire clergy, she would pass in solemn procession through the town until she reached the church, where both she and the ass were triumphantly led inside and placed by the altar. A splendid service would be held (in the intervals of which the singers and entire audience would slake their thirst and feed and water the donkey). After the liturgy everyone mixed together, danced around

The Origin of Parody

the donkey, and the tempestuous merriment soon changed into revelry. One of the participants, who had been dressed in the garments of and appointed bishop, mounted the ass, facing the animal's tail, and rode through the town to the merry jokes of the crowd, accepting bread and beer. The finale was a merry and tempestuous procession with torches and the improvisation of obscene farces (Frazer, 335s). The "La mère folle" festival developed, during which a man mounted backwards on an ass rides around a town, through a masked and fantastically dressed crowd, while his wife slaps and beats him (L'origine des masques, by C. Noirot, 1609, Collection de Leber, Vol. IX). Simultaneously, there develop sotties, comedy-farces, which are already barred from church, all with the same character of merry satire, masquerade, and excess. A prince des sots is chosen, on whom a donkey's ears are hung, and he passes in triumphant procession on an ass (Petit de Julleville, Les comédiens en France au Moyen Age, 1885). What do we say about all this? How do we explain the appearance of an ass in the role of the Lord, the liturgy translated into the language of buffoonery and farce, the church as milieu for carousers and a dirty animal? What we are dealing with is a parody not so much of the liturgy as of God himself. And who is it that is parodying him with the participation of all the higher clergy? An ass. Certainly this is the kind of joke no mortal of today would bear!

3.

Yet it was specifically the highest representatives of the church and of secular authority who did bear this, eagerly and with reverence. More than that, the mockery of divinity took place during major religious feasts and coincided primarily with Christmas, with feasts of the Virgin, and with Easter. It is obvious for whom it was intended. But there is also a list of other rituals in which we encounter parody of church hierarchs as a kind of parody of God himself in the person of his servants. With impunity a little boy imitates a bishop, dressing in episcopal vestments and in his mitre, performs the mass in the bishop's place, and parades through the town in the company of others like himself, thus parodying a church procession (Disraeli, 261). And what of the "drunken deacons" feast in ancient France? Or the elections of an "abbott of fools," "a pope of dolts," even a "pope of jesters," whose procession, in the midst of thieves and drunkards, was described with such historic fidelity by Victor Hugo in Chapter III of Notre Dame de Paris?

Let us not forget that all these parodies of divine services, called sotties, emerged from the church itself and, when they were driven out of it, retained the right to mock all that was sacred: their participants took the titles of the clergy, and no hierarch was spared (Petit de Julleville, Les comédiens en France au Moyen Age, 1885, pp. 30, 37, 40, 248; Gaston Paris, La littérature française au Moyen Age, p. 282).

Thus a parody of God? Of the highest clergy? Within the walls of the church? Involving the clergy itself as performer and accomplice? But in this case what we are dealing with is not the idea of imitation or mimicry, and, in any case, is not the fruit of the fantasy of some merry author.

4.

In medieval England's law schools, the young students and the representatives of already studied law openly hold, during the Christmas holiday, a jesters' parliament, a jesters' court, and imprisonment in jest (Disraeli, p. 264).

Let us go further. Here are parodies of officials of the highest ranks, of rulers; here is a parodied court; here are popular representation and jurisdiction, all of it in active comic depiction, but with the observation of all forms and done in all seriousness (Disraeli, pp. 264-65). Astounding! And no one arrests these bold mockers-actors. Quite the contrary, in historical epochs of monarchy and ecclesiastical authority, fancies of this kind are sanctified with traditional connivance, even encouragement and love, on the part precisely of the monarchs, precisely of the court and of jurists (op. cit., p. 272). And what is even

The Origin of Parody

more amazing, these parodies of the highest governmental and state authorities were rigorously associated with the celebration of the greatest holidays. It was precisely during a holiday that parodies of the sacred were presented: the archaic connection of parody with the most sacred is made explicit.

The fact is that parody perceived this way begins to shed light on itself in an entirely new fashion. Now I recall weddings — those innumerable weddings encountered in the folklore of the entire world, with the ossified motif of "metamorphosis": he loves her and she him; but there occurs a shuffling, a change of clothing, a substitution, and the viewer is present at a sham wedding, with a substitute hero and sham ceremony. A sham wedding! The participants seriously going through the marriage ritual are neither groom nor bride! Medieval literature is full of such plots, which rest on ritual. And what are we to make of performed funerals in which there is no corpse and the only persons present are participants in the ritual dressed in mourning and dissolved in tears? Consider Boccaccio, the fabliaux, the Thousand and One Nights, the Seven Wise Men, and you will be astounded by this seemingly absurd play, this simulation of death reproduced with the full accuracy of all forms and overt lack of content. Let me recall an ancient English miracle play in which birth is simulated: a woman feigns groaning in bed, a young lamb is wrapped in diapers and imitates a newborn baby with its bleating, the husband deceptively rocks it and calms it; and this entire scene, with complete adherence to the norms of everyday life and with conscious emphasis of the deception, is associated with the birth of Christ and the appearance of the shepherds (the so-called Towneley collection, about which one may read in the Jahrb. f. Rom. u. En. Lit., 1859, I). But I am no longer paying attention to this, but rather to the following: if we have conscious simulation, if we are faced with the totality of sacred or legitimized forms with an illusory content, then are we not facing the same parody in these rituals and plots as in the Batrachomyomachia? Liturgical melodies with preposterous lyrics, a service over an ass, a funeral without a corpse, a wedding without the couple, birth without the newborn: it is the same Batrachomyomachia, in which we find a well-known and rigorously canonical form along with total absence of an appropriate content.

5.

And in antiquity? There we see the identical phenomenon, but so archaic that antiquity in it is no younger than the Middle Ages. By way of example I cite only two parodies: of kings and of the royal entrance. In the latter case I propose to recall the Roman triumphal marches of jesters, such as those described by Suetonius, for example, or the principle of parody and farce in the serious triumphal processions of military leaders and emperors, also described by him. There is much more archaic evidence of parodies of kings: in Babylonia, Persia, Judaea, Rome, and Greece there were established festivals of jester kings, who were recruited on holy days from among criminals and were clothed in royal dress. They were granted the right to the use of the royal harem and the royal authority, after which they were stripped of their finery, lashed, and hanged or driven away. In their mocking triumph, in their victorious procession through the city escorted by the highest authority and entire population, we find a parody of the entry of a conquering king, of divinity, and of the sacred person of the king.

Now here is an ancient Attic comedy. It has become the custom to view it as political and to see in the writings of Aristophanes a satire of power. But what endlessly amazes me in Aristophanes is precisely his atheism, openly mocking all forms of religion and power. If we consider his attitude toward Zeus, Poseidon, Dionysus, and Hermes, we cannot understand it merely as the boldness of thought of classical antiquity. It is necessary to pay attention to the fact that Aristophanes leaves untouched the grandeur of the form, depriving it only of its content. Consider in The Birds the legend of the kingdom of birds cast in solemn form and presenting a comic plot of paltry significance (688 ss). What we are dealing with is a parody of

The Origin of Parody

theogony, which in itself is a sacred genre. Or consider in Aristophanes the numerous parodies of prayers, paeans, sacred hymns, ritual songs, and playlets: for example, the choruses of the farmers in The Peace, and concluding hymeneal songs both there and in The Birds, the invocations in The Frogs, Zeus's majestic appeals in The Clouds, the rituals and songs in honor of Dionysus in The Acharnians, etc.

Here a smile is often present only because the author is Aristophanes and the lips on which it plays are concealed by a comic mask. These passages of lofty lyricism, transferred in toto from customary religious usage, provide a valuable indicator of the former nature of parody. It was based not on jest or imitation but on its contiguity with the exalted. Thus there is nothing funny in the chorus of the clouds (275 ss; 299 ss) or in the paean to the Thesmophoria (295 ss). Nor would I be so bold as to regard as imitation those numerous sacred choruses and individual sacred passages that are so often incorporated by Aristophanes in their original form. They are comic only in their placement, in the fact that lofty content and paltry surroundings do not coincide. Here it is not form alone that is parodied, as in the Batrachomyomachia or the medieval liturgies: the content is permitted to retain all its majesty, without any "quotidian" imports. The entire scene of celebration of the Thesmophoria is particularly instructive (and if explained in any other way, incomprehensible). What we are witnessing, no more and no less, is a reproduction of the mysteries. A female herald sings a paean that is preceded by a ritual exclamation and a majestic prayer to the Thesmophoria, to Demeter and Kore, Plutus, Kalligeneia and the Kurotrophos Gaea, Hermes and the Charites — a severe prayer to severe gods, gods not of jest but of death (295 ss). The chorus of praying women responds with sacred hymns (312 ss). The female herald again speaks out with prayers to the bright gods and goddesses (322 ss). Only in the portion of the prayer that pertains to human relationships is parodic content introduced (334-52), but the same sacral form is adhered to. The participants in the mysteries respond with choral prayers (352 ss), and then the messenger opens the meeting of women with a solemn formula (372 ss). The parody of sacred service is finished, and a parody of community begins.

But are not Aristophanes's favorite parodic descriptions of the court and the popular gathering the same as the medieval parody of parliament, the tribunal, and the court? And does not the absurd wedding of a pitiful human to the daughter of Zeus, a wedding at which a hymeneal song is sung in honor of the sacred marriage of Zeus and Hera, or the parodic wedding of the goddess of peace provide a bridge to the wedding rituals of antiquity and medieval times, in which a sham content is introduced into the rigorous forms of the wedding ceremonial? Of course: Aristophanes's parodies of sacred legends, prayers, and religious services do provide a complete parallel to the medieval parody liturgies and parodies-plots, with a general parodying of all the statutory norms of daily life, above all those of secular power.

6.

Observation of examples of parody shows that its connection with religious rituals and words, or its coincidence with religious feasts, is no accident; for what was originally parodied was precisely what was most sacred — the gods and worship; the transfer of parody to "the powers that be," to kings, rulers, and the popular assembly (the parliament), the judges, and to all the major civil forms, was secondary. Just as in the Middle Ages the dramatis personae of parody are God and the Mother of God, so in Aristophanes does one have, in rudimentary form, introduction of Dionysus (The Frogs), Poseidon (The Birds), Hermes (The Peace, The Clouds), Plutus, Polemon, Irene, Opora, etc. We also encounter in Aristophanes Prometheus (The Birds), Heracles (The Birds, The Frogs), Charon, Aeacus, and others. This ought to remind us of earlier examples of so-called "old comedy," i.e., Epicharmus with his The Wedding of Hebe and ridicule of the supreme gods headed by Zeus, or Crates with his Dionysus, or Cratinus, in whom we can still

The Origin of Parody

find Dionysus and the Trojan heroes among the major dramatis personae. At the opposite end, for the sake of contrast, we place Menander, as depicter of everyday life pure and simple and of human characters. In sum, while it has long been known that the most archaic comedy began with the parodying of myth and that only with the passage of time did it proceed to humanize its characters, Greece confirms this path of comedy from the god, through the hero and sacred legend, to simple and mortal man, a path not of comedy in our contemporary sense, but of parody in its old, sacral significance. This genesis of parody out of all that is holy explains to us, together with Cratinus and Aristophanes, such an incomprehensible phenomenon as the genre of tragicomedy and hilarotragoedia. Now we understand that if Dionysus is portrayed as the central character, and Zeus, Poseidon, Hera, and others appear episodically or indirectly, even the ruler of the gods, Zeus, is from time to time depicted on stage (compare the Ζευς κακουμενος of Plato the Comedian), and that a literary form existed — once again scenic, i.e., fundamentally ritual — which made special use of lofty form and sacred legend to deprive them of content and render them in comically paltry form: all of this long before Rhinthon or Pomponius. This compels me to refute two current opinions. The first holds that the appearance of gods in a laughable situation is a late phenomenon of religious decadence. On the contrary, the association between divinity and the principle of parody dates specifically to the most archaic religious conception. The second opinion has to do with the influence of tragedy on Aristophanes. A wholly different view is held by Aristotle when he speaks of the emergence of tragedy from the humorous. This view finds support specifically in parody. The features of tragedy that are so evident in ancient comedy and their contiguity in composition, choral parts, and language are to be explained by the fact that they have a single, common origin and a single, common nature. Hilarotragoedia is one of the direct signs of this earlier identity with each other. Its antiquity is also indicated by its dramatis personae (gods and heroes), by sacred plots, and by its closeness to phlyákes and farce, as we know, the most ancient dramatic forms of folk ritual creation.

7.

We cannot ignore the kinship of the tragic and ludicrous, which is revealed to us by the idea underlying every parody. It is no accident, of course, that parody is companion not to comedy but specifically to tragedy. Nor is it accidental that in Menander or Roman comedy we do not find the element that we very imprecisely call satire and that "ludicrous tragedy" comes down to us in the shape of an entire genre, albeit understood in distorted fashion. For those who have long grasped the primitive error of all division into "periods," a parallel with European tragedy will not seem useless. Let me recall that in Shakespeare, Calderon, and Lope de Vega (I must qualify this: and all playwrights of less genius) the tragic conception goes hand in hand with the comic, both in their story-lines and in overall composition. It has childishly been said that this follows from a brilliant knowledge of life, which yields the quality of tragedy side by side with that of comedy. No, the substrate is more prosaic and more concrete and lies in the origin and history of drama. Both Shakespeare and the Spanish tragedians have a legitimized literary tradition that requires the creation of two conceptions (the tragic and the comic), two story-lines, two courses of events, and two types of personages in one and the same work. Long ago, Ticknor, distinguished connoisseur and father of the history of Spanish literature, directed attention to the role of servants in Spanish drama and came to the conclusion that they represented parody (i.e., imitation and caricature) of the principal dramatis personae. When I studied the genesis of the role of the jester, I became convinced, on the basis of a long list of examples, that the nature of the so-called "servants" lies in the idea of a double of the hero himself. This idea of doubling, i.e., of the introduction of a second aspect, constitutes the nature of all parody. We encounter it, without exception, "paired": without chiaroscuro, without something to be contrasted

The Origin of Parody

to something else, it does not exist. As a consequence tragedy, not comedy, is its realm, which is why epic and theogony are the forms to which it gravitates in the period of conscious application. And it is because of this that parody does not die over many centuries: in Western drama in the parallelism of tragic and comic plots, in dual situations, and in the roles of servants, parody retains its archaic nature even more purely than in the comedies of Aristophanes.

8.

But once I began to speak, albeit in passing, about servants and jesters in connection with parody of the hero, I started, without being aware of it myself, to think about the study written as far back as 1897 by Albrecht Dieterich on the subject of Polichinelle. This is all the more pleasant for me, since it is precisely this book which can provide confirmation and support for my views. I would group Dieterich's observations in three ways: First there are the depictions of Pompeian frescoes and Greek and Italian vases and masks, in which one comic face appears among the tragic ones. Next, there is classical drama, which offers high tragedy along with mythological travesty parodying it. Finally, there are tragic figures, among whom one invariably finds one (at least) comic figure, as companion to or shadow of the hero. This is the role of the "merry servant." Even such a comparison of Dieterich's materials points to parallelism in origin, genre, and personage, and to the unity of parodic nature whether manifested in tragedy or in the individual hero. It is all the same, in the final analysis, whether we are studying ritual, an entire literary genre, a single work, or a single role in that work: We, in any case, discover the nature of parody as a particular system of archaic thought true to itself even in all its particulars. And parallels immediately suggest themselves: from the world of classical antiquity, the Roman "mythological" Atellana and exodium, parodying the tragedy which it immediately followed in performance, and the Greek satirical drama that closed the lofty trilogy in the form of jest. Parallels from the Middle Ages also come to mind. Here we encounter the same hilarotragoedia in the form of Pia Hilaria, a merry facetia on the subject of piety (not even to mention mysteries with a comic element or interludia on Biblical themes). As Lucian's atheism was prepared by the sacred character of parody, so in the tenth century the religion of the nun Hrosvitha permitted her to author a comedy based on a vita of "holy virgins." But particularly indicative is an example from an entirely different realm: from the world of situations and characters. Exactly the same is true of Hindu dramaturgy, in which the so-called parahasana is the same one-act play of smiles, laughing at the very highest ruling and sacred class. The role of the vidūshaka, the jester servant, carries with it the comic aspect of tragic situations.

9.

Indeed, we need only attempt to uncover all the simulations parody offers us and we are immediately persuaded that there are "essences" underlying them. I will not touch the matter of the jackass — I studied it and found in it the prehistoric divinity of intense heat, the sun at its apogee, with later elements of fertility and a saving element. It is clear to me that the Golden Ass, the ass under a golden blanket, deservedly receives the mass in the milieu of his age-long worshippers, who had long ago forgotten the hot sands of the desert and who had built a city temple. Just as the travesty of myth and of the individual hero-god conceals nothing but the genuine religious conception of the god-hero, just as Amphitryon merely provides a screen for Zeus, the servant for the hero, the mock king for the real king, so do all "fool" rituals contain religious belief, which is merely temporarily masked by its own "likeness." I have deliberately saved for the end one ancient description of a jester's mass. The church is in the possession of gardeners, tramps, cooks and dishwashers, and orchard keepers. They all fill the church and hold a service lasting a whole day. They are dressed in sacred vestments torn to shreds or turned inside

The Origin of Parody

out. In their hands are prayerbooks either upside down or with the binding facing the "reader." On their noses are enormous spectacles made of orange peel, without lenses. They shake the censers so hard the ashes fly all over the church and onto each of them. They sing neither psalms nor hymns but speak gibberish in penetrating voices and squeal like a herd of whipped pigs. This is what they sing:

> Haec est clare dies, clararum clara dierum.
> Haec est festa dies, festarum festa dierum.
>   (Thiers, Traité des Jeux, 449. Disraeli, 259-60)

They greet the ass with "Hez! Sire Ane, hex!" "Huzza! Seignior Ass, Huzza!"

Here, consequently, is the single front of the archaic system of thought: the religious service, hymns, clothing, prayerbook, and even voices turned inside out (equally, the clergy turned socially upside down). Yet all this is merely the "wrong side" [iznanka], which in fact is the nature of parody, like a song turned inside out. But do we not find that on its opposite side lie always its true face, its meaning and essence? The voices are those of people but not of piglets; it is a hymn and not a bellow; the clerical vestments, the clergy, and the Mass are all genuine. And consequently, even the clergy itself, parodying God, somewhere and in something is the same God; and the mock king, in a certain sense, is the same king. What is the sotte chanson in the Middle Ages and later if not a religious song, not a love romance topsy-turvy, not a "parody" in the literal meaning of the word? Or in Aristophanes's parodic comedies? In their most archaic portion, the parabasis, we still encounter appeals to the divinity; and it is precisely here that the axis of jibes and satire is found. In other words, the divinity is called into the milieu of scoffers to be present right among the obscenities and jibes often directed at the gods themselves. And in this we see yet another confirmation that there was a time when gods played the principal role and staged parodies, that the mockery was aimed at them, and that its role was

Semiotics and Structuralism

sacred. Comedy is the handmaiden of tragedy. Parody is that same sacred appeal, that same song of psalm or paean. It is only the presence or absence of "a being" that makes the difference. The switching of roles is one of the religious topics of ancient man, corresponding to a comic line. Consider the wedding in which substitutes replace groom and bride; recall the substitute personalities and the entire chain of these "pseudos" who screen the real central figures — all of this is invariably with the most meritorious of purposes: to conceal temporarily what really is, to protect from it and put in its place one of its "likenesses," something that is the same but in which the thing itself is lacking, the identical but without its essence. This is, in our eyes and in our consciousness, what is termed form without content, grandeur in the presence of the insignificant, lack of correspondence and dualism. What a mistake! For this dualism and lack of correspondence are the result of the archaic conception, but not its cause. On the contrary, the unity of the two bases, the tragic and the comic, the absolute unity of these two forms of thought and, consequently, of the word and the literary product — the internal identity — this is the nature of all parody in its pure form. This is the nature not only of ancient comedy, the ancient servant in literature, the ancient religious ritual: this is the idea underlying each mask and each double. Parody is also linked with a holiday (as a nuptial metamorphosis is with a marriage ceremony) by its religious content, by the religious idea of benefaction. For the very element of benefaction is laughter and deception. What lies in parody is not camouflage, in our present understanding of it, and not lack of content, as seems to be the case. What lies in it is intensification of content, intensification of the nature of the gods; and it laughs not at them but only at us, and does so with such success that to this day we take it for comedy, imitation, or satire.

Thus parody is not the product of someone's individual invention or someone's merry fantasy. Parody is not imitation, ridicule, or mimicry. Parody is the archaic religious conception of "the second aspect" and "the double," with a total unity of form and content.

The Origin of Parody

The fundamental religious difference consists of two conceptions — ridicule of the lofty or its affirmation by means of the beneficent element of deception and laughter. The first idea is the result of the decline of religious consciousness. The second is its apogee, the moment of creative living faith, still hoping and vigilant. That being the case, we cannot explain certain literary forms by the weakening of religious thought, or by atheism, or by political freedom. We must draw a boundary between the lofty religious conception which has engendered the traditional literary form and the life of that very literary form, which has forgotten its religious origin and has turned to the service of a new content.

The Art of the Word and the Culture of Folk Humor (Rabelais and Gogol')

M. M. BAKHTIN

In our book on Rabelais (1) we sought to demonstrate that the basic principles of that great artist's creation were defined by the culture of folk humor [narodnaia smekhovaia kul'tura] of the past. One of the most significant shortcomings of contemporary literary scholarship lies in the fact that it attempts to confine all literature — including, particularly, that of the Renaissance — within the framework of official culture. However, the creation of that same Rabelais can actually be understood only within the flow of folk culture, which always, at all stages of its development, has resisted official culture and developed both its distinctive point of view of the world and distinctive image forms in which this view is mirrored.

Literary scholarship and aesthetics usually take as point of departure the narrowed and impoverished manifestations of laughter in the literature of the past three centuries and attempt to force the laughter of the Renaissance into these narrow conceptions of laughter and of the comic. Yet these conceptions are far from adequate even for understanding Molière.

Rabelais was the heir and culminator of millennia of folk laughter. His work is an irreplaceable key to the entire European culture of laughter in its most powerful, profound, and original manifestations.

Rabelais and Gogol'

Here we shall deal with the most significant phenomenon of the literature of laughter in modern times — N. V. Gogol's creation. Our sole concern is the elements of the culture of folk humor in his work.

We shall not touch on the question of the direct and oblique influence of Rabelais on Gogol' (through Sterne and the French natural school). Of importance to us here are those elements of Gogol's work that — independent of Rabelais — are determined by Gogol's direct linkage to folk-festival forms on his native soil.

Ukrainian folk-festival and fair life, which Gogol' knew superbly well, organizes the majority of the stories in Evenings on a Farm near Dikanka: "The Fair at Sorochintsy," "A May Night," "Christmas Eve," and "St. John's Eve." The themes of the festival itself and the free-jolly festival atmosphere define the plot, images, and tone of these stories. The festival, the beliefs associated with it, and its distinctive atmosphere of freedom and merriment take life out of its usual routine and make the impossible possible (including also marriages that were previously impossible). Jolly deviltry, profoundly kin in character, tone, and functions to the gay carnival visions of the nether world and to diableries, plays a vital role both in the purely festive stories we have already mentioned and in others. (2) In these stories food, drink, and sex life are marked by a festive, Shrovetide-carnival character. We emphasize, further, the tremendous role played by disguises and all sorts of mystifications, as well as by beatings and debunkings. Finally, Gogolian laughter in these stories is pure folk-festival laughter. It is ambivalent and elementally materialistic. This folk foundation of Gogolian laughter is retained in it to the very end, despite its substantial subsequent evolution.

The introductions to Evenings (particularly to the first part) resemble Rabelais's prologues in construction and style. They are written in a tone of markedly familiar chatter with the readers. The introduction to the first part begins with a rather lengthy passage of abuse (true, this is not the abuse of the author himself but the anticipated abuse of the readers): "What kind of nonsense is this? 'Evenings on a Farm near Dikanka'? What kind of evenings? And pushed into the world by some beekeeper!...." And further we find characteristic curses ("some ragamuffin: look at the trash that rummages in the back yard..."), swearing and cursing ("Strike me dead!" "May the devil shove his father off a bridge!" and so forth). One also encounters the following characteristic image: "Foma Grigor'evich's hand, instead of making a fig [shish], reached out for a knish." A story about a schoolboy who tries to latinize everything is inserted (compare the episode with Rabelais's student of Limousin). Toward the end of the introduction there is a depiction of a number of dishes, i.e., feast images.

Let us present a very typical image of dancing old age (virtually dancing death) from "The Fair at Sorochintsy":

> Everything was dancing. But an even stranger, even more puzzling feeling would have been aroused in the depth of one's soul at the sight of the old women, on whose ancient faces lay the indifference of the grave, who pushed among new, laughing, living people. Careless! Without even the joy of childhood, without a spark of sympathy, compelled by drunkenness alone, as by a mechanic with his lifeless automaton, to do something that seemed human, they quietly rocked their tipsy heads, dancing after the merry crowd, without even casting a glance at the young couple.

In Mirgorod and Taras Bul'ba features of grotesque realism emerge. In the Ukraine (as in Belorussia) traditions of grotesque realism were very strong and viable. They were disseminated primarily by religious schools, seminaries, and academies (Kiev had its own "Mont-Sainte-Geneviève" with analogous traditions). Wandering schoolmen (seminarians) and the lesser clerics, "itinerant scribes," spread the oral recreational literature of facetiae, anecdotes, minor verbal travesties, parodistic grammar, etc., throughout the Ukraine. School recreations, with their special mores and rights to freedom, played in the Ukraine a significant role in the development of culture. In Gogol's time, and even later, the traditions of grotesque realism were still alive in Ukrainian educational

Rabelais and Gogol'

institutions (not just religious ones). They lived on in the dinner-table conversations of the Ukrainian raznochintsy intelligentsia (which came chiefly from the priestly milieu). Gogol' must have known them directly in their living oral form. In addition, he had an exceptional knowledge of them from literary sources. Finally, he took over essential elements of grotesque realism from Narezhnyi, whose work was shot through with them. The free recreational laughter of the seminarian was kin to the folk-festival laughter that resounded in the Evenings, and at the same time, this Ukrainian seminary laughter was the remote Kievan echo of the Western "risus paschalis" (Paschal laughter). This is why the elements of folk-festival Ukrainian folklore and those of the seminary grotesque realism combine so organically and rigorously in "Viy" and Taras Bul'ba, in the same way as, three centuries earlier, analogous elements organically combined in Rabelais's novel. The figure of the kinless seminarian of democratic origin, of a Khoma Brut, who combines knowledge of Latin with folk laughter, heroic strength, and boundless appetite and thirst, is extremely close to that of his Western brothers, Panurge and, particularly, Frère Jean.

Careful analysis would show that Taras Bul'ba contains, in addition to all these factors, images of jolly heroism akin to Rabelais, as well as hyperboles of bloody battles and feasts of the Rabelaisian type. Finally, in the depiction of the specific order and existence of the free Sech', such analysis would also discover profound elements of folk-festival Utopianism, of a type of Ukrainian saturnalia. In Taras Bul'ba there are also many elements of the carnival type; for example, at the very beginning of the novel we find the arrival of the seminarians and the fist fight between Ostap and his father (carried to its limit, this is the "utopian cuffs" of the saturnalia).

In the St. Petersburg Stories and all of Gogol's subsequent work, we find other elements of the folk humor culture primarily in his style. Here we cannot doubt the direct influence of public-square and puppet-show folk comedy. Of course, the images and styles of "The Nose" are associated with Sterne and Sternian literature. They were then current images. Yet at the same time, Gogol' found both the most grotesque nose, which strove for an independent existence, as well as the themes of the nose, in the puppet show of our Russian Pulcinello: at Petrushka's. In the puppet show he also found the style of discourse of the puppet-show barker, which breaks into the course of the action, with its tones of ironic publicity and praise, its alogisms and deliberate absurdities (elements of "coq-à-l'âne"). In all these phenomena of Gogolian style and imagery, Sternianism (and, consequently, the oblique influence of Rabelais) combined with the immediate influence of folk comedy.

Elements of the coq-à-l'âne — both isolated alogisms and more developed verbal absurdities — are quite widespread in Gogol'. They are particularly frequent in descriptions of lawsuits and official red tape, and in the depiction of tittle-tattle and gossip, for example, in the officials' assumptions about Chichikov, in Nozdrev's expatiations on this score, in the conversation between the two ladies, in Chichikov's conversations with the landlords about buying dead souls, etc. The connection of these elements with the forms of folk comedy and with grotesque realism is beyond doubt.

Finally, let us deal with one more factor. Close analysis would reveal at the foundation of Dead Souls forms of a gay (carnivalesque) journey through the netherworld, through the land of death. Dead Souls is a most interesting parallel to Rabelais's Fourth Book, i.e., to the travels of Pantagruel. Of course, the factor of life beyond the grave is present for a good reason both in the very conception and in the title of Gogol's novel (Dead Souls). The world of Dead Souls is a world of gay nether regions. Externally it more nearly resembles the netherworld of Quevedo (3), but in its internal essence it is closer to the world of Rabelais's Fourth Book. In it we find both the rabble and trash of the carnival "hell" and a whole series of images that have the realization of abusive metaphors. Close analysis would reveal here many traditional elements of the carnival netherworld, the terrestrial and bodily lower

Rabelais and Gogol'

stratum. And the very type of "travel" ("journey") undertaken by Chichikov is a chronotopic type of motion. Naturally, this deep traditional basis of Dead Souls is enriched and complicated by much material of a different order and from other traditions.

In Gogol's works we find virtually all the elements of folk-festival culture. A carnival perception of the world characterizes Gogol', although it certainly is romantically tinted in most cases. He gives it diverse forms of expression. Here we cite only the famous purely carnival description of the fast ride and of the Russian: "And what Russian does not love a fast ride? Does not his very soul, which hungers to go for a spin, to go on a spree, sometimes say, 'Devil take it all!' Does not his soul love it?" And, somewhat farther on: "The entire road flies no one knows where into the disappearing distance, and something terrible is concealed in that rapid flashing in which one cannot make out the disappearing object...." We must emphasize this destruction of all the static boundaries between phenomena. The special Gogolian perception of "the road," which he expresses so often, also has a purely carnival nature.

Nor is the grotesque conception of the body alien to Gogol'. Here is a very characteristic draft for the first book of Dead Souls:

> And really, what kinds of faces doesn't one find on this earth! No matter the mug, it certainly isn't like any other. On one it is the nose that is the commanding officer; on the next, the lips; on the third it is the cheeks that have spread their dominance even at the expense of the nose itself, which as a consequence is no bigger than a vest button; here's one with a chin so long that he has to cover it with a napkin every minute so as not to drool over it.... And how many there are who don't look like people at all: that one is such a perfect dog in a morning coat that one wonders why he carries a cane in his hand; it looks as though the first person he meets will grab it.

We also find in Gogol' an extremely consistent system of

transforming given names into nicknames. With what almost theoretical clarity is the very essence of the ambivalent, laudatory-abusive nickname revealed by the Gogolian name for the town in the second volume of Dead Souls — T'fuslavl'! We also find in him such vivid examples of a familiar combination of praise and abuse (in the form of an enraptured, blessing curse) as: "The devil take you, steppes, how beautiful you are!"

Gogol' profoundly sensed the acutely perceptive and universal character of his laughter and at the same time could not find either an appropriate place or a theoretical foundation and sanction for this kind of laughter under the conditions of "serious" nineteenth-century culture. When in his arguments he explained why he laughed, he clearly did not dare to fully disclose the nature of laughter, its universal and all-embracing folk character. He often justified his laughter in terms of the limited morality of the times. In these justifications, aimed to meet the level of understanding of those to whom they were addressed, Gogol' involuntarily lowered and limited, and at times sincerely attempted to incorporate within official limits, that enormous transforming force which was rising to the surface in his humorous creation. The first, external, "ridiculing" negative effect, offending and refuting accepted notions, did not permit direct observers to see the positive essence of this force. "Why does my heart grow sad?" asks Gogol' in "Leaving the Theater" (1842); and he answers, "No one observed the honest character in my play." Revealing, further, that "this honest, noble figure was laughter," Gogol' continues: "He was noble because he decided to step forward despite the low value ascribed to him in society."

It is precisely the "low," lower-class, folk significance which gives this laughter, in Gogol's definition, a "noble visage." Gogol' could have added: a divine face, for thus laugh the gods in the folk-humor element of the archaic popular comedy. Such laughter (the very fact of its being a "character") found no place in explanations then existing or possible.

"Laughter is more significant and profound than is thought," Gogol' wrote in the same place.

Rabelais and Gogol'

Not the laughter that is born of temporary irritability, of a bilious and morbid cast of characters, nor that easy laughter serving the vain amusement and entertainment of men, but the laughter that arises in its entirety out of the bright nature of man, and arises out of it because at its bottom there lies the "eternally flowing spring that is its source...."

No: unjust are those who say that laughter perturbs. Only what is gloomy perturbs, and laughter is bright. Much would upset a man were it presented in all its nakedness. But, illuminated by the power of laughter, it already carries reconciliation into the soul.... But the powerful force of such laughter is not heard. Society says, "What is funny is base"; only what is uttered in a stern, tense voice is designated lofty.

Gogol's "positive," "bright," "lofty" laughter, which grew out of the soil of the culture of folk humor, was not understood (in many respects it is not understood to this day). It is this laughter, incompatible with the laughter of a satirist, which defines what is fundamental in Gogol's creation. One could well say that his inner nature compelled him to laugh "like the gods," but he found it necessary to justify his laughter in terms of the limited human morality of his time.

However, this laughter revealed itself to the full in Gogol's poetics, in the very structure of his language. Into this language freely enters the verbal life of the people untouched by literature (its nonliterary strata). Gogol' uses unpublished realms of discourse. His notebooks are literally packed with unusual, mysterious words, ambivalent in meaning and sound. He even intends to publish his own "Explanatory Dictionary of the Russian Language," in the introduction to which he asserts: "The need for such a dictionary seemed all the more necessary to me because, within the foreign life of our society, which accords so little with the spirit of the land and the people, the direct and genuine meaning of indigenous Russian words is distorted; and some of them are ascribed different meanings, while others are entirely consigned to oblivion." Gogol' acutely perceives the need for a struggle of the folk speech element with the dead, externalizing strata of language. The absence — typical of the Renaissance consciousness — of a single, authoritative, unchallengeable language finds its echo in his creation in the organization of the comprehensive, humorous interaction of speech realms. In his discourse we observe, as a consequence, a steady release of forgotten or prohibited meanings.

Meanings lost in the past and forgotten begin to communicate with each other, to emerge from their cocoons, to seek application and attachment to others. Semantic connections that had existed only in the context of particular utterances, within the bounds of particular verbal realms, indissolubly associated with the situations that had generated them, obtain, in these conditions, the opportunity for rebirth, for becoming part of a renewed life. Otherwise, they remained, after all, invisible and, as it were, ceased to exist: they were not, as a rule, preserved, did not become fixed in abstract, semantic contexts (worked out in written and printed speech). It was as though they had been lost forever and barely combined for the expression of a living, unique instance. In abstract, normative language they had no rights to enter into a system of world view, because that is not a system of conceptual meanings but the very life which speaks. Usually appearing as an expression of extraliterary, extrapractical, extraserious situations (when people laugh, sing, curse, loaf, and feast — in general, take themselves out of the established routine), they could not claim to be represented in serious, official language. However, these situations and turns of speech do not die, although literature may forget about them or even avoid them.

Therefore, a return to living, folk speech is necessary; and this is accomplished in a way that is perceptible to all in the creation of such spokesmen of genius for the folk consciousness as Gogol'. Here the primitive notion, which commonly takes shape in norm-setting circles, that some kind of linear forward motion exists is rejected. It turns out that every truly significant step forward is accompanied by a return to the beginning ("primitiveness"), or more exactly to a renewal of the

Rabelais and Gogol'

beginning. Only memory, not forgetfulness, can go forward. Memory returns to the beginning and renews it. Of course, in this understanding the very terms "forward" and "backward" lose their self-contained absoluteness. Rather they reveal by their interaction the living, paradoxical nature of motion, which has been studied and variously interpreted by philosophers (from the Eleatics to Bergson). As applied to language, this return signifies the reestablishment of its active, accumulated memory in its full semantic scope. The folk culture of laughter, so vividly expressed in Gogol', is one of the paths to this restoration-renewal.

In Gogol' humorous discourse is organized in such a way that its object is not a simple indication of individual negative phenomena but a revelation of a special aspect of the world as a whole.

In this sense in Gogol' the zone of laughter becomes the zone of contact. The contradictory and incompatible are combined here, and they come to life as a linkage. Words carry with them the total impressions of contacts — special genres, which are almost always very remote from literature. The simple chatter (of a lady) sounds in this context like a problem of discourse, as significance coming through verbal litter, which, it would appear, has no meaning.

In this language a continuous dropping-away from the literary norms of the epoch and a correlation with other realities that explode the official, direct, "decent" surface of the word are achieved. The process of eating, in general the various manifestations of material-corporeal life, some extraordinarily shaped nose, a bump, and the like, all require language to denote them, demand various new turns of phrase, agreements, a struggle with the need to express oneself accurately and without offending the canon. At the same time, it is clear that such manifestations cannot offend the canon. There arises a dichotomy, a leap of meaning from one extreme into another, a striving to keep balance and, at the same time, discontinuities — a comical travesty of the word, which reveals its multidimensional nature and shows the path for its renewal.

Semiotics and Structuralism

The same object is served by unconstrained dancing, by animal traits that emerge in man, and so forth. Gogol' pays special attention to the gestural and abusive stock, not ignoring any of the specific peculiarities of humorous folk speech. Life outside the uniform and rank attracts him with extraordinary force, although in youth he dreamed of a uniform and rank. The violated rights of laughter find in him their defender and spokesman, although he thought throughout his life about serious, tragic, and moral literature.

Thus we see the clash and interaction of two worlds: a completely legalized, official world, put in order through ranks and uniforms, vividly expressed in the dream of "life in the capital," and a world in which everything is funny and unserious, in which only laughter is serious. Incongruities and the absurd introduced by this world prove, on the contrary, to be true, unifying, inner principles of the other, the external, world. This is the jolly absurdity of folk sources, possessing a multiplicity of speech correlations that are precisely fixed by Gogol'.

Consequently, Gogol's world is always in the zone of contact (as is every humorous depiction). In this zone all things once again become tangible. Food, depicted by devices of speech, is capable of stimulating an appetite; and analytical depiction of individual motions that do not lose wholeness is also possible. Everything becomes real, contemporary, actually existing.

It is characteristic that nothing of significance that Gogol' wants to transmit is presented by him in the zone of recollection. Chichikov's past, for example, is presented in the zone of distance [dalevaia zona] and on another level of discourse from his quests for "dead souls" — here there is no laughter. Where character is genuinely laid bare, there constantly acts the element of laughter — unifying, collecting, contrasting with everything around it.

It is important that this world of laughter lie permanently open to new interactions. The usual, traditional conception of the whole and the element of the whole, which gains its meaning only within the whole, has to be reexamined here and considered somewhat more deeply. The point is that each such element is

Rabelais and Gogol'

simultaneously a representative of some other whole (for example, folk culture), in which, above all, it gains its meaning. In this way the wholeness of Gogol's world is fundamentally not closed, not self-satisfied.

Only thanks to folk culture does Gogol's contemporaneity partake of the Great Time.

Folk culture gives depth and a connection to the carnivalized images of collectives: to Nevsky Prospekt, to officialdom, to the chancery, to the government department (the beginning of "The Overcoat," a curse: "the Department of Meanness and Nonsense," etc.). Only within it can we understand the gay demise, the jolly deaths in Gogol': Bul'ba, who has lost his pipe; the jolly heroism, the transformation of the dying Akakii Akakievich (the delirium at the point of death, with curses and rebellion), his adventures in the afterlife. In essence, folk laughter removes carnivalized collectives from "real," "serious," "proper" life. There is no standpoint of seriousness counterposed to laughter. Laughter is "the only positive hero."

Consequently, in Gogol' the grotesque is no mere violation of the norm but a denial of all abstract and inflexible norms that claim to be absolute and eternal. The grotesque rejects obviousness and the world "of what is self-evident" for the sake of the surprises and unanticipated quality of truth. It appears to say that good is to be expected not from the stable and the customary but from a "miracle." The grotesque contains the popular renewing and life-affirming idea.

The buying up of dead souls and the various responses to Chichikov's proposals also reveal, in this sense, their link to folk ideas about the connection of life and death and the carnivalized derision of these ideas. Also present here is an element of carnival play with death and the boundaries of life and death (for example, in Sobakevich's arguments that the dead are not much use, Korobochka's fear of corpses, and the saying: "A corpse can be used even to prop up a fence," etc.). There is carnival play in the clash between the insignificant and the serious, the terrible; the conceptions about infinity and eternity are played up in carnival fashion (unending lawsuits, interminable absurdities, and so forth). Thus even Chichikov's journey is uncompletable.

In this perspective we also see more accurately the comparison with real images and situations of the serf system (the sale and purchase of human beings). These images and themes cease with the end of the system of serfdom. Gogol's images and plot situations are immortal; they exist in Great Time. A phenomenon that belongs to profane time may be purely negative, only hateful; but in Great Time it is ambivalent and always beloved, as involved in existence. From a plane where one can only destroy them, only hate them, or only accept them when they are no longer there, all these Pliushkins, Sobakeviches, and the like have passed onto a plane on which they remain eternally, on which they are shown with their involvement in the eternally becoming, but not dying, existence.

The laughing satirist is not jolly. In the extreme case he is gloomy and sullen. In Gogol', however, laughter triumphs over everything. In particular, it creates a kind of catharsis of vulgar banality.

The problem of Gogolian laughter can be correctly posed and resolved only on the basis of a study of the culture of folk humor.

Notes

1) M. M. Bakhtin, Tvorchestvo Fransua Rable i narodnaia kul'tura srednevekov'ia i Renessansa, Moscow, "Khudozhestvennaia literatura" Publishers, 1965. The present article is a fragment of the dissertation on Rabelais that did not become part of the book.

2) Let us emphasize the utterly carnival image of playing durachki [a card game] in the netherworld in the story "Propavshaia gramota."

3) See Quevedo's Sueños (written in 1607-13, published in 1627). In it representatives of various classes and occupations and of certain vices and human weaknesses pass through hell. The satire is almost without deep and genuine ambivalence.

Gogol' and the Correlation of "The Culture
of Humor" with the Comic and Serious
in the Russian National Tradition

Iu. M. LOTMAN

1. M. M. Bakhtin's exceptionally profound work "The Art of the Word and the Culture of Folk Humor (Rabelais and Gogol')" (1) reveals previously uninvestigated aspects of the comic element in Gogol', placing the writer's creation in the context of folk-festival, humorous, and carnival culture. In revealing the link with this popular and democratic tradition, Bakhtin justifiably protests against one-sided reduction of Gogol's laughter to satire. Developing Bakhtin's thoughts, one might point to yet another tradition, besides folk-humor and accusatory-satirical traditions, that supplements the complex of Gogol's attitude toward laughter.

2. The attitude toward laughter and toward the carnival tradition in western Russian regions touched by the culture of the baroque (particularly in the Ukraine), which Bakhtin discusses in connection with the "grotesque realism" of the recreational seminary literature and the carnival elements of Ukrainian folklore, was different in Great Russian regions. The tradition of medieval Eastern Orthodoxy separated the divine principle, as real, from the apparent, the imaginary, the

"dreamy," and the diabolical. The former is constant, the latter is many-faced and variable. Therefore, the attitude toward play, theatricality, various forms of change in appearance, mummery, and masks was utterly unambiguous. The "as if existence" of theatrical life was identified with diabolical "flattery" and "dreams."

From the inner point of view, the world of carnival gaiety could appear to be beyond valuation, to be ambivalent. In Western culture it could successfully impose its inner position on the culture as a whole, since it was permitted during specific calendrical periods as a form of obligatory social behavior, a humorous catharsis of the serious medieval world. In the Orthodox culture of medieval Eastern Europe the opposite occurred: the official evaluation of carnival as demonic play-acting penetrated into its inner self-evaluation. Permission for carnival behavior at certain times was linked with the belief that at that time God permitted the Devil to rule the world. (2) Thus the fact that participants in carnivals were engaging in legitimate behavior did not eliminate the fact that this behavior itself remained sinful. Whereas in the tradition studied by Bakhtin laughter abolishes fear, in our case laughter implies fear. The world of masks and mummers turned inside out was funny and frightening at the same time.

3. Gogol' is the writer who synthesized the most diverse elements of national life. The acute contemporaneity of his works was combined with a capacity to penetrate into deep strata of the archaic folk consciousness. Thus Gogol's works can serve as the foundation for reconstruction of the mythological beliefs of the Slavs, which go back to the most distant antiquity (3) and which, of course, were unknown to Gogol' at the level of self-awareness. The connection with the deep strata of the pre-Petrine national cultural tradition also emerged in a special treatment of the concept of the comic: European culture of the new era had legitimized two functions of laughter: accusatory satire and amusement, entertainment. Bakhtin noted the presence in Gogol's laughter of a third principle: ambivalent carnival laughter. But Gogolian laughter has yet

Gogol' and "The Culture of Humor"

another aspect: it is inseparable from horror; it is related to the world of diabolical confusion. The changing of masks, theatricality which had penetrated into life, is funny and frightening at the same time: "Our world is wonderfully constructed! Every thing that lives in it, everything seeks to imitate and mimic something else." (4) The theatricalized world, in which there are "some kinds of pig snouts instead of faces" (5), is at the same time a diabolical, illusory world, in which "the demon himself lights the lamps in order to show everything not in its true form." (6) Andrei Bely long ago directed attention to this aspect of Gogol's laughter.

4. Linked with this treatment of laughter is the effort to overcome the comicality, theatricality, and seriousness of the liturgical attitude toward art (compare the second variant of "The Portrait" or the comment of the painter A. A. Ivanov, who was very close to Gogol' in those years and who, when shown an album of caricatures, "looked at them for a long time and, suddenly raising his head, muttered: 'Christ never laughed' "). (7)

Of course, also inherent in Gogol' was a positive experience of gaiety and a dream about the utopia of the carnival world (Taras Bul'ba, "Rome"). (8) However, one also cannot forget that aspect of laughter which induced horror in Gogol' and which he tried to "neutralize" by the serious culture of utopia and homily.

Notes

1) M. M. Bakhtin, "Iskusstvo slova i narodnaia smekhovaia kul'tura (Rable i Gogol')," in the collection, Kontekst 1972, Moscow, 1973.

2) See, for example, Kievskaia starina, 1889, No. 9, pp. 5-6.

3) See, for example, Viach. Vs. Ivanov, "Ob odnoi paralleli k gogolevskomu 'Viiu,'" Trudy po znakovym sistemam, Tartu University, 1971; same author, "Kategoriia 'vidimogo' i 'nevidimogo' v tekste: eshche raz o vostochnoslavianskikh fol'klornykh paralleliakh k gogolevskomu 'Viiu,'" Structure of Texts and Semiotics of Culture, Mouton, 1973.

4) N. V. Gogol', Poln. sobr. soch., Vol. I, 1940, p. 204.
5) Ibid., Vol. IV, p. 93.
6) Ibid., Vol. III, p. 46.
7) I. S. Turgenev, Sobr. soch. v 10 tt., Vol. X, Moscow, 1956, p. 337.
8) See Iu. M. Lotman, "Istoki 'tolstovskogo napravleniia' v russkoi literature 1830-kh godov," Trudy po russkoi i slavianskoi filologii, Tartu University, 1962.

On the Reduction and Unfolding of Sign Systems
(The Problem of "Freudianism and
Semiotic Culturology")

Iu. M. LOTMAN

1. The Freudian psychoanalytical model is constructed as a chain at one end of which are subconscious libidinal notions and at the other the verbal testimony of the patient. Between these extreme points lies a sequence of symbolic equivalents, transformations, and sign substitutes. Both criticism and isolation of the most interesting aspects of this model from the standpoint of semiotic theory have frequently been undertaken. (1) Without touching on the entire complex of varied problems that arise in connection with the discussion of this theme, we will attempt to shed light on but a single aspect: to what degree the complex of initial sexual motifs underlying the entire construct is in fact primary, reaching into the depths of child psychophysiology, and to what degree it arises as a secondary fact — the result of translation of complex texts, received by the child from the world of adults, into the considerably simpler language of specifically child ideas.

1.1. The world of the child of the very earliest age (and it is specifically such an age that Freud had in mind when he wrote: "The physician engaging in psychoanalysis of the adult neurotic, uncovering psychic formations layer by layer, ultimately arrives at certain hypotheses about child sexuality, in the components of which he sees the productive force for all neurotic symptoms of later life" [2]) is characterized by a limited set of persons (in fact, three: "I," mother, and father) and objects. This world is described by a language whose nouns are proper names. (3) However, even at the earliest stage "the child's world" and "the child's language" are not a self-sufficient and isolated system. Next to them there exist the world and language of adults, which make a constant and broad intrusion into the first.

1.2. The child's contact with the world of adults is constantly imposed on him by the subordinated position of his world in the general hierarchy of the culture of adults. However, this contact itself is possible only as an act of translation. How can such translation be accomplished? On the basis of some contextual-situational equivalence (situations: "good," "pleasant," "bad," "dangerous," etc.) the child establishes a correspondence between some texts familiar and comprehensible to him in "his" language and the texts of "adults" (for example, on the principle "incomprehensible but pleasant" or "incomprehensible but frightening"). In such translation of a whole text by another whole text, the child discovers an extraordinary abundance of "superfluous" words in "adult" texts. The act of translation is accompanied by a semantic reduction of the text. In the process a tendency clearly appears to substitute referents borrowed from the child's world for the meanings of words that have no correspondent in the child's lexicon. We know of cases in which a child has believed that "poison" means an old piece of felt lying behind the buffet in the dining room. There is also another tendency: thus the word "fire" can signify "an event unknown but so terrible that it is frightening to establish its meaning."

The child reduces the semantic model obtained from natural language (which appears as the language of adults) in such a way that translation into his own language of the texts flowing in from without is possible. However, it is not only natural language that realizes this modeling intrusion: conversations

Reduction and Unfolding of Sign Systems

of adults that introduce an entire world of secondary models — ethical, political, religious, and so on, burst into the child's consciousness. Fairy tales and other artistic texts introduce an enormous quantity of signs — from entire texts to individual words (and also depictive signs), the meaning of which the child has yet to establish by identification with the content units of his world. The contemporary urban (and even rural) child hears the word "wolf" in a context that leaves no doubt that the thing under discussion is scary and dangerous long before he has an idea of the social semantics of this word. One has often heard a child pointing out to its mother various things it regards as scary and asking, "Is that a wolf?"

1.3. Not only the system of nouns in "adult" texts but also the system of plots is reduced in such a situation. When a child hears the fairy tale about "Little Red Riding Hood," he does not introduce additional personages into his world but identifies the characters of the fairy tale with names from his child's world. In this case it is natural to identify "Red Riding Hood" with oneself, the grandmother with one's mother, and the wolf with one's father. The point here is not latent hostility toward one's father but the need to retell the plot of the fairy tale in an alphabet in which there are only three nouns: "I," mother, and father. In this situation there is no need to invent an Urszene in which the infant supposedly witnessed coitus a tergo, as Freud assumes, to explain the identification of the father with the wolf. (4) It is simply that the child derived from the fairy tale a ready-made plot scenario and assigned the roles to the personages present in his own world, in the same way as a director "translates" the list of dramatis personae of a play into the language of the list of the names of actors in his group. By identifying the father with the wolf in the fairy tale, the child is certainly not externalizing the supposedly primeval hostility toward his father (after all, he is not inventing a negative role for his father but seeks in his tiny troupe a performer for a negative role imposed from without). On the contrary, he transfers into the interior of his "child's world" the role of the "villain" presented by the plot models. Of course, for the average child the gradation of proximity between father and mother is such that, since the role of "villain," "bandit," and "wolf" is obtained from external texts, its distribution among the available characters, is, as a rule, unambiguous: it is the "not-mother," i.e., the father. When the signs "to love" and "to kill" enter the child's world from the linguistic and plot models of the surrounding world, he naturally distributes them between father and mother. Consequently, the notorious "Oedipus complex" is not something spontaneously engendered as the expression of the child's own sexual attractions and aggressive drives but is the fruit of the recoding of a text with a large alphabet into a text with a small one. Something else is related to this: the signs "to love" (and derivatives from them, such as "mistress," etc.) and "to kill" lose, in such a recoding, that specific sexual or aggressive meaning they had in the original language. It is extremely naïve to assume that we understand the texts uttered by a child who used these words when we substitute in them the meanings of the language of adults.

In connection with this, I should like to make a comment. Freud's interpretation of the subconscious is astounding in its straightforward rationalism: it does not differ in content from the categories of texts of consciousness, merely masking them in other symbols of the expression plane. The psychoanalyst deciphers dreams, unintentional utterances, and other involuntary texts; and he finds, upon substitution of a system of symbols, a content adequately expressible in the terms and categories of the language of consciousness. The Freudian subconscious is a masked conscious. It belongs only to the expression plane and is totally translatable into the language of consciousness. This also reveals its nature: it is constructed by the investigator's metamodels and, naturally, is translated into them. What Freud regards as spontaneous features of children's thought proves, in fact, to be an extract, by means of the codes of adult thought, from the child's consciousness of what adult thought itself had previously put into it. Furthermore, in the middle link of this chain — the link of the child's consciousness — texts lose those features that, in Freud's

Reduction and Unfolding of Sign Systems

opinion, specifically characterize the child's consciousness. These features arise with reverse translation of the texts of children's thought into the language of psychoanalysis.

2. The impossibility of adequate translation of texts from a language "with a large alphabet" into a language "with a small alphabet" means that whereas the spontaneous texts of the child's consciousness acquire definite expression in the child's language, texts translated from the language of adults retain a certain indefiniteness, simultaneously being primitivized. Many texts simply do not submit to translation and prove to be introduced into the memory of the "small world" in the form of integral textual inclusions of an unclear semantics. It would seem that the presence of such texts, essentially extrasystemic from the standpoint of the child's sign world, can acquire only negative characterization, inasmuch as these texts are alien to the context surrounding them and, from the child's point of view, are not obligatory.

2.1. However, the uselessness of inclusions of this type is only illusory: in their subsequent development these inclusions perform the role of unique "spores" — folded programs; and it is precisely thanks to them that the accelerated development that characterizes the psychology of the childhood years occurs.

3. One might draw an analogy between this process and the phenomenon of accelerated cultural development characteristic of particular moments in the development of some national cultures. (5)

3.1. As in the "child-adult" system, in this case as well there is a clash between a system with "a large alphabet" and one with a "small" one. One observes broad penetration into the culture of "foreign texts," the impossibility of adequate translations, and an accumulation of untranslated textual inclusions. Moreover, along with the accumulation in the small internal cultural space of untranslated texts of "external culture" one constantly senses in that space an orientation toward such translation.

3.2. The parallel between the "child-adult" system and "small alphabet culture-large alphabet culture" is also manifested in the fact that the period of aggression of texts from the latter sphere into the former is followed in explosive fashion by a period of accelerated development of the former region. Examples of such a process could be the abundant intrusions of external texts during the period of baptism of Rus' or during the Petrine epoch, followed by periods of headlong movement in the eleventh and twelfth and in the eighteenth and nineteenth centuries.

4. In connection with this one can hypothesize that along with the law of the shift of semiotic periphery and the core of the sign system in the process of automatization-deautomatization described by Iu. N. Tynianov and V. Shklovskii, (i) the pulsing, rhythmic movement, constructed as an alternation of reductions and unfoldings of the language of culture, and (ii) the acceleration of the rate of development of culture by recoding of large systems into small ones constitute some general regularities in the dynamics of self-developing sign systems.

4.1. Modern comparativistics is ruled by the idea that the objective foundation for the penetration of texts of one culture into another is reciprocal isostadiality of the two cultures. The latter case, of course, creates certain premises for the circulation of texts and can be compared with that communicative schema in which participants in the intercourse strive for maximum approximation of codes (ideally for the use of one united code). In this situation the addressee receives the new text in a previously given language, not a new language. In such a process the message is transmitted and not transformed in the course of an act of communication; no new message arises. The texts received enlarge the world of the addressee culture only quantitatively and correspond to the needs of a superficial stratum of culture. Of considerably greater significance in the overall cultural sense is the process of obtaining texts from a culture at a different stage — more developed or more primitive. In this case there takes place reduction or complicating unfolding of the received text, as well as an accumulation of untranslated texts (compared the accumulation of French texts in the Russian cultural consciousness during the latter half of the

Reduction and Unfolding of Sign Systems

eighteenth and the beginning of the nineteenth centuries). The result is an abrupt transformation of the internal semiotic order of the perceiving culture, which is accompanied by explosive acceleration of the flow of cultural processes.

4.1.1. From the foregoing emerges an explanation for a well-known fact: closed, immanently developing cultures can sharply slow the rate of development (compare the slowing of cultural processes in Rus' during the period of the "Moscow as Third Rome" conception, and the coincidence of periods of pulsation of closedness and openness with slowing and acceleration in the history of Russian culture). At the same time, one might observe that upon immanent description of a single national culture, the indicator of the speed of its movement drops from the field of vision.

4.2. Traditional comparativistics, noting empirically the difference between particular national cultures, immediately sets itself the task of determining which of them is "backward" and which "advanced" and assumes that the natural destiny of the former is to come to resemble the latter as soon as possible. However, a glance at the culture of an area (and, in the final analysis, at the general culture of the earth) as at some working mechanism persuades us of the necessity of unevenness and diversity of organization of the sign mechanisms of the diachronic movement of culture as a whole.

4.3. Apparently also related to this is the empirically observable constant violation of the isostructural nature of sublanguages of each culture, the heterostadiality of the separate component sign systems of the culture. It would be possible to show how, in a number of cases, literature anticipates the depictive arts, the cinema runs ahead of literature, and so forth, and how subsequently their intrusion into adjacent or remote realms of semiotic activity causes revolutions in the latter. Within the confines of each of the cultures it might be possible to isolate and describe mechanisms working both in the direction of a leveling of separate sign systems and in the direction of increasing the differences between them.

5. The assimilation of foreign texts is not reducible to the

Semiotics and Structuralism

introduction of new sign units — it also lies in the assimilation of new rules. A child obtains from adults not only symbols not yet having significance for him/her but also rules. Yet another dubious proposition of Freud's is associated with this. The author of The Psychoanalysis of Childhood Neuroses noted the child's early tendency toward indecent gestures, exposure, and the "improper" aspect of human behavior; and he drew from this a hypothesis about spontaneous sexual impulses that are later suppressed by the system of culture and subjected to various substitutions and displacements.

5.1. One could assume that something directly opposite takes place: the child's sexual curiosity is generated by the culture, just as the first clothes on a female penguin in Anatole France's Penguin Island led to sexual curiosity about her on the part of her tribesmen, who gazed with indifference at her naked female friends.

5.2. The child obtains from the world of adults the first rules of culture, among which the rules of shame and fear are the most powerful. (6) The assimilation of rules always occurs as a game with them, and play violation of the rules is "naughtiness." It is precisely the assimilation of the rules of shame that evokes play attempts to violate them, attempts which later fill the formal norms of semiotic behavior and give it content — not Nature but Culture. Erotic emotions develop spontaneously in the child; but language for consciousness of self, language that anticipates inner development and stimulates it, he acquires from without. For the child plays equally with fear, evincing curiosity about the mysteries of death, flirting with danger to life. A child's attraction to anomalies is not evidence, as is alleged, of the primordial perversion of his nature but, with respect to semiotics, is mastery of the Norm and, with respect to psychology, is the striving to convince himself of the firmness of this norm (the shifting of anomalies into the world of play). The rule of Sex and Fear in the history of world art thus gains an explanation directly opposite to that provided by Freud.

Reduction and Unfolding of Sign Systems

Notes

1) See V. N. Voloshinov, Freidizm, Moscow and Leningrad, 1927; on this book, see Viach. Vs. Ivanov,* "Znachenie idei M. M. Bakhtina o znake, vyskazyvanii i dialoge dlia sovremennoi semiotiki," Trudy po znakovym sistemam, VI, Tartu, 1973; E. Benveniste, Problèmes de linguistique général, Gallimard, 1966, chap. VII; Jacques Lacan, Ecrits, Paris, Seuil, 1966; J. Lacan, "Réponses," Scilicet, No. 2-3, Seuil, 1970; A. Green, "Le psychoanalyse devant l'opposition de l'histoire et de la structure," Critique, 1963, No. 194 (July); J. Kristeva, "Idéologie du discours sur la littérature," La Nouvelle Critique, 1971, No. 39 bis (Cluny II, Littérature et idéologie); a number of articles in the collection Littérature, 1971, No. 3 (October) (littérature et psychoanalyse); Teksty, 1973, No. 2 (8), and others.

2) S. Freud, Psikhoanaliz detskikh nevrozov, Moscow and Leningrad, 1925, p. 1; compare, further: "The first information about Hans pertains to the time when he was not quite three years old" (p. 2), followed by reconstructions pertaining to the ages of 2.5, 1.5, and even 0.5 years, although here one also finds the qualification that the arguments are "of considerably lower probability" (pp. 127, 129).

3) See Iu. M. Lotman and B. A. Uspenskii, "Mif — imia — kul'tura," Trudy po znakovym sistemam, VI, Tartu, 1973.

4) Freud, op. cit., pp. 127-29.

5) See G. D. Gachev, Uskorennoe razvitie literatury, Moscow, 1964.

6) See Iu. Lotman, "O semiotike poniatii 'styd' i 'strakh' v mekhanizme kul'ture," Tezisy dokladov IV Letnei shkoly po vtorichnym modeliruiushchim sistemam, Tartu, 1970, pp. 98-101.

*This essay appears on pp. 310-367 of the present volume.

The Significance of M. M. Bakhtin's Ideas on Sign, Utterance, and Dialogue for Modern Semiotics (1)

VIACH. VS. IVANOV

1. Bakhtin's is the achievement of having brought forward, as far back as the 1920s, those ideas which only today are becoming central in the concerns of students of sign systems and texts. In particular, he pointed to the direct connection between the study of signs and the general science of ideologies (2) he proposed to create: all forms of ideological activity are united by their sign — bilateral — character. According to the formulations in his first books, "Where there is no sign there is also no ideology" (5 [3], p. 15); "Everything ideological possesses semiotic meaning" (5, p. 17); "All products of ideological creativity — works of art, scholarly works, religious symbols and rituals, and the like — are material things.... True, they are things of a special kind, and inherent in them are meaning, sense, inner value. But all these meanings and values are given only in material things and actions" (3, p. 15). During the same years, trying to find a theoretical sense of how "in the givenness of a single material sign, a word, are incarnated and condensed the unity of cultural sense and subjective content" (4) was the object of G. G. Shpet, who also had in common with Bakhtin the study of the problem of social valuation (value) of the sign-word.

M. M. Bakhtin and Modern Semiotics

But they differed in their understanding of the relation between value ("comeaning" [soznachenie], according to Shpet) and meaning, which Shpet, unlike Bakhtin, "places in different spheres" (5, p. 128). In the spirit of recent works combining the semiotic (sign) approach with the axiological (value) (5), Bakhtin asserts that the meaning of a sign is formed by valuation: "Change in meaning is, in essence, always revaluation: the shifting of a word from one value context to another" (6) (5, p. 127; compare 3, p. 162). Bakhtin criticized the first edition of Saussure's Cours de linguistique générale because in it "linguistic connections have nothing in common with ideological values" (7) (5, p. 69). Meanings and values "become ideological reality only when implemented in words, in actions, in clothing, in manners, in the organizations of people and things, in a word, in some sign material" (3, p. 16). Bakhtin used this thesis primarily to demonstrate "the material embodiment and totally objective givenness of all ideological creativity" (3, p. 17). This determines the accessibility of ideological creativity to the objective method of cognition and study: "Each ideological product and everything in it is 'ideally meaningful,' not in the soul, not in the inner world, and not in the reflected world of ideas and pure meanings, but in the objectively accessible ideological material — in the word, in sound, in gesture, in combinations of masses, lines, colors, living bodies, and the like" (3, p. 17).

In singling out as the object of study of semiotics "the philosophy of the sign" (5, p. 42) and of the science of ideologies "a special world — the world of signs," which exists "alongside natural phenomena, objects of technology, and objects of consumption" (5, p. 16), Bakhtin established the presence in signs "of different types of connection of meaning with its material body... in art meaning is totally inseparable from all the details of the material body incarnating it. A work of art is meaningful all the way through. The very construction of the body-sign [tela-znaka] is of first-rank importance. Technically subordinate and therefore replaceable elements are here reduced to a minimum" (3, p. 22); "it is impossible to draw an absolute boundary between body and meaning in the realm of culture"

(13, p. 240). What follows from this is the importance of establishing, above all, the connections between the various levels of aesthetic texts, not the importance of isolating the individual levels, as was done (with respect, for example, to the level of sound organization in poetry or with respect to plot in prose) in those works of OPOIaZ with whose orientations Bakhtin was in disagreement (3). In recent years among specialists in structural poetics, which came to replace experiments in formal analysis, the interest has concentrated on study of interlevel relationships. This is why, for example, people study sound instrumentation not independent of meaning but in relation to it (which Saussure anticipated in part in his Anagrams). Isolated study of separate higher levels is suggested only by a few scholars who are oriented toward the experience of studying synonymic transformations occurring during transition from the highest to the lowest levels in linguistic semantics. However, judging by the mixed character of early systems of writing based on the combination of "highest" level (semantic) signs with "lowest" level (phonetic) signs, it appears that various degrees of bringing parts of the utterance being generated to the actually uttered sign are interwoven in the process of synthesis of the text. The possibility of separating various stages in the process of synthesizing an artistic text becomes all the more problematical, since in it the surface structure, determined by formal restrictions, may affect the deep image structure, for example, because with an increase in the number of formal restrictions, as in terza rima, an increase in the number of synonymous expressions is imperative, and that is achievable thanks to metaphorical and figurative word usages, unusual word combinations, and so forth. The measure of such expressions remains given within certain limits only in scientific or neutral texts, with which primarily linguistic semantics deals.

   According to Bakhtin, many additional factors are introduced into a scientific text, unlike a work of art. Thanks to this, translation from one language to another is facilitated. Toward the end of the twenties, Bakhtin considered the basic task of the science of ideologies, of which he regarded literary studies to

M. M. Bakhtin and Modern Semiotics

be a branch, the "detailed study of the specific peculiarities, of the qualitative distinctiveness of each of the fields of ideological creativity — science, art, moral philosophy, religion" (3, p. 11). "After all, each of them has its own language, its own forms and devices in that language" (ibid.). Through the example of the language of the carnival Bakhtin studied this very problem of the relationship between different systems of signs in his latest concrete literary and historical-cultural works, in which, in accordance with the idea of dialogue between various realms of culture, he comes to the conclusion that "carnival developed an entire language of symbolic concrete-sensual forms — from large and complex mass performances to individual carnival gestures. This language differentially, one might say, articulately (like any language), expressed the unitary (but complex) carnival perception of the world that permeates all its forms. It is impossible to translate this language completely and adequately into a verbal language, and even less into a language of abstract concepts; but it is amenable to a certain transposition into the language of artistic images related to it in concrete-sensual character, i.e., into the language of literature" (8, p. 163). Bakhtin called this transposition the carnivalization of literature. Its analysis makes up the principal content of his book about Rabelais.

According to Bakhtin, each field of ideological creativity "forms its specific signs and symbols, which are not applicable in other fields. Here the sign is created by a specific ideological function and is inseparable from it" (5, p. 21). Such "basic, specific ideological signs" cannot be replaced by others, but they all "rest on the word and are accompanied by the word, as singing is attended by accompaniment" (5, p. 22).

Anticipating the distinction, now widely used in contemporary semiotics, between natural language and supralinguistic (secondary modeling) sign systems, he noted that only the word "can bear any ideological function: scientific, aesthetic, moral, religious" (5, p. 21); "the word accompanies and comments on every ideological act.... Speech elements flow around all manifestations of ideological creativity, all other, nonverbal signs;

they are immersed in it and are not subject to complete separation and detachment from it" (5, p. 22). Therefore, Bakhtin regards the word as the principal object of the science of ideologies and sign systems.

As with all other signs, Bakhtin studies the word in the context of concrete forms of social intercourse (1; 5, pp. 28-29). This viewpoint, based on the communicative view of art and other cultural phenomena, is counterposed to the usual one, which has come to be taken for granted: "We most readily see ideological creativity as some kind of internal matter of understanding, perception, and penetration, and do not observe that in fact it is entirely displayed on the outside — for the eye, for the ear, for the hands — that it is not within us but between us" (3, p. 17). In essence this anticipated that use of the general model of communication which was broadly adopted only after information theory was created. As a particularly vivid example of investigation of a social (communicative) situation (8) determining the structure of utterance, one must note the very profound understanding of psychoanalysis presented by Bakhtin in his first book: "All these verbal utterances by the patient (his verbal reactions), on which Freud's psychological construction is based, are scenarios primarily of that immediate, tiny, social event in which they were born — the psychoanalytic session" (2, p. 119). (9) Proceeding from the communicative approach to the subject of psychoanalysis, Bakhtin was one of the first (10) to mark the way toward its semiotic reinterpretation, which in those years was proposed by E. Sapir and was later developed in the school of Lacan and also by Shands and a number of other present-day investigators. (11)

Bakhtin extended the communicative approach to all sign phenomena of intellectual life: "The inner world and thought of each person have their stabilized social audience, in the atmosphere of which that person's inner arguments, inner motivations, evaluations, and the like are constructed. The more cultured the particular person, the more the given audience approximates the normal audience of ideological creativity" (5, p. 102). Study of art in its communicative aspect made particularly important

M. M. Bakhtin and Modern Semiotics

for Bakhtin the discovery of "forms of artistic intercourse in the defining of the structures of works of art" (3, p. 24). "Outside these unique forms of social intercourse there is no poem nor ode, no novel, no symphony" (3, p. 22). Iu. N. Tynianov followed a similar path in his works at the close of the 1920s, particularly in his study of the ode as an oratorical genre. A certain similarity in the approach to the problem of genres may also be discovered in comparing Bakhtin's ideas about the interaction of literary genres (particularly the novel) and extraliterary forms — mundane [zhiznenno-bytovye] and ideological (12, p. 116) — with the concept of canonization of the "lower" genres used in the historical-literary works of OPOIaZ. Suffice it to mention, as one of the most successful examples, the comparison of some of Akhmatova's poems with recitative folklore, of the chastushka type, made by B. M. Eikhenbaum. (12)

For Bakhtin, "speech genres," the identification of which is also necessary for study of genres of verbal art (1; 5, p. 115-116; 8; 9; 12), are linked to definite situations of communication. But the literary genre is not derived directly from the life form but is linked to the past of the same literary genre: "A genre lives by the present but always remembers its past, its beginning. Genre is the representative of the creative memory in the process of literary development" (8, p. 142). The latter thought, admitting a reformulation in the terms of cybernetic models, accords with the very latest theories of literary communication, which simultaneously take into consideration the modern literary situation and the "development series" (vývinový rad), which jointly shape the literary context. (13) At present, given developed conceptions about the role of memory as a component link in the channel of communication, such a model seems natural or even obvious. Introduction of the conception of genre memory as key in historical poetics must be recognized as an outstanding achievement on the part of Bakhtin, who thereby succeeded in eliminating the opposition between historical and synchronic poetics. This concept helps describe the transmission in time of genre structures previously formed under the conditions of direct communication which in themselves are "constitutive

Semiotics and Structuralism

only for certain artistic genres" (3, p. 23).

2. The boldest thought in the general conception of the sign, developed in Bakhtin's first books and flowing from his advancement of the communicative aspect into the foreground, was his understanding of the relation between sign and utterance. Although the concrete conclusions he drew pertaining to the structure of utterance exercised undeniable influence on a number of linguists and literary scholars, nevertheless this conception was, on the whole, far in advance of its time, and therefore found no response. In the words of G. Dumézil in the preface to one of his last books, the return to what had been discovered fully thirty years ago and then remained unnoticed has become normal in the humanities. (14) Virtually word-for-word correspondence with this conception in Bakhtin's early books appears in a number of recent articles by the most prominent Western European linguist of the older generation — E. Benveniste (to whom these books were unknown). In spite of the fact that as a pupil of Meillet he may be regarded as a direct heir of Saussure in the second generation, Benveniste has opposed the one-sidedness of that understanding of language which originates with Saussure. According to Benveniste, the development of the semiotic study of language "was inhibited, paradoxically, by the very tool that had created it: the sign." (15) For further research it is essential to create, along with the semiotics of the sign, a semantic theory of utterance. This is demanded both by the goals of properly linguistic investigations and by the tasks of comparing language with other systems. Benveniste's thought may therefore be clarified by an example borrowed from the semiotics of film language. In the works of S. M. Eisenstein and other theorists of the time, the montage silent film of the 1920s was comparatively easily described as an analogue of verbal language because every montage "sentence" was divisible into individual units — shots, which could be correlated with the signs of verbal language. Therefore, for example, the same Eisenstein could set himself the task of transmitting a verbal image by means of a montage sentence ("bloody slaughterhouse" in The Strike, etc.). Many films in today's sound cinema are

M. M. Bakhtin and Modern Semiotics

characterized more by a tendency to maximize the shot-episode, i.e., to exhaust a whole episode within the limits of a single shot, hence also the role of such devices as the travel shot — uninterrupted movement of the camera at the same angle between its optical axis and the series of things being filmed (for example, horizontal travel of the camera along a street on which a character may walk for as long as desired, accompanied by the traveling camera). It would be artificial to describe the macrostructure of such films in terms of units smaller than a whole shot-episode. It turns out that, with respect to verbal texts as well, the real unit of description should be a complete utterance, sometimes quite lengthy. In asserting this idea, directed polemically against the promotion of the sign as principal and sole unit of description in the Saussure school, Benveniste speaks of the investigation of the structure of the utterance in linguistics and of the "metasemantic" study of the structure of text in other fields of semiotics as two principal tasks of "second generation" semiotics. (16) But it is precisely these two problems that not only were formulated on the basis of similar general semiotic ideas but were also concretely resolved in the works of Bakhtin published forty years before Benveniste's articles. While many of the problems examined in Bakhtin's works were posed by him only in general form, as a program for a future philosophy of language (17), the problem of the structure of utterance (particularly in connection with transmission of someone else's word [chuzhoe slovo]) and "metalinguistics" — the scholarly discipline concerned with dialogic relations (6; 8, pp. 62-64) — were given amply detailed and concrete study in his words. In this sense his works considerably anticipated the most recent studies in the realm of discourse analysis (18) and translinguistics, differing from them (and from traditional rhetoric [19]) also in the respect that, for Bakhtin, the major difference between "metalinguistics" and linguistics lies not in the scale of the object of study (in linguistics the sentence, in translinguistics a text of many sentences), but in the nature of the approach: in "metalinguistics" one studies the communicative aspect. Therefore, according to Bakhtin, the

Semiotics and Structuralism

object of study of metalinguistics may also be the individual sign-word, appearing in the context of real communication, while Benveniste continues to use the term "sign" only in the sense that Saussure gave it.

Like Benveniste in the articles cited, Bakhtin pointed to the limited nature of this Saussurean understanding of "utterance" (parole), which set it outside the limits of systemic research (4; 5, pp. 96-98). Anticipating the recent discussions concerning Cartesian linguistics in its relationship to Humboldt and Saussure (20), Bakhtin asserted that the roots of the rationalist conception of language as a system of signs "lie in Cartesian soil" (4, p. 124 and fn. 11; compare 5, p. 70 and fn. 11). "Rationalism as a whole is characterized by the idea of the conventionality, the arbitrariness of language, and is equally characterized by the comparison of the system of language with the system of mathematical signs. It is not the relation of a sign... to the individual who generates it, but the relation of a sign to a sign within a closed system, once adopted and admitted, that interests the mathematically oriented mind of the rationalists. In other words, they are interested only in the internal logic of the system of signs itself, taken, as in algebra, absolutely independent of the ideological meanings that fill the signs" (5, p. 70). This purely syntactic (in the broad logical-mathematical and semiotic sense) approach to language and other signs, which is characteristic of many trends in twentieth-century science and art (such as OPOIaZ in the initial period of its activity), was criticized by Bakhtin, who started with a more general semantic and pragmatic (sociological or communicative) examination of utterances.

Basing himself on the fact that every utterance has a "theme" or "thematic unity" (5, p. 119), Bakhtin proposed an understanding of meaning as the "technical apparatus for realization of a theme" (5, p. 120). In this one could see a similarity to that trend in the most recent linguistic semantics which builds a model of transition "from sense to text," but here Bakhtin brought to the fore "multiplicity of meanings — the constitutive feature of the word" (5, p. 121). Therefore, his ideas are closer

M. M. Bakhtin and Modern Semiotics

not to a description of meanings for a discrete case of single-valued meanings of words in a scientific text, toward which linguistic semantics has hitherto oriented itself, but to the model for the continuous case that it has recently been proposed to construct for describing meanings in poetic language. (21) According to Bakhtin, "There is no continuous transition, and no connection at all, between the linguistic forms of the elements of an utterance and the forms of its whole. Only by a leap can we move from syntax to questions of composition" (5, p. 94). Similarly, Benveniste, describing the tasks of study of speech activity that creates a message, says that "a message cannot be reduced to a sequence of elements, each of which can be independently recognized; sense is not formed by some addition of signs; on the contrary, sense ('that which is understood'), examined as an integral unity, is embodied and divided into individual 'signs' making up words" (22); "The world of the sign is closed. There is no transition from sign to sentence." (23) While Bakhtin disputes the orientation of rationalism toward comparing language with a system of mathematical signs, at the beginning of the articles referred to above, Benveniste speaks of the difficulties arising upon application to natural language and other semiotic systems of that logical-mathematical conception of the sign used by Ch. Peirce (24) (who differs from Saussure because signs for him are far from all being conventional). As Bakhtin had done earlier, Benveniste emphasizes the difference between recognition of a repeating sign — "signal" in Bakhtin's terms (5, pp. 81-82, in which a flexible sign in a concrete utterance is counterposed to a fixed signal) — and his conception of utterance: "The semiotic (sign) should be recognized (reconnu), while the semantic (utterance) ought to be understood." (25) Similarily, Bakhtin, whose formulations correspond literally to Benveniste's cited idea, took it as point of departure that "the process of understanding ought in no case be confused with the process of recognition. They are profoundly different. Only a sign is understood, while a signal is recognized. A signal is an internally immobile, single thing that actually reflects nothing but is merely a technical means of indicating a

Semiotics and Structuralism

particular object (specific and immobile) or some action (also specific and immobile)" (5, p. 82). This distinction is used in his book (5) to criticize that reflexological explanation of language (26) which was advanced in the 1920s and which had much in common with the behaviorist conception of it in descriptive linguistics, which battled with mentalism. (27) A distinction similar to the above-cited delimitation between signal and sign in an utterance was suggested at that time by Eisenstein, who counterposed to the ossified sign-conventional symbol the living "symbol in formation" (Symbol im Werden), which he studied in connection with the "formation of an image." (28) For him this difference was variable: "With the passage of time and under specific conditions, the image can freeze into the immobility of a symbol, while the symbol can become permeated with dynamism and return to being an image." (29) For Bakhtin "an ideological sign should be immersed in the element of internal subjective signs, resound with subjective tones, so as to remain a living sign and not fall into the venerable status of an incomprehensible museum relic" (5, p. 51).

According to Bakhtin, "the constitutive factor for a linguistic form as a sign is not at all its signal self-identity but its specific variability, and for the understanding of the linguistic form the constitutive factor is not recognition 'of the same thing' but understanding in the strict sense, i.e., orientation in the given context and the given situation, orientation in formation and not 'orientation' in some immobile existence" (5, p. 83). These ideas were based on a consistent differentiation between the point of view of the listener (toward which, in Bakhtin's view, linguistics had traditionally oriented itself) and the point of view of the speaker, the role of which was emphasized by Bakhtin, who in this respect anticipated one of the fundamental ideas of the linguistic conception of Chomsky (as well as those of many other contemporary linguists, who have advanced to the fore the linguistic intuition of the speaker, the formal description of which makes up the principal goal of generative grammar). The relationship between these two viewpoints was studied, following Bakhtin, as one of the fundamental problems of general linguistics

M. M. Bakhtin and Modern Semiotics

and poetics by R. O. Jakobson, who built a communicative model to describe linguistic communications and poetic texts, and by his followers.

3. According to Bakhtin, "to understand someone else's utterance means to orient oneself with respect to it, to find for it the proper place in the appropriate context. It is as though we layer on each word of the understood utterance a series of our own responding words.... Every understanding is dialogic. Understanding is opposed to utterance as a remark is opposed to a remark in dialogue" (5, p. 123). To use Bakhtin's terminology, dialogue is unquestionably the dominant of his scientific creativity, the central and key concept around which his principal themes and achievements are grouped. According to Bakhtin, "dialogic communication is the realm of the true life of the word" (7, p. 270); dialogic relationships are revealed both in those types of speech that presume orientation toward someone else's word and in the forms of organization of the text of the paragraph type (5, p. 131-34), which have recently again attracted the attention of linguists. (30) All the tasks of "metalinguistics" are subordinated to investigation of the realm of dialogic relationships. Various aspects of "two-voiced" discourse [dvugolosaia rech'] (with an orientation toward someone else's word) were first systematized by Bakhtin. In the classification he proposed (8, pp. 266-67), which is something like a periodic system of the elements for the description of prose, such types of prose narration as the skaz, which had previously been studied by members of OPOIaZ, particularly Eikhenbaum (31), but were unrelated to the problem of someone else's discourse [chuzhaia rech'], found their place. This example clearly shows the continuity between members of the OPOIaZ group and Bakhtin, who, despite all his theoretical disagreements with the OPOIaZ school, assimilated and developed its achievements. The problem of quasidirect discourse [nesobstvennaia priamaia rech'], to which a special part of the book (the last part) is devoted (5), appeared in a new way in Bakhtin's general conception. The results achieved by that time in this field, which interested many literary scholars and linguists at the beginning of the

Semiotics and Structuralism

twentieth century, were interpreted by Bakhtin in the light of his concept of "speech about speech," "utterance about utterance" (5, p. 136), or "message referring to message" (32), as Jakobson wrote thirty years later, rephrasing the terms of the work in the spirit of information theory (5). Bakhtin's achievement also lay in the fact that he also associated this phenomenon, which was to a high degree characteristic of avant-garde prose (33), with those features of "the social destiny of an utterance" thanks to which, in most fields "of verbal creativity, what predominates is not the 'pronounced' but the 'made' word. All speech activity is reduced here to the placing of 'someone else's words' and 'seemingly someone else's words [kak by chuzhikh slov].' Even in the humanities there is a tendency to replace a responsible utterance on an issue with a depiction of the current status of a given issue in a field with calculation and inductive derivation of 'the presently prevailing viewpoint,' which is sometimes considered the most reliable 'solution' of the question.... Artistic, rhetorical, philosophical, and scholarly speech in the humanities becomes the realm of 'opinion' " (5, p. 188). Therefore, the role of quotation, the problem of which has recently again begun to be posed in semiotic research, becomes particularly important. (34) Bakhtin sheds light on this problem from the standpoint of the role of someone else's word. He notes that "one of the most interesting stylistic problems of Hellenism is the problem of quotation. Infinitely varied were the forms of explicit, half-hidden, and concealed quoting, forms of framing quotations in context, forms of intonational 'quotation marks,' various degrees of alienation or assimilation of the cited someone else's word. And here a problem often arises: Is the author quoting reverently or, on the contrary, with irony, with a sneer? Ambiguity in the attitude toward someone else's word is often deliberate" (11, p. 16). "The attitude toward someone else's word in the Middle Ages was no less complicated and ambiguous." With almost Rabelaisian richness of epithet he enumerates the types of quotations in medieval texts: "The role of someone else's word, quotation, explicit and reverently emphasized, half-concealed, concealed, half-conscious, unconscious, correct, deliberately distorted, unintentionally dis-

M. M. Bakhtin and Modern Semiotics

torted, deliberately reinterpreted, etc., was grandiose in medieval literature" (11, p. 17); "the boundaries between someone else's word and one's own discourse were flexible, ambiguous, often intentionally devious and tortuous. Certain types of works were constructed, like mosaics, from someone else's texts" (11, p. 17). Similar "collages" of quotations, like the cento, mentioned by Bakhtin, from someone else's verses and hemistichs again became commonplace in modern artistic prose (for example, in the works of J. P. Faille), in which quotations may be regarded as metonymic substitutes for an entire text. In this way they enter the metonymic system of prose narration. The post-Cubist function of quotations in collages emerges with particular clarity in the early notes of Eisenstein, who wrote in 1928 that "an entire treatise can be made by composition of quotations." (35) In his later works, in which compositions of quotations are often used, he himself explains them (in the spirit of the "linear style" of quotation) by a desire for "minimal distortion of the very objects from which the montage image is made up." (36) Similar thoughts may be found in Thomas Mann, who gradually was arriving at a striving "to regard life as a work of culture in the form of a mythological cliché, and to prefer quotation to one's own invention." (37) During the same years Mandel'shtam, in whose creative work the significance of hidden quotations is particularly great, described the similar "keyboard of mentions" [upominatel'naia klavatura] in Dante in connection with the role of quotations in his works (which in part continued the medieval tradition investigated by Bakhtin). (38) It is no accident that in the 1930s the theme of "counterpoint" (the title of a novel by Aldous Huxley), or the dialogue of the component parts of a cultural tradition or various cultures counterposed to each other (3; 13, p. 240), is posed simultaneously both in the humanities and in verbal art, where it determines the structure of many works.

According to Bakhtin, the advancing of dialogic relationships into the foreground is characteristic of artistic prose, while in poetry, prior to its "prosaization" in the twentieth century, a considerably larger role is played by the word which is direct and immediately oriented toward its object (8, p. 267). It is no accident that a major poet like Lucian Blaga, whose words are cited by the Romanian mathematician S. Marcus in a book on mathematical poetics, could assert that "a genuine dialogue between two people is essentially impossible. Any dialogue amounts to two alternating monologues." (39) But another poet — T. S. Eliot, who made a detailed analysis of the relationship between the first, second, and third person in a poetic text — came to the conclusion that "in any work of poetry, from private meditation to epic or drama, more than one voice can be heard." (40) However, only in prose does the two-voiced word become the basic factor in narration. Thanks to this, authorial speech can also be perceived as someone else's, which "often finds compositional expression in the appearance of a narrator who replaces the author in the usual sense of the word," as "in Dostoevsky, Andrei Bely, Remizov, Sologub, and the modern Russian novelists" (5, p. 143; 6 and 8). In other words, someone else's word as a theme also determines even composition. Borrowing from Wölfflin's works on the arts, which he held in high esteem (3, p. 19), the distinction between "linear style" and "pictorial style" (5, p. 142), Bakhtin counterposed to the linear, rationalist style of transmission of someone else's discourse (in the seventeenth and eighteenth centuries) the pictorial style that erased its boundaries, as with the listed Russian writers. But in the paragraph structure of other prose writers as well, Bakhtin saw "dialogue which had seemingly weakened and which had entered monologic utterance" (5, p. 133).

In general Bakhtin conceives of the monologue as dialogue which has entered inside ("interiorized," in Piaget's terminology, which is used in another work on this subject by Benveniste, who here again fully coincides with Bakhtin). (41) "The word had first to be born and mature in the process of social communication among organisms in order subsequently to enter the organism and become an inner word" (5, p. 50). This idea, first clearly expressed in Bakhtin's investigations in 1926-1929 (1,2, and 5), was later (in 1934) propounded by L. S. Vygotskii in connection with the findings of Piaget's work in experimental psychology on the egocentric speech of children. Vygotskii's hypothesis that the latter is an intermediate stage between dialogic speech and inner speech was confirmed by tape recordings of a child's monologue before falling asleep, uttered in the absence of an adult. (42) Vygotskii's conception "of the functional diversity of speech" (43) — "speech genres," which according to Bakhtin depend on concrete communication situations — of the primacy of dialogue over monologue (44), and of the relation of inner speech to monologic and dialogic speech not only corresponds in many respects to the conclusions of Bakhtin's earlier works but also reveals their influence. One becomes convinced of this, specifically, by comparing the analysis of the identical passage in Dostoevsky's The Diary of a Writer in Bakhtin (5, pp. 124-25 ff) and in Vygotskii. (45) In turn, Eisenstein, who met with A. R. Luria, N. Ia. Marr, and Vygotskii just before the latter's death to work jointly on psychological problems in the arts and language, was obviously under Vygotskii's influence. Eisenstein's movement from study of signs in montage film language to attempts to penetrate through both the techniques of film and scientific methods into the structure of inner speech is to a certain degree analogous to the movement, examined above in terms of the works of Bakhtin and Benveniste, from the rationalistically (logically) understood sign as the principal subject of semiotics in the first stage of its development, to the utterance, including the interiorized utterance. In Eisenstein's words, "Our epoch — acutely ideological and intellectual — could not but read in the shot primarily its property as an ideological engram — a sign; could not fail to see in the juxtaposition of shots the appearance of a new qualitative element, a new image, a new concept." (46) However, further development of the theory of film language led Eisenstein to the necessity to compare it not so much with written and spoken speech as with inner speech, "where the affective structure functions in an even more full and pure form. But the formation of this inner speech is already inalienable from that which is (enriched) also termed sensual thinking (thought)." (47) Eisenstein's theoretical studies in the 1930s in the realm of inner speech, devoted primarily to analysis of interior monologue

Semiotics and Structuralism

in Joyce (particularly the stream-of-consciousness of Molly Bloom in the last chapter of Ulysses), were associated with his intentions to reproduce interior monologue in the film (in his scenario for An American Tragedy), which were later realized by Fellini, Bergman, and Alain Resnais. Turning later to the same problem in his book Method, Eisenstein remarked how Dostoevsky, in "A Gentle Spirit" (48), overheard "the magic of the true flow of inner speech." The same story and the author's preface to it are analyzed by Bakhtin in his book on Dostoevsky to illustrate how the character's "inner word" about himself becomes in turn the ultimate objective of the construct (7, pp. 72-74). (49) From attempts to re-create the interior monologue through the devices of cinema, Eisenstein proceeded to establish a general aesthetic theory based on the idea that "the regularities of constructions of inner speech prove to be the very regularities that underlie the entire diversity of regularities, in accordance with which the form and composition of artistic works are constructed. And... there is not a single formal device that is not a copy made from one or another regularity, by means of which inner speech, unlike the logic of external speech, is constructed." (50) In his book Grundproblem Eisenstein studied "the fundamental problem" of the theory of art, which lies in the fact that the structure of a work reflects deep layers of sensual thought (associated with inner speech), but that at the same time in art there occurs an elevation "to the highest ideological levels of consciousness." (51) Description of this dual process may be linked with the conception of inner speech developed by Vygotskii, who regarded signs as instruments for the control of behavior. From this point of view man's use of inner speech, which retains the "function" of communication, is "a unique form of collaboration with oneself" (52); "regulation of someone else's behavior by means of the word gradually results in the development of verbalized behavior of the personality itself." (53)

Of particular importance to the treatment of these problems in Bakhtin's study of Freudianism, written several years before the cited works of Vygotskii, is the conclusion that "within the

M. M. Bakhtin and Modern Semiotics

verbalized realm of human behavior, quite severe conflicts occur between inner and external speech and between different layers of inner speech" (54) (this accords with Eisenstein's idea about the conflict that is the essence of the principal problem of art). Beginning, like Vygotskii (55), with a critical reinterpretation of the ideas of such thinkers as Dilthey (5, pp. 34-36) and Scheler, Bakhtin arrives at a semiotic conception of the higher psychic functions, which always "exist only in the sign material" (5, p. 37). Bakhtin proceeds from the role for emotion of its "sign incarnation, ... the organizing and shaping center lies not within (i.e., not in the material of inner signs) but without. It is not emotion that organizes expression but, on the contrary, expression that organizes emotion" (5, p. 101). Therefore, along with the "we — experience" (the highest psychological functions, in Vygotskii's terms) there emerge lower sensations ("I — experiences"), which in their extreme forms lack communicative manifestation: "With respect to the potential (and sometimes the explicitly perceived) listener, one can distinguish two poles, two limits, between which an experience, now tending toward one, now the other, can be realized and ideologically shaped. Let us tentatively call these limits 'I — experience' and 'we — experience.' The 'I — experience' yearns for annihilation; as it approaches its limit, it loses its ideological form, and consequently its awareness of self, approximating the physiological reaction of an animal. In striving toward this limit, an experience loses all potentials, all shoots of social orientation, and therefore loses its verbal aspect as well" (5, p. 164). In particular, groups of sexual experiences can drop out of their social context and thus lose verbal awareness of self (2, pp. 136-37). Bakhtin regards Freud's unconscious as "unofficial consciousness" (2, p. 128); "the wider and deeper the chasm between official and unofficial consciousness, the more difficult it is for the motifs of inner speech to move into external speech" (2, p. 134). Consequently, in the early work devoted to reinterpretation of the findings of psychoanalysis from the semiotic standpoint, that problem of the relation between official and unofficial consciousness is formulated which constitutes the content of a series of Bakhtin's later cultural-historical works devoted to the opposition of "official monologue" to dialogue (6 and 8) and to the unofficial carnival cultural tradition of the Middle Ages and the Renaissance (8, pp. 162-83; 9; 11). In the book on Rabelais, the "unofficial elements of speech" or "the unpublishable realm," freed from the hierarchy and prohibitions of offical language, are counterposed to it as a special language with which a special group is linked — the carnival "crowd on the square" (9, p. 203). The very content of the images of the grotesque body which are studied in the book about Rabelais is close to that range of symbols investigated by Freud and his school. The thesis of the ambivalence of public-square words and the carnival image also has something in common with Freud. But Bakhtin's point of view is fundamentally different from the Freudian: he analyzes that unofficial folk language which formed within particular — holiday, carnival, market — situations of unofficial communication. This language of the carnival uses, specifically, a set of symbols that can have a great deal in common with the "I — experience" (images of the lower part of the body); but with respect to this language (as, apparently, in general with respect to the creativity of Rabelais and his contemporaries) one cannot speak of the "unconscious" (even of the collective unconscious of Jung), because in Rabelais the symbols of carnival appear in the capacity of a conscious communicative medium.

From the standpoint that Bakhtin developed in his early works, biological and biographical factors are significant only for "lower strata in the ideology of life" (5, p. 111). "That which is usually termed 'creative individuality' is an expression of the basic, firm, and constant line of social orientation of the particular individual.... There we find words, intonations, and intraverbal gestures that have undergone the experience of external expression on a more or less broad social scale, as though well polished socially, ground fine by reactions and replies, by the rejection or support of the social audience" (5, pp. 110-11). Therefore, carnival language is a means of connecting the lower strata of inner speech with the broad social milieu (in other words, a means of retranslating the individual-biological into

M. M. Bakhtin and Modern Semiotics

the social). Thus the general question of "the mundane genre," constituting part of the social milieu, which was formulated even in Bakhtin's first works (1; 5, p. 116), is solved in the material of the festival celebration. This shows how unified is all his creative, scholarly work, which is inseparable from the social context of the epoch and which explains many striking similarities both in the formulation of problems and in their resolution by the outstanding contemporaries we have already named. (56) In the 1940s the idea of the "counterpoint" of various languages becomes one such central idea of the epoch. This is why, in the book on Rabelais, the language of carnival is examined not so much on the level of the correspondence between festival speech genres and the speech of the given author — Rabelais — as in the broader aspect of the carnivalization of literature, i.e., the relation between the language of carnival and the language of literature. (57)

5. Anticipating that understanding of semiotics as the science of relations between systems of signs, and linguistics as the science of relations between languages, which developed in the 1960s, Bakhtin first expressed the idea of the role of multilingualism in the development of the awareness of language and in verbal linguistic creativity, above all for the novel genre. He discovered the role of "someone else's word" for the first philological and linguisitic experiments and for the most ancient philosophy of language. Recent works in the field of the sociology of writing (58), a skill that appeared only in those societies in which the priesthood existed as a separate social class, have confirmed his thesis that "the first philologists and the first linguists, everywhere and always, were the priests" (5, p. 88); for it was their task to comprehend the sacred text that was in a foreign language. To this it may be added that this text, even if it was not always in a foreign tongue, consisted of signs of a type different from the usual spoken language. In particular, it could be a written utterance. The role of someone else's word in the appearance of conscious thought about language is similar to the manner in which Bakhtin conceives of the appearance of the novelistic word [romannoe slovo] under the influence of

Semiotics and Structuralism

comparison of different languages: "There occurs the transformation of language from an absolute dogma, which it is within the limits of self-isolation and deaf monolingualism, into a working hypothesis for the attainment and expression of reality" (11, p. 11). Bakhtin associates the very appearance of the novel with active multilingualism, i.e., with the "counterpoint" of different languages (10, pp. 101-2). "Every novel is to a greater or lesser degree a dialogized system of images of 'languages,' styles, of consciousnesses concrete and inseparable from language. Language in a novel not only depicts but itself serves as the object of depiction" (10, p. 89). If the metalanguage (59) of linguistics (particularly, ancient Indian) began to take shape to interpret an alien language (for example, Sanskrit), then in the novel metalinguistic use of the word is revealed thanks to multilingualism. From this standpoint Bakhtin proposes a new interpretation of parody-travesty forms, according to which their subject is always "language itself in its direct functions" (11, p. 10). This reveals the place of the genres that prepared the way for the novel in the history of language as a semiotic means that initially was not differentiated from the concepts and denotata it signified. The parody-travesty forms "freed the subject from the power of language in which it was tangled as in a net; they destroyed the total power of myth over language, freed consciousness from the power of the direct word..., and a 'distance' was created between language and reality" (ibid.). Bakhtin sees parody as the result of a crossing of two languages, i.e., as an "'intralinguistic' hybrid" (11, p. 21); in other words, as a "creolized" text, to use the term proposed in works on semiotics in the 1960s even before publication of the cited work by Bakhtin (which had been written considerably earlier). Interlinguistic creolization, i.e., multilingualism (bilingualism as a special case), both in Russian literature (60), in other European literatures (61), and also in "Third World" literatures (62), is also quite characteristic of the novel.

In his critique of the early works of OPOIaZ (3), Bakhtin pointed to the fact, as one of the significant charges against the formal (morphological) school, that its means were inadequate

M. M. Bakhtin and Modern Semiotics

to describe so important a genre as the novel. Bakhtin's literary studies (6, 8-12) are all devoted to this theme, which is basic for him. He studies the novel in its sources or through material that has already become classic. But for him the novel is primarily a genre which takes form before the eyes of history, an experiment done by literature (not the dead heritage of the past). One cannot fail to see the very deep inner parallel between the laws of the novel he formulated and the structure of such twentieth-century novels as Joyce's Ulysses, which was written during Bakhtin's youth. The interweaving and dialogic juxtaposition of different speech genres, their conflict within the novel, many of the features of the novel genre that made it similar to the parody-travesty forms, attained what was perhaps their ultimate perfection specifically in Ulysses, the very structure of which is a parody-travesty (for it parodies the structure of Homer's Odyssey).

Bakhtin's ideas are also of no less significance for study of the most recent genre, the film novel, in which a dialogic, and often also a carnival, structure is given in particularly clear-cut form. (63) Such a novel as Evgenii Onegin, "the emphatically novelistic principle" (12, p. 112) in which was revealed by Bakhtin (10; 12, pp. 112 ff.), becomes an example for the modern novel, particularly the French, in which quoted someone else's word emerges in the foreground. (64)

Particular significance in study of the contemporary novel (and to an even greater degree the film novel) attaches to examination of its structure in the light of the viewpoints from which the narration is conducted. Recently this approach to the novel, suggested by Bakhtin and carried out by him in detail in his book on Dostoevsky (6 and 8), has been set forth in technically more advanced form: a monograph by B. A. Uspenskii, who uses more specialized language to describe the principle of shift in point of view in prose, is devoted to it. (65) In a general essay on structural poetics, Tsvetan Todorov comments on the similarity of this aspect of the conception of Bakhtin's book on Dostoevsky, "undoubtedly one of the most important in the field of poetics" (66), to the formulation of the same problem of viewpoint by Lubbock (67), who followed and studied Henry James, and by Pouillon, who distinguished three principal types of point of view (68), of which the point of view that is identified with the point of view of a character (vision avec) is particularly important for the conception offered by Bakhtin. (69) But it is necessary to emphasize that, unlike the indicated recent works on structural poetics, the problem of point of view in Bakhtin's book on Dostoevsky did not become technical or technological (for him the technical aspect of the study of art was always secondary). A less technical treatment of exposition was supplemented by the depth with which the question was formulated. This formulation was associated with the theme of another man's world-view, which undoubtedly brings the book (6), published in 1929, close to such later works as Sartre's L'être et le néant, which summarized what had been done in this field in existential philosophy. (70) Bakhtin's formulation "[his] awareness of self constantly perceives itself against the background of another's awareness of him — 'I for myself' against the background of 'I for another' " (8, p. 277) coincides entirely with Sartre's assertion: "I need the other so that I can fully comprehend all the structure of my being. For oneself refers to For another." (71) As we have already had occasion to observe, Bakhtin's discoveries pertaining to Dostoevsky, the founder of the modern European novel, are in natural accord with Sartre's ideas about the novel, in which, as in the world of Einstein, there is no privileged observer. (72) In the second edition of his book, Bakhtin himself compares Dostoevsky's dialogic polyphony with the Einsteinian world, in which the multiplicity of frames of reference is admitted (8, p. 361). The idea that "the scientific picture of one and the same reality may and must be multiplied — not at all at the expense of truth" (73) — has been confirmed in such disciplines in the humanities as structural linguistics, where it was first formulated (74) by representatives of those Eastern cultural traditions in which the presence of several equally acceptable pictures of the world has long been recognized (75) (it is characteristic that Niels Bohr saw in Hokusai's "100 Views of Fuji" a clear-cut embodiment of the principle of complementarity broadly under-

M. M. Bakhtin and Modern Semiotics

stood). It is characteristic that it was precisely the Orientalist F. I. Shcherbatskoi who, in the 1930s (virtually simultaneously with the publication of the first edition of Bakhtin's book on Dostoevsky) at the end of his Buddhist Logic [Buddiiskaia logika], revives the form of the Socratic dialogue, in which the voices of various Indian and European thinkers are combined and contrasted. (76) Revealing the new contribution of Dostoevsky's polyphonic dialogism to the European tradition, Bakhtin wrote: "Faith in the self-sufficiency of the consciousness alone in all areas of ideological life is not a theory created by some thinker, no — it is a deep structural feature of the ideological creativity of modern times, which determines all its external and internal forms" (8, p. 108). In the polyphonic world of Dostoevsky, "the monologic substance" of ideas is less important than their "function" in dialogue (8, p. 123). Singling out a character's self-awareness as an artistic dominant that dissolves the monologic unity of the work, Bakhtin clarifies his thought by counterposing Racine and Dostoevsky: "Racine's hero is all being, stable and firm, like a plastic sculpture. Dostoevsky's hero is all self-awareness. Racine's hero is a static and finite substance; Dostoevsky's, an infinite function" (8, p. 68). In Dostoevsky "the culminating points... — the peaks of dialogues — rise above the plot in the abstract realm of pure relationship between person and person" (8, p. 357). Here we see that fundamental aspect in the conception of the theme of "another man" in Dostoevsky which joins Bakhtin not with existentialist philosophy but with Pasternak's early "Liuvers' Childhood," which is devoted to the appearance of "the other person" in the heroine's self-awareness. Citing a passage from "Stavrogin's Confession" that corresponds almost literally to one from "Liuvers' Childhood" (77), Bakhtin says that "this other person — 'stranger, a person you will never know' — performs his functions in the dialogue outside the plot and outside his plot definition, as a pure 'person in a person,' the representative of 'all others' for the 'I.' As a consequence of such a formulation of 'the other,' communication takes on a special character and becomes something outside all real and concrete social forms" (8, p. 356). According to Bakhtin, in such passages from novels there occurs an emergence into mystery-carnival space and time.

Understanding Dostoevsky's ideas always as a dialogue of ideas (sometimes as an internal dialogue in the self-awareness of the hero — as "ideologue"), Bakhtin observes that in Dostoevsky's novels it is impossible to isolate individual thoughts or their internal system: he thought in personalities — in integral positions of personality and their combinations (8, pp. 123-24). The semiotic idea of the personality as a sign, previously advanced by Peirce, or of man as message, suggested by Wiener, here acquires a quite clear-cut sense. Even in Bakhtin's early works one can trace an understanding of the personality as the theme of language: "The inner personality is the word expressed or driven within" (8, p. 181). This thought is concretized in the study of the personality and self-awareness in Dostoevsky, whose sense of community [sobornost'] Bakhtin understands as "a world of contiguous intellectual human positions. Among them he seeks the highest, the most authoritative position, and he perceives it not as his true thought but as another genuine man and his word. In the image of the ideal man or in the image of Christ, he sees the solution of ideological quests" (8, p. 170).

6. In Dostoevsky the dialogue of personalities aware of themselves is synchronous: "Dostoevsky provides in artistic form what amounts to a sociology of consciousnesses, true, only on the plane of coexistence" (8, p. 44). Bakhtin reveals Dostoevsky's fundamentally synchronistic orientation, which essentially brings him close to many currents in the humanities during the twentieth century and to the modern European novel, because the "interior dialogue" (a term introduced with respect to the novel by Bakhtin long before Claude Mauriac) always develops in a single temporal segment. "The fundamental category of Dostoevsky's artistic vision was not becoming but coexistence and interaction.... Dostoevsky, contrary to Goethe, sought to perceive the stages themselves in their simultaneity, to compare and counterpose them dramatically, not to arrange them in an emerging series. To understand the world meant for him to think of all its contents as simultaneous and to guess their inter-

M. M. Bakhtin and Modern Semiotics

relationships at a single moment in time" (8, p. 38). Artistically perceptive is the idea that this explains "Dostoevsky's passion for journalism and his love for newspapers, his profound and subtle understanding of the newspaper page as a living reflection of the contradictions of social contemporaneity in the cross section of a single day" (8, p. 40).

Dostoevsky's time, which is taken out of historical time (78), like the peculiarities of the category of space in his novels, is explained by polyphonic dialogue: "The occurrence of the interaction of equally valid and internally imperfect consciousnesses requires a different artistic conception of time and space, a 'non-Euclidean' conception, to use Dostoevsky's own expression" (8, p. 237). The category of space in Dostoevsky is revealed by Bakhtin in pages written not only by a scientist but by an artist: "Dostoevsky 'skips' over the internal space of houses, apartments, and rooms, lived in, well arranged, and stable, far from the threshold...Dostoevsky was least of all an estate-domestic-room-apartment-family writer"(8, p. 228).

The systematic examination of the value aspect of the model is a peculiarity of Bakhtin's description of the categories of space and time, the study of which in various models of the world has become one of the principal trends in research into secondary modeling semiotic systems. In his paper read in 1938, Bakhtin deduced the properties of the novel as a genre in large measure from "the revolution in the hierarchy of times," the change "in the temporal model of the world" (12, p. 114), the orientation toward the incomplete present. This examination — in accordance with the ideas analyzed above — is simultaneously semiotic and axiological, since "value-time categories" are investigated (12, p. 107), which determine the significance of one time relative to another: the value of the past in the epic (79) is contrasted to the value of the present for the novel. In the terms of structural linguistics one could talk about a change in relationships of times with regard to markedness (presence of a feature) and unmarkedness. In reconstructing the medieval picture of the cosmos, Bakhtin concluded that "this picture is characterized by a particular value accentuation of space: spatial steps, going from the bottom upward, strictly corresponded to value steps" (9, p. 395). The role of the vertical is associated with this (ibid.): "That concrete and visible model of the world which underlay medieval imaged thought was fundamentally vertical" (9, p. 436), a fact traced not only in the system of images and metaphors but, for example, also in the image of the way in medieval descriptions of journeys. P. A. Florenskii came to similar conclusions when he observed that "Christian art advanced the vertical and gave it a considerable preference over other coordinates. . . .The Middle Ages magnify this stylistic peculiarity of Christian art and give the vertical complete dominance, this process being found in the Western medieval fresco...."; "the choice of the dominant coordinate determines the most important foundation of stylistic uniqueness, and the artistic spirit of the age." (80) This idea is confirmed by Bakhtin's analysis of the transition during the Renaissance from the hierarchical vertical medieval picture to the horizontal, in which movement in time from past to future became basic (9, p. 395).

7. One of the principal features of Bakhtin's book on carnival culture, making it indubitably structural in its principal attitudes, is the fact that the book is built on analysis of several fundamental binary oppositions, particularly the top — bottom opposition, examined simultaneously on various levels — the social, hierarchical, spatial, bodily (81), etc. It must be emphasized that the binary nature of the major oppositions that determined the structure of Rabelais's world is not a tribute to a preconceived notion but something objectively given. This is proved by the coincidence between this thesis in Bakhtin's book and the results of the studies by Paris, who found in the Rabelaisian world series of binary oppositions corresponding precisely to those which Lévi-Strauss finds in myth. (82)

Essentially, the book (9) might have been titled Top and Bottom in the spirit of those oppositions (of a more concrete character) which title the volumes of Lévi-Strauss's Mythologiques. The way the author "immerses himself" in the archaic tradition (mythological in Lévi-Strauss; carnival in Bakhtin) makes Bakhtin's book akin to Mythologiques. One could say, paraphrasing

M. M. Bakhtin and Modern Semiotics

Lévi-Strauss, that the carnival culture itself speaks through the author of the book. However, aside from this characteristic combination of the rigor of the conceptual structural basis of the book and the artistic language of imagery, which fits the very subject of research, the books of Bakhtin and Lévi-Strauss reveal much in common in their view of the functioning of oppositions either in ritual or carnival (which orginates historically in the ritual performance). For Lévi-Strauss the principal goal of ritual and myth is the finding of an intermediate link (mediation) between binary oppositions. Structural analysis of the ambivalence of "the language of the public square" and of the image led Bakhtin (independently of structural anthropology and earlier than its founders) to the conclusion that "the carnival image seeks to embrace and combine within itself both poles of the formation or both terms of the antithesis: birth and death, youth and age, top and bottom, face and backside, praise and abuse" (8, p. 238). From this standpoint Bakhtin attentively studied the various forms of inversion, of reversal of the relationships between bottom and top — "displacement of the hierarchical top to the bottom" (9, p. 91) in the carnival, particularly in the ritual of proclaiming the jester king or in "changing clothes, that is, the renewal of clothes and their social image" (ibid.; 9, p. 214): "Therefore, in carnival images there is so much inside-out, so many reversed faces, so many deliberately violated proportions. We see this primarily in the dress of the participants. The men are dressed as women and vice versa..." (9, p. 447). E. Leach, one of the most prominent structural anthropologists, has devoted a work solely to problems of the carnival, particularly that of the Middle Ages, which was published two decades after Bakhtin completed his dissertation on Rabelais (1940). In it Leach almost literally repeats Bakhtin's conclusions: in the words of Leach, during carnival celebrations "the individual, instead of emphasizing his social personality and official status, seeks to disguise it. The world goes in a mask, the formal rules of orthodox life are forgotten...." (83) He notes "an extreme form of revelry, in which the participants...play-act a role precisely opposite what they really are: men play the role of women, women, the role of men; kings become beggars, servants, masters." (84) The structure of a situation in which participants in such pairings as "prince and pauper" change places was studied by Eisenstein at approximately the same time as Bakhtin wrote his work on the carnival. In Eisenstein's opinion, "This theme touches on one of the most profoundly mysterious situations of the exchange of social positions (slave and sovereign) in rituals, and of sex by means of disguise in saturnalia and even in historical-political cases — the mysterious story of Ivan the Terrible and the Tatar princeling Semeon Bekbulatovich, who temporarily replaced the tsar of all the Russias on the throne." (85) By the admission of Eisenstein himself, in Part II of his film Ivan the Terrible, in which Ivan places Vladimir Andreevich on the throne and orders that he be dressed in the royal clothing, "this situation is transferred to the death of Vladimir Andreevich.... This exchange of clothes (and places) is on a par with other exchanges of clothing. But the principal change of clothing is the exchange of male and female clothing between men and women. The carnival tradition, growing into a universal disguise" (86), was reproduced by Eisenstein in this film, which first presents the carnival situation Eisenstein regarded as "basic" — initial: Fedor dancing in female clothing and a woman's mask, followed by the exchange of clothing between the tsar and his subject and the murder of the carnival king, Vladimir, which fits the very tradition described by Bakhtin in connection with the killing of the jester king (9, p. 220; compare p. 225 on the decoration of the laughter sacrifice). It must be emphasized that Bakhtin's book also points to the presence of a carnival element in the oprichnina (9, p. 294), which historians have only begun to study. (87) Analysis of the motif of the androgyne in connection with the idea of a dual body resulting from the elimination of binary oppositions (such as life and death, male and female) is one of the themes that unite Bakhtin's work with the cited notes of Eisenstein: "The events of the grotesque body always unfold on the boundary between one body and another, as though at the point of intersection of two bodies: one body yields its death,

M. M. Bakhtin and Modern Semiotics

the other its birth, but they are fused into a single, dual-bodied (in the extreme case) image" (9, p. 349). Eisenstein's drawing "Leonardo" suggests a drawing by Leonardo da Vinci referred to in this connection by Bakhtin (9, p. 350). (88) The ecstatic connection in Leonardo of different poles of binary oppositions, about which Eisenstein wrote repeatedly (citing other investigators) (89), is in this drawing denoted both plastically and symbolically — by the ancient Chinese spiral — by means of joining two opposite principles (binary oppositions), yin and yang.

8. But the most vivid parallel to the entire conception of Bakhtin's book and the individual illustrations preserved in it is the way in which Eisenstein investigated laughter at death in folk rituals, which he reproduced at the end of the film Que viva Mexico! (90) Bakhtin provided a very profound interpretation of laughter at death in folk rituals, showing that this image is in the category of the ambivalent, in which two opposite poles are united (9, pp. 444-45). In one of Jakobson's best articles, in his analysis of the Old Czech medieval mock mystery, which has common features with the farce The Living Dead [Zhivye mertvetsy] studied by Bakhtin (9, p. 324), a similar conclusion is drawn about the role of laughter in the ritual triumph of life over death (91), suggested by an article by V. Ia. Propp. (92)

If one accepts that contrast of "pure" formalism (more exactly, morphological descriptivism) and structuralism advanced by Lévi-Strauss in his article on Propp's first book (93), then both Propp himself in his works of the 1940s and Bakhtin have to be classed not with the formal but with the structural trend in study of the semantics of myth and ritual, a trend which in many respects anticipated structural anthropology. O. M. Freidenberg's work (94) (concluded in 1927), the significance of which Bakhtin noted (9, p. 62, fn. 1), moved in the same direction. But unlike the orientation toward the prelogical characteristic of Freidenberg and of the Marr school in general, as well as of Eisenstein in his Grundproblem, Bakhtin insisted on the length of the path separating carnival from "primitive" rituals (9, p. 306). This does not prevent him from recognizing that the carnival tradition, in Shakespeare, for example, studied from the same standpoint by Freidenberg and Eisenstein, has its roots in the prehistoric past (13, p. 239), i.e., goes back to cultural archetypes. But Bakhtin continued to be interested not only in diachronic problems but also in questions of synchronic functional text analysis, which made him similar in this regard to scholars such as G. A. Gukovskii, Eikhenbaum, and Tynianov, who during the same period used their experience in studying text structure in works devoted to the history of literature. Each of these scholars resolved in his own way the problem of combining diachronic and synchronic research.

It is no accident that in his study of the carnival tradition Bakhtin tries to trace it to our day — to its literary reflections in Hemingway, for example (8, p. 215, fn. 1). The role of the circus, which is quite significant in the artistic creativity of the twentieth century (95), also justifies the recent interest among scholars who apply semiotic methods to circus. (96) In this connection it should be noted that the circus, as the most recent continuation of the ancient carnival tradition, was studied by Bakhtin, who made subtle observations about "the organization of puppet-show and circus space" in comparison with the stage of the theater and the mystery play (9, pp. 383-84), about the contrasting pairs in puppet-show and circus comedy (9, pp. 218, 472). In essence, these pairs historically correspond to the dual twin pairs that embody two series of binary oppositions (such pairs continue to exist in dramaturgy, for example, in Becket's Waiting for Godot), just as "the four devils," analyzed by Bakhtin (9, pp. 353, 289-90), ultimately originate in the guardians of the four "points of the compass," which correspond to the elements.

Returning to the theme of ritual laughter at funerals in one of his last articles (11, p. 8), Bakhtin observes that "everything serious had to have and did have a circus double. Just as in saturnalia the jester doubled for the king and the slave for his master, so in all forms of culture such comic doubles were created" (11, p. 9). "Echoes of this humorous parallelism are alive even today, for example, in the rather common doubling by a circus clown of the serious and dangerous numbers on the

M. M. Bakhtin and Modern Semiotics

program" (11, p. 24), which is comparable to "the secondary level of the fool in Shakespeare's dramas and comedies" (11, p. 23) and to the fourth drama among the Greeks (a contemporary example of such doubling was also analyzed in Jakobson's work).

In the book on Rabelais certain other forms of sign systems are studied — such as games (97) or city "cries" (the "cries of Paris," for example), analogous to the shouted advertisements investigated by Bogatyrev on the basis of later materials. It is characteristic that in this connection Bakhtin recalls the role of sound media in the age of the radio (98) (9, p. 197). But particular interest for general semiotics and the individual semiotic disciplines attaches to the conclusions drawn by Bakhtin in his study of the symbolism of body images as a special language. As Bakhtin himself observes, applications of these ideas can also prove significant for analysis of such sign systems as clothing and fashions, and dances (9, p. 349, fn. 2). The mythological and ritual aspect of the same problem was noted by him in the example of such images as Purusha in the Vedic hymn (9, p. 381), to which typlogical parallels may be found in African (99) and other mythologies. For sociological interpretation, exceptional significance attaches to the conclusion about the character of the "combination of the dismemberment of the body and the dismemberment of society" (9, p. 381), i.e., the establishment of mutually single-valued correspondences between "the grotesque body" and the system of social ranks. In view of the evolutionarily early nature of the language of body images, the conclusions of this part of the book are of major interest to diachronic semiotics. The typology of these images proposed by Bakhtin may help in pursuing many still obscure questions, especially in the history of literature. (100)

The very logic of Bakhtin's movement from the formulation of general semiotic problems considered above to concrete studies of semiotic systems of this type is highly instructive for contemporary semiotics, one of the basic tasks of which remains the development of a general semiotic set of concepts and correspondences suited to the description of various sign systems, including those structured quite differently from natural

Semiotics and Structuralism

language. Bakhtin is one of the first investigators of sign systems who also enriched the science of language by broadening its horizons, which were thus illuminated in a new way by comparison of language with superlinguistic (secondary) semiotic modeling systems. Just as, in accordance with the ideas presented by Bakhtin, multilingualism creates the premises for the science of language, and the contrasting of different cultures establishes the conditions for understanding each of them, the semitoic multilingualism of the epoch made possible the perception of each of the systems of signs within the bounds of the general science of such systems, one of the creators of which in its modern form was M. M. Bakhtin.

Cited Articles and Books by M. M. Bakhtin

1. V. N. Voloshinov (101), "Slovo v zhizni i slovo v poezii," Zvezda, 1926, No. 6.
2. V. N. Voloshinov, Freidizm, Moscow and Leningrad, 1927.
3. P. N. Medvedev, Formal'nyi metod v literaturovedenii. Kriticheskoe vvedenie v sotsiologicheskuiu poetiku, Leningrad, 1928.
4. V. N. Voloshinov, "Noveishie techeniia lingvisticheskoi mysli na Zapade," Literatura i marksizm, Book 5, 1928.
5. V. N. Voloshinov, Marksizm i filosofiia iazyka. Osnovnye problemy sotsiologicheskogo metoda v nauke o iazyke, Leningrad, 1929 (reissued by Janua Linguarum, Series Anastatica, 5, Mouton, The Hague and Paris, 1972).
6. M. M. Bakhtin, Problemy tvorchestva Dostoevskogo, Leningrad, 1929.
7. V. N. Voloshinov, "Konstruktsiia vyskazyvaniia," Literaturnaia ucheba, 1939, No. 3.
8. M. M. Bakhtin, Problemy poetiki Dostoevskogo, Moscow, 1963 (work 6, revised and supplemented).
9. M. M. Bakhtin, Tvorchestvo Fransua Rable i narodnaia kul'tura Srednevekov'ia i Renessansa, Moscow, 1965.
10. M. Bakhtin, "Slovo o romane," Voprosy literatury, 1965, No. 8.

11. M. M. Bakhtin, "Iz predystorii romannogo slova," Uch. zap. Mordovskogo un-ta, No. 61, Saransk, 1967.
12. M. M. Bakhtin, "Epos i roman," Voprosy literatury, 1970, No. 1.
13. M. Bakhtin, "Smelee pol'zovat'sia vozmozhnostiami," Novyi mir, 1970, No. 11.

Notes

1) This article is the revised and expanded text of a paper delivered in November 1970 at a meeting devoted to Bakhtin's seventy-fifth anniversary of the Association for Structural Linguistics of Moscow State University's Laboratory of Computational Linguistics.

2) This aspect of Bakhtin's works is particularly stressed in a series of recent publications by J. Kristeva, who constantly cites them. See, for example, J. Kristeva, "La sémiologie comme science des idéologies," Semiotica, I, 1969, No. 2, p. 197, note 3; same author, "La Sémiotique, science critique et/ou critique de la sciences," in J. Kristeva, Σημειωτική, Recherches pour une sémanalyse, Paris, 1969, p. 32, note 32.

3) Here and subsequently in the text, Bakhtin's works are indicated by the numbers within parentheses according to the list appended to the article. In the quotations, emphasis here and below is always Bakhtin's own.

4) G. G. Shpet, Vnutrenniaia forma slova (etiudy i variatsii na temy Gumbol'dta), Moscow, 1927, p. 203. For further detail on Shpet's views on general semiotics (as compared with the ideas of Bakhtin and Western linguists today), see the section on general semiotics by the present author in Kibernetika na sluzhbu kommunizmu, Vol. 5, Moscow, 1967, pp. 371-72. In the study cited therein, "Germenevtika," completed as early as 1918, Shpet wrote about the division, introduced by St. Augustine, into the teachings about things or teachings about signs, that this division "must be made the basis for the classification of sciences, but...to this day has not been fully considered in all its fundamental meaning..." (Shpet archive).

Semiotics and Structuralism

5) C. Morris, Signification and Significance. A Study of the Relations of Signs and Values, Cambridge, Mass., 1964. The book by Morris, who is one of the founders of modern semiotics in the variant that continues the ideas of Peirce, is particularly interesting because it is oriented toward the description of works of art in their axiological [value] aspect.

6) As a particularly vivid illustration, one may cite the analysis of words having the meaning "unfortunate, bad": H. Schuchardt, Izbrannye stat'i po iazykoznaniiu, Moscow, 1950, pp. 232-34. Also compare the terms "deprived," "poor," "wretched" of the type of the Slavic *u-bog, *ne-bog, the Hittite a-šiu-ant (poor) <*n-d(e)i-u-ont *(godless), the Greek ἄ-θεος in the sense of "abandoned by the gods" in Sophocles's Oedipus Rex (E. Laroche, "Les noms anatoliens du 'dieu' et leurs dérivés," Journal of Cuneiform Studies, Vol. 21, 1967, p. 174); the development of the meanings of words signifying "orphan" (W. Porzig, Chlenenie indoevropeiskoi iazkovoi oblasti, Moscow, 1964, p. 182), "Fool in Christ" (L. H. Gray, Foundations of Language, New York, 1939, pp. 259-60; the development of "sacred" > "stupid," opposite to that which is presented in Dostoevsky's Idiot or Wordsworth's Poor Idiot Boy). In this connection Schuchardt (Izbrannye stat'i po iazykoznaniiu, p. 234) recalled Nietzsche's proposal to proclaim a competition for a composition on the theme "What Does Linguistics, and Particularly Etymological Research, Provide for the History of the Development of Moral Concepts?"

7) It must, however, be observed that at the present time, after the publication of all the sources for Saussure's text, this criticism must be directed more at the publishers of the posthumous Course in General Linguistics than at Saussure himself, who asserted, "Ce système d'unités qui est un système de signes est un système de valeurs" ("This system of units, which is a system of signs, is simultaneously a system of values"), F. de Saussure, Cours de linguistique generale, critical edition by R. Engler, fasc. 2, Wiesbaden, 1967, pp. 254-55; see ibid. (p. 255) on the social predetermination of value that Saussure (unlike Bakhtin) felt was entirely conventional for sign systems, unlike economic value, which partially depends on the corres-

ponding objects (ibid., p. 178). Also compare below on the axiological aspect of the categories of time and space investigated by Bakhtin.

8) Study of situation, along with analysis of the act of exchange of signs (acte sémique), is being carried out in Prieto's investigations into general semiotics: L. J. Prieto, Messages et signaux, Paris, 1966. But Prieto separates these two aspects, while Bakhtin proposed to study their interconnection.

9) In connection with some of the deep similarities between the concepts examined below and the views of S. M. Eisenstein, it must be remarked that it is precisely the cited passage in this book which attracted the attention of Eisenstein, who in those years was engaged in a reconsideration of psychoanalysis. On a copy in Eisenstein's library there is the notation "19 — 6.I — 28. Moscow. Genlin" (a reference to the film The General Line — The Old and the New, for the interpretation of which Eisenstein used a system of concepts developed in the course of his acquainting himself with psychoanalysis).

10) The anticipation in book (2) of later sociological criticism of Freudianism was noted by R. O. Jakobson more than once at semiotic symposia.

11) H. C. Shands, "Psychoanalysis and the Twentieth Century Revolution in Communication," in Modern Psychoanalysis, ed. J. Marmor, New York, 1968. For subtle ideas on the role of utterance, of speech (discourse), for psychoanalysis, which echo the ideas of book (2), see E. Benveniste, "Remarques sur la fonction du langage dans la découverte freudienne," in his book Problèmes de linguistique générale, Paris, 1966, pp. 77-78. This article demonstrates, in particular, the inaccuracy of those linguistic arguments Freud used in his judgments about the ambivalence of word meanings. Nevertheless, his guess with respect to this ambivalence was correct, as Bakhtin demonstrated in (9), his study of the language of the "public square," when he accurately referred in this respect to the particularly archaic nature of cursing. Compare, in this regard, the typologically important material in the article by M. J. Meggitt, "Male-Female Relationship in the Highlands of Australian New Guinea,"

American Anthropologist, Vol. 66, No. 4, 1964, Part 2, special publication, New Guinea. The Central Highlands. In the ambivalence of "the language of the public square" we find an exact analogue, on the one hand, of the phenomenon of neutralization of linguistic oppositions, and on the other, of that elimination of the contrasts between binary oppositions in ritual and carnival which is discussed below in connection with books (8) and (9).

12) B. M. Eikhenbaum, "Anna Akhmatova," in Eikhenbaum's O poezii, Leningrad, 1969, pp. 89 and 114-15. From this standpoint, poems written by Akhmatova in her last period ("Za takuiu skomoroshinu" and others) are particularly interesting.

13) F. Miko, Text a štyl. K problematike literárnej komunikácie, Smena, 1970, p. 121. This book synthesizes the Czechoslovak tradition, in which an original theory of literary development was combined with the influence of works (6) and (7) and with Tynianov's Arkhaisty i novatory. See, particularly, M. Bakoš, "Problém vývinovej periodizácie literatúry," in A. Popovič, Strukturalizmus v slovenskej vede, Martin, 1970, pp. 95-101. Analogies between Bakhtin's ideas on the dynamics of genres and the conclusions of other Czechoslovak scholars, particularly Mukařovský, are pointed out in the essay, by D. Okáli, "Michal Bachtin o epose a románe," Slovenská literatúra, XVII, 1970, No. 6, p. 671.

14) G. Dumézil, Heur et malheur du guerrier, Paris, 1969, Preface.

15) E. Benveniste, "Sémiologie de la langue (2)," Semiotica, I, 1969, No. 2, p. 134. It must be emphasized that the entire program of development of semiotics set forth in this article is astonishingly similar to that which had been presented forty years earlier in book (5). There is coincidence not only in the emphasis on analysis of the utterance as the basic unit (7, p. 66) but also in the understanding of language as the principal ("model") object of semiotic research, and in the identification of the objectives of "metalinguistic" (according to Bakhtin, "metasemantic," in Benveniste, p. 135) research, and so forth.

16) E. Benveniste, "Sémiologie de la langue (2)," p. 135.

17) It should be noted that "the philosophy of language," a discipline whose tasks and history were outlined by Bakhtin (5, pp. 55 ff.), finally took shape under this very name only in recent decades. See, particularly, The Structure of Language. Readings in the Philosophy of Language, ed. J. A. Fodor and J. J. Katz, New Jersey, 1964.

18) Z. Harris, Papers in Structural and Transformational Linguistics, New Jersey, 1970, pp. 313-79.

19) These departures from traditional rhetoric, which was incorporated by Bakhtin (with this significant reorientation of it) into the realm of metalinguistics (1; 5, p. 116), should be particularly borne in mind in connection with efforts at a new interpretation of rhetoric in the light of structural science: W. O. Hendricks, [review of] "G. N. Leech, A Linguistic Guide to English Poetry," Lingua, Vol. 25, 1970, No. 2, pp. 175-76.

20) N. Chomsky, Cartesian Linguistics, New York and London, 1966. Chomsky holds, however, that the idea of language as a means of self-expression was advanced in Cartesian linguistics from the very outset. This differs from Bakhtin's characterization of Cartesian linguistics. The principal distinction between Chomsky's conception of the history of Western European philosophy of language and similar sections in Bakhtin's early works is that the latter underscores the difference between Cartesian rationalism and the romanticism of Humboldt, while the former emphasized that which united them (see ibid., pp. 21 ff.). Furthermore, Bakhtin (particularly in connection with Shpet's interpretation of Humboldt in the book cited above) pointed to the complexity of Humboldt's ideas, as a consequence of which the latter could "be made the mentor of widely differing trends" (5, p. 59). In that context of philosophical anthropology which was particularly essential to Bakhtin's ideas, it is important that the creative nature of language and thought, which Chomsky emphasizes in the wake of Humboldt, is transferred by Bakhtin to other aspects of human activity studied by Humboldt in his Ideen zu einem Versuch die Grenzen der Wirksamkeit des Staats zu bestimmen (1972). See N. Chomsky, Cartesian Linguistics, p. 91, notes 50-51; same author, Language and Mind, Harcourt,

Brace, 1968; same author, "Notes on Anarchism," The New York Review of Books, Vol. XIV, 1970, No. 10, p. 32, note 11. Of recent works of criticism evaluating Humboldt's linguist theory and its interpretation by Chomsky, see, particularly, E. Coseriu, "Semantik, innere Sprachform und Tiefenstruktur," Folia linguistica, Vol. IV, 1970, 1/2; ibid., p. 61, see for the conception of transformational grammar as "the grammar of the functioning of the individual language in the process of speaking," which makes it similar to "metalinguistics" in Bakhtin's sense. Furthermore, Coseriu cites Sechehaye's idea, important in this very regard, on the transition to "the organized utterance" (parole organisée) as the goal of linguistic description.

21) S. Marcus, Poetica matematică, Bucharest, 1970, p. 133. In the very same way one may differentiate the discrete case of structures like the Propp fairy-tale schema or the detective story from the continuous case of Dostoevsky's novels (studied by Bakhtin). With respect to prose, a sufficiently rigorous conception of the continuity of the artistic text may be proposed on the basis of establishment of connections between images discovered within text excerpts of any length. See, with regard to Mertvye dushi, Andrei Bely, Masterstvo Gogolia, Moscow, 1934 (continuous sound linkages deriving also from Saussure's idea of "anagrams" are assumed here as well). The assertion about the role of continuity of message in a work of art is particularly valid for the contemporary film, in which one finds the plot of a film like Antonioni's Blow-up constructed on this basis: the metonymic detail of an image can be blown up as many times as desired, thanks to which the image is fragmented into its smallest parts but retains its multiple meaning, i.e., whatever the fragmentation (and enlargement of details), single-valued fragments of the whole do not emerge. Whereas in language words themselves are discrete (in their signifying aspect), in film both the signifier and the signified can be continuous.

22) E. Benveniste, "Sémiologie de la langue (2)," p. 133.

23) Ibid., p. 134.

24) E. Benveniste, "Sémiologie de la langue (1)," Semiotica, I, 1969, No. 1, pp. 2-3. It should, however, be noted, that ad-

vancement of the utterance to the foreground does not contradict the conception of language as a totality of chains of signs in logic and mathematical linguistics.

25) E. Benveniste, "Sémiologie de la langue (2)," p. 134. According to Benveniste, both of these aspects exist only in language, while systems such as etiquette possess only the semiotic aspect, and the semantic exists only in art.

26) Compare the partially similar objections to such description of language in terms of a second signal system, in which all words (including abstract ones of the type of again, or, which are the principal subjects for investigation by modern linguistic semantics), are regarded as the results of "element-by-element projection" (in which each word is placed in a mutually unambiguous correspondence with some element it signifies), in the articles by N. A. Bernshtein, Ocherki po fiziologii dvizhenii i fiziologii aktivnosti, Moscow, 1966, pp. 285 and 305.

27) A consistent justification of the validity of the mentalist point of view in the light of the contemporary science of language is found in the above-cited works by Chomsky. This standpoint was not taken into account in the critical comments that Kristeva made (in a behaviorist spirit) in the preface to the French translation of Bakhtin's book on Dostoevsky, with regard to his use of such words as "consciousness" [soznanie]: J. Kristeva, "Une poétique ruinée," in M. Bakhtine, La poétique de Dostoïevsky, Paris, 1970, pp. 10, 21.

28) Dnevnik of S. M. Eisenstein, Vol. V, p. 63, Sect. 32 (Archive of P. M. Atasheva). It should be noted that Eisenstein arrived at his semiotic concept of art after his involvement in the 1920s with attempts at describing art in purely reflexological terms.

29) S. M. Eisenstein, "Rezhissura," in Izbrannye proizvedeniia, Vol. 4, Moscow, 1966, p. 669. Also compare the opposition between ossified "cultural-poetic" images and the image-tool born of the clash of its component parts: O. Mandel'shtam, Razgovor o Dante, Moscow, 1967.

30) See the most recent works on the structure of the paragraph, listed in Iu. M. Lotman, Struktura khudozhestvennogo

teksta, Moscow, 1970, p. 371, fn. 7.

31) In addition to Eikhenbaum's early works on the skaz, related to the experience of our prose of the 1920s and used at that time by Bakhtin (6; 8, pp. 256-57), it is also necessary to take note of his later articles on Leskov, containing interesting thoughts on Leskov's parodying of dialects and styles (including that of verse), which accord with Bakhtin's range of ideas: B. M. Eikhenbaum, "'Chrezmernyi' pisatel'," in B. Eikhenbaum, O proze, Leningrad, 1969, pp. 341-44. On the types of "two-voiced word" [dvugolosoe slovo] in modern literature, compare the articles by the present author: "Poetika," Literaturnaia entsiklopediia, Vol. 5, Moscow, 1969, p. 938.

32) R. Jakobson, Shifters, Verbal Categories, and the Russian Verb, Harvard University (Cambridge, Mass.), 1967, p. 1; see R. Jakobson, Selected Writings, II, Word and Language, Mouton, The Hague and Paris, 1971, p. 130. Also see the presentation of this work in an essay by the present author: "Kod i soobshchenie," Biulleten' Ob''edineniia po mashinnomu perevodu, 1957, No. 5.

33) See an interesting book written under the influence of works (6) and (7): L. Doležel, O stylu modernÍ české prózy, Prague, 1960, devoted to this problem in its entirety. The new literature on the question is also listed in A. Neuber, Die Stilformen der "Erleben Rede" in neueren englischen Roman, Halle (Saale), 1957, and in the article: Iu. Ia. Nikulikhin, "Spetsifika nesobstvenno priamoi rechi i ee mesto sredi drugikh vidov vyskazyvaniia (na materiale proizvedenii nemetskoi khudozhestvennoi literature)," in Problemy nemetskogo iazykoznaniia i metodiki prepodavaniia nemetskogo iazyka, Uch. zap. fakul'teta in. iaz. Tul'skogo ped. in-ta, Issue 4, Tula, 1970.

34) Anna Wierzbicka, Dociekania semantyczne, Wrocław — Warsaw — Cracow, 1969, Ch. IX ("Deskrypcje czy cytaty?"), pp. 177 ff.; also compare the final section, "The Problem of Quotation," in the collection, Sign, Language, Culture, The Hague and Paris, 1970. Also compare the interpretation, close to Bakhtin's ideas, of the role of quotations in Avvakum (first studied by V. V. Vinogradov), in B. A. Uspenskii, Poetika kompozitsii, Moscow, 1970, pp. 62-63.

M. M. Bakhtin and Modern Semiotics

35) Dnevik of S. M. Eisenstein, Vol. V, p. 14, Sect. 14 (Archive of P. M. Atasheva).
36) S. M. Eisenstein, Izbrannye proizvedeniia, Vol. 2, Moscow, 1964, p. 334. The structure of the present article is determined by this principle.
37) Thoman Mann, Gesammelte Werke, Vol. 12, Berlin, 1956, p. 204. For more detail on Mann's views, see V. Mikushevich, "Problema tsitaty ('Doktor Faustus' Tomasa Manna po-nemetski i po-russki)," in Masterstvo perevoda 1966, Moscow, 1968. In the light of Bakhtin's ideas, it is necessary to compare this role of quotations in Mann with recent conclusions on the function of quasidirect discourse [nesobstvenno priamaia rech'] in his novels (5, p. 180) by Iu. Ia. Nikulikhin, "Spetsifika nesobstvenno priamoi rechi" (which has a bibliography on this question). G. Fourrier's observations on the Polyphones Gewebe in Mann's novels are similar to Bakhtin's ideas on polyphony in the novel (Fourrier, Thomas Mann, Paris, 1960, pp. 85, 265; F. Dabèzise, Visages de Faust au XX-e siècle, Paris, 1967, p. 377).
38) O. Mandel'shtam, Razgovor o Dante, p. 11.
39) "Un adevărat dialog între doi oameni este în fund cu neputință. Orice dialog se reduce la două monologuri alternante," cited from S. Marcus, Poetica matematică, p. 134.
40) T. S. Eliot, "The Three Voices of Poetry," in his On Poetry and Poets, New York, 1961, p. 109; compare the discussion (p. 106) of the applicability to Rilke's and Valéry's verses of Gottfried Bann's definition of the lyric as the poetry of the first person (Probleme der Lyrik).
41) E. Benveniste, "L'appareil formel de l'énonciation," Langages, March 1970, No. 17, "L'énonciation," p. 16. The article is an exact analogue of the section on utterance in work (5).
42) R. H. Weir, Language in the Crib, The Hague, 1962; see, in same source, the article by R. Jakobson, "Anthony's Contribution to Linguistic Theory," p. 18 (R. Jakobson, Selected Writings, II, p. 285), which discusses Vygotskii's theory. Compare L. S. Vygotskii, Psikhologiia iskusstva, 2nd ed., Moscow, 1968, p. 501. On the interiorization and explanation of inner speech according to Vygotskii, also see H. C. Shands, Semiotic Approaches to

Psychiatry, The Hague and Paris, 1970, p. 295a, 10. The role of study of inner speech for semiotics has recently been commented upon by R. Jakobson, "Language in Relation to Other Communication Systems," in Linguaggi nella società e nella tecnica, Milan, 1970, pp. 4 (also about Vygotskii) and 9, R. Jakobson, Selected Writings, II, pp. 698, 702.

43) L. S. Vygotskii, "Myshlenie i rech'," in L. S. Vygotskii, Izbrannye psikhologicheskie issledovaniia, Moscow, 1956, p. 360.

44) Ibid., with reference to L. V. Shcherba and L. P. Iakubinskii (compare 5, pp. 137 and 172).

45) Ibid., pp. 361-62. In Vygotskii's book, the first edition of which appeared in 1934 after the author's death, there are also several other instances in which the sources of the corresponding passages in the book are not indicated. On p. 334 a quotation from Vossler (about Descartes) is not put in quotes. See K. Vossler, "Grammaticheskie i psikhologicheskie formy v iazyke," in Problemy literaturnoi formy, Leningrad, 1928, pp. 188-89. Nor is the source of the epigraph to Chapter 7 given (which is from Mandel'shtam; on this see L. S. Vygotskii, Psikhologiia iskusstva, p. 507). It would be desirable for all similar instances to be specified in the commentary to the Vygotskii Sobranie sochinenii now in preparation.

46) S. M. Eisenstein, "Dikkens, Griffit i my," in Izbrannye proizvedeniia, Vol. 5, Moscow, 1968, p. 171. Here and below the italics in the quotes are Eisenstein's.

47) Ibid., p. 176.

48) Eisenstein held, however, that in Dostoevsky's "A Gentle Spirit" there are "only two or three passages in which...real examples of 'the other syntax' emerge" (Metod, chapter "Frenk Bedman," Archive of P. M. Atasheva). This concentration on the form, and not just the content, of the interior monologue, of which Leo Tolstoy's early attempt "History of Yesterday" (with the recording of "flow of consciousness" while dreaming) is also an example, represents a path, particularly important for twentieth-century art, which is fundamentally different from the objective presentation of the interior monologue (in "linear style"). On this last, see B. A. Uspenskii, Poetika kompozitsii, pp. 60,

M. M. Bakhtin and Modern Semiotics

71. If quasidirect discourse, according to work (5), which Uspenskii follows (Poetika kompozitsii, pp. 91 ff.), is defined formally as speech that can by means of one series of transformations be translated into direct discourse, and by means of another into indirect, then interior monologue "in the painting style" (in the stream-of-consciousness school) is not translatable into either indirect or direct discourse without loss of its essential compositional properties. In Doležel's apt formulation, underlying the interior monologue in contemporary prose is the tendency to transmit inner speech directly. See L. Doležel, "O stylu moderní české prózy," p. 159 (see ibid., p. 158, on polyphony in Bakhtin's sense). Compare J. Mukařovský, "Dialog a monolog," Kapitoly z české poetiky, I, Prague, 1948. Molly Bloom's interior monologue, studied from this point of view by Eisenstein, is analyzed in connection with the problem of semidirect discourse in A. Neubert, Die Stilformen der "Erleben Rede," pp. 143-44. For analogies with the film and polyphony, compare I. Gurvich, "Kinomontazh i sovremennaia zarubezhnaia proza," in Iz istorii zarubezhnykh literatur, Nauchn. tr. Tashkentskogo un-ta, Tashkent, 1970. Eisenstein's ideas pertaining to cinematographic analogues of Joyce's interior monologue are employed in the second part ("Thetechnics") of R. Humphrey's book, Stream of Consciousness in the Modern Novel, Berkeley and Los Angeles, 1953 (in which the corresponding passages of Ulysses are examined). The interaction of the devices of montage cinematography and modern prose (Faulkner, in particular) is cited in modern semiotics as one of the most persuasive examples of that contact between different realms of culture which is associated with the general semiotic problem of their specificity. See C. Metz, "Spécificité des codes et spécificité des langages," Semiotica, 1969, No. 4, pp. 380-81; compare above on Bakhtin's formulation of this problem.

49) This is not contradicted by the fact that, from the biographical standpoint, the reflection in this novella of certain motifs experienced by the author himself is not excluded. Compare the coincidence between the beginning of the preface to "A Gentle Spirit": "Picture a husband whose wife is lying on

the table," and the beginning of Dostoevsky's note written
April 16, 1864 (the day after the death of his first wife): "Masha
is lying on the table...." There is not only a correspondence
of the external situations but of the internal one: a husband who
has just lost his wife tries to clarify the truth for himself (in "A
Gentle Spirit" about the deceased, while in the earlier author's
note, about immortality).

50) S. M. Eisenstein, Izbrannye proizvedeniia, Vol. 2, p. 109.
51) Ibid., p. 120.
52) L. S. Vygotskii, Razvitie vysshikh psikhologicheskikh funktsii. Iz neopublikovannykh trudov, Moscow, 1960, p. 451 (written in 1929-1930).
53) Ibid., p. 194 (written in 1930-1931).
54) Unfamiliarity with this early book explains those observations on the monologue from the standpoint of psychoanalysis that Kristeva offers in her enthusiastic article about Bakhtin, while criticizing and supplementing his understanding of the monologue: J. Kristeva, "Le mot, le dialogue et le roman," in J. Kristeva, Σημειωτική, Recherches pour une sémanalyse, p. 155, compare p. 149; also compare her preface to the French translation of Bakhtin's book on Dostoevsky: J. Kristeva, "Une poétique ruinée," in M. Bakhtine, La poétique de Dostoïevsky, Paris, 1970, pp. 13, 15. In reality, however, Bakhtin's theory was created thanks to the overcoming of psychoanalysis from that semiotic point of view which remains the most persuasive to our day; he was not a forerunner of Freud's discoveries (ibid., pp. 7 ff.) but their interpreter, who described them in a new way.
55) The semiotic approach to the higher psychological functions is set forth in L. S. Vygotskii, Razvitie vysshikh psikhologicheskikh funktsii. For a critical examination of the views of Dilthey and Scheler regarding the higher sensations, see L. S. Vygotskii, "Spinoza i ego uchenie ob emotsiiakh v svete sovremennoi psikhonevrologii," Voprosy filosofii, 1970, No. 7 (chapter from Vygotskii's last book, written in 1934, providing a detailed study of the problem of the relation between affect and expressive manifestation. The same problem was attentively studied on another level in the 1920s in biomechanics, from the

M. M. Bakhtin and Modern Semiotics

postulates of which N. A. Bernshtein and Eisenstein started: each of them arrived at the necessity of isolating a semiotic level of mental functions — Bernshtein's level E).

56) In connection with the other parallels noted, it is necessary to point out that Eisenstein, according to entries in his diary of 1928, "immersed himself in Rabelais" and, anticipating a film on Levenshtein, dreamed of presenting a contemporary Gargantua, in which, in a "tragic grotesque" (une grotesque tragique — the note, made while he was reading Rabelais, was in French), the war with Picrochole would have been interwoven with the war of 1914-1918 (Eisenstein's Dnevnik, Vol. Va, p. 84, Sect. 88, Archive of P. M. Atasheva). Eisenstein himself, like Rabelais, is characterized by the absence of boundaries between the conscious and the unconscious in the Freudian sense, a condition which can be demonstrated by analysis of his diaries, autobiographical and scholarly notes, and drawings. The elimination of these boundaries appears to be one of the most characteristic features of the Renaissance type of personality. Therefore, "unpublishable fields" (9, p. 459, fn. 1) play a special role in it. The historical role of such personalities can be interpreted in the sense of Bakhtin's ideas about the carnival and its connections with critical (crisis) transitional situations, including the development of science (9, pp. 57 and 414).

57) Therefore, the objections raised from a narrow standpoint of academic Rabelais scholarship are not persuasive. See F. Yates, [review of] "Mikhail Bakhtin. Rabelais and His World," The New York Review of Books, Vol. XIII, 1969, No. 6. In this review the semiotic aspect of the book, accurately emphasized by K. Pomorskaia in her introduction to the translation into English, is contrasted with the traditional literary-history aspect, although Bakhtin's service consists precisely in synthesizing synchrono-functional description with diachronic. In even more obvious form (thanks to the absence of references to other contemporary works on Rabelais, to a survey of which Yates's article is essentially devoted), the failure to understand the semiotic tasks of this study is revealed in the critique by V. B. Shklovskii, Tetiva, Moscow, 1970, pp. 257 ff.

Semiotics and Structuralism

58) Iu. V. Knorozov, "Drevniaia pis'mennost' Tsentral'noi Ameriki," Sovetskaia etnografiia, 1952, No. 3; same author, Pis'mennost' maiia, Moscow, 1963.

59) Here and below "metalanguage" is understood in the usual and generally accepted meaning (as a language used to study another language), which originated in logic (from Tarski and his school). Accordingly, the term "translinguistics," introduced by R. Barthes to denote the learned discipline studying the structure of texts longer than a sentence, is to be preferred to the term "metalinguistics," proposed earlier by Bakhtin in another meaning (compare "metasemantics" used in the same sense by Benveniste).

60) On War and Peace, see B. A. Uspenskii, Poetika kompozitsii, pp. 73 ff.; on Anna Karenina, R. Jakobson and M. Halle, Fundamentals of Language, The Hague, 1956, p. 18; R. Jakobson, Selected Writings, Vol. 1, 2nd ed., Mouton, The Hague and Paris, 1971, p. 476.

61) The Swedish-French bilingualism in the prose of J. Almquist offers interesting material for comparison with the Russo-French bilingualism in the pertinent chapters of War and Peace. Mehring's The Golem, which reproduces the motley multilingual milieu of Prague early in the present century, is of considerable interest for study of the connection between the multilingualism of the novel and that of a large city (one must, however, make the qualification that the multilingualism of a city like Ugarit is far more ancient than the novel; however, there was no preurban multilingualism).

62) Compare, particularly, the use of the French language in one of the best novels of the new Vietnamese literature: Vũ Trong Phung, Số dỏ, Hanoi, 1957 (1st ed., 1937).

63) As an obvious example, Kristeva ("Une poétique ruinée," p. 30) has already pointed to Fellini's Satyricon, whose literary prototype, the novel by Petronius, had been studied in detail by Bakhtin (8, pp. 151, 157, 158, 161 ff.; 12, pp. 109 and 112). The role of late antiquity in Bakhtin's constructs in the realm of the history of the novel can be compared with the theme of late antiquity in the poems and novelistic prose of K. Vaginov (in the

case in question, in the light of the existence of biographical ties between scholar and writer, one is dealing with more than just typological similarity).

64) See on this the present author's above-cited article, "Poetika," p. 938; same author, "O tochnykh metodakh v literaturovedenii," Voprosy literatury, 1967, No. 10, p. 124; L. S. Vygotskii, Psikhologiia iskusstva, p. 517.

65) B. A. Uspenskii, Poetika kompozitsii. Compare Iu. M. Lotman, Struktura khudozhestvennogo teksta, pp. 320-35 (particularly pp. 333-34 on the film) and p. 380, fn. 27 (on the works of M. M. Bakhtin). As applied to Chekhov's prose, this method of description is used in A. P. Chudakov, Poetika Chekhova, Moscow, 1971.

66) T. Todorov, "Poétique," in O. Ducrot, T. Todorov, D. Sperber, M. Safouan, and F. Wahl, Qu'est-ce que le structuralisme?, Paris, 1968, p. 158.

67) P. Lubbock, The Craft of Fiction, London, 1965 (1st ed., 1921). Compare W. C. Booth, The Rhetoric of Fiction, Chicago, 1961.

68) J. Pouillon, Temps et roman, Paris, 1946. This work's ideas on time are of interest in the light of Bakhtin's conclusions on time in the novel (8 and 12).

69) T. Todorov, "Poetique," p. 159; compare pp. 117-18.

70) J.-P. Sartre, L'être et le néant, Paris, 1943, pp. 275-367 (the section "L'existence d'autrui").

71) Ibid., p. 277. At the same time, one cannot fail to note the very significant differences between Bakhtin's conception and Sartre's ideas, both in connection with the problem of "the other" (see below about "the other" as "the stranger" — the representative of man in general — as about a pure relationship) and in other matters discussed by both thinkers: the problem of negation, studied in detail specifically on the material of linguistic negations, is resolved by Sartre on the purely logical level (J.-P. Sartre, L'être et le néant, pp. 39 ff.), while Bakhtin (9, pp. 446-52) demonstrates precisely by this example the inadequacy of the purely logical approach.

72) This comparison of the ideas of Bakhtin and Sartre on the

novel was made, independently of each other, in 1968, by T. Todorov ("Poetique," p. 159) and the present author in his article, "Ob analogiiakh mezhdu buddiiskoi logikoi i sovremennoi evropeiskoi naukoi," in the collection Materialy po istorii i filologii Tsentral'noi Azii, 112 (Tr. Buriatskogo in-ta obshchestvennykh nauk, Issue 1, Seriia vostokovedeniia), Ulan-Ude, 1968, p. 145. J. Kristeva writes differently on the echoing of ideas between Bakhtin and Sartre, "Une poétique ruinée," p. 16, where she notes the similarity with the semiotic conception of the role of "the other" in psychoanalysis. Compare E. Benveniste, "Remarques sur la fonction du language dans la découverte freudienne," p. 77.

73) P. Florenskii, Mnimosti v geometrii, Moscow, 1922, p. 7.

74) Yuen-Ren Chao, "The Non-Uniqueness of Phonemic Solutions of Phonetic Systems," Readings in Linguistics, 2nd ed., New York, 1958 (reprint of article of 1934).

75) J. Ziman, Public Knowledge. The Social Dimension of Science, Cambridge, 1968, p. 22. Ziman emphasizes the need to select one of the alternative descriptions in European science. This possibility remains in the world of Dostoevsky as well. See below on his "most authoritative position," the limit of which is given in the image of "the ideal man."

76) On this, see for greater detail the present author's note, "Fedor Ippolitovich Shcherbatskoi," in Narody Azii i Afriki, 1966, No. 6, p. 148. The study by G. V. Chicherin, written in the late 1920s but only recently published, devoted to a comparison between Mozart and the music of the twentieth century, provides a vivid analogy to the work of Bakhtin on the polyphony of the novel. Moreover, Chicherin, like Bakhtin in his first books, took as his point of departure P. Bekker's attempt at historical examination of musical forms (Musikgeschichte als Geschichte der musikalischen Formwandlungen, Berlin and Leipzig, 1926). Chicherin compared the structure "opera — game" with that of the nineteenth-century novel: "The Mozartian picture of the world and his perception of the world are deeply problematical, encompass all contradictions, and each living character appears to him to be a similar bundle of contradic-

tions: each is problematical...it is precisely this that brings him close to the nineteenth-century novel, particularly Balzac and even Dostoevsky" (G. Chicherin, Motsart, Leningrad, 1970, p. 210, compare pp. 95, 134, 251 ff.).

77) This similarity is determined by deeper causes than literary influence, since "Detstvo Liuvers" was written prior to the first publication of "Ispoved' Stavrogina." The similarities in the ideas of Bakhtin and Pasternak are not accidental, as is evident also from the evaluation of book (3) in Pasternak's letter (in connection with the evaluation of the philosophical side of the book in this letter, it is necessary to note the role of the Marburg school in the formation of both thinkers). See the text of the letter in Trudy po znakovym sistemam, V (Uch. zap. Tartuskogo un-ta, Issue 284), Tartu, 1971, pp. 528-29.

78) In this connection it seems possible to recall Rilke's opinion on Dostoevsky's attitude toward time: "Er zuletzt selbst die Zeit anschauen durfte (in seinmen Tagebuch des Schriftstellers), weil er ihr nicht in den Arm fiel, sie aufzuhalten, sich ihr nicht in den Weg stellte, sie zu überreden, sondern sie auslegte wie ei äusserst vorläufiges Bild für das unendliche Geschehen, dessen Schauplatz, für eine Weile Gottes, in unserem inneren Dasein ausgespart worden ist" (R. M. Rilke Briefe aus den Jahrn 1907 bis 1914, Leipzig, 1933, p. 327).

79) It should be noted that the problem of time in ancient epic was first posed in the spirit of modern scholarship by Bakhtin's university instructor F. F. Zieliński at the very beginning of the century, in his article "Die Behandlung gleichzeitiger Ereignisse im antiken Epos," Philologus, Suppl. to Vol. VIII, 1901, No. 3. This article has influenced both recent literary studies (see the references to it in E. Lämmert, Die Bauformen des Erzählens, Stuttgart, 1955, which in many respects is close to Bakhtin's works on the novel) and works on semiotics. In particular, citing Zieliński's article, Jakobson, as far back as the 1930s (in his article, "Úpadek filmu," Listy pro umění a kritiku, I, Prague, 1933), noted the similarity between the presentation of time in the epic and in silent film; and he pointed in this con-

nection to other possibilities, realized in recent films (see R. Jakobson, Linguística, Poetica, Cinema, São Paolo, 1970). Among subsequent works on the category of time in narration, mention must be made of H. Weinrich, Tempus: Besprochene und erzählte Welt, Stuttgart, 1964.

80) P. A. Florenskii, Analiz prostranstvennosti v khudozhestvenno-izobrazitel'nykh proizvedeniiakh, the section "Vremia i prostranstvo," Sect. 58 (P. A. Florenskii Archive). The typology of these fundamental images is the subject of another work by Florenskii, "Symbolarium." See Trudy po znakovym sistemam, V, pp. 521-27 (on the vertical, see p. 526). In the light of other comparisons presented here, it should be noted that Eisenstein often talked about the historical role of vertical composition, both in his theoretical works (starting with his well-known speech on the shape of the screen, delivered in Hollywood: S. M. Eisenstein, "Dinamicheskii kvadrat," in Izbrannye proizvedeniia, Vol. 2, pp. 318-19) and in connection with the attempt to reproduce a medieval myth in Die Walküre, in which the principal theme is "activity, scenically resolved vertically upward." S. M. Eisenstein, "Voploshchenie mifa," in Izbrannye proizvedeniia, Vol. 5, p. 342. Among the universal images studied by Bakhtin, as well as by Florenskii and Eisenstein, there is the opposition between the convex and concave, which is essential to Bakhtin's concept of the grotesque body (9, pp. 344 ff.). In his Analiz prostranstvennosti, Florenskii, like Eisenstein, used this opposition in his classification of the different types of aesthetic attitudes.

81) One of the principal reasons for Shklovskii's failure to understand Bakhtin's book (see V. B. Shklovskii, Tetiva, pp. 284-85) is the fact that, of all these aspects, he (probably for polemical purposes) chose only the last [body], which he interpreted, moreover, in that spirit of primitive hedonism which had also in his earlier, incomparably more meaningful works (before Shklovskii left OPOIaZ) evoked Bakhtin's criticism (3) and that of Vygotskii (L. S. Vygotskii, Psikhologiia iskusstva). From a critical assimilation of what OPOIaZ had accomplished, Bakhtin took a stride forward to structural poetics, while Shklovskii's book can only be characterized negatively in all respects.

M. M. Bakhtin and Modern Semiotics

82) J. Paris, "La mode, la rupture," Change. 4. La mode, l'invention, 1969, p. 167. The same conclusion, arrived at before he was familiar with Bakhtin's book on Rabelais, is repeated in his next book: J. Paris, Rabelais au futur, Paris, 1970, pp. 117-18, in which the bibliography does cite Bakhtin's book. Paris particularly had in mind the passage in Rabelais where the combining of the criteria "left" and "odd," which originate in the Pythagorean reflection of the ancient Greek mythological series of binary oppositions (see G. E. R. Lloyd, Polarity and Analogy: Two Types of Argumentation in Early Greek Thought, Cambridge, 1966; compare I. D. Rozhanskii, Anaksagor, Moscow, 1972, pp. 14, 170), is reinterpreted in the carnival spirit: "Si les syllables du nom estoient en nombre impar, soubdain, sans voir les personnes, il les disoit estre maleficiés, borgnes, boiteux, bossus du cousté dextre. Si elles estoient en nombre 'par,' du cousté gauche" (F. Rabelais, Oeuvres, Vol. 3, "Pantagruel," Paris, 1935, p. 26; in the Russian translation by Liubimov: "If the syllables of these or other names made an odd number, he knew without looking that these people had a crooked right eye, were lame in the right leg, and had a hump on the right side. But if they were even in number, it was the left side, however, that was imperfect" [F. Rable, Gargantiua i Pantagriuel', trans. N. Liubimov, Moscow, 1961, p. 480]).

83) E. Leach, Rethinking Anthropology, London, 1961, p. 135.

84) Ibid. According to Leach, inversion of roles is the opposite pole of "formal" ("official" in Bakhtin's terminology) behavior; a masquerade occupies an intermediate position between these poles. It seems in this case it is possible to establish direct links with the conclusions of the structural-functional sociological school, which is engaged primarily in the study of social roles, particularly in the value aspect. In order to solve the diachronic problem posed by Bakhtin of the significance of carnival in crisis (turning-point) periods, particular importance attaches to the hypothesis that the identification of intermediate links ("mediation") between opposite social roles in the ritual act, which is the source of the carnival, can be linked with culture changes: N. Ross Crumrine, "Ritual Drama and Culture

Change," Comparative Studies in Society and History, Vol. 12, 1970, No. 4, pp. 361-72 (see this work also on another type — the traditional, unchanging society, into which a repeating ritual act is "built," as in the case of medieval carnival).

85) S. M. Eisenstein, Grundproblem (Archive of P. M. Atasheva).

86) Ibid. Also see the present author's article "Eisenstein et la linguistique structurale moderne," Cahiers du cinéma, 1970, No. 220-221. The virtually literal identity of the closing lines with Bakhtin's thoughts, and a long list of other analogies noted above, are of interest from the standpoint of the typology of ideas arising in identical historical situations during one and the same time (notwithstanding the polar opposition of concrete biographies of the thinkers who uttered them); also significant, naturally, is the similarity of the initial cultural and scientific impulses (in the given instance, psychoanalytical) reworked and overcome by both scholars. At the same time, it is also necessary to pose the question of the anticipation, in the cited works, of the different contemporary forms of carnival (particularly the "happening") and of carnivalized art, etc.

87) R. B. Skrypnikov, "Oprichnyi terror," Uch. zap. Leningradskogo ped. in-ta im. A. I. Gertsena, Leningrad, 1969, pp. 162-63. In the light of the peculiarities of the carnival attitude toward the "unprintable" words of the public square, pointed out by Bakhtin, particular interest attaches to the story of the Piskarevskii chronicler (see ibid., p. 163, fn. 1) about how the tsar ordered "to be written down secretly" "the obscene words" uttered by those who frolicked at his feast, "and in the morning ordered the record of their words brought to him and was amazed that these wise and moderate persons from his royal council had uttered such plain words...," after which he himself showed them these notes. Also compare the depiction in folk songs and tales of Ivan the Terrible as a mountebank [skomorokh] and excellent connoisseur of "buffoonery" in S. Shambinago, Pesni vremen Ivana Groznogo, Sergiev Posad, 1914, p. 201 (compare what is said about the oprichnina in connection with jesters' frolics and changing of clothes in travesty: ibid., pp. 17,

23, 29, 56-57, 66). Compare A. N. Veselovskii, "Skazki ob Ivane Groznom," in Sobr. soch., Vol. 16, Moscow and Leningrad, 1938 (first published in 1876), in which one should note the motif of Ivan's changing clothes and the quest, characteristic of the carnival image, for the conjoining of the two poles in the task set by Ivan: to come to him "not on a horse, not on foot, not in clothing, and not naked."

88) The drawing is reproduced in the album, S. M. Eisenstein, Risunki raznykh let, Moscow, 1968, Sheet 2. Bakhtin writes about Leonardo's carnival perception of the world (9, 58). Compare the comments on Leonardo in connection with the problem of the unification of opposites in G. Chicherin's book Motsart.

89) See, for example, S. M. Eisenstein, "Rezhissura," in Izbrannye proizvedeniia, Vol. 4, Moscow, 1966, p. 667 ("such was Leonardo in the unity of yet another antithesis..."). On the ancient Chinese spiral symbol, see ibid., pp. 653-54 and Fig. 1. The theme of the androgyne is developed by Eisenstein in detail in a special chapter of Grundproblem.

90) See, in particular, S. M. Eisenstein, Montazh, in Izbrannye proizvedeniia, Vol. 2, pp. 365-66. Similarity to carnival as Bakhtin understood it is also evident in the presentation of authority (including Mexican ministers) as a carnival effigy (compare 9, p. 231). In the art of the 1940s there was a revival of certain other grotesque images studied at this time by Bakhtin in his scholarly works; in particular, the sculptured figure of a laughing old woman (compare 9, p. 31) became the image of the era to Barlach.

91) R. Jakobson, "Medieval Mock Mystery (The Old Czech Unguentarius)," in Studia philologica et litteraria in honorem L. Spitzer, Bern, 1958, p. 263. In addition to the work by P. G. Bogatyrev cited by Jakobson in this connection, another article of his should be mentioned: P. Bogatyrew, "Zur Frage der gemeinsamen Kunstgriffe im alttschechischen und im volkstümlichen Theater," Slavische Rundschau, X, 1938, No. 6 (Franz Spina zum Gedächtnis), pp. 158-59; P. G. Bogatyrev, Voprosy teorii narodnogo iskusstva, Moscow, 1971, p. 154.

92) V. Ia. Propp, Ritual'nyi smekh v fol'klore, Uch. zap. LGU,

No. 46, 1939. Compare the remarks about laughter in myth in a book by a pupil of Lévi-Strauss: M. Guyot, Les mythes chez les Selk'nam et les Yamana de la Terre de Feu, Paris, 1968.

93) See E. M. Meletinskii, "Strukturno-tipologicheskoe izuchenie skazki," in V. Ia. Propp, Morfologiia skazki, 2nd ed., Moscow, 1969, pp. 143-44 (in which further bibliography may be found); L. S. Vygotskii, Psikhologiia iskusstva, p. 511.

94) Specifically, in the light of the foregoing it is necessary to note the precise formulation of the exchange of roles between a king and a slave who is later executed in saturnalia: O. M. Freidenberg, Poetika siuzheta i zhanra, Leningrad, 1936, p. 88; on laughter at death, compare, ibid., p. 106 (Freidenberg's book is discussed in Eisenstein's notes for his Grundproblem). "Displacement," "the motif of inverted relationships" in ancient carnival, was investigated at the same time in an article developing the ideas in Zielinski's works on ancient Attic comedy: A. Piotrovskii, "Teatr Aristofana," in A. Piotrovskii, Teatr, kino, zhizn', Leningrad, 1969, pp. 178-82 (the dual character of these rituals is noted there). Shklovskii, in quoting from this article passages that are undoubtedly the most valuable part of the corresponding section of his book (V. G. Shklovskii, Tetiva, pp. 267-68), did not observe that they deal with a phenomenon analyzed in detail by Bakhtin, who for some reason he counterposes to Piotrovskii. Among later works anticipating structural analysis of the ancient myth, note should be taken first of all of Ia. E. Golosovker's monograph Logika antichnogo mifa (Archive of Ia. E. Golosovker), in which one finds, in many respects, similarity to the methods of investigation of the transformation of groups of myths in Lévi-Strauss's Mythologiques (it is characteristic that Golosovker also concerned himself with the philosophical structure of Dostoevsky's novels).

95) Compare, on this, in the author's article "Ritmicheskoe stroenie 'Ballady o tsirke' Mezhirova," in Poetics. Poetyka. Poetika II, Warsaw, 1966, and in the book by K. I. Rudnitskii, Rezhisser Meierkhol'd, Moscow, 1968, p. 34.

96) P. A. Bouissac, "The Circus as a Multimedia Language," Language sciences, 1970, No. 11 (bibliography therein). Same

author: "Pour une sémiotique du cirque," Semiotica, III, 1971, No. 2; "Le statut sémiotique de l'affiche de cirque," Semiotica, III, 1971, No. 4; "Les avatars du clown," Semiotica, V, 1972, No. 3. Here, too, Eisenstein was a forerunner of contemporary scholarship, for he made a detailed analysis of the basic features of the circus and the causes of its influence in the introduction to his Grundproblem, and of a series of circus motifs in his own work in the text of this book. Like Bakhtin's, Eisenstein's approach is fundamentally diachronic.

97) The corresponding chapter of the book was incorporated, in the English translation, in the collection, Game, Play, Literature, Yale French Studies, No. 41, 1968, which is an experiment in structural description of play in various aspects (see ibid., p. 168, for a high evaluation of the works of Bakhtin). On play, in connection with Bakhtin's book, compare J. Paris, Rabelais au futur; A. Ia. Gurevich, "Smekh v narodnoi kul'ture Srednevekov'ia," Voprosy literatury, 1966, No. 6, p. 213, where the question is posed of the relation between laughter and play; compare the thesis that play is an "inverse image" of the sacred, similar to Bakhtin's idea of "laughter doubles" [smekhovye dublery], in E. Benveniste, "Le jeu comme structure," Deucalion, 1947, No. 2, pp. 161-67; also see the note on the role of play in connection with the grotesque in the critical article by L. M. Batkin, "Smekh Panurga i filosofiia kul'tury," Voprosy filosofii, 1967, No. 12, p. 120.

98) The thesis expressed by Bakhtin on the greater role of sound devices in previous centuries could interestingly be compared with the data on archaic cultures oriented to sound means of communication: P. L. Kilbride and M. C. Robbins, "Pictorial Depth Perception and Acculturation among the Baganda," American Anthropologist, Vol. 71, 1969, No. 2, p. 299.

99) G. Galame-Griaule, Ethnologie et language: la parole chez les Dogons, Paris, 1965 (in which coincidence with the Vedic can be seen even in the number of members of the grotesque body: $22 = 21 + 1$). Bakhtin's idea about a special understanding of the boundaries between the body and the world, stated in connection with study of the grotesque body (9, pp. 341-43 ff.),

is of particular interest in the light of the posing of the same problem in modern social psychology and linguistics (particularly in the study of the category of inherent belonging, which usually pertains to such parts of the body as the nose). Compare the explanation (particularly close to Bakhtin's ideas) of tabooing ("unprintability") of linguistic denotations of the human bodily excretions, through their ambivalence, which is connected to their intermediate position between the body and the world, i.e., to mediation between the terms of a binary opposition: E. Leach, "Anthropological Aspects of Language: Animal Categories and Verbal Abuse," in <u>New Directions in the Study of Language</u>, ed. by Lenneberg, Cambridge, Mass., 1964, p. 38.

100) See, for instance, certain examples analyzed in the author's article "Ob odnoi paralleli k gogolevskomu 'Viiu,'" <u>Trudy po znakovym sistemam</u>, 5, Tartu, 1971. As Bakhtin observed (8, p. 210, fn. 1), "Gogol' still felt the significant direct influence of Ukrainian carnival folklore." Even greater interest attaches to comparison of the carnival images he adopted with those he created according to the carnival type of symbols of the grotesque body — such as <u>"Nos,"</u> which can be explained by the general regularities identified by Bakhtin (9, p. 343). Compare also his observations on the universal symbolic significance of the nose image, which are important in interpreting this image in Gogol' (and in other writers, particularly Catullus in the thirteenth poem of his anthology) (9, pp. 97 and, particularly, 342).

101) The basic texts of works 1-5 and 7 are by M. M. Bakhtin. His students <u>V. N. Voloshinov</u> and <u>P. N. Medvedev</u>, under whose names they were published, <u>made only small insertions and changes in particular parts</u> (and in some cases, such as [5], in the titles) of these articles and books. That all the works belong to the same author, which is confirmed by the testimony of witnesses, is evident from their very texts, as one may easily convince oneself by the quotations presented.

After finishing the present article, the author had the opportunity to familiarize himself with two responses to French translations of books by Bakhtin, each of which particularly confirms the need for everyone who wants to understand this scholar's

M. M. Bakhtin and Modern Semiotics

entire system of views to study the book <u>Freidizm</u>. Thus Frioux's observation (C. Frioux, "Baktine devant ou derrière nous," <u>Littérature</u>, 1971, No. 1, p. 111) about the similarity between Bakhtin's ideas and Jung's thoughts on archetypes (and, let us add, to an even greater degree — the understanding of genre as archetype by such literary scholars as Frye, who were influenced by Jung) remains incomplete because he did not know how Bakhtin viewed the interrelation between group and individual psyches. This also applies to the observation that a psychoanalytic interpretation of the theory of the grotesque body in the book on Rabelais is conceivable (S. Gabay, "Rabelais: des annees 30 à 1970," ibid., p. 118). In both cases (as in the corresponding passage in Kristeva's introduction, cited above, with which Frioux takes issue on other gounds) it is suggested to Bakhtin that he return to what was the starting point of his evolution in the 1920s.

About the Editor

Henryk Baran is currently an assistant professor of Slavic languages and literatures at the State University of New York at Albany. He received his B.S. in Mathematics from the Massachusetts Institute of Technology and his M.A. and Ph.D. degrees in Slavic languages and literatures from Harvard University. Professor Baran has published several articles on twentieth-century Russian poetry.

F. W. Galan
5720 Solway Street
Pittsburgh, PA 15217
Tel: (412) 521-9077